13.50

Fritz Lang

083314

KT-486-756

In memory of my old friend
Fritz Lang
whom fate did not enable to
hold this book in his hand.

WITHDRAWN FROM
ST HELENS COLLEGE LIBRARY

.004

.004

Fritz Lang 1974: photo by John Gray

Fritz Lang

by

Lotte H. Eisner

A DA CAPO PAPERBACK

Acknowledgements

All my thanks go first to Fritz Lang for his thorough comprehension, his patience, his interest, his sympathy and deep understanding of my work, as well as for the beautiful stills and the scripts he put at my disposal.

Then, many thanks go to the Cinémathèque Francaise and to Henri Langlois who enabled me to see all the Lang films over and over again; to the photothèque of the Cinémathèque Francaise (there especially to Miss Sybille de Luze and the photographer Mr Jack Salom) for finding and allowing me to use many rare Lang stills. I thank also Mr Herman G. Weinberg for the use of his filmography, and for the use of stills the following people and institutions: Mr Charles Hofmann, Toronto, Ontario, Canada; Mr Phillip Chamberlain, then of the Los Angeles County Museum; the Museum of Modern Art Film Department (especially Mrs Adrienne Mancia); The British Film Institute; Mr Wolfgang Klaue of the Staatliches Filmarchiv, East Berlin; Mr Eberhard Spiess of the Deutsches Institut für Filmkunde, Weisbaden; Bienbrich; the Deutsche Kinemathek, West Berlin; Mr John C. Koball, London, Mr Howard Vernon, Paris, Mr Eric Rhode; and for the portraits of Lang, Mr Axel Madsen, London, and Mr John Gray, Moorpark, California.

I especially thank Mr David Robinson, London, for his invaluable editing of the English version, and Mr David Overbey, Paris, for his important editorial assistance in forming the final version of the book with me over endless pots of tea.

Library of Congress Cataloging in Publication Data

Eisner, Lotte H.
  Fritz Lang.

  (A Da Capo paperback)
  Reprint. Originally published: London: Secker and
Warburg, 1976.
  1. Lang, Fritz, 1890-1976—Criticism and interpreta-
tion. I. Title.
PN1998.S3L3577 1986   791.43′0233′0924   86-11466
ISBN 0-306-80271-6 (pbk.)

This Da Capo Press paperback edition of *Fritz Lang* is an unabridged republication of the edition published in London in 1976. It is reprinted by arrangement with Secker & Warburg Ltd.

Copyright © Lotte H. Eisner
This translation copyright © Martin Secker & Warburg Limited 1976
Published by Da Capo Press, Inc.
A Subsidiary of Plenum Publishing Corporation
233 Spring Street, New York, N.Y. 10013

All Rights Reserved

Manufactured in the United States of America

ST. HELENS
COLLEGE

791.4302 33

83314

JUN 1996

LIBRARY

Contents

Part III: The Second German Period: 1959–1960

Preface

It is much more difficult for me to write about Fritz Lang than about F. W. Murnau – the subject of an earlier book. Murnau I never met: when I came to films in 1927 he had moved to the United States. In order to find out about his working methods I had to spend two or three years interviewing people who had worked with him. Scripts in his brother's possession, written by Carl Mayer, Henrik Galeen, Thea von Harbou, Willy Haas and Hans Kyser, with Murnau's own notes and modifications, gave me new insights, or confirmed impressions of his style derived from repeated viewings of his films. After all this quasi-archaeological excavation, I confined myself to a description of his style and working method, in order not to fall into the trap indicated by Goethe: 'If you cannot interpret, read into it'. I never attempted, then, subjective interpretation of the 'eternal emotional themes' in the work of this long-dead artist, which was the aim of an author of a monograph on Murnau that succeeded my own. For my biographical chapter I had the good fortune of the assistance of Murnau's brother.

In the case of Fritz Lang the undertaking is much more complicated. I have known Lang for many years, and have had opportunities in Paris and Beverly Hills to discuss his films with him, ask him questions, argue – and even occasionally quarrel – with him. In addition we have been able to clarify many points by letter. Lang, moreover, entrusted all his American scripts to me and to the Cinémathèque Française.

Each chapter as finished has been submitted to him for approval and for verification of dates and facts. While never attempting to influence my critical point of view, Lang commented extensively on those facts which had on occasion been misrepresented.

Because he is so intensely alive, Fritz Lang and his films cannot be summed up under one heading or given a simple label. My training as an art historian often tempts me to write about aspects and developments of styles. In answer to this Lang points out to me that every film takes its specific style from its subject matter. Though I believe that he is right in his criticism of an exclusively stylistic interpretation of his films, I had nevertheless occasionally to use this approach, particularly when dealing with his German films, in order to pinpoint, for my own and the reader's understanding, certain tendencies, correspondences of differences in his film work.

Sometimes too I may have yielded to the temptation of ascribing to him certain passages in the American scripts to which Lang rarely signed his own name, since anyone familiar with his methods knows that during preparation for shooting he always brought his own stylistic initiative to bear on the script – even though the final drafts do not tell us anything about his modifications (as do Murnau's hand-written notes).

Much has been written about Lang. It is not my concern to criticise the monographs that have been published on him, all of which Lang himself considers inadequate. For my own part I do not claim to have produced a definitive study. I know that after me there will be others who will arrive at different conclusions about many aspects of his work. This book is, I believe however, the first attempt to do justice to a creative artist who always strove for perfection, and who meditated deeply about himself and about others; without pursuing false illusions; and a fighter who was interested in the battle rather than in the victory.

Fritz Lang: Autobiography

I was born on 5 December 1890, in Vienna, Austria. My father, Anton Lang, was an architect and Stadtbaumeister (municipal architect); my mother's name was Paula, née Schlesinger.

My father wanted me to become an architect too. Yet I had heard too many of his complaints about the disadvantages of his profession to feel much enthusiasm at the prospect of a career as Stadtbaumeister, which would have forced me to spend my whole life in Vienna. I had different plans, yet in order to keep the peace, I agreed to attend lectures in engineering at the Technische Hochschule. In spite of all my good resolutions I only lasted a term there, because I wanted to become a painter.

To begin with I should say that I am a visual person.

I experience with my eyes and never, or only rarely, with my ears – to my constant regret. I love folk songs, but nothing would ever induce me to go to a concert or an opera.

The most important of my childhood memories is the Christkindlmarkt (Christmas Fair). This market is something very special. On a low wooden platform only a step or two higher than the cobbled pavement, there were simple wooden stalls filled with cheap Christmas stuff. As the passage ways between the stalls were roofed over also, it was possible even during a snow storm to walk about the stalls amidst the light of many colourful candles and oil-lamps. There were wonderful things to buy: gay Christmas tree decorations, glass balls and stars and garlands of silvery tinsel and red-cheeked apples and golden oranges and dates; fantastic toys, rocking horses and puppets and Punch and Judy and tin soldiers; toy theatres with characters and scenes for many different

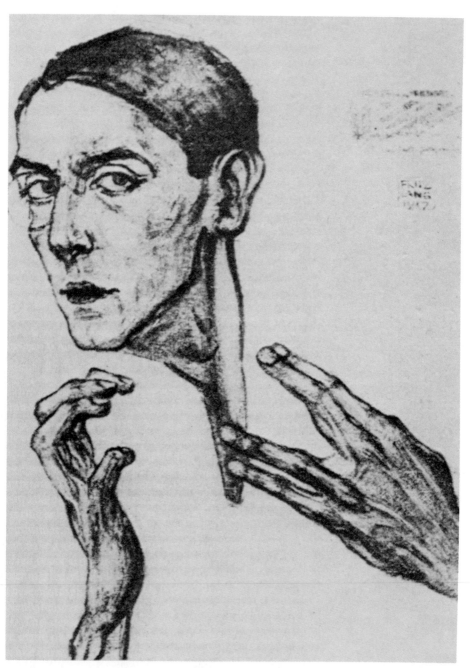

Self-portrait (*above*) in style of Egon Schiele (*opposite*)

plays. With these theatres one could stage real fairy-tale shows, with changing sets. Then there was the Wurstl-prater with a ferris wheel, shooting ranges, side-shows and merry-go-rounds.

I have always been an enthusiastic theatre goer – tickets for the fourth gallery or for standing room were cheap. In those days it never occurred to me that I might one day become a film maker. I wanted to be a painter.

During my school years I read a lot and indiscriminately – good literature and popular stuff alike. But gradually I became more discerning in my reading. I still continued to read whatever I could lay my hands on – theosophy, history, Schopenhauer, Kierkegaard, Nietzsche, the German and Austrian classics; Shakespeare, Hans Sachs, books on occultism, Karl May and Jules Verne, Mayrink's *Golem* . . .

And then I got interested in women. I was precocious and started having affairs very early. Viennese women were the most beautiful and the most generous women in the world. It was the custom to meet secretly in a Viennese café during the interval of the theatres or accidentally after

11 in a cabaret or night club. Women have always been my best friends, right down to the present day.

In spite of my interest in women I have always been a very shy person, even today, though now less so. I found it difficult to make new friends, was always something of a loner, and was considered arrogant as a result. In reality I was probably trying to find myself; and even making films, which later became my over-riding passion, was at first perhaps only an adventure.

At the time I definitely decided to become a painter, and my models were Egon Schiele, who unfortunately died all too early, and Gustav Klimt.

There was trouble when my father learned that I had already worked in two Viennese cabarets – 'Femina' and 'Hölle' – and since I could not convince him that I would make neither a good architect or a successful engineer, I ran away from home – something every decent young man should do. First I went to Belgium, and from there my wanderings took me over half the world, to North Africa, Turkey, Asia Minor and even as far as Bali. Eventually I ended up in Paris. I earned my living by selling hand-painted postcards, my own pictures, and occasionally cartoons to newspapers.

In Paris I went to Maurice Denis's painting school, and in the evening to the Academie Julien to study drawing the nude.

When I had money I went in my spare time to the cinema, because I was already very interested in films from a professional point of view. When I painted or sketched, my subjects were, so to speak, un-animated. We sat, for example, in front of a model and it did not move; but the cinema was really pictures in motion. There I already subconsciously felt that a new art – later I called it the art of our century – was about to be born.

I lived in Paris until August 1914. I remember that in those days nobody really believed in a war between France and Germany. I was sitting in a small café on Montmartre with some friends, when somebody stormed in: 'Jaures assassiné par un camelot du roi'. This was the prelude to the end.

On 5 August I arrived back in Vienna as a refugee from Paris, rented a studio, but did not manage to do much work before I was called up, as a one-year volunteer. At the front, I was promoted to officer rank, was wounded several times, and received some medals. In 1918 I was declared unfit for further front-line service.

All this time I was preoccupied with the new medium of film. In military hospital I wrote some film scenarios – a were-wolf film I did not manage to sell and eventually two scripts, *Wedding in the Eccentric Club* and *Hilde Warren and Death*, both of which I sold to Joe May, then a very well-known producer and director in Berlin.

A few months later, back in Vienna on leave, I saw a newspaper announcement of *Wedding in the Eccentric Club*. I was very proud of my success and invited a number of friends and my girl-friend, too, of course, to come to the opening night. There I received the first shock from the profession that was going to be my life. When the film began I did not find my name credited as the author – though the script had been filmed scene by scene as I had written it. Instead, Joe May figured as author as well as director.

I did not like the direction of the film, and had imagined things differently. I think I must have decided then, sub-consciously, to become a film director. This decision that was to determine my whole life was hence not taken after a lengthy weighing of the pros and cons, but emerged with the same curious, almost somnambulant certainty which I later felt with all my films right to the present day.

This curious instinct that made me feel that I was right in choosing the cinema has never left me. I was completely immune to any criticism of my films, whether good or bad. This is not arrogance or megalomania on my part, and requires explanation: films are, or rather were, until the end of the Second World War, made by a group of people to whom cinema was not only the art of our century, but also the sole purpose of their lives. Among these film-obsessed mortals I count both myself and the members of my crew – whether lighting engineers, studio workers, property men; whoever worked on my films always considered them *their* films. When my crew – author, architect, cameramen and the rest – had worked with me on the preparation of a film, completely giving up their private lives, and then on the shooting and again on the cutting, for months more; and finally at the first showing of the film a critic sat down, after having seen it, to write a review in a hurry because it had to be in next morning's paper; when he condemned the work it had taken a group of men months to do, then I just could not accept his criticisms.

And if I cannot accept a bad review, then, equally, I must not accept a good review.

Early in 1918 I was invalided home to Vienna from the Italian front, to spend two months in hospital. After that I was allowed to leave the hospital during the day, reporting back at eight o'clock in the evening.

One day I found myself in a Viennese café, when a gentleman came up to me and asked if I would take the part of a lieutenant in a play called *Der Hias*. I demanded 1,000 kronen instead of the 800 offered.

At one of the performances I was noticed by Erich Pommer, who offered me a contract with Decla in Berlin. That was in August 1918.

In Berlin I first worked as a script reader, and wrote scenarios. Erich Pommer was more of a friend than a boss to me. I earned little, but I was happy to be able to make films. In order to earn a few extra marks, I played three parts in a film for which I had written the scenario, under the direction of Otto Rippert: a German courier, an old priest and Death. When the Spartacus rebellion began in Berlin I was directing my first film, *Halbblut (The Half Caste)*. On the first day of shooting my car was repeatedly stopped on the way to the studio by armed rebels, but it would have taken more than a revolution to stop me directing for the first time.

Two years later I married the German writer Thea von Harbou, and from then on all my German scripts were written in collaboration with her. Since I now made films in Germany, I acquired German citizenship, of which I was deprived in 1933 by the Hitler regime.

After the Nazis had come to power, my anti-Nazi film, *The Last Will of Dr Mabuse*, in which I put Nazi slogans into the mouth of a pathological criminal, was banned of course. I was called to see Goebbels, not, as I had feared, in order to be called to account for the film but to be told by the Reichspropaganda minister to my surprise, that Hitler had instructed him to offer me the leading post in the German film industry. 'The Führer saw your film *Metropolis* and announced, 'That's the man to make national socialist film . .!'

I left Germany the same evening. The 'interview' with Goebbels had lasted from noon to 2.30 p.m., by which time the banks had already closed and I could not withdraw any money. I had just enough at home to buy a ticket to Paris, and arrived practically penniless at the Gare du Nord. In Paris I met Erich Pommer who had left Germany some weeks before. Friends succeeded in getting me a *carte de travail* and for Pommer, who represented the French branch of Fox, I made the film *Liliom*, based on the play by Ferenc Molnar.

After this film I was offered a contract to work for Metro-Goldwyn-Mayer in Hollywood, so I left France.

Here Fritz Lang's autobiography, which provides important clues to his development, ends. He originally intended to give me an additional chapter on his father's history, but has now had second thoughts. It would in fact have been rather the story of his father's mother, Lang's grandmother, who had come to Vienna from a rural background to work as housekeeper to an upper-class family. The son of the house fell in love with the young girl, and soon she was pregnant. Class barriers in those days were as rigid as castes in India; but she married an honest man who gave her child his name. (Lang likes to recall this story to demonstrate that he is a mixture of peasant stock and haute bourgeoisie.) Despite her Jewish descent, his mother, Paula Schlesinger, was brought up as a Roman Catholic, so that Lang grew up in a thoroughly traditional Viennese Catholic environment.

Lang explained his change of mind about continuing this autobiography: 'A chapter like this would delve deep down into one's private life. And I have always insisted that my private life has nothing to do with me or with my films. If my films do not add up to an image of myself, then I do not deserve the book you are writing about me.'

I have respected Lang's wish, and have not written his personal biography. Instead there are the two chapters on working methods and style, culled from an analysis of his films, from comments of people who worked with him, and from occasional passages in his letters to me. These chapters reveal more about Lang as a human being than the small surface details of his private life or business affairs.★

★The troubles this perfectionist had to survive are in any event illustrated by his numerous movements from one production company to another.

Part I: The German Films Before Hitler and *Liliom*

After the defeat in World War I, and after the obligatory but senseless, because emotional social upheaval, followed by an equally obligatory but much more successful counter-revolution by the reactionary forces, because the counter-revolution was cold-bloodedly conceived and executed – Germany entered a period of unrest and confusion, a period of hysteria, despair and unbridled vice, full of the excesses of an inflation-ridden country.
Fritz Lang: Lecture for the University of California Extension, Riverside, 28 June, 1967

1 Lang's Early Scripts and Films

The First World War brought changes to the Western world. In Europe an entire generation of intellectuals embraced despair. In America, too, intellectuals and artists turned to a rocky wasteland, trying to outdo each other in pessimistic outcry. All over the world, young people engaged in the cultural fields, myself among them, made a fetish of tragedy, expressing open rebellion against the old answers and outworn forms, swinging from naive nineteenth-century sweetness and light to the opposite extremes of pessimism for its own sake.

Fritz Lang: 'Happily Ever After', *Penguin Film Review*, No 5, 1948

With the exception of *The Indian Tomb* and *Plague in Florence*, little is known about Fritz Lang's early scripts for films by Joe May and Otto Rippert. Film was not yet respectable enough to merit reviews in the big daily papers – despite the celebrity won by *The Student of Prague* (1913) and *The Golem* (1914). The trade journals had their own distinctive publicity jargon, whose inadequacy I was able to test in preparing my book on F. W. Murnau. In this case I was lucky to find a few original scripts by Carl Mayer. We would have a totally false idea of these if we had only the clumsy and sentimental plot descriptions of third-rate critics which are our only evidence for most of the lost Lang scripts and films.

Not even this much survives in the trade journals for *Wedding in the Eccentric Club* (1917) an early Lang script filmed by Joe May; or for another May film of the same year, *Hilde Warren and Death*. A fragment of the latter film survives in the East German Staatliches Filmarchiv; but the scenario reveals little apart from Lang's interest, so early, in the death motif.★

The trivial reviews of a lost Otto Rippert film reveal little beyond the standards of reviewing then prevalent: *Kinematograph*, No 149 (1919) says of *Totentanz (Dance of Death)*, using the style fashionable at the time:

★Lang does not recall any other titles from the period, though according to Albin Pötzsch there was a script entitled *Die Rache ist Mein.* Lang does not agree with Eibel that there was also a scenario called *Die Peitsche.*

★★There was no censorship immediately following the World War.

Sascha Gura has splendid costumes which – she doesn't wear most of the time. Shows a lot. If we had a censor★★ he would be in a rage most of the time. The audience is calm of course. Grateful admiration. Occasionally the director Otto Rippert should have avoided too scantily dressed legs. In spite of his preference for such effects. Otherwise his work is almost perfect. He has honest collaborators.

As one of these 'honest collaborators', Fritz Lang called the film 'a nocturne in five acts', which suggests that it was

Mia May in *Hilde Warren and Death* (1917); *The Indian Tomb* (1921) (*opposite*)

intended to possess a certain atmospheric quality. *Film*, No 23 (1919) provides a synopsis:

The novelty of this film is its subject matter . . . The setting . . . is the strangely laid house of an even stranger cripple, Dr Sephar (Werner Krauss). He hates the world and 'She' (Sascha Gura) is the tool with which he wreaks destruction and lures people to their death. 'She' dances, her body attracts men as light attracts insects, though they know that they will suffer death. One assumes that many others have already been destroyed when she makes Harry Free die. Dr Sellin and Frederic die, the latter without ever having enjoyed her. The first man she loves is Stuart O'Connor. She plans to escape with him. The ever-present Dr Sephar, forever spying on her, learns about this. He promises Stuart his freedom if he can find his way out of the maze under the house. Stuart dies of his guilty conscience: he has murdered Hennekemper. Sephar wants to possess 'Her'. This revolting old man on crutches wants her beautiful body, and tries to rape her. They fight, wrestle; she is almost overcome and has been forced down on the divan when the apache steps out of a niche and strangles Dr Sephar. Free at last, she runs to the coffin of Stuart, the man she won by her dancing; and dances until she is exhausted, collapses, dies.*

*F. W. Murnau filmed a similar story, though with a happy ending, in *Der Bucklige und die Tänzerin*, from a screenplay by Carl Mayer. The hunchback's 'strange house' could even have been suggested by Lang's scenario, and would be an example of the influence of his visual ideas on contemporary film-makers.

This inadequate and ill-written plot description gives little indication of the quality of the scenario. The synopsis in *Lichtbildbuhne* No 24 (1919) is not much more help:

In his hands the beautiful woman is a helpless tool . . . and brings death and destruction without showing any emotion of her own . . . until finally she is on fire herself and prepares her escape with her lover. Yet her torturer gets there first, sends the happy rival to his death and makes a grab for the beautiful victim himself when revenge at last strikes him down. He is strangled by the apache, while the woman dances round the corpse of her lost lover in despair until she sinks down dead at his side.

We are left to speculate on such apparently characteristic touches as the house and the Lulu figure of the *femme fatale*, which was to recur in many later Lang scripts.

An advertisement for *Totentanz* in *Film,* No 23 (1919), shows that Lang was already a well-known film writer: 'Four of the big names in modern film are responsible for this work: Werner Krauss, Sascha Gura, Fritz Lang, Otto Rippert'. Yet as late as *Pest in Florenz (Plague in Florence)* we find reviews which do not mention the author's name at all. This film, of which fragments survive in the Staatliches Filmarchiv of the DDR, is a little better documented. *Der Film* No 44 (1919) reports that its first screening at the prestigious Marmorhaus was an event; and there is a sentence, usual at that time, soon after the defeat, about the resolution of the German film industry to 'concentrate its efforts on the competition with other countries in which it has a fairly good chance to conquer'. Similarly, *Neue Berliner 12-Uhr-Zeitung* of 24 October 1919 describes it as: 'A film that testifies to the achievements of German film industry and that can become a fine representative example of German film in the international market'.

The description of the film suggests it was a kind of prelude to Lang's Venetian Renaissance episode in *Destiny*: 'The film, which Lang has divided into seven parts, shows us Florence at the time of the Renaissance in a series of colourful and evocative scenes; splendid festive sequences, large-scale mass scenes and dramatic events to keep the eyes riveted from beginning to end.' Lang had already begun his practice of giving very detailed indications of the action. He recalls how he tried in one of these early Rippert scripts to confine himself to a single sentence: 'Here an orgy takes place', without going into details. Rippert came to him and asked, 'But what shall I do there?', so from then on Lang made a habit of describing every sequence in great detail.

Der Film relates the content in highly-coloured prose:

A courtesan of irresistible beauty comes from decadent Venice to the pious town of Florence, which is governed strictly by the council of elders. Cesare, the master of the town, falls for her charms, but his handsome son also falls in love with the glorious woman. The whole of Florence lapses into debauchery; the town's youth flocks to the courtesan's house, which is the centre of vice, lust and love. Too late, Cesare recognises that he has been overcome by the woman's arts, that she rejects him and prefers his own son. Embittered, he sends her to the torture chamber. The son then kills the father, the churches are turned into places of lust, all Florentines have become licentious. The hermit Franciscus calls in vain for people to search their souls and repent. He, too, falls victim to the immoral woman and he, too, kills his rival. The population becomes wilder and even more licentious. Then the ghost of Death appears; Plague. Yellow grinning Death rises up in the midst of debauchery. It visits the palaces of the rich and the hovels of the poor. It demands its victims inexorably. Nobody can resist it, nobody can escape. The town of joy and pleasure is transformed into a scene of horror. All perish miserably.

Again in this script – perhaps inspired by Poe's *The Masque of the Red Death* – Lang associates a fateful woman and death.

Little is known about Otto Rippert, apart from a few surviving episodes from *Homunculus* (1916), whose powerful crowd scenes and effects of light suggest that the youthful Lang could have learned a few things from the older director. Contemporary reviews of *Pest in Florenz* praise Rippert's 'highly developed artistic sense'. *Die Welt am Abend* (24 October 1919) goes so far as to say 'The Good Friday procession easily surpasses the mass scenes in *Dubarry* (directed by Lubitsch). *BZ am Mittag* of the same date praises the gay festive scenes and the Dantesque hell of the raging epidemic. It is hard to know what was Lang's contribution. *Lichtbildbühne* No 49 (1919) speaks of the astounding images that show Lang's exquisite sense of style and artistic understanding.

No reviews have been traced for another Rippert film from a Lang script, *The Woman with the Orchid*, although the title seems to suggest another *femme fatale* theme. Of *Lilith and Ly*, a Lang script filmed in 1919 by Erich Kober (a director apparently unknown outside Austria) Walter Fritz says that only a few stills have survived. Fritz* gives

* *Filmkunst*, No 4, 4a, 1965

the following summary of the plot:

Frank Landow, a scholar and ladies' man, is at work on an invention –
a television mirror. During a pleasure trip to India he discovers
fragments of a parchment roll from which he learns the secret of
creating life. Returning home, he brings to life a statue, the work of a
school friend, with the help of a ruby. It is the creature Lilith, with
whom Landow falls in love. He continues to work on his invention,
and soon the mirror is ready to be set up. By now Landow, who never
keeps the same woman for long, is in love with Ly. But Lilith changes
into a vampire. In his mirror Frank becomes a passive witness of her
murder of one of his friends. The vampire grows more and more
powerful. As Landow lies ill in bed with glandular fever, Lilith appears
to him in the form of Ly; and also threatens Ly herself. In utmost
despair, Frank destroys the television mirror in which he was forced to
witness the horrible spectacle, and smashes the statue from which
Lilith was made. Yet only after he has thrown the ruby, the vampire
stone, into the river, can he and Ly be saved from the horror of
supernatural forces.

The television mirror anticipates *The Spiders, Metropolis*
and particularly *The Thousand Eyes of Dr Mabuse*.

The last script which Lang wrote for another director –
this time in collaboration with Thea von Harbou – was the
two-part Joe May film, *The Indian Tomb* (1921). By this
time, since *The Half-Caste* (1918), Lang was a director in
his own right, and understandably disappointed that the
Joe May film company gave the subject to the older and
apparently more experienced director rather than giving it
to him, the young author. *Der Film*, No 41, 1921, calls *The
Indian Tomb* uncompromisingly 'the world's greatest film'
and speaks of 'the immense expense': the two parts cost 24
million marks:

Again, unfortunately, the Joe May film does not manage to avoid an
error which seems to be common to all costume films; i.e. to use a
script that is logically and psychologically weak. The story by the
competent authoress whose writing during the war constituted part of
the 'lay-it-on-thick' kind of literature and is now as resolutely film-
orientated, presents an India that is too close to the ideas of the man in
the street, quite apart from the psychological blunders which one does
not expect in an author as experienced as Fritz Lang. Or does he think
it natural that the Indian prince should tell his newly appointed
architect intimate details about his married life? And similar episodes.
The apologetic prelude is most inartistic, too. Why not simply have an
Indian market with fakirs showing their magic tricks (if it is considered
necessary at all to give an explanation?)

The review praises the stunt work (which may or may not

have figured in the scenario), but calls Conrad Veidt a western-type neurotic who completely lacks the proverbial majestic solemnity of Indian royalty. The critic finds the second part, *The Tiger of Eschnapur*, more powerful than the first, though,

the script's weaknesses affect this part, too. Joe May's direction has to make up for this by using strong and effective detail . . .

The review concludes:

The Prince's collapse by the corpse of his still ardently beloved wife is of great human beauty. In between are coldly theatrical splendours, in particular the totally unnecessary scene of the sacrifice to the God of the Penitents, with its sentimental ending, 'Your sacrifice was to make me into your God. Through the sacrificial ecstasy of your soul, I wanted to recover . . .'

EARLY FILMS

Halbblut (The Half Caste, 1919)

Little evidence survives of lang's earliest films. His first work as director, *Halbblut*, made for the so-called Ressel-Orla Serial, was premièred at the Marmorhaus, a prestigious cinema that still stands on Berlin's Kurfürstendamm. The *Kinematograph* gave the following summary:

It is the story of two men and a woman, called *Halbblut*, and demonstrates the consequences of marrying a half-caste. 'You may take a half-caste for mistress, but you should never make her your wife', the young husband is told by a friend. The girl, a whore from a Mexican opium den, hears these words and decides to take revenge for the insult. The revenge makes up the story of this tragedy.

The review mentions as the centre of interest the rewarding title role played by Ressel Orla, the Decla star. The most interesting part of this clumsy notice is a rather curious passage, which follows mention of the actors of the main roles, and the writing and direction of Fritz Lang:

Why shoot scenes which are meant to take place in the open air in the studio? People permitted themselves such jokes in the past. Nowadays one is irritated by open-air scenes which have been shot in the glass-house.

From this we can gather that even at this early stage Lang was shooting outdoor scenes in the studio, as he was later to do in *Destiny* and *Nibelungen*, for better atmospheric effects; and also that the critic believes he is criticising a solecism instead of understanding that Lang, the landscape

23

painter, had to work as he did. Apart from this the critic confines himself to a complaint about the trade-mark 'Decla Filmgesellschaft' on all the titles, which allowed pranksters to read the words out loud along with the rest of the text, for comic effect.

We learn a little more about the story of *Halbblut* from a review in *Der Film* (no 141) of 1919:

The film has Ressel Orla playing the part of a woman of dubious character, a cross between two races, who inherits only the worst characteristics of both. Cunning bitch! She ruins two men, one of whom dies in a lunatic asylum, the other in a penitentiary, and only a *mestizo,* a kindred spirit, finds happiness with her. Together with him she engages in card sharping in their own establishment until their game is up. Before they succeed in fleeing from Europe, intending to escape to Mexico with all their spoil, fate catches up with her in the shape of a bullet from the revolver of a man whom she has cheated, but who has still sufficient presence of mind to exterminate 'this flower of civilisation'.

The script is dramatic and of flawless logic . . . Fritz Lang's direction shows taste, expert knowledge, and a rare instinct from tonal values that are so effective cinematically that success is automatically assured.

Lichtbildbühne (No 14/1919) writes:

A characteristic merit of the film is the dramatic quality of its plot, which increases from act to act. This, and its rather good direction and impeccable treatment makes it into a feature film of top quality.

Der Herr der Liebe
(Master of Love, 1919)

Lang's next film was written not by himself but by Oscar Koffler; and the director also took part as an actor (since *Der Hias* in the theatre, he had acted in a number of the films he had written himself, in Berlin). The *Kinematograph,* Düsseldorf edition, No 664, 1919, says very little about the content of the film except that the plot of *Der Herr der Liebe* manages to break with the conventions of society drama:

The director tries hard to find images unusual in the medium of the film for his plot, Gilda Langer* shows a roguish charm and passionate devotion in the intimate scenes with her husband; she is as perfect in expressing secret jealousy and long suffering as in expressing hatred and the emotion of gratified revenge. Her partner de Vogt tries to emulate Gilda Langer's masterful artistry . . . A number of successful masks are lifelike copies of members of the leisured aristocracy. Direction and photography are impeccable . . . The film may be counted among the pearls of a programme, though not one of the most precious ones.

* This actress was to have played Jane in *Caligari,* but died just before the film was shot and was replaced by Lil Dagover.

Harakiri 1919

Between the two episodes of *The Spiders*, Lang filmed *Harakiri*, an adaptation of *Madame Butterfly* by Max Jungk. *Der Kinematograph* (31 December 1919) discusses the fascination of exotic films, the clever handling that takes the spectator straight into other people's lives and customs, the images of 'astonishing fidelity to nature' (a number of Japanese extras were used). The house in which the little geisha spends the honeymoon of her 999-day marriage to the European naval officer 'lies in the midst of flower dreams like a fairy-tale house'. There is praise for the festival of falling leaves, with the melée of little boats with lanterns for the Yoshiwara of Nagasaki. 'Pretty lighting effects heighten the charm of street life in the evening.' As in *The Spiders*, the authentic costumes and decorations were supplied by the Ethnographical Museum run by I. F. G. Umlauff.

Harakiri (1919)

The review in *Der Kinematograph* goes on to tell us that 'Fritz Lang's direction renders all the subtleties of the plot with loving attention and takes good care that taste is never offended, even in minor details.' *Der Film* (Volume 4, no 51) gives a summary of the story that had been lengthened to six (one-reel) acts from the four acts of the opera. A lecherous priest intends to make the girl a temple prostitute, thus causing her father to commit harakiri. O-Take-San consequently seeks refuge with a Danish naval officer, and so into the story.

The reviewer remarks that 'a careful dramatic preparation of the plot would certainly have made things easier for the direction (Fritz Lang) and the actors'. Surprising as this is in view of Lang's habitual care over preparation, it may refer to the scenario, which was not his. Moreover it must be remembered that he shot no less than six films in 1919, three of which he also wrote.

The *Berliner Börsenzeitung* of 21 December 1919,

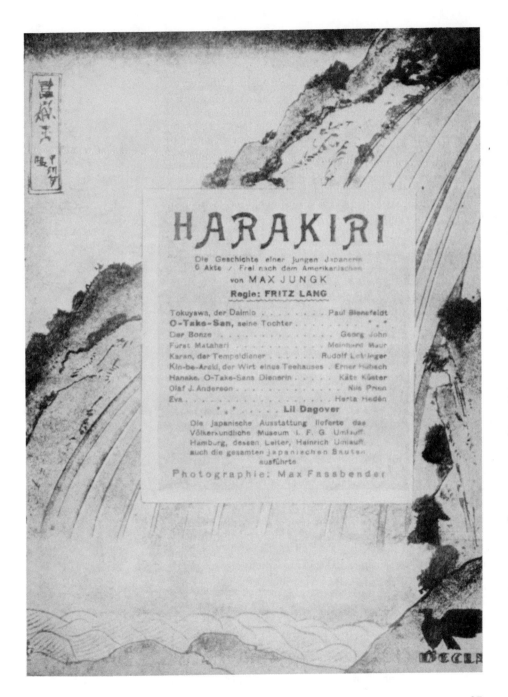

HARAKIRI

Die Geschichte einer jungen Japanerin
6 Akte / Frei nach dem Amerikanischen
von MAX JUNGK

Regie: FRITZ LANG

Tokuyawa, der Daimio . . . . Paul Bienefeldt
O-Take-San, seine Tochter . . . . " "
Der Bonze . . . . Georg John
Fürst Matahari . . . . Meinhard Maur
Karan, der Tempeldiener . . . . . . Rudolf Lettinger
Kin-be-Araki, der Wirt eines Teehauses . Ernst Hübsch
Hanake, O-Take-Sans Dienerin . . . . . Käte Küster
Olaf J. Anderson . . . . Nils Prien
Eva . . . . Herta Hedén
" . " . . . . . . **Lil Dagover**

Die japanische Ausstattung lieferte das
Völkerkundliche Museum I. F. G. Umlauff,
Hamburg, dessen Leiter, Heinrich Umlauff,
auch die gesamten japanischen Bauten
ausführte

Photographie: Max Fassbender

praising the film's 'vivid realistic picture of life as it is', affords more positive comments:

There is now much talk of the film which is nothing but pure film and sticks to the limits set by the possibilities of the screen, using the latter to the full. This is such a film. It is strange how close the Japanese subject seems to come to the essential nature of film . . . the silent mime . . .

The plot is gratifyingly progressive; only people expecting crass literalness could call it boring . . . the more profound person will find richness and much pleasure in scenes that resemble miniature paintings.

The outdoor shots are quite splendid and very picturesque, particularly those of Japanese festivities. One would not have thought the happy grounds of Woltersdorf could produce all this . . . a film product of the highest rank.

Das Wandernde Bild
(The Wandering Image, 1920)

The outdoor scenes of Lang's next film may also have been shot in Woltersdorf. *Lichtbildbühne* of 1 January 1921 gives the following summary:

Mia May, who plays the female lead, has surrendered herself to a disciple of free love, and, having given birth to a child, marries the twin brother and *Doppelgänger* of her chosen lover, in his name. When the philosopher finds out about this, he retires into the mountains, vowing not to return to civilization until a statue of the virgin which he passed on his way in the snow begins to walk. His brother pursues the woman he married, but she is saved by an unknown relative and escapes. Pursued, she meets the hermit. The pursuer goes mad and perishes. The lost girl devotes her life to the poor. One stormy night when the statue of the virgin is destroyed by the elements she brings a strange child back to her home. The hermit takes her for the walking statue of the virgin and is reunited with his companion.

The review continues:

The film's best moments are the splendid nature shots in impeccable photography, snow landscapes and in particular the storm scene. The most artistic of all is a scene where the door of the hut is opened and lightning lights up the snowscape.

The action is said to be punctuated by an explosion, avalanches, cliff-hanger chases, a fall from a mountain – 'almost too many good things'. Of the script by Lang and Thea von Harbou, *Film-Kurier* (January 1921) says:

What seemed like promising signs of profound insight and real

Das Wandernde Bild (1920): Mia May and Hans Marr (*above*)

Das Wandernde Bild

problems in the first two acts turn out to be nothing but plot motivation, and are carried along vaguely by diluted mysticism and religion. Sentiment is called into play when Frau von Harbou is at a loss for a rational solution . . . Is the happily reunited couple intended to be a symbolic answer to the ethical question? . . . Too easy.

So much on a subject that demands a proper and serious discussion. As I said it has weaknesses and faults and yet it is very effective. This is mainly due to perfect staging. The script is exemplary in the composition of its dramatic structure, due probably to the director's collaboration, and achieves a much higher artistic level than the plot because of the genuinely tasteful means by which tension and interest is maintained . . . Fritz Lang's direction is outstanding, particularly the crowd scenes, e.g. the peasant wedding on the Bavarian mountain lake, the peasant dance, the changing group scenes with ever-new types, all very colourful and vivid. The careful distribution of effects ensures that every one of the five acts is equally lively.

The review is notable as the first time a distinction is made between the work of Thea von Harbou and Fritz Lang's direction and collaboration on the script.

Vier un die Frau
(Four Around a Woman, 1920)

The last of these early Lang films – also known in English as *Fighting Hearts* – was scripted by Ralph E. Vanloo. *Film und Presse* (516; 1921) merely talks about a tasteful feature film,

with an original plot, logical and consistent in spite of a host of disparate themes; dramatically well constructed, interesting right up to its tragic ending that could be called a real film ending. The core of the complicated plot is the struggle of four men for one woman. Chance, kismet and mysterious darkness, heightened by a *doppelgänger*. Final exposure of the evil principle and victory of the good. Contrition.

Otherwise all that we are told is that Lang's direction is 'tasteful, sure in its handling of effects and full of original details. Evening and night scenes are done in superb lighting'. *Lichtbildbühne* (13 February 1921) at least gives the complicated plot:

The dealer Yquem buys his adored wife a precious piece of jewelry with forged money, in a place where thieves and receivers of stolen goods meet, and whither he goes disguised. There he finds a gentleman who looks exactly like a portrait he once found among his wife's possessions. He follows him to an elegant hotel, where he leaves a letter, in a faked hand-writing, inviting the man to come to his house. William Krafft also turns up. Then, for a few hours of the night, Yquem's house becomes the scene of a series of violent acts and crimes in quick succession. Florence is revealed to be innocent; Yquem's friend turns out to be a common criminal and is shot. The gentleman con-man William Krafft is arrested, and Yquem also is punished for his misguided deeds. . . .

Lang achieves good visual effects. Yet not all the implications of the complicated action are worked out clearly.

Little of real importance can be divined from these naïve reviews; and it is from Lang's earliest surviving films, the two episodes of *The Spiders* that we must seek a true impression of the young Lang's work as director.

2 Die Spinnen (The Spiders, 1919)

Episode One: Der Goldene See (The Golden Lake)

The first episode of the adventure series 'The Adventure of Kai Hoog in Known and Unseen Worlds' according to *Der Kinematograph* (8 October 1919), was to be the first film 'produced by Decla Film Company, recently put on its feet again by a massive capital injection'. As customary in the period following the end of hostilities, there is a sentence to the effect that everybody is 'very proud to produce work which may also attract attention abroad'. 'The Decla Company', the notice continues, 'intends with this series to become a rival to the American film industry, which makes mainly Westerns . . . Our film industry can be proud of this film work and other countries will acknowledge with envy the advances we have been making, when they see this film.'

The tone of this article must be attributed partly to its appearance in a trade journal; partly to the massive inferiority complex of a country defeated in the war, and heightened by the difficulties of breaking into foreign markets. (As late as 1921 *Caligari* had to be called Austrian in order to get a showing in Paris.) Hence the talk about 'massive capital injection' and the assertion that people in foreign countries, faced with the brilliant novelties from the German film market would not be able to close their eyes to the fact that in spite of all the fateful happenings of the past the Germans remain efficient and take pride in their work and are 'clever fellows' still.

Now quite obsessed by creating works of art in the expressive new medium, Lang was quite without interest in this side of things.

As for criticism, *Der Kinematograph* acknowledges the

I simply wanted to film adventurous subjects. I was still very young. I loved everything that was exuberant and exotic. And furthermore I was able to make use of memories of my travels.
Fritz Lang: Choix de textes etabli par Alfred Eibel, *Presences du Cinema*, Paris 1964

'scrupulous care' which had gone into the making of this film, including enlisting the services of an authority on ethnography, Heinrich Umlauff, the founder and owner of an ethnographical museum. With his expert advice, it seems, the buildings and sculptures of the Incas were reconstructed, and the authenticity of Inca costumes and customs ensured. The buildings had been built in the grounds of the Hagenbeck Zoological Gardens in Hamburg, thanks to an arrangement made by Umlauff, a relative of Hagenbeck.

Surprisingly the review makes no mention of the comparable American serials – school of Pearl White – or of the French *films aux episodes* of Feuillade. The writer enthuses about the adventurer type presented by Karl de Vogt (who today seems somewhat colourless) as Kai Hoog, praising him for riding 'like a cowboy', swimming and climbing with great daring and skill and even simulating a parachute jump from the basket of his balloon, 'which he had previously courageously climbed into by means of a rope, while it was ascending'. Ressel Orla is admired as his equal in acting and skilful embodiment of an elegant sporting lady and millionairess, daring adventuress and head of the secret society of 'spiders'. Today we are conscious only of a mediocre and rather plump actress, an ideal beauty of the times in long skirts and blouse – the *dernier cri* of fashion.

Der Film (No 41, 1919) approaches the production of the great adventure film in a less nationalist and more factual spirit:

The first step was to make an adventure film deliberately restricted to a thrilling well-made plot without any literary ambitions . . . This was inevitable since the erotic film had lost its attraction almost completely* and the detective film is dying.

The reviewer acknowledges the sources – return to Karl May (*Schatz im Silbersee*) and to Leatherstocking – and remarks that it is:

the first German film deliberately to use the technique of the penny dreadful, by keeping the spectators in suspense, waiting for the next instalment.

* Perhaps an allusion to the so-called sex education films of the type made by Oswald.

The Düsseldorf edition of *Der Kinematograph* (1 October 1919) had more to say about the artistic aspect:

Fritz Lang offers a rich variety of fairy-tale miracles and splendours skilfully woven and structured into an exciting and dramatic plot which retains our interest all the time. The sensational effects which strain the spectators' nerves to their utmost are used so discreetly, naturally and matter-of-fact that they seem never contrived, but are organically and logically developed out of the story and its integral elements.

This reviewer has discovered a characteristic of Lang's style: we shall find such moments of suspense which are organic parts and logical developments of the plot, again and again in his later films.

Alas the faded copies from weakened dubbed negatives which are all that have survived of the film can give little idea of the individual images which, the reviewer continued, 'surpass each other in striking beauty and exotic flavour that occasionally assumes compelling force':

The direction gives perfection to these images with its subtle, carefully considered artistic touches and the sure instinct for cinematographic effect; it gives the plot moments of tension which must be considered extremely felicitous dramatic ideas.

The second part of the series, *Das Brillantenschiff (The Diamond Ship)* was coolly received by *Der Film* (No 7, 1920), as 'quite good', but a second best to a comparable film, *Herrin der Welt*:

Sticking close to its American models, the film is psychologically even less convincing than these. Even the sensational bits are not consistently successful. . . . This may be the reason why Decla brought this film out rather quietly. It concludes, incidentally, the adventure series which was originally meant to have been in four parts. . . . In this last film Fritz Lang, the film writer and director, probably did not have enough funds to enable him to reach the artistic level of his previous work.

Another indication that the producer was less interested in the second instalment is that it was not serialised in *Film-Kurier* as was *Der Goldene See*.

The reasons for the fading away of the serial and the abandoning of the proposed further episodes was evidently internal, and in no way indicated a lack of interest on the part of the audience: indeed, reviewers did not hesitate to predict success for the second film on account of its 'skilful dramatic effects'. But against Lang's protests, shooting of *Das Brillantenschiff* (originally named *Sklavenschiff*) was not begun until the autumn (*Harakiri* being squeezed in between); and because of bad weather conditions filming had to be transferred from the Hagenbeck grounds to the studio. Angry, Lang severed his contract with Decla and signed a new one with Joe May.

The scenario of *Der Goldene See* is more straightforward than the plot of the second part, with its variety and numerous episodes, even though *Der Kinematograph* described it as too vivid, varied and rich to summarise in a few words:

In the beginning, unfortunately, the episodic development was rather erratic and that made it difficult to understand what the film is all about. But as the plot proceeded it gradually became more consistent.

Evidently German audiences of this time were not accustomed to the skilful montages which Lang as scenarist used to build up his stories. The film opens with a ragged old man clambering with difficulty out of a rocky cave on to a cliff overhanging the sea. He writes something on a piece of material, puts it into a bottle, which he seals and throws into the sea. An Inca in full war dress sneaks up behind and kills the old man.

The scene changes to a city and an evening party, much like a party in a Feuillade serial. One chair remains empty: Kai Hoog's. The luscious Lio-Sha is introduced, demonic and mondaine, hair parted like Cléo de Mérode.

Fritz Lang has yet to discover the accelerating power of ellipsis. Kai Hoog's arrival is leisurely in treatment; a servant takes his hat and coat before he finally tells the assembled guests why he is late. A flashback shows him sportily attired in a motorboat, and discovering the letter in the bottle. There is a characteristic piece of Lang documentary detail: in his exotic living room Kai Hoog tries to open the bottle which is encrusted with shells and seaweed, showing how long it has remained in the sea.

A retarding comic interlude: in the cellar, the wine waiter tastes the guests' wine. The young director permits the waiter and the two little servants to overdo their mugging; later Lang will become adept at such comedy scenes. Above stairs Kai Hoog, who has put the piece of material quickly into his pocket to prevent Lio Sha's seeing it, touches glasses with her so violently that his newly filled glass breaks. Hostilities are declared!

The adventure now proceeds in a direct line. Kai Hoog is robbed of the precious rag by figures in masks and black leotards. Knocked out by chloroform, when he comes

Scenes from *Die Spinnen* (1919)

round he discovers a black spider. The similarities with Feuillade serials are apparent, though at this date Lang cannot recall if he saw them: when *Les Vampires* was released, in any case, France was at war with Germany and Lang himself was in the army.

Kai Hoog and 'The Spiders' set out individually to seek the mysterious treasures of the subterranean Inca city described by the rag. They travel by train, balloon and sailing boat. Kai Hoog rescues a beautiful, improbable sun priestess (Lil Dagover) from a snake. The descendants of the ancient Incas kidnap Lio Sha from the Spiders' camp, intending to sacrifice her to the Sun God. Kai Hoog, noble and incautious, cannot help himself from rescuing her. The Spiders invade the sun temple; and there is a massacre. In the golden lake the Spiders find the rich golden treasure of the Incas, and while fighting for possession, kill one another. Their leader (Georg John, an actor who had played in *Harakiri* and whom Lang was later frequently to

use after he had built up his own favourite group of actors)
goes mad. There is a subterranean eruption, in which rocks
fall upon the gang of criminals; and this is followed by a
flood. Kai Hoog and the beautiful sun priestess escape in an
extravagant makeshift ark made of carpets and ropes, are
washed out to sea through a subterranean waterfall, and
saved by a ship. Lio Sha also manages to make her escape,
and gathers a new gang of criminals around her.

She invades the peaceful and exotic home where Kai
Hoog now lives with his Inca wife. Kai Hoog spurns her
threats, but later that day returns home to find his young
wife, whom he left lying on a garden chair, dead on the
lawn, a black spider on her bosom.

Already Lang's style makes itself felt on a film
superficially no different from the run of melodramatic
serials of the 1910s. There is the taste for underground
chambers which leads him from Alberich's treasure cave to
the underground town of *Metropolis,* the old professor's

moon grotto in *Die Frau im Mond,* the leper caves and temple grotto of the Indian films of the end of his career. A psychoanalyst might produce all kinds of interpretations; yet it may be no more than a love of the mysterious, atmospheric and unusual, a curiosity about the mysteries that lurk beneath the surfaces of the earth. The interior of a cave is an ideal location for chiaroscuro effects or, as in the Indian films, colour dissolves and transformations. Mystery, the evocation of atmosphere and a sense of transcendence are better achieved even than in Siegfried's magic forest.

Alongside dream and fantasy there is always Lang's documentary instinct. He engages experts to recreate the Inca temples; the gold treasure is perfectly convincing.

As well as the caves there are the cellars of the secret organisation, the armour-plated vaults which serve the Spiders as conference rooms. Walls glide apart, lifts and trap doors lead downwards, sliding doors afford secret escapes, or traps for the invader. Eminently respectable-seeming gentlemen in top hats and tails go down in the lifts to their sinister conferences (echoes of the nineteenth century 'habits-noirs' gangs who also operated in top hats). In the corner of the lift, cheek by jowl with the world of formal suits and top hats, stands a Chinese guard with a huge scimitar. Lio Sha's boudoir is equally exotic. Her extravagant mechanical armoury includes a desk which can descend like a lift, taking the documents with it; and a circular mirror in which may be seen the proceedings of the conference room – an anticipation of television, of the countless television screens in *The Thousand Eyes of Dr Mabuse*, and the screens over which the foreman (Heinrich George) tells Herr Frederson about the workers' rebellion in *Metropolis*.

The subterranean vaults and caves are supplemented by an extravagant surface world. Through the glass walls of a sight-seeing railway carriage, Lang can reveal to Kai Hoog and his friend the world of adventure. At that period there was no back projection. With the same simplicity as a Lumière cameraman would film the passing scenery from the window of a moving train, Lang's cameraman filmed the view from a scenic railway, without ever looking for the exotic.

A Western sequence has Kai Hoog in a cowboy hat,

looking for all the world like William S. Hart, and a hold-up, in best Western style, in which Kai Hoog retrieves his precious rag. All the Spiders set off in pursuit of him. He barricades himself in a log house, which is besieged. As shots are fired, Kai Hoog escapes through the skylight, and from the roof, with the help of a tree, mounts his horse. The action moves between Kai Hoog's wild dash on horseback and a waiting balloon, with Kai Hoog's friend anxiously consulting his watch. At the last moment, Kai Hoog arrives, seizes the rope hanging from the already ascending balloon, and is saved. 'Such sensation', said the Düsseldorf *Kinematograph*, 'makes heavy demands on the spectators' nerves.'

Das Brillantenschiff is, as I have said, more complex. Indeed, the reviews suggest that Lang's narrative exuberance and rich visual texture provoked a degree of bewilderment. The story begins with a robbery in a London bank, guarded on the street by an unsuspecting policeman. This well-planned and perfectly executed operation recalls *M*, even to the tied-up watchman struggling to break out of his fetters. A tilt-shot, enabling the viewer to take in all the offices at once, adds to the mystery of the operation.

The Spiders are after one particular diamond in their pile of loot – a stone in the shape of a Buddha's head, which is supposed to make the woman who wears it the liberator and ruler of alien-dominated Asia.

Lang employs his whole repertory of adventure techniques. This time Kai Hoog does not use an old-fashioned balloon, but flies by plane over the rooftops of London to find Liò Sha's house, and enter it by the roof. 'A modern razzia' runs the title (surprisingly laconic in view of the long-winded style of most of the titles in the list, fortunately preserved). As with the earlier robbery, the force of Lang's presentation is to give precise documentation to colourful improbabilities. Kai Hoog shoots the Chinese lift attendant; police force their way into the building; sliding doors create confusion; gas is let in; people fight for air; walls have to be broken down.

At an alarm signal, secret doors open and Lio Sha, who has been presiding over a conference with the new gang leader and a high-ranking mandarin (the same actor as the Jewish junk-dealer in the Western episode), escapes with her gang. Kai Hoog only manages to snatch a mysterious document and a strangely shaped piece of ivory from the dead mandarin.

A quaint old professor (closely resembling the thread-bare apothecary in *Destiny* and the mad professor in *Die Frau im Mond*) interprets the document and the ivory: it is the password which admits to the subterranean Chinese town beneath the Chinese quarter. More trap doors, stairs, corridors, and a whole colourful and confusing under-ground world, guarded by Eschnapur tigers behind bars. Kai Hoog, going to observe an assignation between Lio Sha and the captain among the gambling establishments and opium dens, apparently allows himself to be put to sleep after smoking opium. Suddenly, however, he grabs Lio Sha in order to make his escape. (A scene which appears at this point in surviving copies of the film, with Kai Hoog in a narrow dungeon into which water slowly seeps, probably belongs to the razzia sequence and has been cut in by mistake.)

The hiring of the captain of the *Sturmvogel* is characteris-tic. He is first seen sitting in a wine house. A tramp sits next to him and, to the captain's disgust, keeps spitting. Then the tramp dips his dirty finger into the captain's glass and writes the number 100,000 on the table. By the time the bar-maid comes up the tramp has already erased the figure, and remarks impudently that the captain will pay.

A large and mysterious box is stowed in the hold of the *Sturmvogel*. Inside, we see Kai Hoog dressed in Fantomas style (which strongly suggests that the young Lang *had* seen the Feuillade serials). Choosing his time, Kai Hoog will emerge from his box, overpower the radio operator in order to read his messages, and frighten the cook, who takes him for a ghost. Pursued, he will climb on to the masthead and jump into the sea, in order to reach the treasure island.

First, however, the audience is taken to another mysterious continent: Asia. The Spiders are trying to enlist the help of a Maharahja to whom they promise the mysterious stone. Using hypnosis (as Lang would later do in *Mabuse*; had Lang seen Wegener's *Yogi*?) a Yogi endeavours to find out where the diamond is hidden. So the new leader of the gang learns that the diamond is in the hands of diamond king John Terry in London. Before he can tell them more, the Yogi dies of a heart attack.

In London the Spiders try to break into the safe of the absent John Terry, but are surprised by his daughter whom they carry off, rolled up in a carpet. As ransom they demand the stone; but Terry insists – even to Kai Hoog – that he knows nothing about it except that one of his ancestors was captain of a pirate ship. He produces his portrait and the log of his ship, the *Seehexe*, from which some pages are missing. The log mentions a rock cave on the Falkland Islands. In the proper style of the genre, Kai Hoog discovers Terry's servant listening at the door. He tears off the man's wig – it is the notorious Fourfinger John of the Spiders. He is locked up, but releases a pigeon with a message for Lio Sha.

The action moves to the rocky cave on the Falklands, which has the stalagmite look of Alberich's treasure caves. There Kai Hoog finds the diamond among the rich treasure and skeletons of long-dead pirates. The Spiders soon follow him and overpower him. When he denies that he has the stone they declare (title) 'Hunger and thirst will make you come round in the end'. They all lie down to sleep in the cave, but as a title (in the misleading past tense) explains: 'In the night the crater let out poisonous fumes.' They struggle to reach the cave entrance, but only the young gang leader and Kai Hoog, who has by this time managed to free himself from his fetters, escape alive.

Kai Hoog returns with the stone to John Terry, only to learn that the Pinkerton Detective Institute has reported that an old man in disguise has checked into the Hotel Royal with a young lady he calls his daughter, but who is clearly under hypnosis. It is, naturally, the young gang leader and Terry's kidnapped daughter, Ellen. The gang leader is being trailed by two turbanned gentlemen, Indians from the Asiatic committee, which suspects him of double-dealing. His plan is in fact to have a counterfeit diamond made in order to use Ellen Terry (Lio Sha being dead) to steal 'Asia's Imperial Crown'. The turbanned gentlemen force their way into his room, intending to kill both the man and the girl; but at the last moment Kai Hoog rescues Ellen. This dénouement could well come from some Feuillade serial.

It will be clear from this deliberately lengthy rendering of the plot how complex it must have been for a contemporary audience. For us its importance is that in this script, written by Lang alone (he was not to meet Thea von Harbou until 1921 when they worked on *The Indian Tomb*), there are motifs which were to appear again and again in one form or another. Certainly he had a long way to go before the organic and structured scenarios of the two *Mabuse* films. The significant question at this point concerns the extent of von Harbou's contribution to the evolution of Lang's style after *The Spiders*. No doubt it involves the emotional elements, alongside a certain routine expertise. Judging from his known contribution to the American films – of which only the first credits him as co-author – it seems reasonable to assume that the organic and logical sub-structure of the scripts after *The Spiders* may be attributed to Lang himself, as a born author-director.

3   Der Müde Tod (Destiny, 1921)

With this film he has produced something of such artistic purity that it can be compared to Wegener's Golem.
Freiheit, 11 October 1921

. . . It is Fritz Lang's merit to have discovered the genre (of lyrical ballad) for the film.
Herbert Ihering, *Berliner Börsen Courier,* 30 September 1923

Fritz Lang's Film Destiny *opened my eyes to the poetic expressiveness of the cinema.*
Luis Buñuel (quoted in Ado Kyrou's *Luis Buñuel,* 1963)

'The angel who is sent to us in our last hour and whom we harshly call Death, is the gentlest and kindest angel, softly and imperceptibly plucking the dropping human heart from life, to carry it away in his warm hands, without the least pressure, away from the coldness of the breast, high up to the warmth of Eden', writes Jean Paul in his *Leben des Quintus Fixlein.*

Lang writes: 'I feel that in this film (*Destiny*) a certain Viennese tone can be discerned, specifically the *intimacy with death.* This intimacy is found in many Viennese songs' (Lang mentions the *Fiaker Lied,* Raimund's *Hobel Lied* from the play *Der Verschwender,* and other songs). This, then, is the spirit of Lang's 'folk song in six verses' about 'Weary Death'. Perhaps Lang and Thea von Harbou remembered the beautiful fairy tale by Hans Anderson, *The Story of a Mother,* in which Death is 'a poor old man wrapped in a big horse blanket that keeps him warm; and he needs warmth because the winter is cold'. He comes to the young mother who watches by the bedside of her sick child, and rocks himself on his chair, nodding strangely. For three days and nights the mother has watched, and her head is heavy. She nods for a moment, then wakes bewildered to find that the old man and the child have vanished (cf. in Lang's film the young girl's return from the kitchen to find her lover gone away with the strange wanderer).

In Anderson's story the mother now starts out on her desperate search. To discover the way to Death, she must sing to Night, a woman in long black clothes, who sits in the snow, all the songs she ever sang to her child. Then in the dark pine forest, she has to warm the thorn bush at her breast. The thorns pierce her flesh; her blood flows in big

43

Der Müde Tod (1921): The cemetery garden

drops, and the thorn bush grows fresh green leaves and even flowers. In return for carrying her across to the house of Death, the lake demands that she shall cry out her eyes into it. Thus blinded, she reaches the other shore, and here the old graveyard woman who guards the green house of Death, asks the mother to exchange her black hair for her own snow white hair. She explains that every human being has its own tree of life or flower. Death transplants the wilted ones into paradise. The young mother recognises her child's heart-beat in a little blue crocus that is wilting. . . .

Lang or Harbou changed the green house of death ('where flowers and trees grow helter skelter') for the much more powerful image of the cathedral in which brilliant candles – high and straight as stalagmites or flickering stumps almost extinct – symbolise human souls. This image, the scholar of German, André Faure, points out to me, comes from one of Grimm's fairy tales

44

... Death demands the child

Gevatter Tod. In Grimm, however, Death is vengeful and malicious. A doctor who dares to outwit Death, his godfather, twice, is taken by Death's ice-cold hand, and led into an underground cave.

There he saw a thousand lights burning in infinite rows, some large, some medium-sized, some small. Every minute a few of them went out, others revived and the impression was of a constantly changing scene of flickering flames. 'Look', said Death, 'these are the life lights of human beings. The long ones belong to children, the medium-sized ones to married people in the prime of life, the little ones to old people. But often children or young people have only small lights.

These comparisons illustrate how the musical, ballad-like character of Lang's film connects with German romanticism. This quite deliberate intention was not always understood even at the time the film appeared. *Der Film* (No 46, 1921) declares pedantically and chauvinistically, for instance, that a German folk song would not mention the Orient or the Venetian Renaissance, but would have a more 'national' setting – missing the point that the film's romanticism is more concerned with the linking story, set in a small, timeless town in the middle of nowhere – the world of German poetry. It is neither the picture-book mediaevalism of a Moritz von Schwind nor the simplified Biedermeier version of Ludwig Richter. It is not by any means unimportant that the sequence of the little apothecary searching for mandrake roots under gnarled trees by night evokes the enchanted romantic world of the painter Caspar David Friedrich, which is atmospherically related to *Destiny*.

Interviewed by Gero Gandert (*Protokoll zu M*) Lang declared: 'In treating a romantic theme like that of *Destiny* ... the direction had to take into account this romanticism, but that does not mean that the feelings of the characters had to be falsified romantically in any negative sense.' So his characters act 'very simply, every one according to his nature'.

Today it is the linking story of the two lovers, separated by the strange wanderer, Death, which is the most powerful and purest aspect of this many-faceted film. The little town is brought to life by Lang's feeling for realistic detail and his sense of comedy – the young man who teases the goose in the mail coach, the grotesque town dignitaries in the tavern, the little apothecary. Lang's sense of humour had already taught him that tragedy must be complemented by its opposite. He recalls the impression made upon him by the Shakespearean stage direction 'Enter the bear': after the tragic climax, the great dramatist brought on clowns and jugglers to give the audience a necessary relief from dramatic intensity.

In the United States, Lang's style became ever simpler, as he learned to free himself from 'playfulness in the handling of details, secondary episodes, characters and symbols' that in his view resembled the ornate baroque of his native Vienna. At this period however he was still inclined to give symbolic meanings to incidental details. When Death enters the tavern, flowers wilt, the cat arches its back. The handle of the walking stick is seen to be shaped like a skeleton.

Yet the essential elements used to evoke a dense atmosphere are already assembled with mature confidence. A sense of the supernatural is instantly

46

conjured by a swish of sand at the crossroads, heralding the appearance of the figure in gabardine and broad-brimmed hat. When he appears in the wine tavern, the wandering figure seems to carry with him his own solitude, an invisible wall separating him from the living. The majestic figure contrasts with the plain humanity of the comic city dignitaries; the gateless wall rises menacingly up alongside the enchanting little Nuremburg-like toy-town devised for Lang by Herlth and Röhrig.★

The transition to unreality is hardly perceptible. The shadow figures of the dead appear in superimposition before the eyes of the girl searching for her lover, approaching her to go through the wall. The trick of super-imposition (which in those days had to be done in the camera, not in the laboratory) does not intrude itself as a trick and illusion: it is an extra dimension of a surrealist rather than the expressionist world, and we are irresistibly drawn into the spell of Lang's fantastic realm. Pommer had early given the young Lang the advice of studying the camera, 'because it is with the camera that you will write your film'.★★

In the apothecary's dusty little shop, with the phosphor-escent outlines of round-bellied bottles, bundles of herbs, a stuffed owl and a skeleton, there seems a permanent struggle between heaven and hell. There the girl finds the ancient volume in which she reads the Solomonic verse: 'Love is as strong as death'. In her eagerness to save her lover, she takes this to mean 'Love is stronger than death'; and so decides to take the poison on the first stroke of midnight. But between the first and the last stroke of twelve, from the beginning of the night-watchman's song, like *Die Meistersinger* ('Hört Ihr Herrn und lasst Euch sagen . . .') is unfolded the whole trilogy of the woman who claims to defeat death.

The gateless wall opens up for the girl: a gleaming arched door, behind which stand floodlit flights of stairs leading to eternity. Death is no abyss, nor the descent into hell. The realm of death is revealed as the vast expanse of a cathedral in which candles grow up like the pipes of an illuminated organ, reaching into the far distance, their misty vapour intermingled with a streaming flood of light that three years later would be recalled by the light in Siegfried's magic forest.

★ The settings are very different from Röhrig's work as collaborator on *Caligari*. Only one camera angle, from the graveyard (cf. picture) shows, says Lang 'the direct influence of the Caligari architecture: the view into the graveyard garden over the wall where the girl leans in despair. . . . Today we would call this a "perspectival construction"'.

★★ Lang told me how he used to go to the Prater in Vienna as a High School student where he was particularly attracted to the Kratky-Baschik Magic Theatre. On the stage illusionists performed tricks by means of large mirrors which must have been similar to the mirrors used in Méliès' Théâtre Houdin to make devils and ghosts appear and disappear.

Der Müde Tod: The First Light episode

Death graciously allows her three chances to save her beloved; and three flickering candle stumps from which the wax inexorably drips symbolise these three attempts. Three times the beloved is drawn ever deeper into his doom by the efforts of the loving girl.

The three chances and the three stories they introduce give Lang the irresistible opportunity to play freely with one motif, trying out all the possible permutations that lead to the same end result, while constituting variations, as in music. Moreover, in treating a series of three separate episodes, Lang still stays close to the series film, with which he had already experimented in *The Spiders.*

The story of The First Light is set in the world of the Arabian Nights. A Franconian infidel is in love with the sister of the Caliph of Baghdad. The adventure story with its chases, disguises, suspense and exoticism recalls *The Spiders.* An episode of the hero's escape in the stairs suggests reminiscences of Pastrone's *Cabiria*; the most characteristic Lang sequences are the scene on the roof terrace, in a sfumato half-light, and the nocturnal garden where El Mors, the gardener, has dug a grave for the beloved.

The story of the second light is set in Quattrocento Venice. Like Max Reinhardt, Lang delights in the *joie de vivre* and visual exuberance of paintings on old Florentine bridal chests. Scholars in pleated waistcoats lean casually against pillars like some Ghirlandajo painting, or throw their springy bodies like Damascus steel blades against their enemies. Some passages echo Reinhardt productions of Shakespeare, particularly in those moments when the sets are no more than sketches. Dark waves lapping the palace steps reflect the light and the shadow of a gondola pole cast across it; the arch of a high bridge is still half Gothic in its curve; steps are placed at an angle to the picture, for a carnival crowd to come whirling and dancing down them, just as Reinhardt might arrange it. Then the flame of torches, bursting through the darkness. Béla Balász must have had one of these Lang sequences in his mind when he wrote in *Der sichtbare Mensch*:

It is the task of a director to look for the 'eyes' of a landscape: the black silhouette of a bridge and a swaying gondola underneath, steps which lead down into the dark water where the light of a lantern is reflected, produce a more truly Venetian atmosphere – even when shot in the studio – than an actual photograph of St Marks Square.

Ernst Lubitsch's parody of Expressionism in *Die Bergkatze*, directed against the ornate architecture of Ernst Stern, Reinhardt's favourite designer, was superficial, confined only to decor. In Lang's third story, about the Chinese emperor who desires the magician's daughter, the parody of Expressionism has become an integral part of the plot itself. Of course the overturned Baroque roofs built higgledy-piggledy together, the little bridges, the warped trees with their tortured curves and bends, are a good rendering of the bizarre contortions of Expressionism. But Lang's invention goes further: the rolled-up parchment of the imperial letter that orders the magician's death, should he bore the great lord with his tricks, wriggles in expressionist curves, and bows. The magician, turned into a cactus by his daughter, is stretched into a grotesque expressionist diagonal. By means of trick

49

Der Müde Tod: the cactus scene

camerawork, one transformation or whimsical idea
follows another. We see in close-up, under the hem of the
imperial robes, which form a palanquin, an army of
lilliputians on the march, past pillar-like legs and gigantic
slippers (which were built in mammoth proportion on
the lot to produce a trick of scale). The climax of trick
photography is the flying carpet with its unwilling
passengers. Douglas Fairbanks bought the film, which he
never released, in order to be able to adapt the trick work
for *The Thief of Bagdad*. Lang told Herman G. Weinberg,
'Naturally, having much more money and technical
possibilities, he improved on them tremendously'.★

Failing at each of her attempts to save a human life from
extinction, the girl is graciously given one more chance by
death: she may offer another soul in exchange for that of
her beloved. She rushes to find those who seem weary of
life; but the little apothecary is indignant when she asks for
his life; a beggar who had apparently nothing to live for

★ Murnau's sequence of
Faust travelling on the cape
of Mephisto in *Faust* had
the same inspiration.

rejects her pleas angrily, and the old people in the Old People's Home who had been complaining a moment before at having been forgotten by death, run away from her terrified. As they tumble down the dilapidated wooden steps, a lamp is overturned and fire breaks out.

Lang's superb art of lighting is brought into play in all its subtlety. From the Rembrandt chiaroscuro of the evening lamplight in the Old People's Home, a whole spectrum of half-tones is created, right up to the brilliant glare of the fire itself. A baby has been left behind in the Old People's Home; and the girl rushes to snatch it, in order to have another life to offer to Death. But when Death appears, she cannot bring herself to give him the little child. Instead she leans out of the window and hands down the baby to the desperate mother in the waiting crowd. Thus she offers herself to death as the sacrificial victim who can save the life of her beloved – the only solution of implacable fate. As the burning beams crash all about her, salvation is achieved.

In the hospital mortuary – the crypt, so to speak, of the Cathedral of Death, the lovers are united on the bier. Death raises them – as Liliom is later to rise. In superimposition the figures leave behind their own dead bodies, to walk for ever in the realm of the blessed.

'I shall never forget,' writes Robert Herlth, Lang's film architect, in his memoirs:

How Lang, who always did everything himself, worked the trick with the letter sent by the magician to the emperor of China in *Destiny*, with a temperature of 25 degrees centigrade in the old glass-house.

'The letter', the script stipulates, 'bows to the Emperor.' Because in those days there was no such thing as an optical bank or back production, Lang produced this trick 'directly' or 'in the original' on a 9 foot by 12 foot black velvet-covered wall, where the letter, measuring about 15 feet by 12 feet was pinned up in the desired position and moved between every frame. Shooting thus in stop-action, each frame separately exposed, the letter had to be rearranged some 800 times to produce 50 seconds of film. Every time Lang himself jumped up and changed the pins supporting the giant letter. He worked incessantly, the sweat pouring down his face, but he was so involved that he forgot time and place. After this the exposed negative had to be rewound and remain in the camera in order to allow the main action to appear on the same strip. In places where the letter unrolled there had to be no other movement. The scene thus had to be fitted in accordingly. The action had to be played with the letter remaining imaginary. Only Lang seemed able to see it already, and that is why his behaviour seemed to us like magic-making. But how astonished we all were, we who had been in on every phase of the work, when we watched the film re-run, with the superimposition. The letter really unrolled itself, bowed to the emperor, and was read by him.

Herlth's remarks show something of how Lang worked in the studio, trying to do everything himself; though Herlth's memory is at fault: the letter was not directed to the emperor, but was sent by him to the magician.

Perhaps because of the Expressionist parody in the Chinese episode, *Destiny* is often considered in France as an Expressionist film. Lang rejects such an arbitrary label: he is too much of an eclectic, in the best sense of the word, to embrace indiscriminately one particular style of the period. Yet like any sensitive artist, unknown to himself, he was certainly influenced by tendencies of the *Zeitgeist*. The Expressionist experience inevitably left visible traces in his work.

The mode of calling the characters only The Young Man, The Girl, The Wanderer and so on is characteristic of Expressionist drama. The little town in the middle of nowhere, however, smacks more of romanticism than Expressionism. Yet sequences like those in the apothecary's laboratory or the 'Crypt of Death' are only made possible by Lang's deep comprehension of Expressionist effects of light. On this point of lighting, Lang writes to me:

In the Spring of 1919 I made my second film, *Der Herr der Liebe* in a small studio somewhere north of Berlin. The cameraman was Carl Hoffman, who did all my first films, because he had a Decla contract.

We filmed a scene in a big room, such as the Americans would call a living room. On the walls were a number of three-branch candlesticks. I was still very inexperienced, and when we started the shooting and Carl Hoffman shouted 'lights', all the lights were turned on, yet the bulbs in the candlesticks were not burning.

I shouted, 'Stop', and told Hoffman. Little Hoffman replied: 'Doesn't work: it is not tonal'; and I had apparently learned something.

Then we were helped by an accident. It all happened during the Spartacus rising in Berlin. The small studio had hired a number of temporary electricians, and when Hoffman called 'light' again, the electrical candles in the wall came on too. The temporary electrician believed they had to be plugged into the system too.

'Never mind', said Karl Hoffman, 'They won't show; and anyway it will take too long to disconnect them'. We went on shooting. When we viewed the rushes later on, we were astonished: the electrical candles were burning happily and made the whole scene singularly atmospheric.

'Well, well', said Hoffman, 'They are on after all'. And from then on in all the following scenes we had any electric lamps connected up.

This made me think. I had never liked the blue tinting which was used to make scenes shot in daylight look like night scenes.

My next experiment came in *Destiny*. For the fire in the old people's home I shot the scene where the waterbuckets are handed along a chain of people, late in the afternoon. Since the house could only burn down once, and I had to shoot the fire willy nilly, I went on shooting into the dark.

The effect of bright flames clearly picked out against the dark sky was excellent and relatively easy to understand (we had lit up the house with floodlights).

But how atonished we were when the scene which we had shot in late afternoon, with the human chain passing the buckets, also turned out to be a night scene.

The cameraman this time was my beloved Fritz Arno Wagner, who shot many of my films.

From this it emerges clearly that certain scenes of *Destiny* were shot out of doors.

Conversations with Fritz Lang also revealed other new points about *Destiny*. He says, for instance, that he put the Renaissance story first in order because it seemed to him stronger than the Franconian episode, which he felt went better as the middle story. Yet all the copies of the film known to me are in the sequence I have described, and contemporary reviews also confirm this. In the known copies, also, there is no title to explain why the young man 'went with the wanderer'. Before the scene with the old people who complain that Death has forgotten them, however, a title states that a young man who has been run over by the mail coach horses has just died in hospital.

In relation to titles, Lang says that the film had originally three decisive verses though today even German copies have only prose titles. He still remembers the first of these:

There is a little town somewhere
Dreaming in a valley;
In it there lived and loved
Two young people, full of life;

Yet from all the trees
The golden leaves are falling
Like tears in the red glow of dusk,
At cross roads which
Have seen many things,
Stands waiting for them
Lonely
Death

Lang thinks that the second of the three verses appeared after the lover has disappeared with the wanderer, on the return of the young girl to the kitchen:

She looks for her sweetheart everywhere
And roams through all the streets.
She has left the town.
At the graveyard all the graves
Are encircled by a wall.
Cold winds like presentiments
Of death are blowing round her head.
(?)
(?)
Love is fighting
With Death
And believes!

The third verse apparently followed the three episodes; and a film enthusiast, Albin Pötzsch, from the Meissen film school, remembers the opening lines:

Death remained triumphant in the fight
Yet he puts fate,
with a smile
Into the hands
Of her suffering once more.

Despite the musical structure and atmosphere of Lang's film ballad, and the rhythmical sense of Lang's later films, Lang, the painter and architect, believes that he is not musical. He has told me that music – apart from folk-song – is the only art he cannot understand. It might be truer to say that though he never studied harmonics, he uses certain elements of music instinctively through his innate sense of rhythm. (Architecture, after all, resembles in many of its works the structures of symphonies.)

In his interview with Peter Bogdanovich Lang emphasises one aspect of his work which may be the key to this film ballad:

I think the main characteristic of all my pictures is this fight against destiny, against fate. I once wrote in an introduction to a book that it is the fight which is important, not the result of it . . .

Similarly, in the interview with Gero Gandert, already quoted:

The fight of the individual against destiny is probably the basis of all my films, the struggle of a primarily good human being against higher and superior forces, be it the power of a generally accepted social injustice, or the power of a corrupt organisation, society or authority. Or be it the power of one's own conscious or subconscious drives . . .

As for death, I believe that it is sometimes preferable to life lived under inhuman conditions and that one should fight for whatever one considers right, even against superior forces and at the risk of dying. *The struggle,* the (gesture of) *rebellion* is important.

Lessing said that if God held in one hand truth, and in the other the *search* for truth, he would call out: 'Give me the search for truth'. Likewise, the main concern in Lang's first masterwork is the fight against destiny.

APPENDIX: ON BENEVOLENT DEATH, by Fritz Lang – Berliner Tageblatt, 1 January 1927

The childhood dream which most influenced my life and work was concerned neither with friendship nor with love. Yet it awakened in me an emotion of fear, growing into love of such force, that I have never since been able to free myself from its almost mystic force.

I was ill, on the threshold of boyhood and adolescence, and it happened on a night when I was very close to the fulfilment of the saying that whom the gods love, die young. I felt the closeness of death with a kind of drowsy lucidity, yet I was too exhausted by fever to fight the approach of the dark stranger. I was slipping away on my faint breath, which got weaker and weaker, and the tear-stained face of my adored mother was disappearing from my view.

I slept and dreamed – or was I awake? With undimmed eyes, almost too clearly, I saw the familiar room in which I was lying. The shutters of the window were half open – the moonlight was streaming into the room. And I saw myself face to face, not terrifying, but unmistakeable, with Death. Made of black and white, light and shade, the rib cage, the naked bones. On top of it the head, barely recognisable, shaded by the wide-brimmed hat.

Death and I gazed at each other. I don't know whether I should call the feeling I experienced at that moment one of fear. It was horror, but without panic. And even the horror made way for a kind of mystical ecstasy which gave me, boy though I still was, the complete understanding of the ecstasy which made martyrs and saints embrace death.

I raised myself in order to accompany him. In my weak state I collapsed. People came and lifted me up. Death had disappeared.

I recovered quickly. But the love of death, compounded of horror and affection, which the Gothic master depicted, stayed with me and became a part of my films: humanized in *Destiny*, symbolic in *Die Nibelungen*, living Gothic in *Metropolis*.

4 Dr Mabuse Der Spieler (Dr Mabuse the Gambler, 1922)

Film as an archive of its time. That's new, at least. The reflexes of an epoch immortalised in celluloid, preserved for posterity in moving pictures which will convey the rhythm of our present time with much more directness than a book could do . . . The director Fritz Lang presents this panorama of our time with great devotion and a strong gift for observation.
Vorwärts, 30 April 1922

This film is a document of our time, an excellent portrait of high society with its gambling passion and dancing madness, its hysteria and decadence, its expressionism and occultisms.
Die Welt am Montag, 1 May 1922

The director Fritz Lang has tried hard to concentrate the insanity of our period into its characteristic types and milieux. While the novel by Norbert Jacques concentrated on the character of the criminal Mabuse, Lang, himself a restless type who was once a painter in Paris, aims at presenting a panorama of the times and does so with imagination, wit and visual inventiveness. All the

Fritz Lang and Thea von Harbou called the first part of this film, 'A portrait of our time' and the second part, 'Inferno characters of the time'. Two years later, Lang described it unambiguously as 'a document of its time.'

The distributor's hand-out which accompanied the film is not at all characteristic of public relations cliché, and might well have been inspired either by reviews or by Lang himself:

The world which opens up before our eyes in this film is the world in which we all live. Only it is condensed, exaggerated in detail, concentrated into essentials, all its incidents throbbing with the feverish breath of those years, hovering between crisis and convalescence, leading somnambulistically just over the brink, in the search for a bridge that will lead over the abyss. This gambler, Dr Mabuse, was not yet possible in 1910; he will perhaps – one is tempted to say hopefully – no longer be possible in 1930 (sic!) But for the years around 1920 he represents a larger than life-size portrait, is almost a symbol, at least a symptom. Mankind, decimated and trampled under by war and revolution, takes its revenge for years of suffering and misery by eating its lusts and pursuing pleasure . . .

It is illuminating to compare with this Lang's own picture of the age in his talk on *Spies* to the University of California, Riverside Extension. (See p80). Even *Das Tagebuch*, a magazine normally very critical of the cinema, uses words not unlike the left-wing *Vorwärts* and the popular newspaper *Berliner Lokalanzeiger*:

No vice of our time is forgotten . . . It is a mirror of the age, not specially uplifting, not ennobling in its effect. Yet it is genuinely felt, visually powerful in Fritz Lang's direction.

The strictly middle-class *B.Z. am Mittag* declares that here the film:

has understood its true function as the portrait of an age set in motion.

57

Sensations, adventures which follow one another in rapid succession, a condensation of the spirit of the age, a playful re-enactment and a mirror of life.

It points out that Lang's understanding of this essential fact leads to a reworking of the novel that was first published in the *Berliner Illustrierte*, 'according to the highly volatile character of the time, with sure instinct'.

This review, moreover, perceives quite clearly what matters about this film whose infectious vitality bursts the closed form of the drama:

The success of this film does not lie in its plot . . . but in the episodic details, not in the sequence of events as a whole but in the individual events which vividly express an age and are held together by a conscious artistic intention, by rhythm and speed, by style and atmosphere. There is a concentration of dance and crime, of gambling passion and cocaine addiction, of jazz and razzias. Not one important symptom of the post-war years is missing. Stock exchange manoeuvres, occultist charlatanism, prostitution and over-eating, smuggling, hypnosis and counterfeiting, expressionism, violence and murder!

There is no purpose, no logic in this demonic behaviour of a de-humanised mankind – everything is a game. Yet while other people are enjoying themselves in gambling, Dr Mabuse gambles with human lives and human destinies. Everything else is only a means to an end for him . . .

'At last', wrote the *Roland von Berlin* of 4 May 1922, 'a film that has something to say to us':

that represents the present, daringly shot, contemporary history relentlessly photographed. The novel by Norbert Jacques has been reworked skilfully by Thea von Harbou . . . yet it is really due to Fritz Lang's direction that the Wedekind lamps have been kindled to throw a phosphorescent glow of grotesque unreality over the hectic dance of death going on during those unbalanced, hysterical post-war years, over a Marquis of Keith world, immensely exaggerated.

It is marvellous how in his hands architecture and photography have achieved a force of expressiveness hitherto unheard of.

These extensive quotations from contemporary reviews – notably more colourful and informative than most reviews of the period – illustrate how strongly critics felt that the film reflected their own age, and how normally mediocre journalists were stimulated to find the right words to describe it. They somewhat contradict Seigfried Kracauer's assertion, in *From Caligari to Hitler* that 'from these expressionist and similarly stagey products emerged

characters are taken from our hectic, corrupt, confused epoch, and get fused into it again . . . The director tries to visualise the confused and bewitched atmosphere by using a furious speed and an enthusiastic temperament and it seems stimulating merely because over-stimulated people exist in it . . . This film will have an enormous success everywhere, . . . because millions of people who sense dimly the confusion of our time are confronted tangibly and visibly in this visual and highly rhythmic embodiment with the collapse and madness with which we are all forced to live.
Das Tagebuch, 6 May 1922

the overall picture of an emotionally heated pseudo-world'.

According to Lang the film has lost its original introductory sequence: a brief, breathless montage of scenes of the Spartacus uprising, the murder of Rathenau, the Kapp *putsch* and other violent moments of recent history. Lang maintains that when it first opened this sequence was intact; and it is unclear when the prologue was cut – whether in the twenties, when people did not want to be reminded of the troubles of the time, or later, by the East German archive, which owns the negative and may have preferred to excise the Spartacus material.

As it survives today the film opens with a circle of still portraits of Mabuse in various disguises. Mabuse, sitting at his dressing table, shuffles the stills like playing-cards and selects one which he hands to his cocaine-addicted, homosexual mask-maker to indicate his next disguise. Originally, Lang recalls, the opening montage was linked to this scene by two titles: the first,

WHO IS BEHIND ALL THIS?

The second title, a single word which rushed towards the spectator, growing and growing until it filled the entire screen:

I

The most remarkable advance over *The Spiders* is in the characterisation. The characters are no longer conventional figures from conventional serial films but (said the *B.Z.* reviewer) 'representatives of a certain social set-up from our times'. Today they still seem to be well-defined individuals of their own time, decadent and unstable in moral matters, rather than merely types of the richer class during the inflation period.

Countess Told is the sort of woman who might have been encountered at any Berlin fancy-dress ball or first night, yet she has distinctive individual traits. A neurotic, bored, heavy-lidded, hypochondriac, disappointed in love and possibly rather frigid, orchid-like and thus the ultimate in smartness according to the styles of the time. Unable to live the Ibsen life she would wish, she observes other people and their emotions in the gambling clubs where she herself never touches a card. She can establish no contact with these people, and is alarmed when State Prosecutor von Wenck tries to involve her in action as his accomplice. Even her long cigarette-holder – a typical accessory of the sophisticate of the period – serves to distance her, as it were, from her environment.

When she is bored during a spiritualist seance, her fingers trace the outlines of the Soutache pattern on her gown – a detail which Lang characteristically enjoys for its revelation of the superficiality of her character: she is even incapable of concentrating. She resists Mabuse's advances not out of a married woman's propriety, but out of genuine frigidity, the congenital outsider's reluctance to be involved.

Like the Countess, the rich Count Told is a decadent, and probably a latent homosexual. He is 'sensitive', self-centred and spineless. As an art collector he is intoxicated by works of art as if they were opium. Barely participating in his wife's soirées, he only comes to life when he is allowed to show off his collection. Momentarily vitalised, he asks a guest – Mabuse – 'What do you think of Expressionism, Herr Doktor?' – a reference which at the time Lang feared was too obscure.* Exposed, the veneer of *savoir faire* once pierced, this aesthete is a weak and helpless creature: after the incident where, though he normally never plays, he is hypnotised by Mabuse and made to cheat at cards, he runs to Wenck through the rain, to cut a wretched figure in the prosecutor's office.

Wenck himself is a less earthy figure than Lohmann in *M*, belonging to a social class where dinner jackets are worn with nonchalance: Lohmann, with the vitality of a man of the people, belongs to a later period of realist perception. Played by Bernhard Goetzke (Death in *Destiny*) Wenck with his inborn *noblesse* is nevertheless not very scrupulous. As a man of the inflation years, when everyone had to learn to go with the tide, he is essentially an adventurer in his battle against his opponent Dr Mabuse.

As to Dr Mabuse himself, the *B.Z.* called him 'a criminal of genius' while the critic of *Kinematograph* (7 May, 1922) wrote naïvely:

This Dr Mabuse is a kind of ideal figure of our time. He is not like the

*Mabuse's response ('Expressionism is just a game, but, nowadays, in life everything is just a game.') can be seen as double-edged: a remark indicating Mabuse's nature ('The Gambler' in the widest meaning of the term) and an ironic joke from Fritz Lang who has always refused to play aesthetic games.

gangster king of the past with his crude methods; it is not accidental that he is a doctor, and has put all the intellectual powers of his academic training into the execution of his gigantic plans.

Mabuse can be seen as a tragic figure, a fallen angel; and it was not accidental that Lang in one scene puts him beneath the picture of a gigantic Lucifer, lit by the firelight as if by flaming phosphorus. Lang recognises that Dr Mabuse could only have been invented in Germany, the country of *kadavergehorsam* (absolute obedience), where Nietzsche's idea of Superman was born. There is a revealing passage in the original novel:

For the prosecutor Wenck a criminal was no longer an inferior person. In his eyes he turned into a man of higher impulses in the sense of constituting a hellish force whose ever intensifying actions he was trying to stop by demonic means.

The only negative figure in the film is the young millionaire, Hull – a weak image of the so-called Lang hero who was to acquire his full contours in such a character as Mobley in *While the City Sleeps*. Might Hull have been deliberately kept in vague terms ('a young man in his thirties, a touch calloused, a touch casual, with an unusually unruffled and easy-going manner . . .') in order to throw Mabuse into still higher relief?

The *B.Z.* review again:

Yet not only are the characters typical of our age, but their way of life and the environment in which they are placed are also characteristic. Thus the scenic side of the film, its architecture – an astonishing achievement by the architects Stahl Urach and Otto Hunte – gains in importance.

The review also mentions the 'expressionist rooms at the Tolds' and 'the expressionist nightclub'; but it is possible that more Expressionism has been read into the film than was intended. Writing about it, the *Berliner Börsen-Courier* (30 April, 1922) even takes on a touch of Expressionist language:

This film works at breakneck speed, imparts a harassed restlessness. Klein-Rogge's Mabuse is the embodiment of tense will-power; he is concentrated will-power, and, when necessary, shows a mesmerising demonic force.★

★ Cf. page 12/13 of *The Haunted Screen* and my remarks on Expressionism as 'gestraffterwille' (tensed-up will power).

The only genuinely Expressionist feature is the restaurant with its flame walls, where Wenck and his friend (played by Falkenstein) have dinner. The gambling room with its

61

Dr Mabuse Der Spieler (1922): The entrance to the gambling room

'bizarre furnishings' (*B.Z.*), whose round shape Kraucauer interprets as 'the circle as symbol of chaos', rather recalls the ornamental stylisation of the Viennese or Munich workshops. The Viennese Secession style is identifiable also in such features as the croupier who is raised hydraulically from below, and sinks down again on the arrival of the police, or in the lowering of a dancer – anticipation of the false Maria in *Metropolis* – on a kind of giant chandelier. Nor are Told's rooms Expressionist, though some of the works of art in them are. Here, as in the Countess' tea salon, we see the typical Art Deco of the time. The Count's gaming room would be called 'modernist' if it appeared in a film by Marcel L'Herbier; it is the world of Iribe and Lapape, of the year 1910, prolonged, as in France, into the twenties. Only the mood is, at moments, Expressionist: Dr Mabuse under his Lucifer picture, or Count Told roaming his collection at night by candlelight which momentarily picks out a piece

Dr Mabuse: In the gambling room

of sculpture or an African mask which starts like a cry out of the darkness. Later, on the open staircase, there is a similar chiaroscuro contrast that produces the shock effect characteristic of Expressionism in painting. The eclectic Lang uses this style in order to reveal the Count's confusion of mind and despair. He employs it again for the scene of the murder of Hull and his friend, under the flickering gaslight – anticipating also the night streets of *Woman in the Window* and *Scarlet Street*.

One aspect of the film seemed particularly astonishing, indeed almost unbearable to the contemporary spectator. *Berliner Lokalanzeiger* reported that:

The first big applause which spontaneously arose in the large auditorium during the first public showing of *Dr Mabuse* occurred at the night scene in which the cars are racing through the streets, the lights of which can be seen stretching for miles into the darkness like stars.

The same applause was repeated during a similar scene whose effect

Dr Mabuse: Alfred Abel as Count Told

was heightened by an elevated train that passes over a dark viaduct in the foreground, with its windows lit up and flashing out in the dark. . . . In these terms the film of *Dr Mabuse* constitutes a success of German film technique, a triumph of the arc light.

B.Z. am Mittag shared the same enthusiasm:

In this film the techniques of the film camera (Carl Hoffman's brilliant photography) are brought to perfection. The problem of how to film lit-up streets at night has been solved for the first time. It is unbelievably impressive to see the glaring lights of speeding cars flash through the night or the rapid passing of an elevated train or the initially blurred, then gradually focussed glimpse through a pair of opera glasses on to the variety stage, the nuances of light and shade – these things alone prove the value of film documentary.

Although today we take for granted such refinements as the view through the opera glasses or the effect of light and shade, they had to be first 'invented'; and Lang even then knew how to invent. It was immediately recognised that this film was a unique act of cooperation by Lang and his associates – the cameraman Carl Hoffman and the

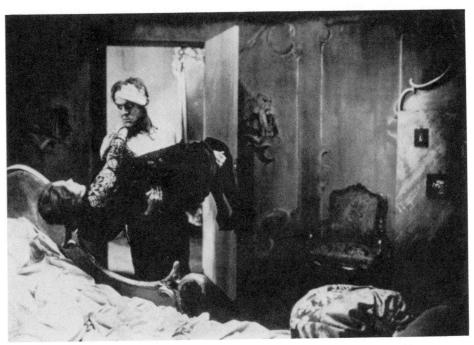

Dr Mabuse: Mabuse and the captive Countess Told

architects. Carl Hoffman, wrote *Vorwärts*,

without toning or touching up a single picture concentrated in his camera work purely on atmosphere and achieved the most refined nuances. Some ideas are utterly fascinating, for example Dr Mabuse's eyes approaching the spectator at rapid speed, the lettering that is gradually enlarged, with suggestive force, the view through a pair of opera glasses which changes from an imperceptible blur to a lucid picture in the course of adjusting the glasses . . .

Berliner Fremdenzeitung (1 May 1922) adds:

Fritz Lang's merit is, however, to have worked out the details in such a way that they fit into the whole like the stones of a mosaic, and yet produce the utmost suspense in the spectator. This director is a master in the way he focusses on apparently minor and unimportant details to an extent that makes them into an experience (like the splendid gambling scene with the Chinese glasses in which the ingenious gambler's suggestive powers, rendering his victims powerless, are felt also by the spectator).

Lang succeeded in making the audience actually feel the

force of hypnotism. 'Fascinating' wrote *Neue Zeit* (4 May 1922):

the fight between Mabuse and the prosecutor, where Mabuse's face gets bigger and bigger and he literally hypnotises the spectator.

The effect still works today. Mabuse plays with the glasses he has taken off, and their sparkle is a true Expressionist shock effect. The head of the old man (Mabuse in disguise) moves forward, growing bigger and bigger until it almost bursts out of the screen. Again, when Wenck, trying to resist Mabuse's will, picks up the cards and the Chinese letters *Tsi Nan Fu* on them light up, expand menacingly, and seem to fog his consciousness, a sympathetic effect is produced in the spectator. Again and again the contemporary reviews return to this; *B.Z. am Mittag* for instance concludes:

It is astonishing how a title is used as an expressive means, how the hypnotic gaze of Dr Mabuse casts its spell over the public as it does over his victim, how psychological processes are externalised.

The reviews also speak of the new and so far unprecedented speed of the film. Thus, *Neue Zeit* (4 May 1922):

Speed, horrifying speed characterises the film. The incidents chase one another. This is the present, the hustle and bustle of its life-style. The six acts take no less than three hours to finish, yet one was not aware of the passing of time until it was ended. Is there better proof of a gripping story?

Unreality and documentation of a *zeitgeist*, at one and the same time, patterned into rhythm and suspense – these were to remain the characteristic features of Lang's films.

Talking about filming the night scenes in *Destiny*, Lang commented (see above, p. 53) 'Yet we still had not really understood what we were doing'. The night scenes of *Mabuse* were filmed in the studio. The elevated train which so thrilled contemporary spectators was a toy train, shot in the studio and subsequently superimposed on to the previously shot scene of the street at night.

Many years later, in *The Last Will of Dr Mabuse*, Fritz Arno Wagner and I discovered that genuine night scenes were best shot with a wide-angle lens during the short moments of dusk, the five or six minutes of transition between day and night; or early in the morning between night and day. We dress-rehearsed the scenes in question carefully before we shot them – never more than one scene in one day. . . .

There is more to say about the animated titles that were so new at the time. They proved a veritable sensation, particularly the hypnotic TSI NAN FU in the playing cards, which puzzled critics and audiences alike. They were simple letters, cut out of a piece of wood-grained paper, lit from underneath.

The greatest sensation was caused by the recurring title MELIOR that ran ahead of Wenck's car, eternally renewing itself and dragging him mesmerically towards the Melior quarry and thus to his death, as planned by Mabuse.

We deviated from the book, using only the fundamental outlines. I seem to recall that a producer friend of mine sent me a book about Al Capone from Hollywood. It may have influenced me a little. I also used a *cause célèbre* of the time: the defensive battle fought by the car-robber Chavrol, beseiged in a Paris house by the police. Yet my main theme was man's helplessness.*

It is interesting to discover Lang, so early in his career, already drawing inspiration from items in news clippings. The seige of Mabuse's house and his escape into the sewers are shot in a pure documentary style. There is the objectivity of documentary, too, in the organisation of the criminal set-up, with its flawless operation in the execution of the trade contract robbery near the beginning of the film. Side by side with this element we have hypnosis, the superimpositions of Told, who resumes the game with his own protoplasm. When Mabuse's madness sets in, we see his victims in superimposition, while the big printing press becomes a giant monster like the machine centre in *Metropolis* that becomes Freder's Moloch. No-one but Lang could arrive at such an alliance of documentary and the fantastic.

The astonishing montage of this film had a profound effect on Eisenstein when it arrived in the Soviet Union; and Sergei Yutkevich has told me that in order to study its sophisticated cutting technique, Eisenstein rearranged the scenes, putting them in new orders, only to arrive back at fitting them together in their original form.**

* Interview with Gero Gandert, in Fritz Lang, *M, Kinemathek* No 3. Hamburg, 1963.

** Echoes of Lang's films are to be found again and again in the work of other film-makers. Among the more obvious from Mabuse are the circle of hands during the spiritualist seance shot from a similar angle in Marcel L'Herbier's *Feu Mathias Pascal* (1925), the use of the stock exchange in a similar way in the same director's *L'Argent* (1928); the battle in the besieged house in von Sternberg's *Underworld* (1927); and the escape of the criminal into the sewers in Carol Reed's *The Third Man* (1949).

Die Nibelungen (1923–24): Siegfried's arrival at Gunther's court (*above*); The flowering tree (*below*)

5   Die Nibelungen 1923–24

From the beginning to the end the films (Siegfrieds Tod *and* Kriemhilds Rache) *possess Greek tragedy, a quality of inevitability, but their emotional impact accrues not so much through specific identification with these abstract characters, but rather from their becoming the embodiment of a stirring saga of profoundly mythical appeal. In this the films resemble the multi-part Japanese period spectacles with their awesome samurai heroes.*
Kevin Thomas, *Los Angeles Times*, 10 October 1969

Thea von Harbou appears to have published the *Nibelungen* script retrospectively, just as she was subsequently to write the novel *Metropolis* after the completion of the film. This published script reveals how over-rich in detail Harbou's language is. For Lang this detail provided a welcome possibility of revealing character and motive, and of developing symbols – and the Lang of the silent German period took it for granted that he had to use symbolism. Without a means of verbal explanation, the symbol was a structural necessity, helping to convey to the spectator the things which could not be spoken. It might be argued that such visual symbolism is necessary to achieve the necessary stylisation in a Homeric and epic sense. Certainly Lang refused to attempt a remake of *Die Nibelungen* in the sixties because the sound dialogue would destroy such stylisation and make the characters appear bombastic and ridiculous.

So when Kriemhild reveals to grim Hagen, before the hunt, where Siegfried's vulnerable point lies, in order as she thinks to protect him, Lang uses a symbolic image to express the presentiment of coming disaster. Kriemhild stands beside a flowering tree, waving goodbye to her smiling hero. A moment later, she sinks desolate into the arms of her mother Ute, because before her eyes and ours there is a terrible apparition: the flowering tree turns into a mass of leafless branches, and finally into a death's head. Thus the spectator is prepared by a symbol for the coming event.

For some curious reason many people still regard the well-balanced, symmetrical, spacious sets as Expressionist. Yet there are none of the ecstatic distortions, the oblique angles of *Caligari* or *Raskolnikoff*. Lang and his architects, Otto Hunte and Erich Kettelhut, inevitably had to pass

69

Die Nibelungen: geometrical design and architectural composition

through the Expressionist experience of their age; but the only trace of it surviving here is a tendency to abstraction, to anonymity and stylisation of form.

For the most part all is harmony, balance, structure. Arcades and niches predominate, with figures practically fitted into them and framed by them. This is particularly apparent in Hunte's sketches now preserved in the Cinémathèque Française (cf. illustration, page 71). Often the figures become part of the decor; for instance the row of soldiers like pillars in the foreground, their backs to the camera, all dressed identically with geometrical ornament, and parallel in posture, one hand on the hilt of their swords, the other holding their shields; and behind this pallisade of bodies the procession of kings and heroes slowly approaches on its way to the cathedral. Lang uses the soldiers here to symbolise the sheer power of the Burgundians. In the use of extras, the anonymity of character may well be a hangover from Expressionism.

Die Nibelungen: the harmony and balance of Otto Hunte's design (*above*) realised by Lang (*below*)

Die Nibelungen: the monumental figure of Hagen

Similarly, when Brunhild leaves her ship, the soldiers line up on either side, visors down and shields held up to form a kind of pontoon bridge. Their helmets and shoulders seem to rise out of the water like decorative railings. On shore other extras, also motionless, silhouetted against the light (Lang explains they were positioned in front of a blue-painted wall) to form a lattice. Yet again, in *Kriemhilds Rache*, when Kriemhild says farewell to her husband's tomb before departing for the country of the Huns, she is surrounded by her women. Faces and figures disappear in the heavy folds of their coats and head-dresses. The bowed heads and shoulders seem part of the curved vaulting, depersonalised into decorative motifs, the mosaic ornaments of the apsis. The people, the extras, appear faceless in this stylised world of heroes because they constitute a kind of chorus, with no motive function in the development of the action.

The main characters too, however, are sometimes treated 'architecturally'. After the Nibelung's gold has been stolen and sunk in the Rhine, the two arch-enemies, Kriemhild and Hagen, are seen standing like pillars, flanking the heavy gate of the treasure-chamber.

Lang chose to divest the Nibelung saga of its Wagnerian pathos. No-one except Hagen wears a beard, or resembles the stout heroes and heroines of the operatic stage. The decadent world of the Burgundians is treated with appropriate stylisation, and the wonderful costumes designed by Guderian resemble early miniatures.*

To portray this world demanded a certain strictness of form. Structure is all. (Heine, talking about the *Nibelungenlied* and its expressiveness cannot find a tower as high, a stone as hard as the grim Hagen and vengeful Kriemhild). Nothing in Lang is façade; everything is three-dimensional and spatial. His *mise en scène* makes constant use of this space and he composes with it. The white-robed followers of White Kriemhild and the dark followers of Brunhild meet to form the shape of a wedge on the cathedral steps, in just the same way that the masses were employed in Reinhardt's Grosses Schauspielhaus productions of Greek tragedy.

The sets had likewise to be structured. Lang says that if he had had the use of the American Redwoods, he might have done the forest scenes in natural exteriors; but as it

* There had been earlier attempts at modernising Wagner's heroes. In 1908, for example, the costume drawings for *Tristan and Isolde* by C. O. Czeschka anticipated the geometrical costumes of *Die Nibelungen*.

Die Nibelungen: atmosphere created by the lighting potential of the studio: Klein-Rogge as Attila

was, the atmosphere he sought was only possible with the lighting potential of the studio. Nothing is accidental: the spirit of the sets is conjured up by Lang's will alone, inspired by pictures he recalled. Though Böcklin may now appear kitsch to us, he was important for his own age, and Lang used his *Great Pan* (also called *Schweigen im Walde*) as inspiration for Siegfried's ride through the mysterious sun-streaked, misty forest. The flowering meadow with the spring where grim Hagen's spear strikes the blond hero is a combination of two other Böcklin pictures; the images of the naked children with wreaths about their hair, and Attila in black armour (*Kriemhilds Rache*) were inspired by an etching by Max Klinger.

These atmospheric landscapes were built in the grounds of Neubabelsberg, since they were too big for the studio itself. The dense tree-trunks of Siegfried's magic forest were made of long wooden frames coated with cement to look like bark, and ending half-way up the trunk. Real soil

74

and moss were heaped about their roots. They were enclosed by a cyclorama which was open only at the point where the camera and lighting equipment were positioned. The top of this cyclorama was covered with laths and bits of sacking.

The shooting began in autumn, and the two parts of the film took about nine months to complete. Lang was therefore able to wait for real snow to cover the earth for the scene where Kriemhild kneels to pick up the soil stained with her husband's blood, to carry it to the country of the Huns, and for real flowers (sown by Vollbrecht) for the flowering meadow in *Siegfrieds Tod*. For the scene where Hagen drops the Nibelung's treasure into the frozen Rhine, the unit waited for a pool in the grounds to freeze over, adding some ice from the Wannsee.

Elsewhere atmospheres were created inside the studio proper. The misty sequence where Alberich, made invisible by the *tarnhelm*, tries to strangle the hero, was shot on a small stage at Neubabelsberg, and the dense mist in which a filigree of twigs can faintly be distinguished was produced by the use of fire extinguishers. Since it was a hot spring day, the wan sunbeams pouring through the glass walls and roof gave the suspended vapour and eerie atmospheric affect. Lang attempted to repeat the effect, but at the next try the fog simply dispersed about the studio.

All the time there were new inventions an experiments. Lang wanted a rainbow for the scene where Kriemhild's ship travels up the Rhine. Carl Hoffman objected that rainbows could not be filmed, but Rittau, the second cameraman, had the idea of drawing a rainbow on black paper and superimposing it. The weird flickering aurora borealis which appears in the sky when Brunhild first sees the heroes' arrival was produced by Rittau with the help of spotlights and a moving mirror. In his programme note to *Die Nibelungen* Lang praises the talents of his cameramen. Carl Hoffman, he said, was able to realise everything the director had imagined visually, by means of light and shadow:

He knew the secret of photographing a woman, so that while looking at her face a light in the corner of an eye, a shadow across her forehead, a luminous line across the temple revealed not only her externals but also the spiritual content of a scene.

Günther Rittau's talents were more experimental:

Together with Carl Hoffman he experimented for entire nights. He approaches the visual aspects of the cinema by way of mathematics. Every third sentence he uttered began: 'What will happen if..?' What happens when mathematics, technology and imagination combine may be seen in the northern lights in *Die Nibelungen* and the petrified dwarfs whose mouths are still moving in a scream while their bodies have already turned to stone.

This petrification of the dwarfs in Alberich's treasure cave is an astonishing feat. As they gradually turn to stone, their faces stay alive for a while before they, too, freeze. Günther Rittau achieved this not by ordinary super-imposition, but by superimposing from below to above – all, it must be remembered, done directly inside the camera by a footage and frame count, since the German cinema did not yet have special effects departments like the Americans. Even the ghostly effects of the silhouette of Siegfried made invisible by the *tarnhelm*, while assisting Günther to defeat Brunhild in the contest, was achieved in this way by superimposition in the camera.

Another technical difficulty was presented by the dragon. At first, Lang recalls, it crawled along 'like a decrepit old man' and, according to Vollbrecht, collapsed the moment it was moved. Finally a mechanism was devised to give it suitably life-like movements.

The narrative flair Lang had displayed in *Destiny* comes into its own in the confrontation of the Burgundian world with three other worlds and three other styles. In 1966 he recalled, in a talk at Yale:

I was interested in bringing to life a German saga in a manner different from Wagnerian opera, without beards and so on. I tried to show in the *Nibelungen* four different worlds: the primeval forest, where lives the crippled Mime who teaches Siegfried to forge his sword, the dragon and the mystic subterranean realm of Alberich, the deformed, dwarfish keeper of the Nibelung treasure, which he curses when slain by Siegfried.

Secondly, the flame-enveloped caste of the Amazon Queen of Iceland, Brunhild.

Thirdly, the stylised, slightly degenerate, over-cultured world of the kings of Burgundy, already about to disintegrate. And finally the world of the wild Asiatic hordes of the Huns, and their clash with the world of the Burgundians (who changed their names to Nibelungen after taking over the treasure).

Brunhild's entourage is shown as less static than the world of the Burgundians. There is movement, a to-and-fro of maidens as Günther performs the tasks in which he is assisted by the invisible Siegfried (perceived by the spectator through superimposition).

Both these worlds are contrasted to the fairytale idyll of Siegfried's magic forest. The highly stylised Burgundian world is, however, softened by the appearance of Siegfried: when the Nibelung treasure is being brought in by carts, Siegfried leaps onto the piles to distribute jewelry to the people, who no longer appear as anonymous faces, but as individuals.

The stylisation of the Burgundian world is again emphasised, however, when Siegfried and his vassal king enter the Burgundian castle, riding in procession over the drawbridge, and reaches its peak in the scene of Siegfried and Günther swearing blood brotherhood, with Hagen towering in the centre and the two royal brothers placed symmetrically to either side; again, too, at the marriage, where Seigfried and Kriemhild kneel with similar symmetry.

The gathering for the hunt – remembered by Marcel Carné in the hunt scene of *Les Visiteurs du Soir* – is conceived with the earthy vitality of a medieval tapestry. When the hunters take their rest, Lang ingeniously brings the forest to life. The final idyllic images of this tragic song shows Siegfried refreshing himself at the spring where Hagen's spear is to kill him. Then, one of the most beautiful passages: shot from beneath, the high drawbridge where earlier Seigfried's vassals and their followers in serried ranks had asked for entry, is again crowded – with Siegfried's funeral cortège. The same wind that a moment before made the curtains of Kriemhild's chamber flap menacingly now tears at the curly hair of the dead hero, lit by a pale light, while Siegfried's white horse rears ominously.

The epilogue in the cathedral shows Siegfried's bier surrounded by candles. To the left is a dark figure, half fallen to the ground; to the right, Kriemhild, still in white, bends over before turning to tell a messenger to bring Günther the news of the Queen of Burgund's death. It is a different Kriemhild from the gentle loving wife, who now kneels at her husband's bier. The static spatial conception is already being broken by passion; we sense Kriemhild as the avenging woman she is to become. Momentarily the scene recalls that earlier scene in the cathedral, the light pouring like a shimmering mantle through the rose window as the closed ranks of the followers kneel in prayer on both sides, and Kriemhild stands between her two brothers.

The second part of *Die Nibelungen, Kriemhilds Rache*, replaces static stylisation with dynamism, as nemesis drives the action onwards, as the introduction of the Asiatic elements destroy the monumental stillness of the heroic epic, and as Kriemhild's revenge acts upon all the other characters like a violent maëlstrom. In Germany at the time the film appeared, critics seemed only to notice the heroic, Teutonic elements of *Siegfrieds Tod*. This approach tended to produce enthusiastic nationalist and ill-written reviews like that in *Filmwoche* (No. 7, 1924) where a positive fanatic maintained that Siegfried was by birth and character 'the most German of men', and thus anticipated the ideology of *Blut und Boden*.

I am indebted to Wolfgang Klaue, director of the Staatliches Filmarchiv of the DDR, for a remarkable quotation from Friedrich Engels, who had a totally different view of the Siegfried figure, stated long before Lang's film:

What can it be that moves us so forcefully about the legend of Siegfried?... It is the deep meaning given to his personality. Siegfried is the representative of German youth. All those among us whose hearts are still untamed by the oppressions of life know what this means. We are all filled with the same thirst for action, the same resistance against the conventional... in us, the eternal weighing up of things, the philistine fear of quick action is something we hate with all our soul ... we would like to tear down the barricade of circumspection.

(Marx-Engels: Uber Kunst und Literatur.
Berlin Ost, 1953)

Small wonder that this German film was the favourite viewing of Hitler and Goebbels, dark-complexioned men who saw themselves as blonde heroes of a heroic race.

Lang and Thea von Harbou were conscious that a Siegfried who betrays to Kriemhild a secret which he should have kept is not entirely without weakness and fault. It is significant of the growing nationalist feeling in Germany that when they discussed this problem in a magazine article, their ideas were not welcome; the magazine itself did not survive its first number. The views expressed then must have been similar to those stated by Lang at Yale in 1966:

It is easy to be a hero when you make yourself invisible with the help of the *tarhelm*. And though it may perhaps be forgivable that Siegfried gets the Virgin Queen Brunhild into the connubial bed of his weak King Günther of Burgund by trickery, it is quite unforgivable that he cannot keep his mouth shut, and brags to his wife Kriemhild about his deeds. The final destruction of the Nibelungen has its origins in this bragging.

Such a realistic view of his hero hardly accords with charges of racism in Lang's portrait of the world of the Huns.

Siegfried Kracauer alleged that Lang's Alberich has markedly Jewish features, and he reads into this a deliberate gesture of anti-semitism. In reality, Lang and his make-up artist Otto Genath were simply influenced by the grotesque character make-up used by the Russo-Jewish Habimah ensemble that was currently visiting Berlin. Alberich was played by Georg John, an actor Lang regularly used; and the mask had to be a total disguise since he also appeared as Mime and as one of the principal Huns, Attila's brother. It was also Genath who discovered how to make Siegfried's blond wig glitter appropriately (it was finally achieved by adding blue streaks to the fair hair) and who created Attila's make-up, giving Klein-Rogge a bald head and false chin.

For documentary accuracy Lang again consulted Umlauff of the Hamburg Ethnographical Museum. Umlauff supplied the barbaric Huns with native African and Asiatic weapons, and dressed them in rags and furs which were strapped to their bodies with leather thongs. The shaggy, bow-legged forest inhabitant Mime is contrasted to the blond Siegfried, and to the decadent and stylised world of the Burgundians; but if anyone at Ufa enjoyed the emphasis on racial differences, it was certainly not Lang or Pommer, who simply followed the action of the saga.

The first premonition of a different world comes with

the scenes where the Huns are seen sitting in the bare branches, spying out the arrival of Kriemhild, and afterwards make off on their horses in a wild chase over the hills and across the steppes. This scene illustrated how generous Pommer was as a producer, even though this was the inflation period, with prices soaring up throughout the period of filming *Siegfrieds Tod*.

Before the sequence was filmed, Pommer asked Lang to think again about whether the scene, involving 400 extras and horses, was really essential. 'It is going to be very expensive and anyway we shall never be able to compete with the Americans with crowd scenes. Let's discuss it again tomorrow.'

Next afternoon, Lang said: 'I think that we do not need the scene. Thea and I will think up something else.'

Whereupon Pommer answered: 'I've done some thinking too. I think we should shoot the scene as it was originally planned.'

Forceful visual contrasts like that between the Huns, crouched and winding along the ground like reptiles after their prey and the Burgundian heroes, as well as with Rüdiger and Dietrich von Bern, are helpful in clarifying the pell-mell of battle; similarly, in *Siegfrieds Tod*, where Lang dressed Kriemhild and her husband in white and Hagen and Brunhild in black. Apart from the obvious symbolism – good and evil, light and dark – it helps to clarify the *mise en scène*: the whole becomes a kind of chess board where black and white become formal adversaries.

In the course of their mortal battle, the Burgundian heroes lose more and more the cold stylisation of the culture they have left far behind. Even their companions-in-arms become more individualized (as the anonymous workers in *Metropolis* will acquire individual faces in the course of their rising).

Attila's tent, his royal palace with its cramped proportions, the mud floor, the animal skins on the walls: all are in marked contrast to Kriemhild's native castle. Conscious of this difference, Attila drops his precious coat before Kriemhild's feet so that she may tread on it on her path to the throne. Attila, God's scourge, is more human than the rigid Kriemhild. He honours the strangers until Hagen, again the agent of nemesis, kills his beloved little heir.

Ruins, smoke and flames constitute the grand orchestration of the fall of the Nibelungs. Fortunately even here there is no trace of Wagner, but something nearer the austerity of the ancient Nordic Edda sagas. The impact *Nibelungen* made on Eisenstein is attested by whole passages in *Alexander Nevski*, as well as by such details as the helmets of the Teutonic knights, so like the angular helmet of Rüdiger. The heroic stylisations of *Ivan the Terrible*, too, are often reminiscent of Lang's *Die Nibelungen*.

Metropolis (1925–26): the design by Erich Kettelhut

6 Metropolis 1925–26

Die Nibelungen is a drama of the past; *Metropolis* is a drama of the future, set around the year 2000; yet we feel much more intensely in this film the twenties style, from which we have not as yet been able to distance ourselves sufficiently to understand its evolution and importance in the documentation of an age.

It is of primary importance to recognise the positive aspects of this film, for instance its grand prelude. In this silent film, sound has been *visualised* with such intensity that we seem to hear the pistons' throb and the shrill sound of the factory siren with their radiating trumpet-like rays of light. There is movement up and down, backwards, forwards; the pistons are placed in three-dimensional space, and are substantial in spite of the misty flood of light, in spite of the superimposition to indicate them as monumental symbols of labour. The wheels turning within wheels and the thudding of the pistons constitute a fusion of surrealist-expressionist vision with the technological achievements of the avant-garde.

In the stylised world of the workers, everything is of an equally intense visual force. The working class is portrayed powerfully – slaves dressed in black, heads bent, anonymous creatures of labour walking through vaulted corridors, rhythmically keeping time like the Expressionist revolutionary choirs, sharply outlined ranks in which the individual no longer counts as a human being. In the machine centre, they turn into hands on enormous dials, jerkily executing their mysterious work to keep the gigantic wheels moving. They are more machines than human beings – more machine even than the robot that struts towards the camera.

There is a transformation which echoes Pastrone's

Metropolis: the underground meeting

Cabiria: in Freder's eyes the machine centre is transformed into the image of the God Moloch, with gaping mouth and gleaming eyes. A new shift of workers march into the threatening maw on their way to the machines, in the same serried ranks.

There is an accident, viewed through a screen of smoke and the horrified eyes of Freder – all elegant in white silk – who is frozen into an Expressionist diagonal as the dark figures bearing the casualties file past, shot against the light. The scene immediately preceding this, with dark figures glimpsed merely as silhouettes in the dusty air and hazy light of the machine room, is again of great visual impact. The scene is presented without symbolism, with just that documentary approach which is Lang's great strength and which succeeds in counteracting the pomposity of much of the film.

The scene in the catacomb where a crowd of dark figures with pale faces is contrasted with the white crosses

I enjoyed it beyond my wildest dreams.
Sir Arthur Conan Doyle (quoted in Ray Lee: *A Pictorial History of Hollywood Nudity*)

The other day I saw the most foolish film. I cannot believe it would be possible to make a more foolish one.
H. G. Wells, quoted in *Frankfurter Zeitung*, 3 May 1927

The narrative is trivial, bombastic, pedantic, of an antiquated romanticism. But if we put before the story the plastic photogenic basis of the film, then Metropolis *will come up to any standards, will*

84

. . . and Maria helping the children

overwhelm us as the most marvellous picture book imaginable. Imagine, then, two antipodean elements held under the same sign, in the zones of our sensibility. The first of them, which we might call pure-lyrical, is excellent; the other, the anecdotal or human, is ultimately irritating.
Luis Buñuel, in *Gazeta literaria de Madrid*, 1927

in the background, and the touching figure of the good Maria, is intensely dramatic. The telling of the parable of Babel, during which the images are lit from the corners and the interpolation is thus visually distinguished from the main story, is experienced as a powerful legend. Along streets resembling the tentacles of an octopus, thousands of shaven-headed slaves drag the great square stones of the tower.

Light is allowed to pour in from all sides; the protesting figures on the steps seem to be surrounded by an aura, their tense bodies picked out in shining contours. The energy of their will, pitted against the bright figure of The Chosen One, is vividly sensed. The tower itself, inspired by Breughel, is very effective.

Effective too is the chase in the catacombs, even though the debutante Brigitte Helm as Maria goes off into strange contortions that anticipate her robot Maria, when the beams of Rothwang's lantern reveal to her the horror of her surroundings, with skeletons and skulls. As Rothwang, Rudolph Klein-Rogge, in fact, is the only actor who never overstates the ecstatic elements of the film. His nervous, transition-less gestures seem appropriate to a magician. He is a seer, outside time and gripped by holy madness. When we see him at work in his laboratory, switching levers or creating flashes of lightning while bright vapours rise from his jars, we are far from the grotesque laboratories of the old Frankenstein films. The futurist fantasies are masterly, controlled, credible.

Lang's vision of skyscrapers, an exaggerated dream of the New York skyline, multiplied a thousandfold and divested of all reality, is splendid. It has become truly the town of the future, reaching up into the sky in luminous immensity – quite unlike Godard's cold Alphaville. Again it is the encounter of Expressionism and Surrealism. Light and fog mingle to produce an atmosphere of weightlessness, of shimmering brightness. Towers soar with the pious thrust of Gothic architecture; corridors and hanging streets link them together prophetically, so that we hardly notice the toy airships from a bygone age.

Freder's fevered dreams are similarly expressionist-surreal. When he runs to his father, with whom the false Maria is coyly flirting, the wheels suddenly begin to rotate around the ill-matched couple. Then Freder seems to be falling through circulating shapes into an abyss; and finally everything is turning about him – a visual effect which would later be echoed in the fainting sequence in *The Blue Gardenia*. Here real pandemonium should have begun; but in the surviving versions only Freder, in his fevered dreams, can see the woman who sits on the beast of the apocalypse during the party. The statue of death with its scythe, in the city cathedral, comes to life, with all the seven deadly sins. Lang had originally planned much more powerful visions of the evil forces loosed by the creation of the robot, but he feared his audience would not have followed him. As well as Freder's visions, he wanted to show demons let loose and death and the deadly sins walk away from the cathedral, where they had been imprisoned by the Catholic faith. Again, fantastic and documentary realism were to have been mingled: the workers were to have destroyed the freeways above the city, overturned cars and set them on fire. The surviving versions of the

Metropolis: The Master, Rothwang and the Robot

film contain only the destruction of the machine centre.

The grimacing gargoyle figures were also supposed to come to life and fly down from the cathedral, attracted by the flames of the welding machines with which engineers were mending the hanging streets. Perhaps this failure to express, as intended, the *mystical* symbolism is the reason why the *sentimental* symbolism favoured by Thea von Harbou seems so embarrassing, striking a jarring note in an otherwise grandiose vision of the world.

Among the other unrealised details is an intended, characteristic von Harbou motif. Abel, the master of Metropolis, and Rothwang once loved the same woman, Hel, who became Freder's mother. The curiously medi- aeval gabled house with the hex sign on its door was intended to contain a gigantic head of Hel, rather like the head of Althea in Pabst's *Die Herrin von Atlantis.*

The excess of emotion, the abundance of stylised-

87

The crew on the set of *Metropolis*; during the flood scene (*below*)

symbolic ornamentalism – for it is the symbolism that counts – have to be judged by the standards of the age that produced them, along with the exaggerated styles of post-Secession design. People are gushingly sentimental and noble, like the characters of D'Annunzio novels; and this extravagance should also perhaps be seen as the consequence of, and the reaction after the unemotional war years. It was common at the time to admire works that now seem to us pure *kitsch* – for instance Stuck's and some of Klinger's pictures, that have a fatal Böcklinesque tendency. 'We were all effusive and sentimental in those days', Lang now recalls.

While Freder's bedroom is designed with extravagant arabesques, the office of the master of Metropolis resembles in its sober simplicity Lang's own study in the twenties (and even now his house has no pictures and hardly any decorations on the wall apart from some African straw shields).

The *kitsch* reaches its extreme in the dance of the false Maria, inspired by the expressive gymnastics of Mary Wigman (and usually aggravated today by being shown at sound speed), while Fröhlich's make-up and playing are typical of the conventional jeune premier of the period.

Yet as soon as Lang escapes from the arts and crafts stylisation and the kitschy emotionalism and 'sophistication', the 'architect' Lang takes over, triumphantly: the workers' sarabande in the destroyed centre; the dance around the bonfire in front of the cathedral; most notably the crowd that pushes forward in a wedge shape near the cathedral; the children who form a pyramid around Maria during the flood. The geometrical or architectural structuring of bodies expresses a conception that has nothing to do with emotional excess. This technique of 'concentration', while still semi-expressionist, is already far on the road to the so-called 'New Objectivity'. Lang moreover complements the formal geometrical structures with individual gestures and montage of actions, as when Maria clings to the attic window, trying to break the lattice, while Freder, hearing her, cries and hammers at the gate, the double movement constituting a counterpoint.

Admirable, too, are the 'documentary' techniques used for the flood-scenes, when the water spouting from the destroyed tanks mingles with the steel structures in the luminous mists, or when the surging flood nibbles at the asphalt in front of the workers' barracks, and begins its gradual rise. Wherever the film concentrates on documentary and technological details, the private sentimentalism of the story is supplanted by genuinely dramatic effect.

The ending of *Metropolis* is, however, overwhelmed by the excess of emotionalism. Fulfilling the spirit of the good Maria's appeal to the mediator between the brain that does the thinking and the hands which put the plan into action – the heart – there is a superficial reconciliation between capital and labour. First Heinrich George has to wipe his sweaty yet honest hands, then put them back into his pocket once more when he gets no response. Finally, however, the good Freder grasps his father's hand and puts it into that of the worthy foreman. Lang had intended a quite different ending; Freder and Maria were to leave the world and go by space-ship to another world – *Metropolis* would have become a kind of prelude to *Frau im Mond* (*Woman in the Moon*).

Even at the time, when people were still close to the ecstatic mood of the preceding years, the film – particularly the ending – was not received uncritically. Lang himself now smiles about the notion of the mediator – a kind of sentimentality far removed from the harsh social criticism of his American films. In an article on Vienna, he seems to attribute the ornamental tendencies, the playful attention to detail, secondary episodes and symbolism to the legacy of the imperial city's convoluted baroque.

Lang has told me that what interested him most in *Metropolis* was the conflict between the magical and occult (the world of Rothwang) and modern technology (the world of Herr Fredersen). In his care – out of deference to the audience, not to go too deeply into the magical and occult, he failed to fulfil his innermost intentions, which may be why he feels that *Metropolis* is not stylistically unified. In later years he would have had the courage of his convictions – a fact which explains certain closely related aspects of his Indian films.

For Thea von Harbou, however, the film's importance lay mainly in the 'motto' notion, which she clearly declares in her book *Metropolis* (possibly written before or during the shooting):

This book is a story based on the idea:
'The mediator between brain and hand should be the heart'.

The old-fashioned emotionalism must not be allowed to obscure the enormous technical achievement of the film. In *Dr Mabuse*, when Wenck's desk explodes, Lang first shows the blast and then the flash of the explosion. For the explosion in *Metropolis*, during the flood, Lang again wanted to show first the blast and then the flash. To achieve this he had the camera fixed on a kind of swing, which first swung towards Freder – before whose eyes the explosion is to be seen. During its forward movement, Freder seems to be compressed against the wall; so that when the camera swung back, the spectator seemed actually to have experienced an explosion. What is important is that at this time such effects, however much we now take them for granted, had to be 'invented'. Eugen Schüfftan's mirror process, for instance, the first successful method of combining models with full-scale scenes, gave Lang wonderful decorative possibilities in this film. Shuftan (as he now spells his name) remembers that the workers' barrack-like houses were built up only half way, and beyond that were 'mirrored in'. Lang however maintains that they were fully built, while the stadium of the rich and the gigantic head of Hel were 'mirrored in' by Schüfftan.

As with the Emperor of China's letter, Lang again helped himself to whatever tricks were necessary. Stop-action shots of aeroplanes and cars on the freeways, filmed in the old glasshouse studio, took six days to film, Lang recalls, and barely lasted one minute in the finished film.

The scene in which Abel sees foreman George on a huge television screen was something completely novel. Lang believes it to have been the first time that back projection was used, although he had tried something comparable in *The Spiders*, when Lio Sha observes on a screen the people gathered in the cellar.

Few critics have ever understood the film better than the young Luis Buñuel, who wrote an exemplary review for a Spanish journal in 1927. *Metropolis*, he concludes, 'is two films glued together by their bellies'. Already at that time he distinguished between the contributions of Lang and von Harbou, attributing to the writer the 'dangerous syncretism'. Yet he is full of admiration for the film's great

Metropolis: studio work for the shots of aeroplanes over and cars on the freeways

moments, the wheels within wheels, the throbbing pistons, the skyscrapers and their transparent fountains of light, in which 'physics and chemistry are transformed into rhythm' and where there is 'never a static moment'. When he saw the film, the titles evidently also formed part of this movement:

Even the titles which ascend and descend, twist round, dissolve into light and shade, fuse with the general movement; they also burn into images.

Buñuel makes a clear distinction between the 'pure lyrical element' and the irritating anecdote:

From the photographic angle, its emotive force, its unheard-of and overwhelming beauty is unequalled. It is of such a technical perfection that it can stand a prolonged analysis without for an instant betraying its model.

APPENDIX: *Walter Schulze Mittendorf: THE ROBOT. ITS BIRTH*

problems of form? No!
Expressionism lived.
Technological form had been discovered as motif for painting and sculpture.
Primary, in this case, was the question,
'Which material?'
Thought – at first chased copper plate to have real metal. That meant – searching for and finding a suitable chaser to execute the work.
'Complicated', I thought – when Fritz Lang tried to interest me in the work.
But which material really?
An accident helped us.
   A workshop making architectural models gave us decisive assistance unintentionally.
I went there because of another job.
   My attention was drawn to a little cardboard box labelled: 'Plastic wood' – 'trade sample' – a postal parcel.
   This 'trade sample' – not interesting for the workshop – was given to me. One trial brought the proof straightaway – the material for our 'machine creature' had been found.
   'Plastic wood' turned out to be a kneadable substance made of wood, hardening quickly when exposed to the air – allowing itself to be modelled like organic wood.

93

Now it needed a procedure that was not very pleasant for Brigitte Helm – namely the making of a plaster cast of her whole body.

Parts resembling a knight's armour, cut out of Hessian, were covered with 2 millimetres of the substance, flattened by means of a kitchen pastry roller.

This was then stuck on to the plaster Brigitte Helm, like a shoemaker pulls leather over his block.

When the material had hardened, the parts were polished – the contours cut out.

This was the rough mechanism of the 'machine creature' which made it possible for the actress to stand – to sit and to walk.

The next procedure – furnishing it with detail – to create a technological aesthetic.

Finally – cellon varnish mixed with silver bronze – and applied with a spray gun – gave the whole its genuinely metallic appearance which even seemed convincing when looked at from close range.

The work took many weeks however. In those days, films were carefully prepared – and thus the realisation of a piece of work unusual for a film like this one was ensured.

In striking contrast to the present-day German film industry!

7 Spione (The Spy, 1926)

The mad Dr Mabuse, 'a symbol, a metaphor of the decaying morality and malaise of postwar Germany' shows at least in one episode of his criminal career . . . something like a human trait . . . Haghi, the master spy, is nothing less than what we would call today a human computer . . . Haghi has no human feelings whatsoever. He has an utter disregard for human beings. They are for him nothing but chess men, which he moves according to his mathematical mind.

Fritz Lang: Introductory speech to *The Spy* at the University of California, 28 June 1967

With Fritz Lang's films it is never a question of being fascinated by the incidents of the 'action', but by the 'succession of images', the impact of visual impression, the consistency of visual events'.

Friedrich Porges: *Mein Film* (123, 1928) *Kritik zu Spione*

An immense wealth of happenings is set in motion already with the first picture. There is so much that every individual event has to appear

When *The Spy* was shown at the University of California (Riverside Extension) on 28 June 1967, Fritz Lang, in an introductory talk, gave a vivid description of the Berlin twenties, the restlessness and despair which was to lead to the Hitler regime:

After the defeat in World War I, and after the obligatory but senseless – because emotional – social upheaval, followed by the equally obligatory but much more successful counter-revolution by the reactionary forces (because the counter-revolution was cold-bloodedly conceived and executed) Germany entered a period of unrest and confusion, a period of hysteria, despair and unbridled vice, full of the excesses of an inflation-ridden country. I remember those times very clearly. I was shooting in those days of inflation in Neubabelsberg, where the Ufa studios were located, half an hour by car from the capital of Berlin.

Money lost its value very rapidly. The workers received their money not weekly but daily, and even so when they arrived home after working hours, shops were closed and the following morning their wives could hardly buy a couple of rolls or half a pound of potatoes for a day's work.

At the same time the nightclubs were in full swing, supported by the easily earned money of uncaring war – and inflation; the profiteers, who thought or knew they could buy anything and everything, including the starved and impoverished women of the former upper and middle classes. In cellars and private flats obscure little night spots popped up nightly only to disappear two or three days later – as soon as they became too well known to the general public and the police.

In these places the up-and-coming classes of the new rich could gamble and the sky was the limit. Their rich and jaded wives visited them too, morbidly looking for unequivocal invitations, vulgar and sordid as they came – every sex deviation found fulfilment.

Crime prospered. From time to time some loner tried to stop this witches' sabbath. One morning there appeared wall posters throughout Berlin showing a half-naked voluptuous woman in the arms of a skeleton with the caption: 'Berlin – you are dancing with Death'. But who cared? After four years of war, Death had lost its terrors.

Religion? God? He had been sent to peddle his heavenly wares elsewhere.

In such an atmosphere of 'And Devil take the hindmost' there thrives the constant, ever-present yearning for the fantastic, the mysterious, the macabre, for the strangling terror of the dark.

During the first half of the twenties, the German film mirrored the sombre, hopeless times and moods in equally sombre and foreboding pictures. The inmates of the weird insane asylum and its sinister director in Dr Wiene's *Cabinet of Dr Caligari*, Murnau's deadly vampire *Nosferatu*, or Wegener's *Golem* could only be created in such an era.

I myself joined these film makers with two characters: the master criminal *Dr Mabuse the Gambler* and the master spy Haghi in *The Spy*.

Lang went on to speak about the story of *The Spy*:

In my work I always used and still use real events, culled from the daily papers. In both of my films that I mentioned before, the *Dr Mabuse* films – four to be precise – and in *The Spy*, I got my first ideas from newspaper clippings . . .

The incident on which *The Spy* was based was the so-called Arcos raid in London towards the middle of the twenties. The Russian Trade Delegation, Arcos – the word stands for All Russian Co-operative Society – under suspicion of being an espionage centre, was raided by a special branch of Scotland Yard. Therefore, as you will see, the invented super-spy Haghi was played by the actor Klein-Rogge in the make-up of the political master-mind Trotsky.

The Spy, like *Dr Mabuse*, goes all out for suspense. Yet the character of Mabuse has much more psychological depth than Haghi, who is simply the criminal mastermind *par excellence*. A woman like Cara Carozza might actually fall in love with the demonic doctor; but Sonja – Gerda Maurus – fears and hates Haghi, who has forced her to work for him, ostensibly to give her a chance to revenge herself for her father and brother. Finally Haghi must replace her with the indifferent Kitty (Lien Dyers) whose avarice may safely be relied on.

Again, as in the first *Mabuse* film, Lang achieves the polished technique of the adventure film in which all the links interlock, one event calling forth and precipitating the next by an association of ideas; the same use of ellipsis to accelerate the action; the same mathematical logic. The only retarding element again is the sentimentalism of a pair

small, marginal, episodic in itself. It is only much later that one realises how all these distinct little episodes constitute in reality the precisely fitting wheels of a super-sophisticated plot.
A. Kraszna-Krauss:
Filmtechnik (no 7, 31 March 1928)

Fritz Lang has abandoned the formalism and stylisation of his Nibelungen *and* Metropolis *films. He has returned to the style of* Dr Mabuse. *He has made a film, a thrilling, breathtaking adventure film . . . Fritz Lang has moved more and more from the pictorial and visual to movement and incident.*
Herbert Ihering: *Berliner Börsen-Courier* (23 March 1928)

Spione (1926): Gerda Maurus as Sonja

of lovers, the contribution of von Harbou – strongly contrasted to the effective episode between Kitty and the Japanese diplomat (convincingly played by Lupu Pick) in which the relationship is based not on love but on cool calculation.

The opening of the film is fascinating for its effortless assembly of exciting events and minor details dashed on the screen like vivid brush strokes. Incidents are just hinted, but never too rapidly, and always logically linked. The theft of a secret document echoes the first *Mabuse* film: mysterious hands open a safe; policemen shout (silently!) into telephones. The close-up of a motor-cyclist, looking like some gigantic spider in the grotesque fore-shortening later to be used in *M* for the celebrated close-up of Inspector Lohmann, is not ornamentally conceived, but an organic development of the action. Lang explains that this exciting evocation of speed was achieved by suspend-ing the motor-cycle on a wooden post and producing dust clouds with a wind machine.

Lang is already a master of suspense. A man calls out that he knows who is at the centre of all the terrorist activities when there is a shot from outside the window, killing him before he can speak the name. Yet Lang allows this secret to be revealed to the audience. Another shot shows Haghi's back, and lined up before him the emissaries who will report to him. Lang, confident that the knowledge does not affect the suspense of the film, will proceed in the same way in *M* and *The Last Will of Dr Mabuse*. In *The Spy* he reveals the man-behind-the-scenes after a title; in the sound films after a spoken question.

Without prejudicing the suspense, the methods of the spies are methodically revealed. A post office; and a mysterious figure removes all the pencils and breaks all the pens, so that Tremaine will be forced to use a particular desk on which to write his coded telegram. The moment Tremaine leaves the office, Haghi's man appears and pulls out a carbon copy from beneath the blotting paper. Again, the spies are shown operating from inside the security police: Tremaine is photographed by a police employee with a button-hole camera, as he enters the office disguised as a tramp.

In these scenes Lang's humour is always in evidence. Fritz Rasp, an elegant Rastaquère in waxed moustache, collects a *poste restante* letter by means of a complicated logarithmic trick, leaving the amazed detective with a piece of paper left blank by vanishing ink. In the cut versions available today Rasp appears merely as an amusing episodic figure. In fact the character was based on the real-life case of the Austrian Colonel-General Redl, who betrayed his country's secrets, and whose tragic story was recorded by Egon Erwin Kisch. Lang was fascinated by the story, and in the original version of *The Spy* it was developed right up to his suicide, at the advice of the general staff (which provided the revolver) to save him from public disgrace.

Even apparently episodic sequences, however, are never irrelevant or unimportant; everything is interconnected. Lang often uses important actors in small roles, since there are really no minor parts as far as he is concerned. Even the little post-office clerk in all his comic self-importance, is developed as a vigorous character. Lang devotes the same

Spione: Fritz Rasp – an elegant Rastaquère

Spione: Lien Deyers as Kitty

care to the tics and idiosyncracies of his main characters, for instance Haghi's habit of pulling his upper lip, lost in thought, as he dictates to Sonja the letter from Tremaine; or the security inspector's way of scratching his nose, or gasping for breath with his fish mouth. Small details support the illusion of reality.

Lang enjoys the use of visual parallels. For Tremaine, disguised as a tramp, has left a dark smudge from his dirty hand on the light-coloured chair of the hotel. The next shot shows the hand of the beautiful Sonja, pointing a revolver at the unseen emissary of Haghi, as if threatening him. Again, Dr Masimoto (Lupu Pick) strokes Tremaine's hand, in sympathy because he is getting blind drunk in a pub after losing the beautiful girl-spy. In the next shot Sonja, captured by Haghi, lovingly stroke a picture of Tremaine secretly taken by a Haghi spy. And this shot of Sonja, in evening dress and filmed at an oblique angle, is directly followed by a shot of Kitty (Lien Dyers) in a similar pose and also in evening dress, lounging on Haghi's desk. Such parallelism is not only decorative but a means of speeding up the movement of the film. It can be ironic too as when Masimoto no sooner warns Tremaine against the beautiful girl-spy than he falls victim to another.

The realist surface, the precise documentation of the incidents in Haghi's labyrinthine spy centre are suddenly contrasted with a dream image, when Lupu Pick, betrayed by Kitty and about to commit harakiri, seems to recognise the emissaries with their bloodstained document, who have gone to their deaths for him: the contours and images are blurred and smudged in Expressionist style, by the spectral lighting.

At once the film returns to documentary realism with the train crash, produced by the machinations of Haghi. This was the first film made by Fritz Lang's own company, for distribution by Ufa, and Lang was obliged to economise wherever possible. The train crash was 'filmically' simulated without an engine, which would have been too costly. Hence the scene was shot at night and in a tunnel. Spotlights were fixed in pairs on a moveable framework to look like the lights of an engine and were quickly moved forward to produce the impression of an approaching engine. Another technical trick was turned to gripping visual effect:

Spione: elements of documentary and impact

I had not yet found the artistic shape fitting the event, the impact of the catastrophe, the mood of those last seconds.

So he showed in the gleam of the approaching spotlights the frightened and horrified face of a passenger who is conscious of the danger and the imminence of death. The scene was completed with clouds of steam, splintering glass and broken fragments of metal thrown before the camera. Economy proved a stimulus to Lang's invention.

Even more than *Frau im Mond, Spione* indicates the imminence of the sound film. To save titles Lang sometimes has Tremaine's servant explain events to his master by gestures very different from the sign language used by Haghi to communicate with the deaf-and-dumb nurse who is, perhaps his mother (and is perhaps *not* deaf and dumb, but another deliberate deception like the apparently lame man). Superimposition is used with characteristic expressiveness. Sonja notices a paper on Haghi's desk, inscribed 'Europa Express 33–133'. When

her train stops at a station she sees her lost lover in a sleeping compartment on the train travelling in the opposite direction; and when his train begins to move she notices the number: '33–133'. As her train moves off, Lang shows how the numbers are hammered into her mind: wheels seen in close-up, rolling on and on, with the ominous numbers superimposed. We seem almost to hear the sound of the thundering wheels. Sonja reacts, too, almost as does Peter Lorre in the sound film *M*, when he presses his hands over his ears to shut out the Grieg music he hears in the garden-terrace of the little cafe. From the wheels Lang makes a transition to the undercarriage of Tremaine's compartment and to the act of sabotage, as Haghi's man disconnects the wagon in the tunnel.

The pursuit of the culprit along country roads is a direct anticipation of *The Last Will of Dr Mabuse*, with the trees turning into blurs; while Lang deliberately uses echoes of *Spiders*, in the scene where Tremaine, searching for the hostage Sonja, explores the walls of the Haghi bank with his hands.

The Spy is accented by Lang's interest in the play of light and shade. As Sonja and Tremaine's chauffeur-manservant, tied to chairs, try to break loose in the gaseous fumes, and when a Haghi man is wrestling with Tremaine's servant, they cast gigantic shadows on the wall. Occasionally shadows precede the event in menacing anticipation – a typically German cinematic effect used by Lang as a means of heightening suspense. Again, in the scene where the spies are arrested when emerging from a sewer, or in the great staircase in Haghi's bank, elements that are at once functional and organic to the narrative, and pictorially ornamental, reinforce the documentary and adventure elements in Lang's film.

Cinemagazine of 17 February 1928 gives a 'studio report' by Robert Spa about the filming of *The Spy*. Lang, he says, was working in a studio four times as large as a French studio; and the reporter was struck by the silence, unusual in the filming of silent films:

Short orders are given with a firm voice

Wagner the cameraman explains that they are shooting an explosion. (*The scene where the wall is demolished in order to break into the headquarters of the spy ring.*)

The studio visitor is 'blinded by the lights'; apparently they are using eight cameras. (*In fact Lang now says he never used more than two cameras in those days.*) A nurse stands by with a first aid kit. The wall collapses.

Lang shouts: 'Once more. Rebuild the wall!'

Lang takes Spa to see the previous day's rushes – the shadow sequence of Gerda Maurus tied to her chair – and explains that it is 'only a small film compared to *Metropolis*, but a film full of action'. The reporter mentions the tremendous uninterrupted work. They snatch ten minutes for a meal, working from nine in the morning till eleven at night. Everybody survives on sandwiches and a little fruit. The electricians and machinists are working three shifts.

Lang sees everything, makes everything himself, supervises the make-up of actresses (actors do not use make-up). He controls all the details of the costumes, furniture and props; he is 'infallible'.

8   Frau im Mond (Woman in the Moon, 1928)

Woman in the Moon cannot be easily dismissed as a modernist re-hash of Méliès' 1902 *Voyage dans la Lune*. Lang anticipated everything. Because of his concern for documentary precision, he consulted experts: two rocket specialists, Hermann Obert and Willy Ley were his advisers. It was to increase the suspense of the count-down that he invented the notion of counting down from 6 to 1 instead of ending on the higher number.

Lang's primary interest was in the rocket sequence, and it is justifiable to assert that a passage in *Deutsche Filmzeitung* signed by him was certainly by a public relations man or by Thea von Harbou:

Four men, a woman and a child – a handful of people brought together by fate. Speeding in a never-before seen vehicle, the space ship, to a never-before entered spot, the infinite loneliness of the moon, they remain yet tied to their fates, to the law of their blood, their passions, their happiness and their tragedy. To bring this out was my dream.

This has the same tone about it as von Harbou's summing-up:

Incomparable opportunity of planting the destinies of human beings onto the flower gardens of the stars, to let them come to a fateful flowering in a new world and – watch them perish, experience their smiles and their tears in face of the immense size of the world as something even bigger . . .

Lang rightly points out that much of this kind of emotionalism has to be seen as a necessary concomitant of the silent film with its need to replace words by facial expression, mime, gesture and posture. A sequence now missing from surviving copies illustrates this: in the space ship Gerda Maurus, wishing to express sympathy with her fiancé who lies in the next room, puts her hand to her heart and her mouth to send him kisses.

Thinking back, I realised to my own surprise that it (the count-down) had first been used in the film Frau im Mond. *This was a silent movie, and at one point the words 'ten seconds to go' flashed on the screen, followed by the numbers, '6-5-4-3-2-1-0-FIRE' Knowing that Fritz Lang had been in the Austrian Army in the First World War, I asked him whether he had adapted some military practice which used a count-down. He replied that he had thought it up for dramatic purposes when working on the film; on a proving ground nobody would possibly think of that side effect!*
Willey Ley: *Rockets, Missiles and Men in Space*

Especially noteworthy were the remarkable, realistic studio-made sets and such scenes as the rocket's departure, scenes inside the rocket, during its flight, and the wonderful luminosity of the lunar landscape.
Paul Rotha: *The Film Till Now*

Frau im Mond (1928)

Another element missing from present-day copies of the film is all those sequences involving men in black leather jackets, who attempt to steal the plans of the space ship; and it is possible that they have been recently cut from the original negative now held by an Eastern European archive, on the assumption that these men in black leather were intended as spies from an Eastern power. The loss includes the introductory sequence of the theft which *Deutsche Filmzeitung* (no 42, 1929) described as having 'an almost unreal stylised shape in its fast-moving actions'; and certainly deprives whole sections of the film of their intended rhythm. The five 'brains', with their cheques – the five financiers – remain; and since they are such useful representatives of capitalism this may be further indication of recent censorship.

Lang, as always, understands how to add poetry to the technological documentary, to create vivid imagery. When the space ship is brought out of the hangar, it is lit up

Frau im Mond: working on the moonscape

by enormous spotlights, whose beams cross in the evening light, to appear like rhomboid figures of light floating in the air. In this light, the moon rocket acquires a strange life of its own. While remaining quite concrete, the technical process is in this way transformed into an optical dream of prophetic quality.

Perhaps the 'luminous' moonscapes too should be seen as optical dreams, rather than as studio sets. Stills of work in progress show how bleached sand was poured over the studio floor, with mountains piled up in the grounds. Inevitably however the most effective features were caves and grottoes, packed with mystery, and the lava soil from which steam rises and bubbles burst.

Originally it was intended that the mad professor should find the gold statuary of a pre-terrestrial culture on the moon; and the rock to which he clings ecstatically still shows some traces of a figurative form. In this cave, too, the professor was to have seen a free-floating crystal ball,

Frau im Mond: working inside the rocket

representing our earth and created many thousands of years ago by the first human beings from Atlantis. When they landed on the moon and discovered that they could not return, this was a wish and a dream of nostalgia, a symbol that they worshipped. Like the pandemonium sequences in *Metropolis,* Lang scrapped these optical parables in deference to the realistic temperament of German audiences.

The film lacks the sustained suspense of *The Spy.* Its most memorable aspects are the photo-reportage of the launch of the rocket, with the clever deployment of the moments of tension, superb orchestration of light and shade, magisterial handling of an immense crowd. (For one shot of the wheeling out of the rocket, the waiting crowd is seen at a very great distance. In this scene, according to Lang, the people were nothing but pins with large glass heads.)

On the night of the première a postal rocket was to be

sent off. The attempt, undertaken rather unwillingly by
Oberth, failed dismally: in those days rockets were even
less predictable than now. The launching of the rocket in
the film however was so authentic in all its technical
details, as were the drawings, still valid today, on which
the trajectory from the earth to the moon was mapped,
that the Nazis withdrew the film from distribution. Even
the model of the space ship was destroyed by the Gestapo,
on account of the imminence of the V1 and V2 rockets on
which Wernher von Braun was working from 1937
onwards. (Willy Ley had escaped to the United States,
while Oberth had become a Nazi.)

9 M (1931)

*For murder, though it have no
tongue, will speak with most
miraculous organ.*
Shakespeare: *Hamlet*,
Act II, Scene 2

*Gradually, and at times
reluctantly, I have come to the
conclusion that every human
mind harbours a latent
compulsion to murder . . .*
Fritz Lang, quoted in *Los
Angeles Herald Express*, 12
August 1947

*I have tried to approach the
murderer imaginatively to
show him as a human being
possessed of some demon that
has driven him beyond the
ordinary borderlines of human
behaviour, and not the least
part of whose tragedy is that
by murder he never resolves
his conflicts.*
Fritz Lang: *Why I am
interested in murder.* New
York, 1947

*Lang's camera seldom shows
any prejudice, whether
viewing the police, the
underworld, the populace or
the child murderer . . . and
because of this impartiality,
Lang's picture is almost
mathematical in structure.*
Joseph Himson: *Fritz
Lang's M*, in *Daily Bruin*,
UCLA, Los Angeles,
7 November 1969

This film was originally to have been called *Mörder unter
uns (Murderers amongst us)*. When Lang tried to hire the
Staaken Zeppelinhalle, which had been converted to a film
studio, to shoot his crowd scenes, he was unexpectedly
turned down: Lang himself ought to know the reason
why, said the studio manager. Astonished, Lang asked
why he should not make a film about a sex murderer?

Ah, well; if it was a film about a sex murderer, Lang
could have the studio, came the answer. Lang understood
this when, in the heat of negotiations he seized the
manager's lapel and discovered the Nazi badge on its
reverse. The Nazis had taken the original title to refer to
them.

In a 1947 article, 'Why I am interested in Murder', Lang
explained how he came to film *M* (about child murder),
Fury (the internal stresses of an intending murderer),
Woman in the Window (the tell-tale fears of a successful
killer), and not least, *Secret Beyond the Door*:

> If I were the only producer to be making murder films or if my interest
> in murder were abnormal or unique there would be no point in
> pursuing the question publicly, but the fact is that millions of people,
> of peaceable, law-abiding American citizens are fascinated by murder.
> Why else . . . would the newspapers devote capitals three inches high
> and millions of words to print the gory details . . . ? It seems there is a
> latent fascination in murder, that the word arouses a tangle of
> submerged and suppressed emotion. Shall I ask, why are we interested
> in murder? First of all, a murder story, whether it is a work of fiction
> or an actual murder case reported in the newspapers . . . is a puzzle
> against which to match the sharpness of the mind.

Yet this, he says, is only the fringe of the matter. The
criminal has brutally outraged a well-established code of
society. First we are 'horrified and disgusted'. Thus our
'emotions have got involved', we are concerned about the

'sanctity of human life'; it is a matter of the 'self-preservation of society'. Then follows a typical Lang idea, expressed again and again in his films: we begin to feel something like sympathy in the strict sense of the word; and Lang quotes his favourite Sanskrit saying, *Tat Wam Asi* – 'there, but by the grace of God, stand I'. Lang again and again reverts to the idea that 'Any one of us might turn a murderer in certain circumstances'.

Has personal experience given Lang this understanding? His first wife committed suicide after she found Thea von Harbou, who was working with him on a screenplay, in Lang's arms; and Lang was at first suspected of murder. For the first time he learned how 'unstable' circumstances and reasons for suspicion can be; and because of this he began his longstanding habit of noting down every event of his day. A fat diary records every event of his day, every telephone call, every visit, even the menu of his meals. Without writing everything down carefully in this way, he believes, it is impossible to remember a few days later what happened on any particular day.

At the same time, Lang looks for an 'explanation of human behaviour', particularly when sex is involved in it:

Nevertheless, though civilization may have tamed us and curbed our destructive desires in the interests of society at large, there is enough in most of us of the wild, uninhibited creature to identify ourselves momentarily with the outlaw who defies society and exults in cruelty. The desire to hurt, the desire to kill . . . is closely joined to the sexual urge, under whose dictate no man acts reasonably.

This feeling explains the sympathy, or rather the empathy that we feel when Peter Lorre calls out to the gangster court:

But can I . . . can I help it? Haven't I got this curse inside me? The fire? The voice? The pain?

Again, . . . again and again I have to walk the streets. And I always feel that somebody is following me. . . . It is I myself. . . . Following. Me . . .

(This monologue of despair was, on Lang's testimony, written without his help by Thea von Harbou; and excuses many of her faults of taste in other screenplays.)

Here also we have the explanation of why Lang allows the police to come in, and why he leaves an open ending after the verdict, 'in the name of the people'. 'The pictures argue', he says simply, 'for a democratic procedure'.

He likes to quote the devil in Lessing's *Faust* who answers, when asked how fast he moves, 'as fast as the transition from good to evil – that's me'. In his interview with Gero Gandert Lang goes even further, when he says that guilt and innocence are in reality one and the same thing. He is interested in man as such, and in the motives behind his actions – 'what makes him tick'. . . . 'And I always feel that somebody is following me . . . It is I myself. . . .'

The murderer in *M* is an inconspicuous man, a man in the street who has to be marked with the chalk sign 'M' on his shoulder in order that he may be recognised. He is not even a Hoffmann 'demonic citizen'; Lorre rightly invests him with a certain amiability as well as a trace of retarded development. Lang's murderer, it must constantly be stressed, is based neither on Haarmann nor on Kürten, who had not yet been convicted when the film was made. In those restless times after the end of the war and the abortive attempts at revolution, the mad investment and the vast unemployment that were to give Hitler his opportunity, there was – what else could be expected? – a crop of mass murderers. In his talk to the students of the Riverside Campus of the University of California, Lang gave the vivid picture of the period already quoted, in explanation of the background of *Spies*.

In his *Why I am Interested in Murder* article, Lang mentions 'the sadistic practices in primitive tribes before the sexual act', calls cannibalism 'the desire to possess the body of another person'; tells of an attorney who had said jokingly, 'everybody is a potential murderer' and admits that he himself enjoys reading the obituary pages. For most people, he concludes, reading about murder in the newspapers or detective fiction is a 'sufficient outlet for their atavistic desires'. There is significantly less interest in bank robbers or burglars. Murder is a dramatic event; 'death makes a climax, death speaks the last line':

Murder springs from the dark places of the human heart; it is born of urges and desires whose fulfilment, as long years of civilisation have shown us, leads us to unhappiness and further frustrations. This is the tragedy of the murderer himself.*

* In this light it is unfortunate that Lang was unable to make the film he had planned before *Fury – The Man Behind You*. This was to have dealt with the problem of the Jekyll-and-Hyde double nature of man. The problem of the *doppelgänger* – which underlies many German films, from Mack Mack's *Der Andere* to the three versions of *Der Student von Prag* – was one of the great themes of German romanticism, and occupied Lang again and again. Lang was, as he admitted in a television interview with Godard, after all, in a certain sense a romantic himself.

The documentary element in M

Lang told Gero Gandert: 'I am a more than attentive newspaper reader. I read more than just one country's newspapers, and especially try to read between the lines.' Even when his sight was failing, Lang still went through an enormous pile of newspapers daily – and particularly on Sundays. He was accustomed almost to eat newsprint, which pours into his house from every part of the world.

Whenever I have started to believe in an idea and to become obsessed by it, I do a lot of research on it. I want to know as much as possible about every little detail (nothing is really a little detail) down to the minutest aspects.

He told Gandert, as he had described in his article 'Some Random Notes About *M*', how he sought advice from the criminal police at the Alex (the nickname given to Berlin police headquarters, at the Alexanderplatz) and was told about their techniques of investigation, and given access to the department's records and memoranda. He talked also to psychiatrists and psychoanalysts, and, not least, to characters from the 'milieu', some of whom he later used as extras in the film, notably for the scene of the gangsters' court.

Interviewing Lang, Gero Gandert suggested that the sequences of the beggars' exchange are 'romantic elements'; but Lang explains that they are based on fact. A beggars' exchange, based on a sandwich currency, really did exist in Berlin, and a crime magazine of the period published articles and pictures about it. Moreover in his article 'Some Random Notes on *M*' he states that he had seen notices in which the gangster organisation offered their aid to the police. In recent times there has been a case similar to Lang's notion: Dutch gangster organisations, the press reported, offered to help the police in their fight against the Provos, the rebellious 'fils a papa', their motive being that they could not pursue their 'trade' in peace because of continued police raids. One might also compare the report in *France Soir* of 1 December 1967, that during the trial of the child murderer Jürgen Barsch, at Gelsenkirchen, a group of upright citizens formed a secret action group, called 'Operation Nemesis' to punish sexual crimes by death or castration, to make up for the abolition of capital punishment in Germany. (It is interesting that

M (1931): one of the designs by Eric Hasler

the news report actually mentions *M*.)

The documentary element that is of decisive importance in this film is achieved not by shooting in actual streets. The camerawork itself is designed to produce the impression that newsreel material has been used – in the shots of the police raids in the allotment gardens; even in scenes where the pictorial composition is emphasised – the singing children and the old organ grinder, or the street where the murderer is confronted by the gang of beggars, filmed from above. Unlike Herlth or Röhrig, Emil Hesler, Lang's designer here, does not seek effects of light and shade; and his cool, precise manner makes for the realism which Lang required.

Ornamental romanticism or realistic detail?

The resemblances between the beggars' organisation in *M* and that in Brecht's *Dreigroschenoper* have often been stressed. Lang does not deny the influence of Brecht upon every intellectual of the period:

Did Brecht influence me? Of course he did. Nobody who tried to come to grips with the time could escape his influence. . . . We develop only with the help of influences received from outside. (Interview with Gero Gandert)

The documentary and the ornamental are indivisible: in the shot of the yard of the flats, seen from above with the circle of children and the miserable row of dustbins, a social indictment of the poverty and lack of sanitation; in the street, also shot from above, with the beggars pitting themselves against the murderer. The celebrated shot of Inspector Lohmann in his office, filmed from above and angled to show up his great belly, and make him look like some enormous toad in the foreshortened perspective, has been assumed to be 'ornamental' in purpose. Yet no shot in Lang is only playful or gratuitous; his compositions always reveal something – here it is Lohmann's earthy vitality.

Lang's love of detail, of human traits, always contributes to the characterisation: for instance when Lohmann, being told that the child murderer is captured, rushes to put his head under the tap; or again, where he corrects a spelling mistake and underlines a couple of words in the report he is reading, revealing his punctiliousness in matters of procedure at the same time as it emphasises a clue. (The words underlined are 'alter Holztisch': the idea of an old wooden table will lead to the discovery of Lorre's rough windowsill.)

When Lang shows a shop window (as he was often later to do in his American films) it is not only for the sake of composition that he shows the objects arranged in it. When the murderer looks into the window of the hardware shop, his face seems to be framed in the light reflecting off sharp knives. This is a portent as well as a symbol. Next he makes the figure of a little girl appear – quite logically – in the same frame; and we see Lorre react to her, wiping his mouth with his hand, his already bulging eyes almost starting out of his head, his breathing growing faster.

Later Lang shows us the window of a shop selling art books: an arrow moving up and down on a spring, a rotating, infinite spiral, is designed to attract the passers-by. For the murderer and the spectator too this latently symbolic decoration assumes a positive sexual meaning.

Other considerations account for the shadow sequence in the scene of the gangsters' council. Deliberately, an abstract, anonymous image is created at the climax of the council's discussion, when Schränker proposes that they shall use the beggars. As when the shadow of the murderer falls on the police poster, and then bends over to his next victim, the sound introduces a new element. A scene like this is not intended to be purely ornamental; its effect is enormously gripping, like the other scene in which the black-gloved right hand of Schränker is seen in close-up, hovering like a menace over the town map.

Sound as a dramatic factor
In his first talking picture, Fritz Lang uses sound with astonishing mastery and maturity. Sound is a central dramatic element, never additional or accidental, never an afterthought, but the counterpoint and supplement of the image. The 'overlapping' of sound which Lang was to use so expressively in *The Last Will of Dr Mabuse* is a material and organic part of the whole, and employed very deliberately. It gives the film speed, and strengthens, rather than blurs the pictorial montage, emphasising its essential structure.

After the murder of Little Elsie, a crowd gathers about a

M: . . . little children playing in the courtyard

new police poster, and since the farthest off cannot see it, they ask for it to be read out. Someone begins to read: 'Once again it has to be stated emphatically . . .'. And the reading is continued – '. . . that it is the most sacred duty of every mother and father . . .' – by a gentleman reading his newspaper in a club restaurant. The cut from one frame to the next is thus bridged, yet by changing the location and at the same time showing a common factor between the two scenes, the action is speeded up by the ellipsis, while we have been made to understand that everyone is equally alerted to the horror of the murder. The same movement is continued: the bald man at dinner in the club who is suspected by a drinking companion of an interest in little girls, cries 'Insult! Slander!' and his words lead into the next sequence where in the midst of a raid provoked by an anonymous denunciation, the accused man shouts 'Slander!' So Lang reveals how the psychosis is spreading.

During the police raid the criminal inspector (who will later contribute to the discovery of the murderer; no detail is wasted in Lang) states, 'Every person in the street . . .' and while his voice continues, '. . . could be the culprit', we are shown one of these persons in the street, a little man with spectacles and bulging eyes and a bowler hat, who stands under a street lamp and is approached by a little girl on a scooter who asks him the time. Imprudently the man asks her where she lives, and a bystander asks fiercely, 'What do you want from the little girl'. A pickpocket who has just been arrested by a policeman on the upper deck of a bus takes up the cry: 'Better catch the child murderer', whereupon the crowd, hearing the ominous word and seeing the arrested man gets out of hand.

This 'better catch the child murderer' cleverly prepares the way for the future idea that it will be the gangsters who catch him, because the outsider interferes with their trade. A similar piece of anticipation is the scene where the bar proprietress tells the police inspector: 'They're all curious about the fellow who is responsible for all the raids. Particularly the girls. They may be whores, but there's a bit of mother in every one of them'; and later, 'I know a lot of rowdies who get wet eyes when they see little children playing in the streets.'

Sound may be carried over more simply. The news-

M: the weary atmosphere of the police headquarters

vendor calls out the headline, 'Who . . .

'. . . is the murderer'; and the murderer whom we have so far seen only as a shadow on the 'Wanted' poster, or as a silhouette, seen from the rear with the balloon-vendor, is seen at his window-sill, writing his letter to the newspapers.

The overlapping of sound in this way is perhaps most intensely dramatic when Schränker says, during the discussion by the ring organisation, 'I request . . .' and makes a gesture which is completed by the president of the police, along with the half-finished sentence '. . . your opinions, gentlemen', during the discussion at police headquarters.

As with sound and content, counterpoint is also applied to atmosphere. The light from the lamp on the round table at which the gangsters sit, barely penetrates the thick smoke; and around the long conference table at police headquarters too the smoke becomes thicker and thicker, as the two conferences drag on. As the discussions grow more heated, both groups disintegrate. The gentlemen at police headquarters have got up leaving most of their seats empty as they walk about or stand about in the background, deep in thought. There is a similar depletion of the gangster table; only Schränker and the pickpocket remain seated.

One word, one sentence can be the trigger for a new scene, without necessarily overlapping directly. As Schränker says 'The beggars; the organisation . . . of beggars', we cut to the beggars' exchange. This corresponds also to the 'illustrated' telephone conversation between the minister and the president of police, in which each measure which has been taken is directly illustrated by a still as the president refers to it. When the president mentions the little crushed paper bag which was found, we see the way in which all the sweet shops within a given radius are investigated.

It is notable that the more the drama of the action itself develops, the less Lang has recourse to the device of overlapping. He reverts to it however when the forgotten burglar is caught, and creeps out of his hole grumbling, 'and this time I was really innocent . . .', the sentence being continued in the next shot in the inspector's office, '. . . like a new-born babe'; and again when the inspector says meaningfully, 'One of the . . . guards', suggesting that the guard might have been killed. At the word 'guards' we are shown the honest guard with an enormous plate of black pudding and sauerkraut, taking swigs of Berliner Weisse – a picture of healthy appetite and vitality (another instance of Lang's regular practice of introducing comedy on the Shakespearean principle of 'Enter the bear').

Much earlier, at the beginning of the film in fact, the cuckoo clock in Frau Beckmann's flat strikes midday, followed by the clock on the tower. Frau Beckmann – whose life consists of washing laundry, standing at her tub – brushes the suds from her hands to begin to make Elsie's dinner. Dramatic irony: in front of the school gates, a kindly policeman stops the traffic to let Elsie cross the street. The unsuspecting child throws her ball against the police poster on the advertising column, just as the shadow of a man in profile falls on it from the right. The voice of the invisible murderer invades the picture, dominates it,

M: the search for clues to the murderer

almost painfully: 'You have got a beautiful ball'. The
shadow inclines more: 'What's your name?' 'Elsie
Beckmann'. So simply is the encounter of murderer and
victim presented.

The next shot shows Frau Beckmann slicing left-over
potatoes into the soup. Hearing two little girls tripping up
the stairs, she asks them if Elsie is with them. In the next
shot the blind hawker sells Elsie a balloon, while the
murderer whistles a few bars from Grieg's 'In the Hall of
the Mountain King', which is to be a sinister leitmotif all
through the film, and eventually leads to his discovery.
The blind man hears the child say 'Thank you'.

As Frau Beckmann is putting the soup in the oven to
keep warm, the doorbell rings; someone is bringing her
the latest instalment of a serial novel. This messenger has
not seen Elsie either. The cuckoo clock shows 1.15; and
stikes once. The mother leans over the balustrade of the
empty stair well and calls 'Elsie, Elsie!' The cry echoes in

an empty attic, where washing hangs on a line; then the camera lingers on Elsie's empty place at table, the unused plate, cutlery, mug: and the empty chair as the cry still echoes, distantly, 'Elsie'.

The sandy ground and straggling undergrowth. From beneath a bush slowly rolls Elsie's ball. Her new balloon is caught in the telegraph wires. Distantly we still hear the mother calling her name.

That is all that Lang shows us of the murder. It is incomparably more impressive than if we had seen the deed itself in all its details. Lang writes of it:

> Because of the loathsome nature of the crime *M* dealt with, there was a problem of how to present such a crime so that it would not sicken the audience, yet would have full emotional impact. That is why I only gave hints – the rolling ball, the balloon caught in the wires, after being released from a little hand. Thus I make the audience an integral part in the creation of this special scene by forcing each individual member of the audience to create the gruesome details of the murder according to his personal imagination.

The telescoping of time is masterly. Instantly following the murder of Elsie Beckmann is a shot of a newsboy running along the street, shot from above: 'News extra! News extra! Who . . . is the murderer?', and so back to Lorre.

It is sound which betrays the murderer. Lang does not stop at the familiar truth that the blind have often unusually acute hearing; but puts it into visual terms and demonstrates it audibly. He first shows the blind hawker in the beggars' exchange. Nearby in the fitting chamber, where the beggars try on their professional wardrobes, another beggar is being shown an organ which is squeaky and out of tune. The blind man reacts at once by holding his hands to his ears. Then, when they try out a better organ, he reacts enthusiastically to the sound, moving his hands like an orchestra conductor.

The murderer's whistling is both a motif and a psychological quirk. It is resumed when he perceives a new victim in front of the window with the knives. We first see the murderer still munching his apple calmly, as he looks at his reflection in the window (the scene provides a parallel to the moment in his room when he grimaces at himself before his mirror). Suddenly he stares mesmerised into the

M: the gang tracking down the murderer

pane, as the little girl's figure appears in the frame of knives. Now he follows the child, whistling the Grieg theme tunelessly.★

Then the child runs to her mother, and the whistling which had increased to a paroxysm, suddenly stops. He stares after the two disappearing figures. In the shop window the arrow now seems to penetrate the rotating spiral. Frustrated, the murderer scratches the back of his hand with his nails.

On the garden-terrace of the restaurant he starts whistling again, only to close his ears with his hands, with a tortured expression. Two glasses of brandy do not, apparently, quench his frustrated desire. Whistling again, he leaves, and whistling still will be heard by the blind street hawker. Thus the circle is closed.

While the beggars are closing in on the murderer, the police are also closing in, tracking down the murderer with their clue 'Ariston'. At the scene of one of the

★ During the shooting, Lorre confessed that he could not whistle; it would have to be dubbed into the sound track. Others tried, including Thea von Harbou and the film's editor, but the results were somehow not exactly what was needed. Finally, Lang himself did the whistle. For once his being non-musical served him well: the off-key, tuneless whistle exactly fitted the unbalanced character of the murderer.

M: the underground trial

murders, three cigarette ends of the brand 'Ariston' were found. The inspector tells Lohmann 'But the table was not an old wooden table . . .' and at that moment his eyes fall on the window-sill: simultaneously there is a close-up of the window sill in the murderer's room. A hand (probably Lang's own) with a magnifying glass enters the picture, searching the woodgrain for pencil marks.

Such elliptical effects speed up the action; but at this point Lang introduces a cleverly contrived and visually impressive *retarding* effect which enhances the atmosphere. The murderer has bought oranges in a fruit shop for his next little girl victim. In the street he takes a knife from his pocket, the blade flicks out audibly, and gleams in the darkness. The spectator – along with the boy on screen, hiding – holds his breath: will he use it? . . .

But Lorre's knife only cuts into the peel of the orange.

The boy jostles against the murderer, to leave a chalk 'M' on his back. The murderer drops his knife in horror; but ironically the polite little girl retrieves it and hands it back to 'uncle'.

Again Lang makes dramatic use of sound. The little girl tells the murderer that he has a white mark on his clothes. Startled, he turns to look at his image in a glass window. There is a whistle. Alarmed, he lets go of the child's hand and runs. The whistles multiply all around: the beggars are signalling to one another.

Finding the street blocked, the hunted man runs into a gateway. Two fire engines race past the gate, screaming and ringing their bells. When the engines have passed, the murderer has disappeared. Once again sound has served to achieve a dramatic climax.

The sound effects of the sequence which follows have so often been described that they need only brief mention. The guard finds the door to the attic of the building open, shakes the wooden partitions to make sure that everything is in order, and calls out 'Is anyone there?'. Receiving no answer, he locks the door. The audience now hears the heavy breathing of the murderer in one of the partitions.

A knocking betrays the murderer to the pickpocket: Lorre is trying to make a skeleton key out of a nail, since his knife is broken. From the moment the gangsters enter the building, sound dominates the events. Noisily, the partitions are broken down and the wooden boards

splinter. Besides the sounds, there is the dramatic use of
light: in the conical beam of a torch, the murderer is
discovered, his face distorted by terror.

Lang and von Harbou allow the pickpocket to describe
proudly to the con man what he has done, and thus distract
his attention from the trussed-up guard, who reaches for
the alarm button. Thus the search for the hidden fugitive is
given an additional dramatic twist. With only minutes
before the police will arrive, there are still six partitions to
be opened and searched. 'Only one minute left', calls out
Schränker; and at that moment the murderer is discovered. The gangsters escape with their captive tied in a
carpet.

The Three Mothers
In the end it is left open whether a legal court will
condemn the murderer to death or put him in a mental
hospital. Lang tells Gandert:

In *M* I was not only interested in finding out why someone is driven to a crime as horrible as child murder, but also to discuss the pros and cons of capital punishment. But the film's message is *not* the conviction of the murderer but the warning to all mothers, 'You should keep better watch over your children'. This human message was felt particularly strongly by my wife at the time, Thea von Harbou.

The copies of the film that are available today no longer contain the shot of three mothers dressed in mourning, sitting on a bench in the corridor of the court-room. One of them is Frau Beckmann, who sighs: 'This will not bring our children back to life! One should keep better watch over them . . .' This last sentence survives today only as a voice-off in the fade-out.

Lang himself clearly wanted to go beyond the 'human interest' and the emotional interpretation of von Harbou. What he wanted to say was that the ultimate reason for the murders is the unequal distribution of wealth. Frau Beckmann is forever at the tub; hence she has no time to look after Elsie properly, or to fetch her from school.

So the film ends as it began: with the misery of the backyard amid the dustbins where children have to play in the dreariness and hopelessness of working-class life.

10   Das Testament des Dr Mabuse (The Last Will of Dr Mabuse, 1932–33)

This film meant to show Hitler's terror methods as in a parable. The slogans and beliefs of the Third Reich were placed in the mouths of criminals. By these means I hoped to expose those doctrines behind which there lurked the intention to destroy everything a people holds dear.
Fritz Lang on the occasion of the film's showing in New York, 1943

The Last Will of Dr Mabuse is much more than a repeat performance of the earlier adventure film, or an epilogue to it. The stylisations of the first *Mabuse*, made little more than ten years earlier, reflected the mentality of the inflation period; *The Last Will* seems the summing-up of these restless years.

Although in the past (cf. Kracauer's *From Caligari to Hitler*) there has perhaps been an exaggerated tendency to see in every German film portents of Hitler's rise to power, *Dr Mabuse the Gambler* was indeed the prologue to an epoch of ferment. Only a few years later, heavy industry, right-wing extremists among the petty bourgeoisie, and the increasing masses of the unemployed were ready and susceptible for the dreams of a new and strong Germany under the Hitler regime.

In *The Last Will of Dr Mabuse,* Lang once again deals with the characters of the age, yet now in a politically and sociologically much more conscious way, no longer purely for the sake of adventure and suspense. He is warning his audience of an imminent menace, which was very soon to turn into a reality. He puts into the mouth of his mad Mabuse words which the Nazis themselves still did not dare speak out aloud, but which were already apparent in their confused thought. It is not a very big step from Wilhelm II's assertion that 'Whoever is against me will be destroyed by me' to the senseless terror, the gratuitous crimes perpetrated for power's sake, conceived in the mad mind of Mabuse and inculcated by hypnosis into Professor Baum.

It was a matter of course, then, that the new Mabuse film should be banned by the new Government as early as March 1933, 'for the legal reasons', reported *Kinemato-*

Das Testament des Dr Mabuse (1932–33)

graph on 30 March, 'of endangering public order and security'. It was significant that instead of its showing planned for 23 March 1933, *Blutendes Deutschland* (Wounded Germany), the film depicting Germany's national rising, was announced for the Ufa Palast. In turn this also had to be put off, for technical reasons, and in the end the nationalist film *Der Choral von Leuthen* was held over for a further period.

Goebbels is quoted in *Dr Goebbels*, a book based on notes made by members of his entourage and edited by Karina Niehoff and Boris von Bonesholm, as saying: 'I shall ban this film . . . because it proves that a group of men who are determined to the last . . . could succeed in overturning any government by brute force'. The *Morgenpost* for 30 March took the same line: 'The presentation of criminal acts committed against human society is so detailed and fascinating that it might well lead to similar attacks against lives and property, and terrorist actions against the state'.

Despite the ban, the director of *Die Nibelungen* and *Metropolis* evidently seemed a useful man to the new masters of Germany – perhaps on the strength of *Metropolis'* welcome message of reconciliation between creative brain and working hands. The banned *Last Will* could be forgotten: Goebbels did not mention it when he invited Lang to see him at the Ministry of Propaganda, and offered him the role of leader of the new racist cinema, on behalf of the Führer. (Even the objection that Lang was half-Jewish could be disregarded. After all, neither Jannings, the idolised German actor, nor Leni Riefenstahl, the ideal of German womanhood, were quite Aryan.)

All the same, Fritz Lang ignored all the marvellous promises of a magnificent future, and took a train for Paris the same evening. As for *The Last Will of Dr Mabuse*, the film's producer, Seymour Nebenzal brought both the German and French versions safely into France when he, as a Jew, was forced to leave Germany.

The forgers' silent workshop from the first *Mabuse* film, with the unspeaking blind workers, has come to life. In the opening of the film we can hear – along with ex-Detective Hofmeister – the noise and rhythmical beating of the machines, which becomes so intense that Hofmeister is dazed and forced to close his ears.

Everything that follows is brief and rapid, geared to suspense and tension. Two gangsters come to get new sheets for the forging of banknotes, and notice the feet of the hidden Hofmeister. The audience nervously anticipates a shooting, but the brighter of the two is against it. The two men whisper together, but their words are drowned by the noise of machines. For a moment, nothing happens. Hofmeister sneaks up and narrowly escapes a series of accidents. A heavy piece of stonework from the roof parapet crashes to the ground just beside him. He hurries on and promptly a group of ominous-looking men appear at the street corner. When he turns back, a barrel falls from a beer-cart standing by, and explodes.

All these accidents are carefully prepared and 'documented' with Lang's characteristic, precise logic, and pared down to the minimum. Hofmeister has to escape, to prepare the spectator for further attacks; and also in order to telephone Police Inspector Lohmann, though he is

The Last Will of Dr Mabuse: a ghostly superimposition

unable to tell him anything precise, but only put him on the scent of the mysterious organisation.

The atmosphere in Lohmann's office is entirely authentic. The Inspector – already familiar from *M* in all his earthiness, humour, Berlin wit, characteristic obsession with his work – is on his way to a Wagner opera. Hofmeister's irritability on the telephone reveals his instability, as he endeavours to ingratiate himself with Lohmann again, following trouble over a bribery affair. He is fidgety, confused, incoherent and it is clear that the organisation will get to him before he can give Lohmann the facts.

We do not see what happens: like Lohmann we hear only a scream from the other end of the telephone, the thud of a chair falling over, and then a silence which leaves Lohmann and the spectator to speculate what horrible thing has happened. After the silence comes the mad, inarticulate, tuneless sing-song of 'Gloria, Victoria'. Only much later in the film is a clue to what happened vouchsafed: when Lohmann and the doctor visit Hofmeister in the madhouse cell he sees, not them, but a superimposed image of the fair-haired murderer and the driver approaching him.

Again, towards the end of the film, the mad professor opens the door of the cell and introduces himself to the frightened Hofmeister who is crouching on the floor: 'Permit me to introduce myself. My name is Dr Mabuse'. At once the image cuts to the corridor with the open door. We do not see what happens, but only hear Baum screaming and Hofmeister shouting 'Mabuse!'. Warders hurry to the scene, but the spectator does not see what they see inside the cell; and is left to imagine that Hofmeister may have attacked the professor and tried to strangle him. The stunned warders lead out the demented Hofmeister; and only in the next shot do we see inside the cell. In place of Hofmeister, the professor now crouches, totally mad, slowly tearing up the leaves which Mabuse had covered with his writing.

Even after the introduction of sound, Lang chose to use visual effects of superimposition to suggest hypnosis in the new *Mabuse* film. Entering the mad Mabuse's room, the professor puts his hand to his head and turns quickly: the ghostly apparition of Mabuse's protoplasm appears on the wall before him. Later, when he starts to read the writings of the dead Mabuse, a superimposed image of Mabuse, his dissected open skull showing the convolutions of his brain, appears in the chair opposite him, half crouching. The atmosphere is heightened by enormous African masks staring from the dark with phosphorescent glow, and pale skulls in glass cases. The ghostly Mabuse rises from his chair and 'enters' the seated professor, becoming one with him. The doctor's ghost reappears later to lead the wild car chase, and again, to open the door and force the professor to go into Mabuse's own old cell, now occupied by Hofmeister.

Today Lang feels that he would no longer use phantomatic superimpositions for a film essentially realist in style, but would represent the voice of the subconscious that dominates the professor, by voice-off. The fantastic element of the superimposition, he considers, offsets the reality.

Even so the atmosphere is richly suggestive. When Professor Baum, whom nobody recognises, leaves the police commisariat, Lang makes him pass, long and slowly, a wall on which are posted the police notices about the murder of Dr Kamm. This slow and solemn progress indicates visually the weakening of the professor's stamina.

Here the soundless image is very impressive; yet as in *M* Lang uses sound expressively. A word in one shot is used associatively in the next, to clarify a situation; a sound effect may overlap into another scene. In the curtained room at the criminals' headquarters where a time bomb ticks menacingly and a voice from a loudspeaker has just told the imprisoned young couple that they will not leave the room alive, Kent taps the wall to seek possible escapes. The tapping carries over into the next shot, where an elegant gangster is daintily tapping his boiled egg. At another point the loudspeaker in the curtained room metallically calls out orders to the criminal action groups. Elsewhere, in the professor's house, the same tones call out 'I do not wish to be disturbed now' when the door handle is turned. Lohmann will later discover the ingenious mechanism which starts off a gramophone whenever an intruder touches the door handle.

One episodic scene, the murder of Dr Kamm, is especially memorable. The doctor is on his way to inform the police of the coincidences between the writings of Mabuse and the robbery, when he stops his car at a red light. Another car stops near him. Someone hoots; and the hooting is playfully taken up by the impatient drivers to become a tumult in which the sound of the gun, pointed by the driver of the second car, cannot be heard. The lights change to green; the cars drive on – except one, which stays behind. The policeman who approaches it finds Dr Kamm collapsed over the wheel. Lang was to repeat this scene, with necessary modifications, in his last *Mabuse* film.

The end of the film is excitingly dramatic, with the chemical factory in flames and one chimney after another collapsing. Smoke belches and hisses from the engine carrying the chemicals away from the danger zone. Fire engines with bells aclatter race to the scene from opposite directions: water squirts from the hoses to mingle with the fire and smoke. There are police signals, enormous searchlights raking the bushes, the rat-tat of motor-cycles revving up, the hooting of cars; a grand finale of light, fire, movement and sound of every kind.

In the chase which follows, the ghostly expressionist-white milestones by the side of the road are eerily lit up by the headlights of the racing car. Bushes seem to give way in bundles, leaves above the heads of the pursuers race along and finally dissolve, impressionistically, into blobs of movement and light. Again the atmosphere is prepared for the ghostly apparition of Mabuse.

APPENDIX I: *Fritz Arno Wagner: Cinema sensations seen from the camera angle*

In all my many years as a cameraman, I never experienced the reality of the words 'fear' or 'getting the creeps' until the day I was standing on the ten-metre practicable beside Fritz Lang and his crew, preparing to shoot the blowing-up of the chemical factory. Beside me was a small, harmless-looking model of a factory, with a number of coloured buttons. From the buttons mysterious leads went out to the real factory that lay spread out before us in the glare of innumerable spotlights. Then Lang started blowing up the factory, simply by pressing the buttons. When the first of the four gigantic chimneys, seventy metres high, fell sideways amidst thunderous noise and enormous clouds of dust and piles of rubble, I realised the

The Last Will of Dr Mabuse: the flood (*above*); the exploding factory (*below*)

great danger we all were in. I must confess that even today, weeks after these sequences were shot, I feel cold sweat pouring down my back when I recall those nights in front of the exploding factory and the individual shots of the whole sequence – but fear? I never felt any sensation like fear in spite of the obvious danger. Because of Lang's presence, his confidence, the calm with which he gave his directions, which had been rehearsed and calculated in their smallest detail, this feeling could never arise. Not even when the shots were made in the mysterious curtain room that was to be blown up by a time bomb. Our architects Hasler and Vollbrecht had built a construction from an amazing array of technical gadgetry that should have eliminated from the outset any anxiety by the participating expert – and yet we were not all very happy. But everything went as planned. The explosion worked; the water that was supposed to enter the room flowed according to plan, and apart from getting soaked through, I did not experience any negative consequences or unpleasant feelings during this sequence. Yet I tried with the help of my camera to catch the inherent suspense of the scene, its immense danger and difficulty.

Die Filmwoche, Berlin, No 12, 22 March 1933

APPENDIX II: *Lotte H. Eisner: Visiting Lang's Shooting of* The Last Will of Dr Mabuse

The Fritz Lang film *The Last Will of Dr Mabuse* which is being shown in France, has been banned in Germany on the order of the Ministry of the Interior, because the film board (Filmprüfstelle) found it dangerous 'on account of its cruel and depraved content'.

I had the good fortune to be present at the creation of this fantastic piece of work. Fritz Lang did not start his film in the studio; the first scenes were filmed at night on an outdoor location.

To get there I travelled by car through a very dark night. I passed quickly through a little town near Berlin, whose small bourgeois houses alternated with public buildings of dimensions reminiscent of the big city. I passed a number of bridges in succession, and the Havel river's reflections gleamed in the darkness.

I arrived at a vast area of wasteland, where the ruins of abandoned factories reared up like phantoms. During the war they had been used as ammunition plants. One of Fritz Lang's associates remembered the spot where he had often been on guard duty as a soldier.

For three weeks the workmen had been at work, and had completely changed the appearance of the forest. They had cut down trees that were in the way and had planted others elsewhere. An artificial forest had been erected, to blend in with the real trees. Some practicables supporting enormous lamps seemed to grow out of the ground, and the moveable bridge with its projectors and ladders added to the impression of gigantic dimensions.

At an order, hundreds of lights went on. The light spread in waves over the forest, and the lighting chief gave orders over a loudspeaker. His men were so far apart from each other that it would have been impossible to direct them only with a megaphone.

The cables stretched in all directions, winding like reptiles over the plants on the forest ground . . .

(The light) . . . detached itself in many silver patches, the tree trunks shone, they cut through to the bottom and the plants received a particular impact from it. Lang's eyes surveyed the whole scene, and he said enthusiastically: 'I have always wished to be able to shoot an illuminated forest in the middle of the night. Nobody has ever achieved that effect!'

The set-up of this natural decor still did not satisfy him. This forest was for Lang what the forest of Dunsinane was for Macbeth. He wanted it changed, and continued to transform it. Again trees were cut down and transported from one place to another. Lang himself took out some bushes, and planted them in places where he thought that he needed them.

He modified, changed, transformed with his own hands; modelled the shape and tamed the scenery according to his will. He climbed on to the practicables with his cameraman, Fritz Arno Wagner, took aim with the camera, and made it slide on the rails. He set it to fix the horizon he wanted to catch. While the shooting went on, he corrected every small detail.

He smiled. 'It is maddening', he said, 'that there is such a disproportion between the visualising power of the eye and the camera. We should have eyes all round the head.'

Intransigeant, Paris, 19 May 1933

11 Working Methods and Style: The First German Period

In dealing with Fritz Lang's first German period, which lasted from 1919 until just before the Hitler regime in 1933, it is important to emphasise that it is not safe to rely on statements allegedly made by Lang at the time – for instance, the often-quoted article in Dr Beyfuss's *Kulturfilmbuch*. Wrapped up in his film work, he frequently signed articles submitted to him by public relation men or written on his behalf by Thea von Harbou. Some of these are undoubtedly fascinating in their own right, for instance the statement about *Die Nibelungen* in Beyfuss's book:

Man as an idea needs to be presented with super life-size emotions . . . He needs the pedestal of stylisation as much as ever he did in past centuries. Statues are not placed straight on the asphalt. To make them effective, they are placed above the heads of passers-by.

Though this was signed by Lang, it was far from his opinion:

In fact I was thinking the exact opposite. I did not intend to blow up the characters in *Nibelungen* into exaggerations, or place them on pedestals, but to get them down from the Wagnerian pathos, back to earth. And the first step in that direction was to take away their Wagnerian operatic beards.

(Letter of 3 October 1968 to the author)

No article is of certain authenticity before the contribution to *The Penguin Film Review*, No 5, 'Happily Ever After', in which Lang discusses his views in retrospect. Even later interviews, where the interviewers may have inaccurately ascribed opinions to Lang, or where Lang himself may have been deliberately reticent, can be suspect.

Critics writing about Lang have frequently pointed out the recurrence of the *femme fatale* who ruins men in his early scripts and the first films he himself directed. It is more important to recognise, on closer inspection, that there is on a deeper level a thread connecting the subject matter of Lang's German films: something akin to Nietzsche's myth of superman, which could only flourish in a world of abject obedience *(kadavergehorsam)*.

Lang's predilection for the exotic, the novel, the strange, his imaginative flair for narrative, his talent for suspense, can be traced through all these so-called 'adventure films'. It is perhaps reasonably safe to quote from an article signed by him which appeared in *Die Filmbühne*, Volume 1, April 1927:

The film director needs speed. That does not mean hastiness, but telescoping, tightening-up, underlining, accelerating, and bringing to the climax.

It is necessary to keep all the strings of the instrument we are trying to master vibrating in tune, because relaxing or overtightening of the strings would mean dissonance and discordant notes.

Lang's films are characterised by their peculiar mixture of realism and fantasy. His American scripts, which have been entrusted to me and to the Cinémathèque Français, invariably contain newspaper clippings which caught his attention and inspired his stories, or at least details for individual sequences. He began this habit in his German period, particularly in *M* and *The Last Will of Dr Mabuse*. Lang's awareness that it is the *faits divers* and the documentary touches which make his films so impressive is revealed when he tells Peter Bogdanovich that he always advised his cameramen to avoid 'fancy photography' and demanded 'newsreel photography'. 'Every serious picture should be a sort of documentary of its time.' Even during his German period, in which so many critics find evidence of Expressionist influence – for instance the three-dimensional effects achieved in *Metropolis* or *M* by means of lighting – the films demonstrate Lang's mastery in combining documentary structures and adventure fantasy.

Again and again Lang declares that every film must evolve its own style according to the subject matter. Yet in every film we encounter the characteristic Lang elements – not only in *Metropolis* where the documentary element is projected into the future, or in *Destiny* where the fantastic elements dominate the realistic. Buñuel once said that in fact an artist always makes the same film; and Lang's films, like those of every great cinema creator, reveal a profound underlying unity.

Lang and Expressionism

Like Paul Wegener, who always insisted that his film *Der Golem*, of 1920, was not an Expressionist film as many critics maintained (mainly on account of Poelzig's sets), Lang rejected the suggestion of an Expressionist influence on his films. As President of a round table on Expressionism arranged in Venice in 1960, he would say, 'What is Expressionism? Neither Brecht nor I was ever an Expressionist'. (Brecht's *Baal*, it must be said, shows Expressionist characteristics. In the first *Mabuse* Count Told asks the sinister doctor what he thinks of Expressionism: 'Expressionism', he replies, 'is only a game ... but then nowadays everything is only a game.'

Like all other artists of his time, Lang went through an experience of Expressionism, moulding it to suit his own purposes and his own style. 'I do not reject Expressionism', he told a later interviewer; 'but I did not follow it for long. All that is passé. When I started to make films in the United States, I shed the uses of symbolism.'

In a very comprehensive interview with Jean Domarchi and Jacques Rivette in *Cahiers du Cinema* No 99, Lang said: 'One cannot go through an epoch without taking something from it. . . . I have made use of it (Expressionism); I have tried to direct it'. That Lang was fully aware of what Expressionism meant is made clear by a contemporary statement on the occasion of the 1924 Vienna Kinoreformtagung (*Film-kurier*, 20 and 21 May 1924), which was clearly not composed by a public relations man or by Thea von Harbou. Speaking of the 'artistic structure of the film drama', Lang states what he will emphasise again and again: every film has its own rules and laws. There are no strict formulas. Every period has its own art forms. Lang describes the havoc caused by the war in all countries, and explains why Expressionism was its apt artistic expression.

If you try to fit Expressionism into a formula, you will find this formula to be the absolute expression of reality. Look at Expressionist pictures and you will get the impression of exploding shells from the colours and shapes.

He points out further that women's clothes also tended to

Fritz Lang

Expressionism. 'It cannot be put into simple words; it is as if their clothes had been torn from their bodies in shreds.'

Screenplays and collaboration with Thea von Harbou
It is very difficult today to distinguish the respective contributions of Lang and Thea von Harbou to their collaboration. The only real clue is the episodic film *The Spiders*, written by Lang alone. Though its original title list still exists, it is hard to determine to what extent Lang was still caught up in the emotionalism of the post-war period which affected generations of young people in all countries. War had demanded a repression of feelings. Now everybody abandoned themselves freely to their feelings. Even taking into account, however, the excessive emotionalism and sentimentality of the period (which can also be seen in the films of Abel Gance and Marcel L'Herbier of the same time), one is still left with the rather sensitive critical problem of the collaboration. Con-

temporary reviews, unkindly if not inaccurately, tended to attribute such excesses to von Harbou and the realistic structure to Lang. The rather embarrasingly non-logical and overly sentimental emotionalism of, for example, the 'head and heart' motif of *Metropolis* and the love story of *Frau im Mond*, do not exist in Lang's work before or after his collaboration with von Harbou; his later Indian films and *The Thousand Eyes of Dr Mabuse* present another problem entirely in this regard, as we shall see. Still, as has been noted, her contribution to *M* seems almost entirely and constructively in keeping with Lang's basic vision. Thea von Harbou was a product of the first decade of the twentieth century. Her photographs show her as the handsome 'Germanic' type, and suggest an Ibsen character, oscillating between Hedda Gabler, Hilde Wangel and Soveig. Feminine and emancipated at the same time; domestic and maternal and yet sophisticated; sensitive and psychologically orientated. The Ibsen reference is suggested because the Germans of that time were deeply interested in Scandinavian literature. Thea von Harbou was one of two popular women authors of the time whose fluent style, which now seems rather conventional, made them what might be considered the Françoise Sagans of their place and period. Vicky Baum was the Jewish counterpart of Thea von Harbou, whose name suggests a descent from Huguenot emigrés – like Fontane, more German than the Germans. The two writers were at opposite poles from Anna Seghers, Annette Kolb or Ricarda Huch.

Few actors recall anything about the Harbou–Lang collaboration, though Lil Dagover recalls the devotion with which his wife assisted Lang during difficult scenes in the studio.

An article in *Filmkünstler* (Sybillen Verlag, Berlin, 1928), 'Wir über uns selbst', purporting to be by Lang, discusses his collaboration with von Harbou, though it is hard to know how far to rely on its statements. In Thea von Harbou, the article states, Lang had

found an invaluable assistant who out of profound understanding of my intentions creates the manuscripts which become the basis of my work.

While this suggests that von Harbou herself wrote the

screenplays, the term 'basis' must be seen in the light of Dudley Nichols's statement (page 370) that the script was for Lang no more than a blueprint. Moreover we have the evidence of Theo Lingen, an intelligent and excellent character actor who worked in *M*; who recalled his first meeting with Lang in his villa at Berlin-Dahlem: The first thing he noticed was an enormous script on Lang's desk:

I had never seen a scenario before, but I never saw one quite like that again. In minute detail, everything was annotated, accentuated, fixed and defined. And I believe that it was just this minute detailing and preparatory work which was the secret of Fritz Lang's success. The work in the studio followed the script to the letter.

Work in the Studio
Lang wrote to me in retrospect about the way he worked in the studio. In one of his letters he says that he always worked out the outlines of every sequence and even every individual camera angle the evening before. In early days, inevitably, there was still an element of experiment and improvisation, for instance in the lighting and shooting of *Destiny*. New territories were being opened up in those days.

Among these experiments are the grand visions for which Lang was obliged to work out methods of realisation within the camera, since the German studios at that time were not yet expert in trick work. Even now he dislikes revealing the secrets of these tricks, because he does not want to destroy their magic; but occasionally he will disclose some secret, such as the way the magic circles around the head of the robot in *Metropolis* were achieved (a silver ball was whirled around in a velvet-lined funnel, and then superimposed) or the effects already described – the magic letter in *Destiny*, the hanging streets in *Metropolis*.

Theo Lingen recalls:

One did what one was told to do to the letter of the time table, by which I mean that no improvisation was tolerated. Everything, from the position of the camera, the sets, the positions of the actors, the accent of the dialogue, the end of every scene and even the montage was fixed and calculated in advance. This might suggest precision work which could have degenerated into pedantry, but that is the exact opposite of the truth: the mastering of all aspects, the intelligent use of this method and the conviction that technology can only be mastered by technology – these were probably Lang's main strengths as a film director.

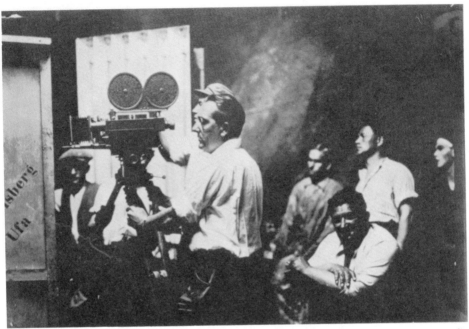

Work in the studio

Lingen is the only actor who worked with him at this time who has so well indicated the essential features of Lang's method. Carl de Vogt, the leading actor of *The Spiders*, says only:

He was dominated by a fanatical love for the cinema and the demands he made on his actors were enormous. He had one great quality: in contrast to other directors he always knew exactly what he wanted. He was indefatigable in his work and was never self-indulgent. This is why I obeyed him involuntarily, even though there were occasional misunderstandings between us. But these were always quickly resolved, because he was a wonderful director, human being and friend.

Lil Dagover (*Der Goldene See, Harakiri, Destiny*) emphasises his dynamism, and above all his obsession with work:

He demanded a lot. One had not to fear fire, water or snakes. These dangerous episodes were always repeated without mercy until his idea of how the scene should be had been realised.

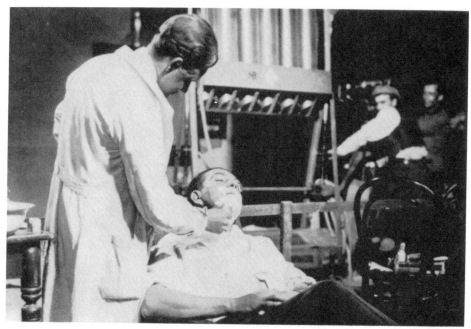

A studio shave

Gustav Fröhlich, the main actor in *Metropolis*, says 'I have never met a work fanatic like him since'. Robert Siodmak, then still an assistant director and assistant editor, recalls:

One was afraid of him because of his particular temperament, by means of which he managed to keep himself and his collaborators in an atmosphere of frenzy and rage.

Siodmak tells how Lang, determined upon perfectionism, refused to show the last reel of *Die Nibelungen* on the opening night, because it was not finished to his complete satisfaction.★

From an account of Ihering we know how much capital and working time was permitted to Lang for his more mature films. Pommer always supported him because he knew the quality of the work he would get. When Pommer left Ufa, Lang also decided to leave. Already before finishing *Metropolis* he had determined to found his own company, in partnership with two acquaintances

★For reminiscences of actors, see Eibel, *Fritz Lang: choix de textes.*

called Fellner and Szomlo, and be independent. (In any case Ufa at this time was in financial difficulties and was to be taken over by a German bank.) The first film made by the Fritz Lang G.m.b.H., though still distributed by Ufa, was *The Spy*.

Les Princes des Années Folles describes how Lang, surrounded by his entourage, drove in style to his own studio. Even allowing for some journalistic exaggeration, the substance of the report is confirmed by Robert Herlth's private recollections:

When Lang turned up on location early in the morning with *three* cars, the rest of his following, technicians, make-up artists and costume designers were already there; and even before he had left his car, we all succumbed to the spell of his authority.

Dictator though he was, he still had to attend personally to everything. He put the finishing touches to the actors' make-up, worked out difficult trick scenes, and even shot the arrows in *Die Nibelungen*.

During the cutting, which in those days was done by the director himself he sometimes did not leave the studio area for weeks. He slept next door to the cutting room because sometimes he got up in the middle of the night to continue the cutting.

He was as extravagant as a renaissance figure. Like Cellini he knew no mercy for himself or for his associates. Hard though he drove his collaborators, he always stuck to them with boyish loyalty and the secret of his success is that his example always won the day.

Outlook

In an article called 'Happily Ever After', written in 1947, Lang discussed his change of views in the United States, due to time and geographical climate. The 'prearranged fate' and the 'man trapped by fate' of his early films, he now considers as a negative attitude, 'showing the triumph of evil and a waste of human life for nothing'. From now on character will determine the fate of man.

He expresses a similar view in a letter to the author – in which we find the explanation of his film *Beyond a Reasonable Doubt*:

I no longer believe in mystical fate. Every human being makes his own fate by the way in which he uses his experience (or does not use his experience), by the choice or rejection of events and situations he partakes in, by what he manages to achieve or not to achieve, for whatever reasons. No mystical fate, no God or whatever is responsible for his fate except himself. And this is why one cannot get away from what one has created for oneself.

Thus character determines human fate: character is the demon of man. All Lang's American films will demonstrate this belief, with their recurrent questions: Where does guilt begin? What is innocence? What is good and what is evil?

12 French Interlude: *Liliom* (1933)

The scenes in heaven, designed in a sort of thirties futuristic, have a great deal of charm, and the echoes on the sound track of earlier happenings on earth are handled with great skill . . . Lang's film never becomes soggily sentimental.
Richard Whitehall, *Los Angeles Free Press*, 3 October 1969

Lang makes this point about the eternity of injustice without indulging Liliom, who, after all was a heel. Liliom with its abundant comic touches, is unique for Lang whose films are characteristically dark-toned. Yet it is the very embodiment of Lang's major theme, the struggle of the individual against an unjust, omnipotent fate. For once, however, that individual succeeds in beating his nemesis to a draw.
Kevin Thomas, *Los Angeles Times*, 3 October 1969

The striking thing about this Liliom is that at this early stage Lang showed no evidence whatever of making a silent film in which occasionally a few people talked, or of a talking picture in which people did nothing but talk. He came

For the Austrian Fritz Lang, the stage play by the Austro-Hungarian Ferenc Molnar is not merely the story of Liliom the incorrigible, but somehow too the bitter-sweet love story of the little Viennese girls about whom Schnitzler wrote, transplanted with striking success to the milieu of a Paris suburb. Lang has an infallible instinct for catching the atmosphere of the country in which he happens to be working: the life of the colourful little suburban fairground is presented with popular humour and much comic detail, at once playful and homely. The joys and suffering of ordinary people are depicted with a musical lightness which Clair could not have bettered, and which mingles earthy reality with the seductive, ephemeral atmosphere of the fairground.

We are never shown more than a small section of the fairground, and everything is achieved without any emphatically virtuoso camerawork. Instead the loving efforts of the studio miniaturist achieves an impression of endless variety. Working for the European branch of Fox, run by his old friend and fellow-emigré Erich Pommer, Lang had to economise, and thus find ever new variations.

This little tragi-comic fantasy in gay picture-book style, rises to a melancholy poetry in the deathbed scene of Liliom, and with the austere loveliness of Julie (Madeleine Ozeray), recalling at once the folk-song qualities of *Destiny* and the ne'er-do-wells of Villon ballads. Lang's Liliom is a *gars du milieu* from somewhere like Belleville or Foire du Trône, purely Parisian, and he provided Charles Boyer with his best role.

In the dusky evening the merry-go-round with its glittering garlands of light turns round and round. The fairground organ attracts the passers-by, dominating

Liliom (1933): the merry-go-round and . . .

every other sound. Liliom, the merry-go-round tout, swings along with it, singing his song in which everyone joins. With such a rival the neighbouring strong man gets no customer for his hammer; and even the drunken sailor is lured to the merry-go-round. Moving shadows fall on the little wooden pay-box and on the buxom figure and round face of the proprietor, Madame Muscat, who casts a proud glance at Liliom – her property too.

She is understandably not pleased when Liliom flirts with a girl, and even gives her a flower. Liliom's character is already revealed. At first he gives way to Madame and agrees to throw Julie and her friend out. But then he is touched by the appalling helplessness of the girl and offended by Madame's undisguised triumph. Resistance is aroused: Liliom does not allow himself to be manipulated, to be considered someone else's property. He prefers to go off with the two girls.

With ruthless realism he appraises his new companions,

to the new form fully prepared to use it for what it was – new. James Powers: *Hollywood Reporter*, 6 October 1969

... the charming love scene

and unhesitatingly indicates to Julie's coquettish and experienced friend that she is not required any more. A charming love scene on a bench dimly lit by a street lamp beside a meagre tree, is not disrupted even by the policeman who warns the little servant girl against the 'Dangéreux séducteur des bonnes'. Liliom does not mince his words or try love talk on the 'drôle de petite fille'. But Julie is from the same mould as the loving girl in *Destiny*. 'When I love somebody I am afraid of nothing', although she proves more real and realistic than the earlier romantic anonymous heroine of *Destiny*. She is not going to die with her lover, for she must bring up his child. Instead, she will lie to her daughter about her splendid father, in pious memory.

Time flies; and other couples' love mementoes have covered the entwined hearts Liliom cut on the bench. Julie has given herself without reservation to her Liliom. She works hard for his aunt in the little photographer's booth. One day she is taking a picture of a well-intentioned shopkeeper, posed with his hat and his dignity against the plaster pillar and the ornamental table. He tells her that he would like to marry her 'in spite of everything'. Meanwhile Liliom is lounging about, his heart secretly longing for the fairground, whose organ sends out siren wisps of sound. He will not hear of the well-paid porter's job the aunt finds for him. He is an *artiste*.

Julie gets to know his tempers. A trivial incident about a coffee pot leads to him boxing her ears. Summoned to police headquarters, Liliom is made to wait for hours in the desolate corridor with 'Défense de . . .' notices plastered everywhere; no smoking, no spitting, no loud talking and so on. Liliom encounters his mate Alfred, who smells out a criminal offence and offers his services as a witness. Liliom accepts. While waiting they start to play a hand of cards on the hard bench . . . But cards are forbidden also.

While Liliom waits, patiently as befits the poor, an elegant gentleman is politely led to the inspector out of turn. The selectivity of justice will determine Liliom's further behaviour. It is a factor already present in *M*, and which will play a still larger role in Lang's American films.

Finally Liliom and Alfred see the inspector. In a characteristic comic touch, Lang manages both to create a realistic human being from a stereotype and to comment lightly on social reality. The inspector attempts to stamp a paper for Liliom's file, but is frustrated by a dried-up ink cushion; he only smiles again when a new cushion allows the stamp to work. Anyone dealing with bureaucrats – especially in France – will immediately get the point.

Allowed to leave, together with his witness, Liliom lies on the lorry with his friend; and Alfred tells him of a profitable prospect: a robbery. Liliom is reluctant to get involved, and prefers to go to the bistro and play cards until the small hours, while little Julie waits up for him. Madame Muscat's raised hopes of winning back Liliom – based on his indifference to the fact that Julie is upset – dwindle when Julie reveals she is expecting a child. Having broken the news, Julie runs away without waiting to see Liliom's reaction – which is an Indian war dance of delight, and the firm dismissal of the overconfident Madame Muscat.

With this prospect of a child Liliom needs money, and he therefore plans with Alfred to rob the payroll-postman.

The scheme is as primitive as Liliom and Alfred themselves; and Liliom rehearses without enthusiasm the charade of stopping the postman to ask the time, to give Alfred the chance to attack him. For the discussion between Liliom and Alfred Lang uses a device which recalls the scene of the gangsters' council in *M*, in which only the shadows on the wall are seen, as voices are heard off. Here we see only the two men's reflections in the water as we hear their discussion.

The gay and fantastic symbol which occurs at this point comes directly from Molnar, but must have pleased Lang's Viennese taste: a knife-grinder with his cart (played by the great writer Antonin Artaud) turns up and asks if anyone needs a knife sharpened. His bell rings merrily; and Liliom, dazed with fear clutches even tighter the knife which he has stolen from the aunt's kitchen. The postman arrives, armed with a pistol, and Alfred takes to his heels. Liliom is about to be arrested, but rather than fall into the hands of the law, plunges his knife into his own breast. At the same instant, in the photographer's booth, Julie anxiously clutches her hands to her heart as if she too felt the thrust.

The death of Liliom provides the film's most intense moments, as Julie's rigidity softens to love and understanding. Madeleine Ozeray – Jouvet's Ondine – manages a transition to the lyricism of the folk song, as we hear the sound of the distant fairground organ, which somehow envelops the dying man. Julie strokes his hand, sitting beside him in self-effacing constancy, revealing the courage of a Solvieg.

It is a tragi-comedy of misunderstandings: Liliom has not had the chance to speak of his love, and Julie only emerges from her rigid daze after Liliom has closed his eyes. Only then is it possible for her to tell him of her love, without knowing of his love for her. But why should a loving woman who only cares for one man in the whole world need an echo at all?

In the fairground Madame Muscat bursts into tears; and requests a few moments silence: one of 'our own people' has died, she says. The merry-go-round turns slowly, the shadows moving; then stops. Everything stops – movement and sound. Like a dark and heavy cloak, a sinister silence settles, almost audibly, upon the fairground . . . It is

Liliom: going up to Heaven

a scene, in terms of visual effects, of movement and sound, such as few directors could bring off today.

Like the couple in *Destiny*, signalled by Weary Death, Liliom sits up out of his dead body as dark-clad figures approach – angels in mufti, with black felt hats. (These figures were to give Cocteau the idea of the dark, motorised messengers in *Orphée*.) Viewed from below, the broad brims of these felt hats look surprisingly like haloes.

Raised up to make a journey through the sky, Liliom looks around him with curiosity and pleasure. In bold camera angles we look down upon the roofs of Paris, the Seine, Notre Dame, the Eiffel Tower – today familiar vistas, but then novel and remarkable photographic tricks. Falling stars and rotating planets mingle with the mist and luminous light in a harmonious fugue, rising up rhythmically and flowing along in streams of darkness and light – tribute to Lang's gift for the treatment of light and shade.

Liliom's heaven could not look different from this, with

155

the heavenly armies innocently showing their baby bottoms and Fra Angelico's heavenly prospects charmingly paraphrased as a great, airy auditorium made out of clouds. Some critics have found the heavenly police station – an ironical copy of the petty bourgeois terrestrial system – too Prussian; but bureaucracy is universal, and the 'Défendu . . .' signs can be found in every police station in the world. Liliom is a simple man; in his childlike belief 'le bon Dieu' is a picture-book notion. In heaven, too, God, the Chief Inspector, with whom Liliom feels he could get on good terms, is not available for a poor man. He must make do with a subordinate; and even for him he has to wait. Here, too, everything is forbidden. Here, too, the business with the recalcitrant rubber stamp is repeated. All is much the same as in Liliom's former, earthly world, apart from the occasional sparkle of stars and the gay little wings of the topless typist and the inspector. Naturally, the under-devil who drags all kinds of documents into heaven looks exactly like Liliom's friend Alfred.

Yet even in this heaven that corresponds to a comic everyday reality there is a serious tone: Lang's perennial motive: where is innocence and where guilt? Is there a social justice, and who is permitted to cast the first stone? What are Liliom's 'mitigating circumstances'; and how much to blame is the environment in which he grew up? There are other things then in this heaven which is so like earth. Liliom is told about contrition, about purification in purgatory. He learns that the knife-grinder was his guardian angel who had come to warn him.

Lang now recalls an episode from Liliom's earthly life; the scene of the quarrel over the coffee pot is shown on a celestial television screen. Wilfully, Liliom refuses to admit his fault, even when the sequence is shown to him again, this time with his own subconscious thoughts, in which he accuses himself as a selfish rascal, superimposed. To the disappointment of the under-devil, he is not condemned to hell, but to sixteen years in purgatory.

Liliom would like to know one thing: will his child be a girl or a boy? There is no answer. Only after the heavy gates of hot and smoky purgatory have closed behind him, does the heavenly policeman with his long white beard, half Santa Claus, half 'Last Man', open the gate a crack to call after him, 'A girl'.

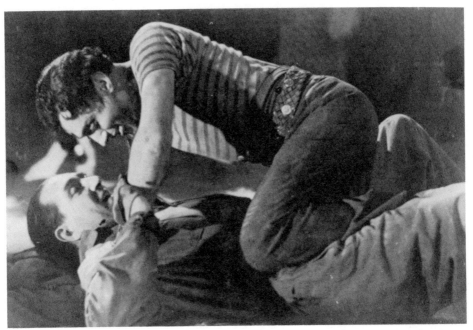

Fritz Lang with Charles Boyer

Grey-haired and parched by purgatory, Liliom is discharged after sixteen years to go down to earth and do a good deed, to give his little girl 'the most beautiful present'. He is led down by the dark-clad figures in felt hats. On the way, the incorrigible Liliom filches a sparkling star to give to his child.

Yet Liliom the incorrigible, despite all his good resolutions, allows himself to be carried away and box the little girl's ears because she does not believe him when he tells her that her father was a selfish rascal. The twinkling star falls into a sewer and is extinguished. The dark-clad figures take the still obstinate man away from earth. The celestial knife-grinder, now turned street-sweeper, picks up the dead star with his pointed stick to carry it back to heaven.

The under-devil/Alfred is already triumphant in anti-cipation as a mighty set of scales is produced in heaven. The side with Liliom's misdeeds sags heavily. But down on earth, Liliom's daughter asks her mother, 'Are there beatings which do not hurt, mother!'; and little grey-haired Julie nods amid her tears. It is those tears which weigh down the other side of the scale to save Liliom from damnation.

Seeing *Liliom* again today, it is a mystery that this film, with its youthful freshness was not more successful when it was first released in France, despite its favourable reviews. Perhaps the French were too Cartesian and rationalist in those days; or perhaps they would have preferred a tragic ending; or perhaps their objection was the same as that of the producer Sol Wurtzel, when Frank Borzage wanted to film Molnar's play (as *Carousel*) in 1929: 'I don't like a picture where the hero dies in the middle'.

Perhaps today the French reaction would be more favourable. Certainly in the United States (where the film was never shown in the period it was made) it has been a popular success in its few recent public screenings. For today's generation, with its healthy mistrust of Establishments, the episodes in the earthly and heavenly police stations have assumed a new relevance.

Part II: The American Period

... When Fritz Lang does a gangster movie or a melodrama, he gets things into it – a mood, a spell or feeling, that an ordinary director won't. This is what *mise en scène* is – the ability to invest this kind of thing on screen with a kind of life and force.

Andrew Sarris: *Symposium on Cinematic Style, Film Culture* No 42, Fall 1966

Throughout Lang's career in Hollywood, regardless of the adverse pressures upon him by studios or the seemingly impersonal nature of some of his assignments, Lang has made films which are unmistakably individual ... Lang's split career between Germany and America (with the one French film in 1934) and his ability to create a coherent thematic continuity over a half century of film-making serves to demonstrate the affinity of his outlook to a variety of social situations. He is more easily characterised as a product of the twentieth century world of mass murder, technological upheaval, and the world war, than as simply a transplanted German director ... In the attempt to recognise the consistencies in his complete ouevre, however, we shouldn't lose sight of the particular, the singularly interesting qualities of each film.

Stephen Mamber: *The American Films of Fritz Lang, Daily Bruin* 15 October 1969

13   Fury (1936)

In France, Lang – still suffering from shock and resentment at having to give up his own place of work – shot *Liliom* before he was really at home in the new environment. Before he filmed *Fury* for MGM in the United States, he had had plenty of time for looking around. Even though he had been invited by David O. Selznick, he shared the experience of many other foreign film directors and stars whose film careers were retarded in the United States.

In collaboration with Oliver H. B. Garret he had written a screenplay based on the Moor Castle ocean disaster. Selznick, in Christmas mood, said he liked it a lot; but three days later, under the influence of others, he found it very bad; intrigue and slander spread quickly in the film world. He had already rejected a previous Lang script, *The Journey to Hell* or *Passport to Hell*. For himself, Lang had written a Jekyll and Hyde plot: *The Man Behind You*. In this modern version, it would have been a very suitable theme for the creator of *M*; but he never presented the script to MGM.

MGM had given Lang only a one-year contract, and had no intention of renewing it. Right at the start he had committed the grave error of slighting Louis B. Mayer; when the producer called, Lang had told his secretary to say he was not home. After that the company considered Lang unapproachable and arrogant, though the truth was he had acted out of shyness in consciousness of his inadequate English.

After about a year without work, Eddie Mannix, a one-time 'bouncer' and former vice-president of MGM, telephoned Lang, whom he liked, to tell him that the studio intended to drop him. Lang fought back. Among other apparently unsuitable scripts he had found a synopsis

The trilogy of Fury, You Only Live Once *and* You and Me *stands in a rather ambiguous relation to the American social cinema of the 30s. In one point . . . they remain its most daringly conceived contribution, in another they scarcely belong to it at all. The difference lies deeper than in the extreme harshness of temperament in the first two films: it is in what the films are about.* Fury *. . . an almost abstract study of mob hysteria; this hysteria has a number of results, of which the attempted lynching is one and the ferocious destructive bitterness it arouses in the victim . . . is another . . .* Fury, *the most realistic of a progressively formalist trilogy, is conceived with an intellectual rigour quite uncharacteristic of the American 'problem' picture. . . .*
Gavin Lambert: 'Fritz Lang's America', *Sight and Sound,* Summer 1955

by Norman Krasna, *Mob Rule*, which interested him. It seemed to be his last chance.

During this period when he had nothing to do but get to know life in the United States, he had continued in his habit of noting everything that seemed different and important to him. He read everything he could lay hands on – particularly newspapers, to learn English and also to understand the mentality of the people. He still insists that comic strips are the best introduction to America, and give the outsider special insights into American life, character and humour, so different from European styles. He at once realised that there must be something especially important about the comic strips, since they are read by so many people from such a wide cross-section of the population, year in and year out. He learned above all American slang, local idiom and stock replies – anything, in short, that seemed typical.

Violent as was his revulsion against the Nazis, he tried to stop speaking German. Though he still retains a trace of a Viennese accent in his speech, he is master of all the nuances and subtleties of colloquial American.

From the moment he arrived, he travelled all over America, talking to everyone; taxi drivers, van drivers, garage hands, shop assistants, bar-tenders and their customers. He went to Arizona, and in order to find out about the Indians, lived among the Navajos for eight weeks. Such experiences help account for the veracity of Lang's Westerns.

From the moment he became interested in *Mob Rule*, which deals with the attempted lynching of an innocent man, he started to add clippings about comparable incidents to his already growing American collection. Even now he regrets that he noticed one of these clippings too late: a report of how San Francisco drivers of long-distance buses would stand by their vehicles attracting customers by shouting: 'Get in, get in! There'll be a lynching in San José at 10 o'clock'.

It is impossible today to disentangle Lang's contribution from that of Bartlett Cormack, to the script that bears both their names, though we know that at that time Lang's English was far from perfect. For his own part he is too modest to lay claim to individual passages, though such an idea as the use of the newsreel film in court to lead to the conviction is very characteristic of his approach. At the time this incident was criticised as improbable; since then film has often been used as courtroom evidence.

Lang recalls that directly after the preview of a two-and-three-quarter hour version of the film (during which he was horrified to hear people whistling at the most interesting bits, until someone explained to him that contrary to European practice whistling in the States signifies approval) he was summoned to the presence of a very angry Eddie Mannix. Mannix accused Lang of making an arbitrary addition to the approved script during the shooting. Lang replied that his English was not good enough for him to improvise any dialogue during the shooting. While the script was being fetched to settle the point, Lang was obliged to wait for one and a quarter hours in the ante-room; no-one spoke to him; he was not offered a drink when they were brought for other people. 'They knew I was in the doghouse.'

Finally he was called into the office. Mannix, with the script before him admitted: 'Yes, it is written down here – but it sounds different on the screen.' Whatever the faults of his English, Lang's ability to bring out hidden aspects of the written word in his *mise en scène* was unimpaired.

The anecdote is significant. A director under contract for a period rather than for one film must learn to submit, to be a mere employee. Lang had been accustomed to the prestige accorded to film directors in Europe. After this experience he was always to contract for single films, until the time when he was blacklisted during the McCarthy witch-hunts, when he signed a yearly contract with Harry Cohn, of Columbia, the only producer with the courage to engage him.

At MGM there were constant harassments in the studio. In Berlin Lang had been accustomed to continue shooting until he was satisfied with the day's work. He would start early in the morning and go on filming obsessively until late at night. The custom was for the technicians to work in shifts, with the lighting men who were not immediately needed, for instance, going for breakfast and then returning to replace the others. Nobody at MGM thought to inform Lang that at certain points of the day the whole crew stopped to eat, and that union regulations stipulated a meal break at least once every five

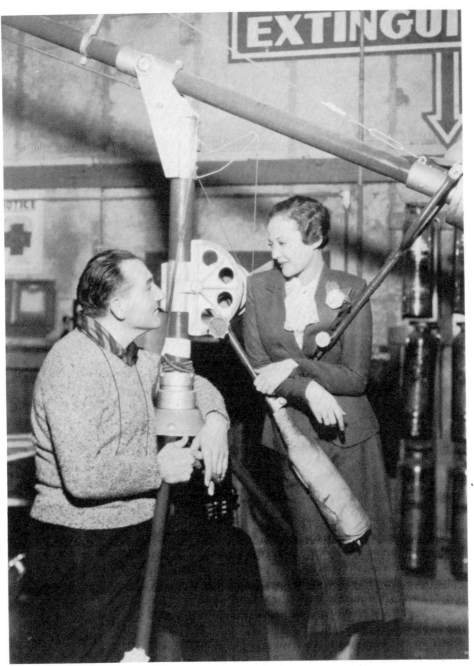

Lang with Sylvia Sidney between scenes of *Fury* (1936)

hours. There was trouble then when Lang became involved in a shot or sequence and went on working obsessively without regard to breaks.

There were other troubles. A disagreement between the producer Sam Katz and Lang's co-writer Cormack over rewriting led to tension in the studio. Nor did it add to Lang's popularity that he was involved in the founding of the Screen Directors' Guild – a sharp thorn in the flesh of the MGM executives, since for the first time it united Hollywood creative workers in a kind of union.

In working on the script Lang learned something of fundamental importance. In the first draft, the hero suspected of kidnapping was made a lawyer, because Lang felt that a lawyer would convincingly be able to defend himself and talk articulately in court. Joseph L. Mankiewicz, who read the first few pages in the producer's office, said that this was impossible. The hero must be an ordinary man of the people, a kind of Everyman or, in the local idiom, 'Joe Doe'. Later Lang recognised that every comic strip has its Joe Doe or Jane Doe. The average American is most interested in things that happen to the average American, people with the same background as himself. The spectator wants to identify with the hero. This is in contrast with German taste. In the land of authoritarianism and 'abject obedience', the country of imperialism and later dictatorship, the hero could be a superman like Mabuse. Such a notion was unthinkable in the United States, where Al Capone was merely a public enemy. Thus *Fury* (the new title for *Mob Rule*) acquired its Joe Wilson, an uncomplicated hero, a Joe Doe.

Nor would it have been acceptable that the man who is almost lynched should be black, regardless of the fact that black lynchings occurred again and again in real life. At MGM Mayer had decreed that 'Coloured people can only be used as shoe-shine boys or porters'.

Other things in the script were excised. A scene in which Joe's fiancée Catherine is reading some of his old letters by an open window, perhaps because outside a young negro boy washing a car is listening to a girl singing a Stephen Foster song as she hangs out the washing:

. . . Oh carry me 'long
Dere's no more trouble for me . . .

Fury: Spencer Tracy as Joe Wilson

I's gwine to roam
In a happy hour
Where all the darkies are free.

Similarly the too-liberal views expressed by the teacher in the barber's chair had to go. In the script, the barber tells him:

... and let me tell you, professor, if you young geniuses at the high school keep trying t'fill our children's heads with these radical ideas, we parents'll have to get a law.

The teacher replies, laughing:

It's not possible to get a law that denies the right to say what one believes. In peace-time, anyway ...
Jorgensen: Who says so?
Teacher: The Constitution of the United States.
Second Barber: You should read it sometime. You would be surprised. ...
I had to read it to become an American.
You never had to b'cause you were born here.

Another excised passage had someone say to the deputy sheriff:

You public servants quit playin' cards all day and maybe you'd bring someone to justice once awhile.

A scene which narrowly escaped being cut is the one which shows an old black man sitting in a dilapidated Ford with a young black couple, listening to the radio. He nods approvingly as the district attorney condemns lynching.

Fury starts off simply: a story of everyday. Joe Doe, alias Joe Wilson, an anonymous young man with his fiancée admires a bedroom suite, 'For the Young Couple' in a shop window. A pair of not very tasteful beds represent for them the embodiment of bourgeois happiness. Spencer Tracy invests Joe with the affected heartiness which paradoxically seems rather effete – chewing peanuts, rather cocky, assured in his stable solidity. All that is lacking is the ultimate embodiment of bourgeois happiness, a bank account. The girl is sensitive, and sufficiently better educated to correct him when he uses 'mementum' for 'memento'.

This might easily remain just an ordinary couple, if fate had not decided otherwise. Joe and his fiancée part at the station, as she goes back West to earn and save a little more money. He dreams of a better job, so that he can marry her. The parting is under a depressing, endless rain. To make matters worse, he tears his rain coat. The girl insists on mending it, even though she has only blue thread in her sewing kit. The raincoat with its blue darn will later play a dramatic part in the story; while Joe's evident embarrassment is already an indication of his character. There is another portent in this parting in the rain, with the atmosphere of melancholy and foreboding accentuated by the weighty close-ups of the engine and the train. Joe misses the last goodbye at the train window when he tries to catch Catherine's hand.

In the original script, this sequence was preceded by a scene in a cinema which vividly revealed Joe's character. Someone in the audience abuses the Americans as 'sheep' and Joe retaliates aggressively: 'I suppose it wasn't the people who made this country what it is today?', at which an elderly black man leans forward and says to Joe:

'Brother, you ought to get around more'. On the way out Joe calls to his opponent, 'If you don't like it in this country why don't you go back where you came from?'; to which comes the answer: 'Not me, Buddy. I came from Scranton, P.A.!'

Again, the original script showed Joe losing his job because he leaves his work to warn his brother, who has become involved with delinquents, of an impending police raid. In the finished film there is no crisis, no unemployment in Joe's world. The decent, hardworking man gets ahead, and within a year Joe's dream of running a filling station has come true. He is even able to take his two brothers in with him, including the one who almost strayed from the straight and narrow. Secure in his possession of a bank account, Joe – a secure, tax-paying citizen – travels West to fetch his girl.

He is not even 'momentarily off guard' as so many of Lang's later heroes fatally are. Camping at night with a clear conscience, he uses a newspaper to kindle the fire. The paper, with the story of the kidnap, is seen by the spectator in close-up.

In fact we know little about Joe's reactions until the moment when, unprepared, he is caught like a fly in the net of so-called justice. Circumstantial evidence mounts up: an ownerless bitch whom he took home after the parting at the station, just for company, turns out to be incriminating; peanuts, small crumbs of which were found in the kidnap note; a bank-note with a number which corresponds to the ransom money and which he must have been given in change on his journey. The upright sheriff stubbornly keeps him locked up in order to verify the evidence.

So far all this is introduction, economically and vividly sketched, to make the audience understand the character and the situation of the man the film is dealing with. Now the acceleration of the mass hysteria builds up. A harmless bit of gossip after the barber's telephone call to his wife starts it off. It continues in the neighbour's kitchen, in the grocer's shop where the neighbour tells another woman of the kidnapper's arrest. The journalist is grateful for material for a big story; in the bar a natural malevolent works on the honest citizens who are delighted with the publicity attracted to their little town, and urges them to

Fury: the gossipping neighbours

go with him to the sheriff and call him to account. Then
the sheriff's office, with the sheriff resisting the over-
excited people who threaten to take the law into their own
hands. Then back to the bar and the honest citizens and a
meddling stranger (characteristically, a strike breaker)
who makes subversive remarks. After that, the street
where the upright bourgeoisie and the workers gather and
start to march. A Jewish mother who wants to prevent her
child from witnessing a lynching, and the boy who begs
her; 'But mother, they are going to ride somebody on the
rail!'

In the Governor's office, politics enter the affair. The
senator advises not to send in troops, because that could
lose votes at the coming election. Finally, in the evening,
the growing and increasingly hysterical crowd and the
hecklers recall parts of the gangsters' court in *M*. The
forward surge of the crowd becomes an uncontrollable

Fury: Lang directing the crowd

mob. Stones are thrown at the window; a battering ram is pushed against the prison gate. The vibrating door is seen from inside, and is finally broken down. The mob surges in, breaking up chairs and piling up inflammable material. The sheriff and his deputy have thrown tear-gas bombs, and smoke adds to the confusion. As Joe waits anxiously behind barred windows, his dog comes running up to him. All is marvellously orchestrated, to bring the suspense to its climax of intensity. Between are the flashes of news cameras, unnoticed by the mob, and close-ups of individuals in the crowd: a man who has climbed a lamp-post, another who amuses bystanders by addressing the sheriff as 'Popeye the sailor-man', a woman who lifts up her child to give it a better view, a man who clutches a hot dog in his hand as he stares into the flames of the fire started by a hysterical termagant. Catherine runs up terrified, sees Joe's figure surrounded by flames, and faints.

Fury: the first flame-thrower

The orchestration builds up to its crescendo with the intensity of a fugue, until the belated arrival of the militia. In the meantime the jail has burned to the ground. The crowd disperses.

In contrast to the *furioso* of this first part, the structure of the second half of the film follows a different rhythm. So far, in revealing how Joe has to learn that his world of respectable bourgeois decency does not exist, Lang's main concern has been mob behaviour; and he carefully notes every detail.

The second part of the film is dominated by cold hatred and bitterness. Without emotion, Joe, who has managed to escape, tells his brothers as they make to embrace him happily, 'Pull down the shades'. He is a man returned from the beyond. His eyes are feverish; he has pain in his side where he was burned by the fire; he is unshaven. At first we see only his silhouette – he will not allow his brother to light a lamp even when the shades are drawn – and the heavy darkness and menacing shadows seem still to belong to the period of Lang's German films.

This scene is the key to the film. The darkness which Joe demands both because the light hurts his smoke-inflamed eyes and because he does not want to be seen by the world outside, is appropriate to his frozen appearance, his abrupt gestures, his shrill, ugly, mirthless laugh. The flames in which we last saw him have destroyed all his human love and confidence. What is the point of being decent and living right. His child-like belief in the American people has been burnt out of him.

He is, by chance, still alive. Yet he has been murdered; and for this the twenty-two people – they at least – must be put on trial. Lynching is first degree murder. Like Kriemhild's his only thought is of revenge. He is just. Again Lang makes believable the reversal of a character; and this single sequence reveals to us 'what makes him tick'.

Even though the dialogue, with its American idiom, is no doubt Cormack's work, we can in retrospect identify elements which *Fury* has in common with Lang's other films. Screen court-room scenes in the films of other directors often appear heavy; but the man who devised the thrilling sequence of the gangsters' court in *M*, in collaboration with Thea von Harbou, knows how to manage his effects, to place his pauses, to show the reactions of Joe, who turns off the radio to which he is listening when Catherine is giving evidence, then turns it on again later, thus creating suspense by ellipsis.

Regardless of who actually scripted the dialogue, the dialectical and sophisticated way in which every detail of the game of question and answer is worked out is unmistakeably Lang, as is the notion of confronting the smug defendants – now converted once more to ordinary hypocritical citizens, with the newsreel of the lynching, in which they behave like wild animals. Here again Lang achieves his effect through variation. We see one defendant, Mr Dawson, who has produced a witness to swear he was elsewhere, at the head of the crowd storming the prison building, and once inside pouring petrol on matchwood beneath a window. A stop action image freezes the hatred on his face. Mrs Humphrey, who has claimed to have been twenty miles away on her fiancé's

Fury: behind prison bars

farm, is seen in the film throwing the burning rag which starts the fire. First seen in longshot, an enlargement picks out her infuriated face, while a close-up contrasts her fear in the court-room. Finally Garret, one of the main agitators, who had 'sat at home peacefully' is seen trying to axe the firemen's hose. Lang and Cormack confine themselves to these three cases: they are sufficient.

In laborious preparation for this court-room sequence, Lang sat in on innumerable court sessions to learn the procedures which are quite different in the States from European practice. He watched and learned, and questioned experts. Happily he did not always follow their advice, for they told him that no judge had ever allowed films to be shown as evidence in a court-room. Though the law still leaves it to the judge's discretion whether film may be brought in evidence, Lang's idea seems to have set an example.

In the trial scene, every link of the chain is established with impeccable logic. Here we have the first of many Lang court-room scenes, foreshadowing in particular the dramatic dialectics of the trial in *Beyond a Reasonable Doubt*.

Other recognisable Lang touches are the radio announcement that the trial is broadcast by courtesy of the 'Magical Desert Homalar Mafat', and the sudden flight of the customer when the barber remarks that an impulse is an impulse and that for twenty years whenever his razor was poised over an Adam's apple he had felt the desire to cut. This is again Lang's sense of 'Enter the Bear'; but the barber incident has a practical dramatic purpose: it provides the opportunity for the barber to telephone his wife not only to tell her the story of the fleeing customer, but at the same time passing on the news that the kidnapper has apparently been arrested. This triggers off a sequence which recalls the backyard gossip in Murnau's *Last Laugh*. Lang yielded to the temptation of cutting from the gossiping women to a flock of cackling hens and ducks – an effect very characteristic of the 1920s (cf. *Strike*; Eisenstein's cross-cutting of murdered workers and slaughtered oxen was admired by critics as 'powerful emotional intensification'). Lang says that he would no longer use that kind of symbolism; and recalls that Sam Katz said to him at the time: 'Americans don't like symbols. They are not so dumb that they don't understand without them'.

Another familiar Lang technique is the use of close-ups of news articles and small ads. Replacing explanatory dialogue, they become focal points which also drive on the action. After the kidnap headline glimpsed at the camp fire, there are two later close-ups in the sheriff's office, one of the peanut crumbs in the blackmailer's letter, the other of a small notice offering a reward of 10,000 dollars and giving the description of one of the gang members, which the sheriff hands to the astonished Joe.

Again in the governor's office after the lynching, the newspaper article with the news that the real kidnappers have been arrested is immediately followed by a close-up of the article which reports that an innocent man has been lynched and burned alive. In the same way Joe shows his brothers the page torn from a legal text-book which we see with them in close-up and which states that lynching is first degree murder. Other comparable examples are the anonymous letter produced in the court-room with the word *mementum* mistakenly used for *memento*; the page of the calendar hanging in the solitary bar, with the ominous number 22.

Lang recalls how during the time he was shooting *Liliom* in Paris he witnessed at first hand the way a mob develops. From a stationary taxi, Lang saw a man rattling a stick along an iron railing. People were laughing at him and stopping to look on; and the more they laughed the more vigorously the man rattled his stick. Then the railings came to their end, and he hit a shop window, breaking it. What had started in a spirit of nonsense now became a riot, and the police moved in. Suddenly the indignant crowd had become a mob; people were no longer individuals. A mob, Lang realised, is utterly without responsibility. But the vivid and graphic way in which Lang shows how a mob is born in *Fury* probes greater depth. I can discover no abstract formula here, as Gavin Lambert does in his *Sight and Sound* article. Lang had been witness to the way the Hitler movement grew gradually from nonsense which no-one took seriously into the terror which did not stop short of murder in the gas chambers. It is not fanciful to find a parallel between the gradual and menacing growth of hatred in a crowd lusting for a lynching, and the Hitler terror.

The associative overlapping, counterpointing and juggling of two interconnected situations – familiar from Lang's German films, such as *M* or *The Last Will of Dr Mabuse* – is in evidence here too. The sheriff tells the crowd that the militia is on its way. The next shot shows the armoury court where the militia are waiting for their marching orders, which will not be issued. A shot of Joe in his cell, terrified as he finally reveals the name of Catherine, whom he had wanted to protect, so that they can ask her to provide his alibi, is followed directly by the shot of Catherine in the highway drugstore where she first hears of Joe's arrest.

The point of one very Germanic symbol (cf. Lupu Pick's *Sylvester*) has been somewhat obscured. Joe, tormented by conscience, stares at the calendar page for 22 November in the lonely bar. The screenplay indicates a previous sequence which was apparently not filmed, in which Joe is frightened by a large '22' on the taximeter. The subsequent apparition of the 22 defendants in the shop window, with ghostly footsteps, as of skeletons, rattling down the street and up the stairs, is yet another reminiscence of the German Lang. Today, many European prints lack this section; even the copy of *Fury* preserved by the Cinémathèque Française, which retains the spectral vision in the shop window, has an altered soundtrack in which staccato music replaces the footsteps. Lang thinks, however, that the American version still retains the original elements.

There is, finally, the question of the happy ending. Joe finds himself again, and renounces his determination to seek the punishment of the 22:

I came to save them, yes. But not for their sakes. Men or women who lynch another human being are a disgrace for humanity. They who pretend to be humans, showed themselves at the first smell of blood to be cruel and brainless beasts.

He does not forgive them:

They lynched what mattered to me . . . my liking people and havin' faith in them.

The decision to present himself in court is taken for himself, not even for Catherine and the brothers who love him. He has realised that he cannot live in isolation, away

from home, without roots, under a false name. This is
what has been symbolised in the walk in the night street,
the escape into the empty bar where the chairs are stacked
on the tables and the only human sound is the radio. It is
therefore untenable to claim that MGM and the demands
of the box office forced a happy ending on Lang. Logic
dictates that Joe cannot go on in exile, unable to see his
family. Only the happy-ending kiss was forced on Lang
against his wishes: originally the script ended with
Catherine smiling proudly through her tears. The question
still remains, whether this kiss *really* constitutes a happy
ending; for Joe after all has been turned into a completely
different person.

The first screening – to which MGM had invited no-one
of any importance – was an enormous success, even
though one of the studio executives had told a journalist
who asked what film was being shown: 'a lousy one from
this lousy German son-of-a-bitch – not worth looking at'.
The studio was astonished with the success and in-
credulously asked journalists, 'You really think it's a good
picture?' Lang (who had been forbidden to touch the film
at a late stage of the editing) went to the opening with
Marlene Dietrich, and left during the applause.

Twenty years later he had an offer to make another film
for MGM, after the departure of both Louis B. Mayer and
Sam Katz. Eddie Mannix engaged him to make *Moonfleet*.

So successful was Lang's first film in the United States
that his second, *You Only Live Once* was announced by the
distributor thus:

'Directing: Fritz (FURY) Lang'.

14 You Only Live Once (1937)

There are again only three characters: the outcast hero, his girl friend, society . . . It is this arbitrariness that gives to the film its curious and memorable force. Critics of the time reproached Lang with sacrificing social comment to melodrama: but they misunderstood, I believe, his purpose. From the opening scene of Eddie's release – asked if he will go straight, 'I will if they let me', he replies – a world of inexorable foreboding and melancholy is created, a world of terrible angst in which guilt and innocence, calculation and fate are confused.

Gavin Lambert: '*Fritz Lang's America*', *Sight and Sound*, Summer 1955

You Only Live Once *was in my view a completely American film without any trace of Europe in it.*

Fritz Lang (Textes, Eibel, p 61)

You Only Live Once is Lang's Song of Songs, his American equivalent, so to speak, of *Destiny*. Man is trapped by fate: the loving woman cannot halt her lover's inexorable destiny; her involvement makes things worse and she must finally perish with him.

Just before the fugitives arrive at the Mexican frontier which means freedom, Jo is recognised as she gets cigarettes from a slot machine. With his sense of the ambiguity of fate, Lang wanted the cigarettes to be 'Lucky Strike'. This ironic symbol and profound pun – worlds removed from his German symbolism – was not permitted by the producer, on the grounds that advertising was not allowed in films.

'The Gods let poor humans err, then leave them to their guilt,' says Goethe. It is the *ananke* of Greek tragedy in its crushing, merciless force. Then secular social justice takes over, without heart, and makes things still more bitter for miserable humans.

You Only Live Once is the first, barely perceptible appearance of the 'Once off guard . . .' motif of later Lang films. At 16 Eddie Taylor (Henry Fonda) beat up a boy because he sadistically pulled off frogs' legs; and was sent to a reformatory. There, through bad influence and resentment, he began on the downward path . . .

The frog story as the fount of a tough career is told in passing in one of the most lyrical love scenes in the cinema. In the garden of the Valley Tavern, an ideal honeymoon setting, Lang, without fear of sentimentality, sets up the young couple's paradise and fulfilment of their love, complete with a background of croaking frogs and in a setting of shrubs and flowers.

They want only to live. 'We may never find happiness',

says Jo (Sylvia Sidney) during the escape in which she has already learnt so much; 'but we have a right to live'. (The French title of the film is *Nous avons le droit de vivre*.)

There is a sudden contrast of mood. The self-righteous middle-class citizens cannot allow a jail-bird to remain under their roof till the next morning. This produces a touch of Lang's humour. The proprietor of the Tavern, a hen-pecked ninny who reads every number of 'True Detective Stories' wants to impress his nagging wife who threatens to burn his magazines if he proves to be mistaken. They come upstairs together; 'When I'm aroused, I'm . . . I'm . . . aroused' he says unconvincingly. The pair of them, something from a Hogarth sketch, hesitate at the locked door. He may be dangerous. The would-be hero falters until the woman loses her patience and hammers at the door. When Eddie appears, the man stammers:

Mr Taylor . . . my wife has something to tell you . . . Tell him Hester.

Whereupon she barks:

Tell him yourself . . .

The man lies:

We-ll – you see, this room was reserv'd – for some folks coming in from Brattelboro . . .

Until finally Hester shouts at him:

Convicts and their wives are not welcome in this Tavern. – So we're asking you in a nice way – to leave at once . . .

Jo tries to calm Eddie:

Darling, you promised you wouldn't let things like this bother you.

Hopeless, Eddie replies:

I must have been hopped up – crazy – to let you marry me.

And again Jo:

What do we care what these people think – What do we care what anybody thinks – As long as we have each other?

The frog story, contrasted to the unpleasantness of the 'decent' couple from the Tavern is more than a mere foil. It introduces a characteristic Lang element into the script. In *Liliom* in the scene where the two no-good friends discuss their robbery we hear their voices but see only their reflections in the water. In a similar manner, we see here only the reflected images of the two lovers in the pond as they talk. Four frogs squat cosily on the water-lily leaves. In 'The Frog and I' (see Eibel, p 84) Lang relates how he struggled to persuade one of the frogs to jump into the water so that the image of the loving couple might be shattered by the splash. This discreet symbol hints at the coming catastrophe – much more effectively than the flowering tree that turns to leafless branches for Seigfried and Kriemhild.

Lang introduces the film's leitmotif: almost shyly Eddie asks Jo:

You know something about frogs? If one dies – the other dies . . .

And then, when Jo smiles, puzzled, and asks:

That's funny. Why?

I don't know, except that they just can't live without each other – You know – like Romeo and Juliet.

Later in the film Jo asks Father Dolan to tell Eddie one thing before he is executed:

Just before the end – not before – at the very last moment – will you tell him . . . that . . . I haven't . . . forgotten the frogs –

The action rapidly shifts location; but the action is linked. As the boss is sacking Eddie for being late (the lovers have been inspecting the dilapidated cottage which is to be their haven) he is shown in a foreshortened angle while he talks into the telephone – a reminiscence of the famous foreshortening of Lohmann in *M*. There the purpose was to reveal the man's earthiness and folksy Berlin style. Here the same device – though this time the man is seen from above – is used to expose the smug incomprehension of the plain, decent citizen when faced with the despair of a man who begs, for Jo's sake, for another chance. It is more important for the boss to discuss with his wife who should be invited to their poker party. His ironical 'If you don't mind – I'd like to speak to my wife' excludes Eddie from any kind of every-day security. The man adds: I'm not running the social system – I'm just running a trucking business'.

Lang and his co-writers Gene Town and Graham Baker stress the failure of imagination and the narrow-mindedness of the socially and economically secure. The stern but kindly warden keeps eating chocolates from an enormous box while handing out good advice to Eddie on his discharge. Ironically Eddie asks his defence lawyer 'Does he know I've been pardoned?' as the warden warns that a further conviction would mean a life sentence. The lawyer explains Eddie has a job with the Ajax Truck Company: 'He'll make good'.

Eddie, without illusions, adds: 'I will if they let me'; to which the warden, unconvincingly, remarks, 'That's up to you'.

There is no false pathos in this. From the start Eddie will encounter people who are no worse than the rest, but simply without understanding of the situation or suffering of others. This failure of understanding is shown continuously in the film, even when Eddie is not on screen – for instance the gum-chewing editor indifferent to which of the headlines will be used: TAYLOR NOT GUILTY, with a happy picture of Eddie; TAYLOR JURY DEADLOCKED, with a non-committal portrait; or TAYLOR GUILTY, with a gloomy face.

When Eddie is pardoned and let out into dubious freedom, Lang sketches a few apparently insignificant details which are nevertheless portents. Bugey, the half-crazy lifer trusty remarks innocently:

So long Eddie – I'll be seein' you

To which Eddie replies:

Not if I can help it.

Then a murderous-looking thug says,

I'll look you up when I get out, Eddie.

which produces a cool reply from Eddie:

Don't do me any favours Monk.

Monk becomes threatening:

Lay off the high hat, Taylor. You're still one of the boys.

Monk will, in fact prove to be Eddie's nemesis.

Father Dolan's first appearance is another such pointer. Eddie tries to avoid the priest; and when his lawyer tells him he owes his pardon to Father Dolan, Eddie's answer is that he is full of 'That love thy neighbour and have faith my son stuff'. This characterises both Eddie's current state

You Only Live Once (1937): the attack on the bank

of mind and Dolan's innocent belief in the goodness of man. Dolan's character and the toughness of Eddie's jail companions is illustrated further in the scene of Father Dolan umpiring a prison baseball game and being ferociously booed when he declares a foul.

When Father Dolan remarks to Eddie that he looks unhappy for a man about to be discharged, Eddie's answer prepares us for coming events:

I cheered the first time I got out – and they rammed it right back down my throat. They're not all like you on the outside.

Like Father Dolan – and like Joe Wilson at the start of *Fury* – Jo believes in justice and man's decency. She has a safe job as secretary to Whitney, the public defender. Her boss is in love with her in a simple way, and is unselfish enough to get Eddie out of jail before his term is up, and help him marry Jo. The Valley Tavern scene shows how their love began.

No sooner have they discovered the cottage ('one thing – nobody can throw us out of it at four in the morning') than Eddie is dismissed, leaving his intransigent, poker-host employer with a crack on the jaw. Before he can tell Jo over the telephone, she excitedly reveals to the desperate man that she has already moved into the cottage. How will he pay for it?

While he is still talking to her on the telephone, Monk, who has moved into Eddie's hotel room, goes down to the street, taking Eddie's hat, with the initials E. T., on which the camera momentarily lingers. Thus the links of the chain are forged.

Again we admire Lang's documentary skill in the attack on the bank truck, recalling the *Mabuse* films and *Spies* with its precise timing. The tension is heightened because we cannot see the bandit's face, and are left to wonder if the gas mask disguises the desperate Eddie. Already we have glimpsed a revolver under his mattress.

Gloved hands lift the blind of a car window and lay Eddie's hat on a cheap suitcase . . . The truck opens up; armed police get out; others approach and clear the passers-by. It is raining. A bomb is thrown and a wall of gas rises. Dimly outlined, police and bystanders are seen grasping their throats, rubbing their eyes, falling suffocating to the ground. Recalling the sound of the second *Mabuse* film, more sirens are added to the noise of a second bomb. Through the clouds of gas and pouring rain the bandit hurries to the truck. As it moves off, the camera rests on Eddie's hat, lying on the pavement.

Fade-in on a detour sign on the highway, at dusk. The truck roars into the picture and disappears around a bend in the road. There is only one more sound – the noise of the truck crashing; and we know that Eddie has lost all chance of proving the identity of the real bandit.

(Films have strange fates, Lang recalls going to see a film called *Dillinger* a few years later on the recommendation that it had an excellent bank raid in it. He was astonished to find that the sequence was in fact some 200 metres of the bank raid from *You Only Live Once,* which fitted quite easily into the new film since the bank raider was unrecognisable in his gas mask. The material had been sold to Walter Wanger and inserted, uncut, into his *Dillinger.* Lang had no remedy.)

When Eddie returns to the cottage, climbing througl the window, after the gas massacre and million dollar robbery, he is changed and tense. The rain is relentless and the swing which Eddie had said would be 'a great place for kids to romp around' sways slightly in the wind.

Jo cannot understand why, since he is innocent, Eddie wants to run away:

Eddie – you can't run. You can't. You'll never be able to prove your innocence then – . . .
Eddie, if you love me, you'll stay and face it.

As a three-time loser, he knows better. He has no alibi; he was wandering the streets in search of work when the raid happened.

O.K., kid. I'll play it your way!
But you're gambling with my life – and if you're wrong –

So Eddie is trapped and led off by the State Troopers, who would have preferred to shoot him while resisting and 'save the State the expense of a trial'

Later, in the Court House hall, Eddie passes Jo who has been waiting to talk to him. He looks hatred and contempt at her, and shakes her off:

Are you satisfied now?

Eddie – please forgive me!

Keep away from me! (and to the cops) Let's go.

There is characteristic overlapping of dialogue. As Eddie is driven away from the Court House he shouts at the mob – hysterical like the crowd in *Fury* and with two maddened women demanding his lynching –

Get a big kick out of me! It's fun to see a man burning!
. . . They're never . . .
DISSOLVE TO CONDEMNED ROW
. . . going to burn me for something I didn't do . . .
CUT TO CLOSE-UP OF EDDIE GRIPPING THE BARS OF THE DEATH CELL, IN FUTILE RAGE:
. . . never, never . . .

So the action is moved forward by ellipsis.

The death cell is seen in its natural abstraction, not in the decorative manner of Mackie's death cell in Pabst's *Dreigroschenoper* (to which Brecht's irony, all the same, adds a certain ambiguity). Lang had researched the

You Only Live Once: the condemned cell

American penal system. He visited San Quentin and Alcatraz; and the death cell is an exact reconstruction of the death cell at San Quentin – filmed by Leon Shamroy, says Lang, 'brilliantly and imaginatively'. The dark, heavy bars form a broad, fan-like pattern of shadows, symbolising disaster even more intensely than the black arrow lines of the prison in *The Cabinet of Dr Caligari*. Fate's inescapable trap is made visible. Through the experience of his German films, Lang manages to create a visual transposition of the message in the script, 'His cage has vertical wooden bars, about two inches apart, and visible from all four sides'. Once this image has been stamped on our memory, when we learn that for five months Eddie has been waiting in the death cell ('waiting, – waiting – just like that') we understand his behaviour towards Dolan after his break-out in the fog. From his use of symbolism in his German films, Lang has progressed in the States to discover the only possible expression of a situation whose symbolic meaning becomes almost painfully real in its visualisation.

Jo learns her lesson. When Eddie is persuaded (by Dolan) to talk to her, she still doesn't quite understand when Eddie whispers desperately:

Get me a gun – a gun!

I can't! You'd kill somebody –

To which Eddie viciously retorts:

What do you think they're going to do to me?

This dialogue is reinforced by a characteristic Lang idea. As Jo hesitates outside the window of the pawnshop (whose crowded display recalls *M*) a newsboy cries out:

Taylor dies to-morrow!
Extra! Extra! Read all about it!

Jo goes into the shop; and we know she will buy the gun.

Jo has learnt her lesson. When Eddie, bewildered, says during the escape:

I can still see Father Dolan's face . . .

she answers

I'm guilty, Eddie . . . not you . . . I pulled the trigger on him. I killed Father Dolan . . . If I hadn't had this silly belief in faith . . . faith . . .

and I had let you go when you wanted to, all this wouldn't have happened. It was my fault. I tell you – my fault, not yours!

The sequence in which Eddie receives the note telling him to get into the hospital isolation ward, where he breaks the coffee pot and where he slashes his wrist, so that blood starts to drip on the ground, recall the *Mabuse* films. The succeeding action emphasises the cruelty of an ostensibly socially minded society. The bleeding man is given a transfusion to save his life for the electric chair. The troubled executioner asks the warden if it will be necessary to postpone the execution; the doctor, with indifference replies that he will be strong enough by then. The warden can announce that 'The execution will go on as scheduled –'

When, in a parallel scene, the warden's smug wife tells Father Dolan,

I still don't understand your feeling for the Taylor boy. I think he was born bad!

Dolan voices the philosophy which could stand as a motto for all Lang's American films:

Every man – at his birth – is endowed with the nobility of a king. But the stain of the world soon makes him forget even his birthright.

Perhaps, he adds, this is the reason for death – just to give men another chance of remembering who they are before they are born again. The warden's insensitive comment is:

Well, father, I hope when Taylor dies tonight he won't be born again. He's caused enough trouble in the world.

At this precise moment the siren starts up shrilly: Eddie has broken out.

In the prison yard there is dense fog; and in the haze are two figures: Eddie, and in front of him as a shield, Eddie's pistol in his back, Dr Hill, the prison doctor.

Searchlights try to track Eddie. The siren continues to blast out. The fog is impenetrable. There are shouts among the guards straining to see down into the yard. The whole is orchestrated with the precision of *The Last Will of Dr Mabuse*.

Like *Fury* the film is divided into two clear sections, in which the tragic reversal of fortune is achieved. At the moment where Eddie Taylor's innocence is established (the truck and Monk's corpse have been found at the

You Only Live Once: the break-out from the prison

bottom of the gorge), he turns murderer, shooting Father Dolan as he makes his break. Now their fate is inevitable, (and this alone distinguishes *You Only Live Once* from the casual, unmotivated activities of *Bonnie and Clyde* with which the film is frequently compared: there is more of Lang's philosophy in Ray's fine *They Live by Night*). Eddie and Jo have no choice: everything is final and without alternative. Every act of violence which is now perpetrated in the country is inevitably blamed on them. When they hold up a garage, merely for petrol, the garage employees quickly empty the till and blame the fugitives. A man speculates:

From all they've stolen – they must be millionaires by now.

His friend replies:

Probably hiding in a swell place and having a real time.

In fact we at once see them shivering in the wind and rain in the car whose windscreen they have had to break

You Only Live Once: the end in the woods

You Only Live Once: Joan (Sylvia Sidney) and Eddie (Henry Fonda)

away so that the bullet holes will not give them away. After the rain, storm and gloom we find them temporarily installed in the sunshine, in the hobo jungle where their baby is born. It is a faint echo of the Valley Tavern idyll.

Whitney, the public defender, is a type such as we meet again and again in Lang films. He loves Jo, and what he does for Eddie is initially for her sake. Yet when he recognizes the judicial mistake, and watches a jury convict a man of murder only on the strength of his record, he decides to devote himself entirely to the Taylor case. When the Inspector reproaches him,

You sound as though you sympathise with that guy –

He answers:

The law condemned him to death. They found out they had made a mistake – And they thought they could straighten it out just like that.

He maintains his resistance when Bonnie, Jo's sister, out of love for Jo, expresses views similar to those of the

189

warden's wife:

You're not helping Jo by trying to keep this case alive. You know as well as I do that Eddie Taylor's been pounding on the door of the execution chamber since he was born.

Lang's sense of justice is clearly expressed when Whitney tells the Inspector:

What do you want me to do? Go out and find him? Get a gun and shoot him. That's *your* job – and I don't envy you.

In *Fury* Joe Wilson becomes more and more embittered, until Catherine makes him realise he cannot continue to live in this way. Eddie is more and more purified during the lovers' escape into nowhere. Lang has been charged with sentimentality in having Eddie hear Father Dolan's voice as he sinks to the ground, clasping the dead Jo in his arms: 'Eddie, you're free – the gates are open!' The script says only: 'CAMERA PANS HIGH . . . over the hill top, over-the-top-of-the-trees. The sun rises higher and higher, casting golden beams of light.' In Murnau's *Faust* also the light of the sun meant salvation. If Lang felt that the beams of sunlight woven among the high trunks of the forest near the frontier that meant freedom was not by themselves enough, it was not out of sentimentality or symbolism. In Goethe's *Faust*, after the declaration 'She has been judged!' comes a voice from above: 'She has been *saved*!' In Germany Lang showed the lovers of *Destiny* walking about in the world beyond. Here, in a far more mature film, Death opens the gates for the two lovers who have been removed from earthly justice.

15 You and Me (1938)

You and Me *was his least
important (film), although it
too was a bold attempt to
break away from Hollywood
formula and to experiment
with sound . . . the story had
moments of novel
treatment . . . there were . . .
many striking camera bits, and
there was the same pungent
characterisation and moodiness
that was evident in Lang's
first two films.*
Lewis Jacobs: The Rise of
the American Film,
Harcourt, Brace and
Company, New York,
1939

You and Me was a failure: perhaps because it was an
attempt at a Brecht *Lehrstück* without Brecht (Kurt Weill's
facility did not compensate for the merciless precision and
harsh rhythm of Brecht); perhaps because – as Gavin
Lambert speculates in his *Sight and Sound* article, 'Fritz
Lang's America' – in contrast to Lang's first two American
films the problem is no longer a fight against social
injustice. Certainly there was no darker under-structure
against which the comedy and irony could reverberate.

The boss of a big department store collects convicts as
other people collect stamps, in order to give them another
chance. The former gaol-bird has, then, none of the
problems of Eddie in *You Only Live Once*, of finding a
decent job to give him the chance to go straight. The
motives are now private ones: the converted gangster goes
back to his former criminal associations because he is
resentful that his sweetheart kept him in the dark about her
own past prison experience.

The opening song,

You can't get something for nothing
And only a chump would try

resembles the rhythmical structure of the original German
of Brecht's:

And as you made your bed
You shall lie there

(It is interesting to note that Weill was accustomed to get
the distinctive rhythm for his songs from Brecht, who
would indicate it on the piano with one finger.) Lang
illustrates the song with a rapid montage of all the desirable
things to be had for money. It is a very different effect from
M's visual illustration of the report on the office break-in,

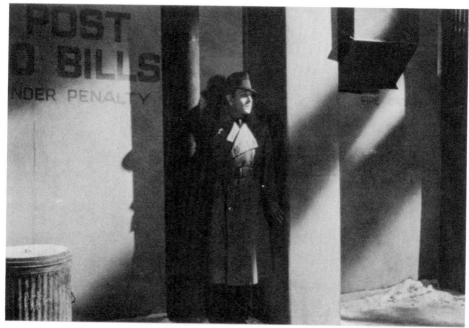

You and Me (1938): studies of the interplay of light and shade

or the police commissioner's account of his force's
investigation methods, in its arbitrary assembly of objects.
Again, Lang's illustration of the business of a sailors' pub,
as the dance hall singer sings:

They call him good for nothing . . .
But he's the right guy for me

is soft and blurred (even allowing for the atmospheric
intention) and uncharacteristic of Lang.

The film's strongest moment is the scene of the
gangsters' Christmas Eve party. One of them sighs as his
eyes fall on the barred window of the restaurant patronised
equally by gangsters and decent bourgeoisie. The bars
recall days of being inside, looking out; and they all start to
reminisce about their times in prison, and the truly festive
Christmas that the one joint of the year represented. Now
that they can buy as many chickens and turkeys as they
please, it does not mean nearly as much . . . One of them

starts to bang the table with his knife, and all the others start up the rhythmic hammering of the prison code. When finally Joe (George Raft) asks to be admitted with the same coded knocking on the door, they all start up in a stylised chorus: 'Stay with the mob. Stay with the mob'. The rhythmic chant appears quite natural in this context, and the desired effect is achieved without Weill's music. (Weill in fact only worked on the film for a short time and abandoned it before it was completed.)

Lang explains that for this remarkable scene he wanted 'something like a song without music, built only on rhythm and sound effects'; though he dislikes the term 'sound effects' and achieved rather a mental association between the nocturnal passing of the code in prison, and the sounds produced by the ex-convicts with the glasses, forks and plates of their banquet.

With his enthusiasm and interest obviously aroused at this point, Lang achieves a convincing poetic movement.

In the soft light we see infinite prison corridors; and everywhere – on the cells, between the corridors, some of which are only blobs of light and lattice made of shadows on the floor. Even the barred restaurant window is suddenly seen to cast a merciless shadow on the wall beside one of the reminiscing gangsters. As in Eddie's death cell, the bars all seem to spell an inexorable doom, the fate of an inescapable incarceration. They all recall the legendary break-out of Number One, the greatest; and all of them are once more pressing against the bars of their cells, vicariously sharing the experience, until the rat-tat of machine guns and the sudden silence of the siren shows that Number One did not make it. This is no longer the case of an arbitrary, accidental, purely decorative illustration, but a forceful and expressive statement.

The scene of the break-in recalls *M*, with the watchman on his rounds, the conspiratorial whistling, the empty entrance railings and drive; and then the emergence of shadowy figures, and the rhythm of people walking upstairs, as if in step . . . Suddenly the light flashes on: the boss and his gunman are lying in wait, take their arms; and the boss remarks that his wife was right after all: he should have collected stamps. Helen (Sylvia Sidney) makes her speech about the unprofitability of crime, and demonstrates on a blackboard that each of them stands to gain 133 dollars and 35 cents: not much for a hunted life. (Brecht's Polly Peachum also dominated the gang by means of simple arithmetic; only she taught that the opening of a bank is more profitable than robbing one: 'Wholesale robbing is better'.)

The film somewhat abruptly changes its mood to gaiety and harmlessness, not much affected even by the scenes which recall *M*, such as the council of gangsters who enquire from house to house and bar to bar for Helen. There is a comic happy ending, as they all sit around in the maternity hospital waiting for the arrival of Helen's baby, incongruously dressed in bourgeois Sunday best. When the nurse calls for the happy father, they all rush forward together. *Lehrstück* as parody, a kind of *Robber Symphony*.

Some of the comic inventions are nevertheless excellent: the shop man who intimidates a fat, spoilt child into choosing the toy she at first rejected, and the unwitting mother who compliments the man's understanding of

You and Me: George Raft as Joe Dennis

child psychology; George Raft's assurance to a sportive lady customer in the sports department that he knows as much about rackets as anyone; the helpful safecracker who deftly shows the boss's wife how to open a tin can; Joe's encounter with an importunate man on the dance floor – knocking him out when Helen is gone, and then sitting him up and straightening his cap.

There is a use of symbolism here, too. A stop/go traffic sign halts Joe in his tracks and sends him back to Helen. But the idyllic relationship lacks the intensity of *You Only Live Once*, because there are finally no tragic undertones; and perhaps because George Raft, with a vapid, gigolo face, cannot believably arouse sufficient interest from Sylvia Sidney.

The film was made under difficulties. Lang did not get on very well with Virginia Van Upp, the screenwriter. George Raft demanded many rehearsals, while Sylvia

Sydney wanted as few as possible in order to keep her performance spontaneous. Americans were not yet ready for the *Lehrstück* film, and to Lang the plot seemed too superficial to warrant a deeper-reaching social treatment.

A script called *Men Without a Country* which Lang wanted to film for Paramount never materialised. It was the story of three adventurers, a Nazi, a Japanese and another international spy who try to get hold of a secret war weapon, a beam which produces blindness. After this Lang tried his hand at a Western script, dealing with a lost goldmine, The Dutchman; and there was an offer by Darryl F. Zanuck, then chief of production at Twentieth Century Fox, to make a sequel to Henry King's *Jesse James*, which would have Frank James, brother of the murdered bandit, as the hero. Lang agreed to make the film.

16   The Return of Frank James (1940)

The fact that, in contrast to so many other films by Fritz Lang, The Return of Frank James has a happy ending, should not be interpreted as a concession to American censorship. Leaving behind moral man, Lang finds sinful man, which explains his bitterness. Yet beyond the sinner there is a study of regenerated man, which intrigues the most Germanic of American film makers. When the fierce individualist Frank James finally finds his happiness, it is only after having first atoned with his pain.
Jean-luc Godard: Fiche U.F.O.L.E.I.S. 1956

I love Westerns. They are based on a very simple and essential ethical code. It is a code which is no longer noted, because critics are too sophisticated. All simple morals are important for the success of a film. Even with Shakespeare the moral is simple. The struggle of good against evil is as old as the world.
Entretien with Fritz Lang, *Cahiers du Cinéma*, 7 November 1959

Approaching his first Western, Lang recognized that for the young American nation the only equivalent to sagas or legends like the Arthurian lore of the English, the Roland Legend of the French or the Nibelungen Saga of the Germans and Scandinavians was the folklore of the War of Secession and the Conquest of the West. History mingles wishfully with myth and legend in the stories of the opening of the unknown and mysterious West, the conflicts with the Indians, the feuds between the pioneers who wanted arable land and the cattle men and cowboys who wanted open grazing land and prairie. The outsiders, the bandits and rebels like Jesse James, were as much romanticised in their own life-times as were the defenders of the established order, marshals and sheriffs. Often the Western gains its vitality from a presentation of the two sorts of folk heroes in conflict.

Lang, having already spent some time living with the Navaho while waiting for MGM to find him work under his contract, accepted the challenge of making a Western as authentic as any native American director could do. As always, he first sought to document every individual detail. In Tombstone, for instance, he found an old theatre still standing, with its narrow boxes and hard benches; contemporary accounts and pictures supplied missing details like the showy chandelier and the stage fittings.

The existing screenplay was good enough to require no more than the usual careful editing and modifications – 'personalising' – which were Lang's invariable contributions to any script. He claims that to ensure the continuity between one film and the other he used the last shots of the Henry King film (*Jesse James*, 1939) as an introduction to his own – the shooting of Jesse James by the Ford brothers after his wedding and just as he is preparing to retire into respectable life under the name of Mr Howard, with a number of killings still on his conscience. However, the scene as it now appears in Lang's film, in which Jesse is shot in the back while hanging up a wall motto inscribed 'God Bless Our Home', is certainly not the scene as it occurs in King's picture, where Jesse is shot while sitting at a table in a wooden-block cabin.

Although it was the first time that Lang had used colour, the technique seemed to come naturally to him. He had always loved to grapple with new problems; and after all he had been used to a whole spectrum of shades and tonal gradations in using black and white film. Nor, for a director who had generally worked in the studio, was he disturbed by the comparatively unusual problems of working out-of-doors in natural exteriors. As he had quickly mastered sound in *M*, so here he learned – helped by his talent as a painter – to cope with the problems of colour, the new techniques of structure, composition and cutting; the need to grade the film carefully so that the spectator's eye is saved the shock of too sudden contrasts of lighting.

The characters have an open-air freshness, and the adventure aspects of the story avoid conventional stylisation, but contribute to the revenge story in which the avenger – unlike other comparable Lang heroes – does not himself have to kill. Frank James, the more moderate of the brothers, had already gone back to his former life as a cattle-breeder and farmer – the life from which the brothers had been inveigled by the intrigues of the railway agents – before Jesse's murder. Thus, the title *The Return of Frank James* carries at least a double meaning: 'return' in the sense of 'revenge'; but more importantly, like Joe Wilson, Frank is able to return to an open life on his farm without the necessity of any longer hiding his identity – 'return' in the sense of 'redemption'.

The revenge motive must have attracted Lang, quite apart from the exotic, mythological and adventure aspects of the story. This is, however, no longer the all-consuming and self-destructive revenge of Kriemhild or Joe Wilson in their determination to have an eye for an eye. Frank decides to act himself only when he sees the court of justice fail him, with the jury, bribed by the railway company,

The clear air and the sweeping landscapes of the West seemed to stimulate Lang only as a painter, for it is in their markedly tasteful and exploratory use of Technicolor that the main interest of both films lies. The landscapes are soft and luminous, they have a rich and idyllic glow . . .
Gavin Lambert, 'Fritz Lang's America', *Sight and Sound*, Autumn 1955

His reputation . . . had preceded him in Hollywood, and it was not until long after his arrival . . . that he had become one of the industry's busiest directors. Later I remember, Darryl Zanuck gave him a Western movie to direct, and I asked him how on earth he could allow a middle European to do an American Western. 'Because he'll see things we don't,' Darryl replied. And he was right.
Joan Bennett: *The Bennett Playbill* by Lois Kibbee, 1970

The Return of Frank James (1940): the sweeping landscape of the West

acquitting the murderers and even rewarding them with their Judas money. He can even rob the Yankee Railroad Company of its money with good conscience and dignity; they have stolen his and his brother's farm. Yet Frank is spared the need to kill the Ford brothers himself. The first of them falls to his death in a canyon during a chase; the other shoots himself after he has been injured and is cornered in a barn by Frank. So, by the laws of American mythology, Frank may have his happy ending and return to the simple life of his little farm – perhaps even first taking a detour by Denver where the amateur girl reporter lives ('mighty pretty country round there . . . Yep, there's lots about Denver I like.').

It must be remembered that the film was made in 1940. The Western *genre*, with its underlying mythus of the American dream, had not yet begun to darken. Still, the laws, for all that, are inexorable. Clem, the ranch hand who is helping Frank, has accidentally caused the death of the railroad man whom Frank had intended to spare. He must pay for his minimal guilt, however accidental. There is an echo of *You Only Live Once* in the situation of Frank's surrender to the court on the advice of the girl reporter, in order to save the faithful Pinky, an Uncle Tom figure in the story. There are important differences, however. The girl is first interested in the case she has rather romanticised, and only later in Frank himself. Frank is rightly named, upright, straightforward, naturally decent, and is more mature than Eddie. Thus he does not bear any resentment toward the girl when things seem to go against him in the court, for her advice coincides with his own conscience. Only when he is officially acquitted can he justify his own deeds to himself and begin a new life. Indeed, it must be remembered that the real Frank James was also acquitted. The happy ending is not a concession either to the box office or the censor, but a meeting of history and Western ideology.

In regard to such ideology as it works within the *genre*, Philip French has made a perceptive observation about casting in the Western:

When Wayne is cast as a criminal there's usually a suggestion that something is wrong with the law in a local, easily resolved way; when Fonda is cast as an outlaw the implication is that there's something basically wrong with society. (Outside the Western, he fulfills this

The Return of Frank James: the court scene

function in, for instance, *You Only Live Once, Grapes of Wrath* and *The Wrong Man*.) The use of Fonda and Wayne proposes fairly immediate social readings of the genre.

Philip French, *Westerns: Aspects of a Movie Genre,* Cinema One, 25 (London, 1973)

Certainly it is more possible thus to interpret *The Return of Frank James*, whose corrupt courts and commercial intrigues of railroad and banks are more dishonest and harmful to society than the outlaw James brothers themselves. To so read the film, however, would be fundamentally to misread Lang's tone here, even if such undertones echo Lang's previous American films and prefigure his use of the *genre* in *Rancho Notorious*. Although Lang is here fully aware of the darker possibilities of the Western, *The Return of Frank James* is a film without pessimism or bitterness. Lang's 'Enter the Bear' humour always counteracts the tragic elements, and in particular gives colour and vitality to the court-room scene. All

The Return of Frank James: the theatrical re-enactment of Jesse James' death

Lang's court scenes are notable for their immediacy and directness, the variations and inventions he is able to bring to this arena, usually so restricted in the films of other directors. Henry Hull is permitted to overact extravagantly his role of newspaper editor and defense lawyer; the court, composed of Southern-sympathizers, takes unconcealed delight in for once being able to cross the Railway Yankees. Such farcical elements override the more sombre implications of the court-room scenes.

There is a happy and joyful earthiness and simplicity in the film which reminds one of John Ford's *My Darling Clementine*. Adventure is interwoven with comic situation, constantly underscoring the humanity of the characters. For example, the encounter of the smirky little detective with Frank and Clem and the hold-up in their room is given a comic dimension by the discovery of the little man gagged and bound to the cupboard door. Even the unpleasantness of the Ford brothers' re-enactment of

The Murder of Jesse James is undercut by the fresh humour of the little theatre with its precarious benches and wobbling scenery.

Lang, after years of working in the artifice of the studio, rejoices here in the exterior work and the breathtaking chases. The familiar Lang style, however, is particularly recognisable in the scene in the barn, with its sense of menace in the isolation of every detail in the impenetrable darkness in which even the change of colour tones seems to harbour an undefined threat. Every small sound – creaking timber, the neigh and stamp of horses, the rustling of the straw – acquires more resonance in the menacing silence. Here the ritardando effect, coming in a film of fast-moving action, is genuinely unnerving.

Courtade, not usually an admirer of Lang, wrote of its 'chanson de geste naiveté which makes for most of the film's charm'. Chanson de geste, perhaps; but not naiveté. Lang was never more deliberate than in constructing this film; thereby establishing himself with authority in a territory which had until now seemed to be the exclusive preserve of native American directors.

17 Western Union (1941)

The box office success of *The Return of Frank James* gave Lang an opportunity to do another Western for Fox, with the possibility of careful preparation. The writer Robert Carson, interviewed by Eibel, said that while he was deeply impressed by Lang's personality and career, his rare encounters with him were not productive from the point of view of the finished script, and that there was no time to make the corrections recommended by Lang for this 'stylisation of American folk-lore'. Lang, to the contrary, remembers that he had time enough to work through the script, making his changes in his accustomed way. The fact that he was given time and opportunity to scout for and choose his own locations would seem to lend credence to the director's memory.

At first glance this subject would not seem to offer the same obvious dramatic possibilities as did the James story. The real-life subject matter – the progress of the Western Union Telegraph Company from Omaha to Salt Lake City at the time of Lincoln's presidency – was so uneventful that, as Lang said later, he needed more time to make a film about it than the Western Union Company itself had taken for the efficiently accomplished laying of the cable. The most momentous historical occurrences were the knocking down of telegraph poles by buffaloes scratching their backs against them.

Nonetheless, Lang saw clearly the possibilities offered by one of the most classic of Western forms, the arrival of an equivocal 'civilization' to the West through 'technological progress' and the linkage of the two American coasts and a concomitant closing down of one sort of code which is to be replaced by another. However, as in *The Return of Frank James*, Lang is not yet ready to allow the celebratory

'To a simple piece of telegraph wire' – this dedication by Zane Grey, one of the most brilliant exponents of regionalist literature, refers to the peaceful epic of the 'Pioneers of the Western Union', who laid the first telegraph wire across the West from 1861 on. The sober tone of the book is also found in Fritz Lang's film, which manages to recreate the simple and hard fight of those men, whose work consisted in 'fitting one piece of iron wire on to another piece of iron wire'.
J.-L Rieupeyrout and André Bazin, *Le Western* (1953)

Lang shooting *Western Union* (1941)

aspects of the coming to the West of eastern 'civilisation' to be more than slightly darkened by undertones of moral and ethical disquiet.★

Hence the need to ornament the theme with classic Western motifs and issues: encounters with Indians, reminiscences of the Civil War, the clash of moral codes. Again there is the characteristic Western motif of the outlaw who wants to go straight: Vance Shaw, the man with a past and a golden heart, is caught in a tragic conflict (*à la* Corneille) of loyalties between Western Union, whose scout he is, and his own brother, whose role as gang leader he cannot bring himself to betray. Such a character, trapped by fate, in conflict with the equivocal justice meted out by the guardians of public order, was obviously irresistible to Lang. There was more for him in the story than the simple fascination of the West, its prairies and its wealth of legend.

Again Lang strove for authenticity, informing himself

★ It is unfortunate that one can do no more than speculate on what Lang might have made of the material he had planned to use for *Winchester '73* in 1948, in which 'technological progress' in the form of a rifle obviously takes on a much darker moral coloration than does the telegraph wire.

minutely on such technical matters as the methods of erecting the poles and tautening the wires, the function of the insulators and the tools which would have been used at the time. Even today he is proud of a letter from some old-timers in Flagstaff, Arizona: 'We have seen *Western Union* and this film is the only one which shows the West as it really was . . . How is this for a European director?' Yet, at the same time, Lang insisted that the film, in spite of the authenticity of detail, did not show the West as it really was: 'It lived up to certain dreams and illusions of what these old-timers *wanted* to remember of the Old West.' No doubt, Lang's ability to discover the spirit and essence of the action made the film appear authentic and credible to the people who remembered the reality.★

Certainly part of the credibility derives not merely from Lang's visual and formal effects, but from the smaller ingenious touches which render each action realistic. There is, for example, the scene in which Vance prepares for his last fight. He tears the bandages from his badly burned right hand and – adding to the script – Lang makes him stretch his fingers to test whether they are ready to pull the trigger of his gun and that 'he can be quick on the draw'. A typical enrichment of the script by Lang with a realistic and characteristically human detail.

In the Western, with its semi-historical, semi-mythological background, and primitive heroic codes, Lang found the possibilities of presenting themes impossible in modern subjects. The cowboy of those days, in all his romantic glorification and his belief in honour and his word of honour, is worlds apart from his present-day counterpart – the Midnight Cowboy who walks the New York pavements without a code to his name. The final gun-battle – in which honour finally forces Vance to destroy his own brother and his gang – has much the same heroic rhythm as the gun battle in *High Noon* despite the more matter-of-fact documentary presentation by Lang. Unlike Frank James, whose robbery of the railroad's money is morally justified, Vance Shaw is required to pay for his bank robber and outlaw past with his life. Too late, he meets the potentially redeeming woman of his life: the end of this Western is tragic.

'The characters of film Westerns', writes Jean-Luc Godard in his analysis of the film, 'are certainly among the

★So effective, indeed, was Lang's recreation of the legendary West, that some of his footage from the film was used by William Wellman in *Buffalo Bill* (1944).

Western Union: on location

most type-cast characters in the cinema, but that means that he (Lang) enters an important part of the mythology by way of their existence.' The typing is an important part of the *genre*. Vance (Randolph Scott) is a simple man of few words, weather beaten, reserved, reticent in his romantic love. His rival and counterpart Tenderfoot Blake (Robert Young) is intelligent, educated, exaggeratedly elegant – in short, an Easterner to contrast with Vance's typical Westerner. Creighton (Dean Jagger) is the professional pioneer who guesses the truth of Vance's past but chooses to trust him nonetheless. He too is a recognisable Western type, as are all the other characters: Creighton's daughter Sue, an idealized and civilizing pioneer woman; the gang of greedy outlaws, the anxious comic cook, the tough, realistic Western Union employees, Homer and Pat. Even if the script at one point speaks of 'savages', the Indians are presented sympathetically. Their chief, Spotted Horse, has a calm dignity; the Indian party which raids the camp does

207

so only after they have been made drunk by corrupt white men.

Again, Lang's use of colour is notable: Vance's ride through the night forest to meet his brother and the attack by the gang; the climactic scene of the burning camp – the sparks and flames, wagons hurtling and tumbling, water splashing up from the puddles, constant movement in which flashes of light and colour mix with shadow – all even more brilliantly orchestrated than the barn scene in *The Return of Frank James*. Further, there is the virtuoso treatment of the moment which announces the start of Indian resistance, an idea which Lang credits to his cameraman Edward Cronjager. The camera pans down the wire hanging loose from the last telegraph pole to the coil still lying on the ground. From the shock of the war spear with its brilliantly coloured feathers, the camera pans rapidly up to the greater shock of two hundred Indians lined up in full war paint. (Lang is particularly proud of the authenticity of this war paint, for which, with the assistance of producer Kenneth MacGowan, he had consulted authorities on Indian lore.) While Lang is usually opposed to tricky and complicated camera work, he used a pan of one hundred and eighty degrees in the shot because he wanted to shock the spectator and to drive the action forward more forcefully than would have been possible with a simple cut.

Lang's first two Westerns reveal a trend towards a new development in the Western *genre* – the 'psychological' Western. His own distinctive manner of balancing right against wrong, of introducing darker undertones to run just under the surface of typical Western action, introduces a new element into the mythology of the Western; and these two Westerns clearly are preludes to the tragic imponderables of *Rancho Notorious*.

18 Man Hunt (1941)

*Early in 1941, I made my
first film with the
incomparable director Fritz
Lang, a circumstance that
would be an important boost
for me as an actress . . . I
played a Cockney, and for
weeks before the shooting
began, I worked on the accent
with Queenie Leonard, an
English music hall performer.
It was the only movie I ever
made in which I knew the
entire script, like a play,
beforehand. Conquering the
dialect was tricky enough, but
the real challenge came in
working with Fritz Lang . . .*

*Fritz was terribly exacting and
demanding and working with
him was sometimes abrasive,
but he commanded great
respect, and I performed better
under his direction than at any
other time in my career.
Almost always I did what I
was told, and we developed a
great working rapport.*
Joan Bennett: *The Bennett
Playbill*, by Lois Kibbee,
1970

Although Kenneth MacGowan, then a producer with Fox, had Fritz Lang in mind originally as director of Dudley Nichol's script for *Man Hunt*, it was offered first to John Ford, who turned it down because he did not like the subject matter. The script was based on Geoffrey Household's novel *Rogue Male* (which was also the original title of the film), and though the dictator who figures in the book is unnamed, both Lang and Nichols naturally saw him as being Hitler. Lang therefore took the opportunity of making his first American anti-Nazi film, to help awaken then indolent Americans to Nazi methods and menace, much as he was to do with *Hangmen Also Die* and *The Ministry of Fear*, although by the time of their release, after Pearl Harbour, America had entered the war. As a kind of final reckoning, in 1946 he made yet another anti-Nazi film in *Cloak and Dagger*.

Dudley Nichols' working methods and conception were very like Lang's own (he was later hired by Lang's own company, Diana Productions, to script *Scarlet Street*); but it is interesting to follow through his original script and discover the extent to which the director himself works over scenarios, revising, improving, testing the credibility of behaviour and dialogue, and finally, in the shooting, adding his own personality to what is written.

It must also be noted that there was much more in the subject that would have interested Lang in addition to the anti-Nazi aspects. Examining either of the film's titles, *Rogue Male* and *Man Hunt*, in the light of the film that Lang made will immediately indicate those areas of the subject which interested Lang. Applying almost any of the alternative definitions of 'rogue' in a standard dictionary to the hero of the film will lead one to those special ambiguities of character and morality which delight the director.

Like most Lang heroes Thorndike will learn about himself, about his own code, and about the code of society which he must either accept or reject, either of which alternatives carries a price. The final title, *Man Hunt*, is not without its ironies, in which, in typical Lang fashion, everything is reversed and the hunter becomes the hunted, is caught in a trap from which he must escape for redemption.

Nichols opens the script with a dramatic introduction, *in media res*. Lang was once again working on the studio lot, in a wood so authentic that it is hard to believe it was an impressive set built by Wiard Ihnen at Fox. The camera slowly pans down to discover enormous footprints in the wet soil. (In Lang's films close-ups are used only when they are vital to the action, as they are here and a little later in the close-ups of a hand adjusting the telescopic sights of a gun.) Near Hitler's Berchtesgaden estate, the British Captain Thorndike (Walter Pidgeon) holds his prey in the telescopic sights of his rifle: the *Führer*. The experienced hunter has stalked his prey without having been discovered by guards or bloodhounds. There is no bullet in the gun when he pulls the trigger experimentally. The hunter's instinct asserts itself; he loads. Is he really going to shoot? Is it merely a matter of proving to himself that he could if he wanted to? By the end of the film, Thorndike will have learned enough about his own motives to give himself the answer: he wished to free Europe of the monster. Then a leaf falls, a shaft of sunlight glints on the gun barrel, and Hitler's blackshirts are alerted.

He is captured and interrogated by a man addressed by the others as Quive-Smith (a cynical and worldly role well suited to George Sanders). A fellow-hunter, Quive-Smith refuses to believe Thorndike's explanations that it was only a sporting stalk for the thrill: there is, after all, a bullet in the rifle. Thorndike in turn refuses to accept that the end (his liberty) justifies the means (the signing of a statement that he was acting on British orders to assassinate Hitler). (The date is 1939 and the British and the Germans are still at peace.) The obstinate man is therefore handed over to the blackshirts. The door slams; there is the 'sound of something being knocked about in the inner room. There is a sickening thud as something falls to the floor'.

Nichols aversion to showing torture coincides with Lang's comparable aversion to violence; but Lang goes further than his writer. Nichols describes at length Thorndike's state after they have tortured and dragged him back in:

He is only half conscious. His arms dangle loosely and his chin is sunk on his breast. His eyes are closed. His fingers look black. His face is battered and across the right cheek is the livid mark of an ugly burn, as if a burning sabre had been slapped across his cheek. Much time has passed, for a stubble of a beard shows on the bruised face . . .

Lang has deleted all this with red pencil, and noted on the margin 'Shadow – don't show Thorndike throughout the whole scene' and 'play the whole scene on Q.S.'. So in the finished film we see only part of the man in close-up as he is dragged in. Lang writes: 'Close shot of dragging feet . . . blood drops could be all.' His legs are limp and his feet dragging on the ground leave visible tracks. Now the scene is concentrated on Quive-Smith and the Nazi doctor. We see only their part of the room, which now seems enormous; we hear the voice of Thorndike, thick and inarticulate, from elsewhere in the room. Then we see the shadow of the armchair, and Thorndike's shadow as he tries to raise himself from it. Lang then adds another shot not in the script: the doctor bends over the tortured man with his stethoscope, and wipes his hands afterwards – presumably because they have been bloodied. In this way, the imagination of the spectator to visualise the effects of the torture, just as the torture behind the closed door was left to the imagination. This is a clear example of Lang's ability to intensify an apparently finished script.

Thorndike's high-level connections (his brother is a Lord, a dim-witted diplomat with faith in Hitler's promises) make it difficult to shoot him 'while escaping', so since he adamantly refuses to sign the confession, an 'accident' must be staged. Only half recovered from his wounds, he is pushed into an abyss by the Nazi doctor. But when an innocent-seeming hunting party sets out to investigate the accident, his corpse can not be found. Only a snapped branch indicates how his fall might have been broken. Lang delights in the tautly cut chase which ensues, through the evocative landscapes that are again constructions on the back lot at Fox, with murky swamps;

Man Hunt (1941): Walter Pidgeon as Thorndike

a dried-out river bed and the cave where Thorndike later seeks safety at the end of the film are also shot on the lot.

Slipping unnoticed past the harbour police, Thorndike reaches a row-boat in the black waters of a port at night (yet another studio set) and is helped by a bright cabin boy (charmingly and unprecociously played by the young Roddy Macdowall) to stow away in a little Danish tramp steamer. But a well-dressed gentleman who resembles a walking corpse, calling himself Mr Jones (John Carradine) has inopportunely turned up on the same boat, bearing Thorndike's passport which was found in the rowboat.

This is all introduction to the nightmare which starts in earnest in London. It is typical of Lang that the well-thought-out documentary detail which creates a sense of reality at the same time also carries a sinister threat. Danger lurks everywhere: the man with the cap who follows him at the port, the little stout man in a bowler, the taxi-driver, the gentleman with an umbrella, all of whom in turn take up the pursuit of Thorndike in the maze of Limehouse night streets. Here Lang brings in screens of mysterious and heavy fog. Walls loom out of the dense fog, as much shadowed as illuminated by feeble lamplight; all much more authentic, more threatening, and less romanticised than the London of Pabst's *Threepenny Opera*. Even such touches of local colour as the pearly king and his entourage who skip by to the accompaniment of a concertina emphasize the nightmare qualities of the dark. Even sound gives volume to the lingering menace as footsteps echo through the fog.

In the original script Thorndike meets Jerry (Joan Bennett) the little streetwalker on the sidewalk. Lang arranges their meeting in a doorway where Thorndike has fled from his pursuers. While it served slightly to obscure her profession for the benefit of the Legion of Decency, for Lang it was only important in providing him with a more dramatic effect. To prevent her from screaming, Thorndike has to clasp his hand over her mouth, later explaining that he is being followed. Slightly to lighten the mounting tension, there is a humorous scene in which Thorndike takes Jerry to visit his brother, whose formal wife, Lady Alice, pleads a headache in the face of Jerry's frank and easy behaviour. Thorndike teases:

Remember she thinks you are a lady. Surely you don't want to disillusion one so young and trusting . . .

Nichols and Lang make the idyll of Thorndike and Jerry subtle and touching, and Joan Bennett plays the little streetwalker with warmth and spontaneity. For Thorndike the affair is merely an amusing and fraternal interlude of companionship forced upon him by chance; when the two have to spend the night in the same room, she in her bed and he on the couch, the girl cries bitterly, because she believes she is being rejected as unworthy of the gentleman. With goodnatured insensitivity (he still has much to learn), Thorndike asks: 'What the devil are you sniffling about?'

(In order to satisfy the moral qualms of the Hays Office, the producers put a sewing machine into the girl's room in this scene, in the feeble hope that the streetwalker might pass for a seamstress. Needless to say, Lang took no notice of the object.)

Lang treats the relationship without sentimentality. For breakfast Jerry buys fish and chips in a newspaper, and Thorndike learns how to eat them with his hands. The girl is touched when he moves up a chair for her to sit on, as a gentlemanly matter-of-course. She reacts again as she had done the previous night when he kissed her hands in open gratitude as she gave him her last ten-shilling note from her stocking. Lang cuts to one of his rare close-ups to show her reaction, and to reveal how all the hardness and obstinacy which she has adopted as armour against the world have fallen away.

The only present Jerry will accept from him is a new hat pin for her tam-o'-shanter to replace the one she lost while running from Thorndike's pursuers. 'Every soldier needs a crest for his cap,' Thorndike says when she chooses a silver-plated arrow from the stock of the old junk and jewelry dealer who turns out to be a German. As he follows the couple with his eyes, the spectator asks himself, along with Thorndike, whether he, too, may not be a member of the Nazi gang.

The story threads are so tightly interwoven that the tension is maintained even in what seem minor or unimportant scenes. The formal 'Mr Jones' is feeding pigeons in front of the house where Thorndike calls to collect money and insure Jerry's future through his solicitor; and then releases a homing pigeon to report Thorndike's whereabouts.

Here follows a breathtaking hunt in the underground, with endless corridors and stairways (all built in the studio) – again demonstrating Lang's ability to mix reality with fantasy. (An equally thrilling variation can be found in *While the City Sleeps.*) The figures of Jones and Thorndike are only dimly seen as they stealthily move through the tunnels; the only noise is the drip of water from the slimy curved ceilings, as specified in the script. Jones holds a torch in one hand and an automatic in the other. Before he has a chance to raise his weapon, Thorndike springs on him. The flashlight goes out and their struggling bodies are only vaguely seen in the dark, with the nearby gleam of the third, live rail. As the ominous roar of the approaching train is heard, one of the figures throws off the other with a grunt. There is a scream, and a flash as a falling body

Man Hunt: Mr Jones (John Carradine) in the underground

Man Hunt: Jerry (Joan Bennett) and Thorndike

touches the live rail. Then the other figure – the spectator cannot make out who it is – leaps to safety as the train thunders by.

A newspaper placard cries: 'Murder in the Underground'; the dazed Jerry buys the paper to find out what Thorndike himself will read aloud a bit later:

Captain Thorndike's body was mangled beyond recognition by the train, but positive identification was made possible by his passport and billfold which he carried.

The tearful Jerry comes back to her room, only to find Thorndike sitting there waiting. She stares as if at a ghost: 'I thought – you was – dead.'

Forced into hiding from the police now as well as from his pursuers, and unable to take the girl with him, he scribbled a poste restante address far from London on a piece of torn newspaper. Their tender parting takes place on London Bridge; the scene has all the tenderness befitting the soft and gentle fog in which it is set. As

... the scene on the bridge

Thorndike wants to give Jerry her first kiss, she sees a policeman. To prevent his recognising Thorndike, the wanted man with the scar, the suspected 'underground murderer' of himself, she must draw attention to herself by playing the hard-boiled tart soliciting a customer. Ignoring Thorndike, the policeman leads her away:

No go Miss . . . you can't be pesterin' gentlemen this time of night . . . Sorry, Sir, if I were you I'd step along. Don't get mixed up with these 'ere girls.

This excellent scene was almost lost. Kenneth MacGowan had already resigned from the film because of Zanuck's interference. Zanuck now opposed the scene: it would, he argued, be tragic if a 'decent' girl had to play the whore in front of a man she loved: but it was not tragic if a whore acted as a whore in the same circumstances. No money was therefore allowed for the scene in the budget.

Lang was nonetheless determined to shoot it all the same. There were existing set materials – paving stones and sidewalks – left from previous studio street scenes. There was even one section of a bridge railing among the sets in storage, but a second one could not be found. Lang therefore paid forty dollars out of his own pocket to have another made. The unit manager, Ben Silvi, was unable to send Lang studio workers. Therefore, Lang and his cameraman shot the scene by themselves at 4 a.m. in the deserted studio. Cameraman Arthur Miller set up the camera, and Lang, instructed by him, hung light bulbs of varying size and strength to give an impression of a perspective line of lights stretching away into the useful London fog, which rendered a backdrop unnecessary. As with the hanging streets in *Metropolis* and the living letter of *Destiny*, Lang was never averse to engaging in the most practical aspects of production; I myself observed this at first hand during the shooting both of *Liliom* and the later *Hindu Tomb*. Zanuck, says Lang, was so impressed with the look of the finished scene that he ordered the set should be retained for a subsequent production. There was, of course, no set.

After the parting, Jerry returns to her room with a certainty that she will never again see Thorndike. Four strange figures are waiting for her in the darkness. She rushes out of the room into the arms of a waiting policeman whom she knows, only to realise that he, too, is part of the gang. Again, we do not see anything of violence or torture. Quive-Smith, who has reappeared, says suavely:

Sit down, girl. We're going to have a long conversation . . . Where have you been so late?

The scene fades out as Jerry gazes at her captors in terror – not for herself, but in her fear of what they may try to make her do to Thorndike.

Evidently the address on the newspaper fragment has been discovered, as Thorndike senses from the hesitation and evident fear of the post office clerk when he asks for his poste restante letters. Alarmed, he manages to make his way back to his cave hide-out, but finds himself barricaded in by Quive-Smith. When he again refuses to sign the confession, Jerry's tam-o'-shanter with the familiar hat-pin is pushed down the air-shaft. Thorndike asks what they have done to her.

Man Hunt: the improvised weapon

She refused to tell us anything . . .
The death of a girl like that can be no loss at all. The police reported
that she had jumped from a window . . .

Now realising in his pain, hatred, and self-discovery
that the affair has gone far beyond a sport, like hunting,
Thorndike agrees to sign the confession in order to gain
time, but asks to read it again first. He has been promised
free passage if he will sign, but outside the cave we can see
Quive-Smith holding his gun at the ready. Thorndike
improvises a crude cross-bow out of a bent tube, his belt, a
shaft, and Jerry's arrow-hatpin, and shoots Quive-Smith as
he comes to retrieve the confession at the air shaft. Before
he dies, Quive-Smith manages to wound Thorndike, who
crawls over to the now dead man, tears the confession
from his hand and destroys it.

The epilogue begins with a series of superimpositions,
scenes of the beginning of the war – R.A.F. attacks, the

German invasion ports – juxtaposed with images of Thorndike in hospital. As we see him recovered and parachuting from an aeroplane, the matter-of-fact voice of a commentator states:

And from now on somewhere within Germany is a man with a precision rifle and the high degree of intelligence and training that is required to use it. It may be days, months, or even years – but this time he clearly knows his purpose.

19 Hangmen Also Die (1943)

*The most remarkable
commentary on the war
produced by the American
cinema . . . Some critics have
seen in this film a melodrama,
forgetting that the melodrama
does not refer to the violence it
presents but to the intrusion of
an unmotivated and accidental
violence into a situation where
an intrinsic conflict does not
exist . . . Like the war itself,*
Hangmen Also Die *is
intrinsically dramatic . . . In*
Hangmen Also Die *freedom
and tyranny are concrete forces
seen in action, and this is
doubtlessly the first film that
ties up personal, collective and
social conflict . . . Lang's film
starts off an historical realism
in place of mystical
idealism . . . Lang's direction
elaborates with superior
artistry the given script, and
does it so well that the film
seems to be the work of a
unique and gigantic will.*
Joe Davidson: Hangmen
Also Die – But the People
Live *in* New Masses, *4 May
1953*

Lang now managed to get free of his Fox term contract. For some time the independent producer Arnold Pressburger, whom Lang knew from their European days in Berlin and Paris, had been asking Lang to make a film for him; but Lang had not liked any of the subjects suggested. Then one day he read in the newspapers that Heydrich, the hated 'Reichsprotektor' of Czechoslovakia had been assassinated. Lang spoke of this as an idea for a film to Bertolt Brecht, who had managed to reach the United States thanks to an affidavit by Lang and Lionel Feuchtwanger, and was a neighbour and frequent companion of Lang. The two of them set to work on a short synopsis which they offered to Pressburger.

Brecht had already tried half-heartedly to sell scripts in Hollywood to keep himself and his family alive; and had written,

Every morning, to earn my bread
I go to the market where lies are bought.
Hopefully
I queue up among the sellers.

This at least was a script that was not in need of lies.

In one of his infrequent mentions of the film in his diaries, Brecht speaks of listening to the roar of the sea in Santa Monica, while Lang was negotiating conditions with the producer. Lang had asked Brecht how much he expected to get for the finished script, and Brecht asked if he thought 3,000 dollars too much. Lang said he would try and get 5,000 dollars for him, but finally asked Pressburger 3,500 – which the producer thought too much in any case for an author who had never before written an American screenplay. Pressburger gave in when Lang said

he would work with no other author, because of Brecht's
unique grasp of the political situations involved; and it was
agreed that Brecht should be assisted by a German
speaking American writer. (Brecht, in his certainty that he
would return to Germany, refused to learn English;
though in 1938 he had published a translation of Shelley's
The Mask of Anarchy into powerful German verse.) John
Wexley, who had just had a success with a play about
capital punishment, *The Last Mile,* was selected as a writer
of sympathetic left-wing tendencies who also spoke good
German.

Lang would meet the two writers every three or four
days to discuss the script as far as it had gone, and after three
months a script of 280 pages (about twice the length of the
conventional script of the period) was completed. Lang
planned to make the necessary cuts in consultation with
Brecht and Wexley. Suddenly, however, Lang was told by
Pressburger that for unforseen financial reasons, shooting
would have to begin three weeks earlier than expected,
and that there were only eight days left to make the cuts.
Lang was thus obliged to make the cuts himself, in
collaboration with a young writer named Gunsburg,
reducing the manuscript to 192 pages. He remembers that
while there were extensive cuts in the hostage scenes, no
really vital scenes were sacrificed.

This then is the origin of the story of an estrangement
between Lang and Brecht over *Hangmen Also Die.* Lang, in
fact, never again saw Brecht after the hearing before the
Screen Writers' Guild, which was called to settle disputes
which had by this time arisen between the two writers.
Wexley had demanded more money for the script – 10,000
dollars – and had asked for sole screen credit. Unjustly, the
Guild decided that Wexley should be credited as sole
author, mainly on the grounds that the credit was more
valuable to Wexley who intended to go on working in the
States, than for Brecht, who would eventually return to
Germany. Brecht and the composer Hanns Eisler pro-
tested in vain against the decision. (As an irony of history,
however, it may be recorded that during the McCarthy
witch hunts Wexley was blacklisted in Hollywood
because, unlike Brecht, he was a member of the
Communist Party.)

It is hard to assess from the final shooting script what

was Brecht's contribution, but Lang attributes 90 per cent of it to him. The ideology expressed in the concentration camp sequences is characteristic Brecht, and the setting, too, was familiar enough to him. It seems unlikely that Wexley would have invented the strangely reticent and seemingly trivial conversation between Professor Novotny and the poet Nezval, or the understatement when Nezval goes to his execution:

... He didn't see why they always have to shoot people at sunrise! Why not at sunset? He said – it didn't make much sense . . .

How typical of the Brecht of the *Kalendergeschichten* are the professor's words to his daughter when he wants to prevent her telling him that she has seen the assassin of Heydrich:

Mascha: I'm sure I saw him . . .

Professor: You have not seen *anyone* . . . it's simply that in such matters one doesn't *talk*. Example: you tell it to A – A entrusts it to B – B confides in C – C deposes the secret to D. It's not very far from E to F – F breathes it to G . . . and G stands for Gestapo!

Even in translation the formulation and the sophistry are characteristically Brecht's. The introductory scenes, in which Heydrich appears in all his Nazi arrogance, his horsewhip elegance and hysterical style of speech, points to Brecht and Lang (who clearly would have made his usual considerable contribution to the script). Sentences like 'This sabotage that stinks to high heaven', 'drastic measures', 'I shall make life hell for these Czech scum and discipline these dregs of mankind in the Skoda works, that they will hear bells ringing in their ears' (Lang marked the last phrase with brackets and a question mark in the script) have the tones of Brecht's metallic voice. The irony of the toning down of the insults by an interpreter for the benefit of the Czechs who do not speak German also seems typical in its manner.

It is much more likely that Brecht and Lang, rather than Wexley, would have thought of the almost Expressionist chorus of voices which rises to a crescendo in the darkness of the cinema where the assassin Swoboda has sought refuge:

Heydrich . . . shot! The Reichsprotektor!
Heydrich . . . ! HEYDRICH ! !

Hangmen Also Die (1943): Swoboda (Brian Donlevy) hiding in a doorway

Applause breaks out on all sides, until the Nazi voice calls out 'Lights on! Stop the film!' (it is typical *Kulturfilm*, a sickly romantic travelogue of the 'Beautiful Rhine Valley') and puts an end to the protective darkness: The response to the angry query, 'Who started the applause' could only have been written by someone who knew the sardonic humour of pre-Hitler Berlin: '*The unknown soldier*'.

There is no reason why the building up of tension should not have been worked out by a writer of Wexley's political experience. The landlady cannot give a room to the assassin because she is 'under orders'. The cafe is closed down and the curfew is already on as Swoboda seeks refuge with Mascha and her family, whom he pretends he has seen at the symphony concert. But the subtle nuances of the conversations, the almost unnoticeable insistence on a specific situation – only the professor and Mascha out of the whole family know what it is about – is the sort of effect that appears again and again in scripts on which Lang has worked, as does the ingenious interweaving of events: Mascha discovers that the man who claims to be an architect must be a doctor because of the professional way he bandages her little brother when he cuts himself on the bread-knife, and because he mentions the chimes of a particular church just beside a hospital. These details, each almost imperceptible, but closely interlocking, push the action forward.

Swoboda, the assassin on account of whom 400 hostages (including Professor Novotny) are to be shot at ever more rapid intervals until the culprit is found, is not allowed to give himself up because of a decree by Dedic, the leader of the resistance. He is still needed and orders are orders: this is the inexorable logic of Brecht's *Jasager*. It is equally consistent that Mascha, indignant at Swoboda's behaviour and out of love for her father, intends to denounce Swoboda to the Gestapo.

The distancing, the 'alienation' of the types whose individual characters are brought out in a gesture or remark, without being analysed must be due to the Brecht-Lang collaboration. 'We didn't want', says Lang, quoted by Eibel,

Analyses of characters, we simply schematised into those who resist and those who organise, those who aspire to freedom but have not yet found or chosen the means of action (*cf. Mascha's fiancé Jan – L.H.E.*) and finally the collaborators, the genuine enemy of the people like Czaka . . .

I don't think it is possible in such a plot to go far into the psychological development because the psychology does not change.

For me psychology is not in the talking, it is in the action, in the movement, the gestures. In *Hangmen Also Die* there is a great deal of detail that makes the personalities come alive . . . It is the behaviourisms which create the character.

Lang instances the behaviour of Gruber, the Gestapo chief, when he discovers in the mirror, by comparison, that the lipstick imprint on Swoboda's face is too regular to be genuine, because the mark on his own face is only a smear. Gruber's recognition that Swoboda's rendezvous with Mascha was a fake, staged to cover up Dedic's presence, at once turns to action. Having incapacitated the obstinate Jan, he hurries to Swoboda's hospital to pressure him into giving information. It is the same kind of fast-moving action based on gestures, images and movement that was already familiar in Lang's German thrillers.

How, Lang asks, should the Nazi psychology be presented? By small touches and understatements – quite unlike the caricature and low comedy of Lubitsch's *To Be Or Not To Be* – corresponding to Lang's mentality and Brecht's concern with epic theatre.

Again as in *Manhunt* Lang is true to his principles of not showing violence for its own sake. As he had done with the sex murder in *M* he shows only the consequences and leaves the rest to the spectator's imagination. He shows neither the torture in the Gestapo headquarters, nor the Heydrich assassination. How very effective this can be is seen in Lang's use of the old rheumatic green-grocer woman who is forced to pick up part of the broken chair again and again. We sense from her haggard face and slow, tired movements what she has suffered; the consequences are here more horrifying than the torture itself, and the action has not been slowed by the inclusion of an unneeded torture scene.

Because the Gestapo men are not crudely portrayed as animals, they appear so much more dangerous. They are civil servants in the traditional Prussian mould, citizens doing their 'duty', who have suddenly acquired a power with which they cannot cope. They are the same people who were to tell the war crimes tribunals that they acted only on 'superior orders', small wheels in an immensely complex instrument of destruction. One of the Gestapo men endlessly and irritatingly cracks his knuckles during the interrogations, a detail Lang had remembered as a habit of one of his more hated schoolmasters. The hoarse-voiced man's continual picking of the pus-filled spots on his face is not in the script: it is pure Lang, a hint that he is probably syphilitic and maybe, with his indifference to women, homosexual too.

In Brecht's *Mann ist Mann* Galy Gay goes out to buy a fish. Mascha goes to queue for potatoes, but gets nothing but turnips. Like Galy Gay her mind is altered on the journey. Caught in the Gestapo web, she realises the import of her first intention of making a statement about the assassin. The Nazis for their part have realised that she can lead them to the man they are seeking.

The search of the Novotny house in Mascha's absence is shown in all its brutality, as part of a method. The interrogation of all the members of the household is shot

Hangmen Also Die: Swoboda and Mascha (Anna Lee) caught in the Gestapo
web (*above*); Gruber and Mascha's fiancé (*below*)

in quick dissolves, with each person answering the question put to his predecessor. The over-lap technique already practised in Lang's German sound films to push the action forward now has an extra purpose in expressing the nervous strain and attrition. Mosaic-fashion, the full picture of Gestapo methods is built up with strict economy, each nuance adding to the panorama of terror.

Gestapo Inspector Gruber is played by Alexander Granach as a kind of inverted Lohmann, a cynical, intelligent and unscupulous sleuth in his world of Czaka beer, schnapps and whores. For the character of the insolent and cowardly brewer, Emil Czaka – a quisling who infiltrates the resistance group in order to destroy it, Brecht wanted to cast Oscar Homolka. This, says Lang, was the source of his only difference with Brecht. Although he admired Homolka very much, his idea was that Nazi parts should be played by refugee actors while the Czechs should all be played by Americans. Thus only the Germans speak with foreign accents, which gives the events a properly three-dimensional atmosphere.

In the scenes of the hostages (which Brecht at one time wanted to expand to use as a separate film for distribution after the war) Lang's concern for documentary corresponds with Brecht's objectivity: we are always aware of a cool detachment, whether in individual characters or the people of Prague seen as a whole crowd, with individuals momentarily picked out. There is no overstatement or sentimentality in the 'Never Surrender' song, even in English pure Brecht, with its forceful musical accompaniment by Hanns Eisler;

Brother – the time has come!
Brother – work to be done!
Take hold of the invisible torch, and pass it on!
. . .
Maybe you will die, maybe you will not,
But never let them take you brother, if you
Shoot or you are shot . . .

The same Brechtian style informs Professor Novotny's 'Letter to my Son' which he asks Mascha to learn by heart after she has been called by Gruber to visit her father who is apparently on the point of being shot, in the hostage camp:

Those will be good days to live! It will be a land where all men and women and children will have enough good food to eat, time to read and to think – and to talk things over with one another, for their own good. When such great days do come, don't forget *Freedom* is not anything one possesses like – a hat or a piece of candy. *Real* freedom is *Fighting for Freedom*! And you must remember me – not because I've been your father, but because I died in this great fight . . .

It is credit to Lang's objective direction that the three pivots on which the plot turns seem plausible and historic realism, even though they are patently 'staged'. The first is where the Nazi's listen-in on the apparent love talk between Mascha and Swoboda (an anticipation of the post-Hitlerian *The Thousand Eyes of Dr Mabuse*). The Nazis hear, expectantly, Mascha's exclamation, 'You killed . . .', but are disappointed when she continues '. . . every feeling – I ever had for you'. They do not see that Swoboda has held up his prescription pad on which he has scribbled 'Microphone! Be careful!'

The second pivot is the staged rendezvous between Mascha and Swoboda in the latter's flat, to conceal the presence of the wounded Dedic, hidden only by a curtain from the Gestapo men. A spilt glass of red wine covers up the slowly dripping blood. The cunning Gruber has brought along Mascha's fiancé Jan, hoping that the apparent infidelity will irritate him into collaboration. In fact Jan's feelings throughout remain remarkably cool and without passion. Equally the authors are at pains not to allow any love element to enter the relationship of Mascha and Swoboda. It is their recognition that in times like these people's personal lives are secondary, their refusal to allow it to become a complicated affair of individual emotions, that lends a directness and authenticity to the film.

The third pivot, at which the film reaches a crescendo, all the threads of the action join up, is the killing of the traitor Czaka. The resistance group wants to know if Czaka is in fact the traitor who betrayed a group in Pilsen two years ago. Czaka, who claims not to speak German, gives himself away when he laughs at a Hitler joke told in German by the waiter, Rudi. Czaka is now finished off by the false evidence of a few individuals – a waiter, a cloakroom woman, the landlady, a cab driver who pretends to have driven Czaka after the murder of Heydrich, and his own servant. Thus the Gestapo is convinced that Czaka is a double agent and the assassin of Heydrich.

The most deadly factor in the case against Czaka is the absence of Gruber, who could have spoken for him. After trying to interrogate Jan in a cabaret, he lies snoring in a pile of beer bottles in Jan's flat, sleeping it off. Waking, he dashes to the hospital because, alerted by Jan's laughter, he realises that the lipstick stains were faked, and also that the fact that doctors wear masks when operating invalidates Swoboda's claim that at the time of the murder he was performing surgery.

In the hospital there is a climactic battle. Gruber holds Swoboda and the doctor who stood-in for him on the day of the assassination in the operating room in check with his revolver while trying to ring the Gestapo headquarters. Suddenly Jan leaps at him from behind. This time Lang deliberately shows violence. Gruber is suffocated on the table with sheets. His hands fall; his dangling legs go rigid. To keep the spectator in the grip of dramatic tension, aware that Gruber might still destroy 'the conspiracy of the people of Prague', there are constant flashback cutaways to people giving evidence to Gruber. The tension is relaxed with the certainty of his death. His round hat slowly rolls forward on the floor. This touch was not in the script: Lang remembered the ball of the murdered child in *M*.

The cutaways to people giving evidence against Czaka is shot very differently from the blow by blow affair of the interrogation of the Novotnys. Here the rhythm is deliberately slow, in order to interweave a parallel action and to contrast with the rapidity of the Gruber sequence. Into these two parallel strands a scene from the hostage camp is effectively cut in. So the spectator is thrown into new suspense as to whether the conviction of Czaka will in fact halt the killing of the hostages. Some copies of the film circulating in France do not, in fact, show the death of Novotny and the remaining hostages; but in the original version of the film the fact of the shooting of the professor was shown, followed by the flower-decked graves of the hostages, to indicate that the Nazis in fact broke their promise after the (apparent) surrender of the assassin. In the French copies, we see the town of Prague as we hear Lang's summing-up, Brecht's song:

Maybe you will die, maybe you will not,

But never let them take you brother, if you shoot
Or you are shot

The end title is prophetic – the war was still on:

NOT
The End

Thus the film does not show the ultimate victory of resistance, it only promises the continuation of resistance. There will be new ranks of fighters 'to take the invisible torch and pass it along'. The pass-word is 'Never Surrender'. It was to remain relevant to Czechoslovakia's tragic history.

What really mattered to Lang in this film was the force of facts. Inevitably there are characteristic pictorial images – the precise instinct for composition; Mascha's reflection in a puddle during the getaway, or again when she has been arrested and the railings cast parallel stripes of shadow, as if inexorably crushing her; the giant shadows which overcast Novotny's interrogation. Yet for the most part Lang is not interested in effects of mood and atmosphere and chiaroscuro as in *Man Hunt* or *The Ministry of Fear*; he concentrated clearly and precisely on the facts; the political events are shown in all their variety, without decorative effect. However, beyond the political facts, one must not lose sight of certain moral ironies and ambiguities which mark every Lang film. While Lang's sympathies are fully with the people of Prague, he shows them turning into something akin to the mob in *Fury* when they discover Mascha is asking directions to Gestapo headquarters. The ironies of a conviction through false and circumstantial evidence against Czaka are not lost on the director who had already made *Fury* and would later make *Beyond a Reasonable Doubt*.

APPENDIX: BRECHT ON *HANGMEN ALSO DIE*

Brecht's recently published work diaries (Suhrkamp Verlag, Frankfurt u. Main, 1973) throw some light on his collaboration with Lang and with Wexley on *Hangmen Also Die* during 1942–3. The diaries are almost daily notes, written in his characteristic handwriting, without any capitals, and perhaps not intended for publication. (Lang and Marta Feuchtwanger, widow of Lionel Feuchtwanger, both believe that they have been polished up by some other hand for publication). If Brecht seems particularly hard on Lang, we must take into account his natural irritability due to external circumstances. The notes reveal that he lived a very precarious existence in a narrow, petit bourgeois room (the sickly pink doors got on his nerves especially), supported by other people. Wexley – whose role in the entire affair seems ambiguous – told Wolfgang Garsch (recorded in 'Der Fall *Hangmen Also Die*', in *Kino und Fernseh-Almanach*, Berlin 1972) that Brecht could not get used to the ideological methods for which this moment in history called, nor to the general commercial outlook on life which he found in America.

Whilst not by any means a conservative and though full of sympathy for the Left, Lang's position could not be regarded as very left-wing, according to the view of the Communist Wexley. There were heated discussions between Brecht and Lang in which he, Wexley, tried to mediate: otherwise the film might never have passed beyond the preliminary stages. Brecht, for his part, knew little about films.

Wexley says that the work was conducted with a daily three- of four-hour conference, sometimes at Brecht's house, in Santa Monica, sometimes at Lang's but mostly in the studio. Then Brecht would go away and Wexley would write down the agreed text as a draft. Many such conferences were held without Brecht, who was more interested in the design of the plot than in the film to be shown on the screen.

Brecht's irritation that – for the very practical reasons already explained – Lang could not accept his suggestion that Oscar Homolka should play Czaka, was aggravated when (for the same reasons) Lang would not give Brecht's wife Helene Weigel the part of the green-grocer which Brecht had designed for her. On 24 November 1942 Brecht complains that he has expressly made it a part without words, while Wexley (and this is the first time we sense resentment against Wexley's behaviour) had 'scribbled' superfluous dialogue into the role. Lang had held a superficial sound audition with Weigel, but the proper screen test that Weigel had expected and prepared for never took place, and another, American actress was chosen for the part.

At first everything had seemed to go well. On 8 May 1942 Brecht notes that he had discussed with Lang on the beach a hostage story in connection with Heydrich's murder in Prague. On 5 July he writes that during lunch at Lang's they discussed a film version of his theatre sketches *Fear and Misery of the Third Reich*. He also attempted a story with Lang about Prague, the Gestapo and the hostages, *Silent City*; 'but all this is Monte Carlo' (i.e. a gamble). On 27 June however it seemed that the story looked more promising: Lang had even talked about it to a producer. Brecht added a touching personal note: 'How I hate these small heat waves which get hold of one when there is the prospect of money: secure working time, a better flat, music lessons for Steff (*his son*) and no more accepting of charity.'

On 29 June he writes interestingly about his work with Lang. At this time he was working with Lang on the hostage story from nine in the morning till seven at night. An interesting term recurs when they came to the discussion of the logic of an incident: Lang's test was 'The audience will accept that'. It emerges at this point that the incident of the wounded resistance leader hiding behind the curtain was Lang's, worked out by the test of audience acceptance.

Brecht remarks that Lang was 'buying gags' such as corpses of criminal inspectors falling out of wardrobes, or secret gatherings of people under the Nazi terror. 'It is interesting, too, how he is much more interested in surprises than in tension.' Evidently the scene in which Czaka makes himself suspicious in the eyes of the resistance group was not in Brecht's plan.

In an entry for 5 July Brecht writes that while he dictates the story to his secretary, Lang has to negotiate with financiers. Astronomical figures and agonising cries can be heard above as if from a propaganda film: '30,000 dollars minus 8 per cent' – 'I can't do it!' Brecht moves with the secretary into the garden . . . 'Gunshots from across the sea!'

By 27 July Brecht is complaining that the hostage film is a 'sad confabulation' with its phantoms, intrigues and falsities. It belonged strictly to the context of a bourgeois and middle-class rebellion. It was now a question of casting, and he had been looking at a book of actors' photographs – faces from the company of the Ulm municipal theatre.

Wexley is mentioned for the first time on 5 August. Brecht is now working in a hot United Artists office in Las Palmas Street, Hollywood, together with secretaries and this American writer who was considered very left and very decent and was being paid 1,500 dollars a week. Their method was for Brecht to go over a scene with Wexley who then dictated to a secretary. The first incident arises when Brecht asks for one of the four copies that have been made, and Wexley only hands it over after some childish excuses. The copy is headed with John Wexley's name. When Brecht retained the copy with his own hand-written corrections and additions, there was frantic telephoning that Wexley could not continue working unless he had it back. 'It appears', remarks Brecht wryly, 'that such tricks are well paid.'

By 14 September, however, relations seemed to have improved. Work was progressing better. Brecht was discussing the transpositions of the outlines into a finished script with Wexley rather than with Lang, and writes that this enables him to correct Wexley's work at the same time. Above all he had persuaded Wexley to cooperate in the writing of an 'Ideal Script' in his own house, which would be shown to Lang on completion. Inevitably Brecht put most of the emphasis on the crowd scenes, and indeed would have liked to call the film *Trust the People.* (The first title given to the film was *No Surrender* or *Never Surrender,* but before shooting was concluded a book of a similar title appeared. Hence Lang and Pressburger organised a competition in the studio to find a new title, and a secretary won the prize of 100 dollars for *Hangmen Also Die.)*

On 5 October, Brecht notes, he hears that Wexley has asked for and received a bonus for evening and Sunday work. Lang has advised him to ask for the same bonus, which he also receives after a lot of trouble. Wexley seems to have remained fairly conciliatory, but Lang with his technical experience and knowledge of script writing, as well as his awareness of the behaviour of producers when trying to get them to accept a script, takes a different position. Lang now wants them to write the outline treatment in the evenings and keep the revising (Brecht calls it 'polishing') for later. In fact Wexley is no longer cooperating on the 'Ideal Script', of which only 70 pages have been completed.

On 16 October 1942 Brecht writes that he and Wexley are still working to the best of their knowledge on the script of *Trust the People*, but that Wexley has told him that Lang dragged him into his office, locked the doors and yelled at him that he was shooting a Hollywood picture, and to hell with crowd scenes (one gets the feeling that Wexley understood how to keep the quarrel alive). Brecht, who a few months earlier had talked about the 'heat waves' which the mention of money produces in people and wrote 'only he who lives in riches . . .' now speaks bitterly about Lang, mentions '70,000 dollars or thereabouts,' talks of dictatorial attitudes behind the boss's desk, of keeping an eye on the box office and so on.

On 12 October Brecht notes down that he would publish some scenes from the screenplay of *Trust the People*, if he could continue with his 'experiments' – for instance the first scene just before the assassination, in which Heydrich shows a Czech industrialist some leaflets found in munitions factories, using the symbol of a tortoise, and urging Czech workers to slow down. Thus a modern tyrant was shown intelligently; the German terror was an impersonal thing in response to the sabotage of production, just as the assassination is an impersonal riposte to terror. Brecht also refers to a few hostage scenes, which showed the class differences still surviving in the camp. Minutes before being taken for execution, the hostages were still throwing anti-semitic insults at each other and so on. The construction he intended for the film was epic, with three interwoven stories: of an assassin, of a girl whose father is taken as a hostage; and the story of a quisling who is brought to summary justice by the town as a whole. From this we can assess to what extent the bite of the script was due to Brecht, and understand that Lang could not accept the too abstract epic elements, nor, perhaps, the anti-semitic incidents, at least if the hostage scenes were to have a positive effect for his audience.

Other entries for 19 and 22 October indicate Brecht's

dissatisfaction with what he saw as commercial compromises: he left it to others 'to find slick lines for the transition from nothing to nothing', states that he does not like the surprises and tensions which make the impossible happen and keep the audience in the dark, characters that are distorted into stereotypes.

On 2 November Brecht records that Eisler brought Wexley along – 'a living picture of a guilty conscience'. Having heard nothing for two weeks he had been telephoned by a secretary who informed him that shooting had begun and that he was 'invited, more than invited!'

In the studio, the first scene Lang shot was one that Brecht and Wexley had cut, in which the heroine – played by an anodyne British actress – is quarrelling with her aunt about the décolleté of her bridal nightgown. Lang he says, had waved to him with affected naturalness; tomorrow he would get the manuscript.

On 4 November 1942 Brecht writes that Wexley, for two weekly cheques of 30,000 dollars, had demolished everything he had built up in ten weeks; and everything that he, Brecht, had thrown out was now back in again. In the studio Brecht watches the shooting of a scene in which the assassin, having walked about aimlessly for hours, comes to seek refuge in the flat of the historian. (Since he does not criticise the scene he probably wrote it.) The studio hairdressers rush at the assassin to prepare him for the shot, and in this commonplace production procedure, Brecht detects the same 'Hollywood glamorisation' happening to everyone and everything.

On 15 November he writes that he occasionally goes to the studio. When Lang directs a fight between a Gestapo commissar and Jan, the result is almost art, he notes. The work has the dignity and respectability of a craft. He would rather have seen the fight, however, in a scene where the kitchen staff of a restaurant prevent the Gestapo from arresting members of a resistance cell.

On 13 December Brecht writes down the words of a song which Eisler's music made the theme song of the film *Trust the People.*

On 17 December Brecht complains that Lang had used a highly-paid hit parade writer to translate the song, and had paid 500 dollars for a travesty. Lang is now combining this version with some lines by Wexley, and the flag which was handed on has become an invisible torch. Brecht's remarks that invisible bulbs were not particularly clear were ignored. The song is now supposed to have been written by a worker in the hostage camp, and who reads it to a famous poet, who ponders for a moment whether he should correct an expression like 'invisible torch', but then leaves it as an adequate and noble document. Brecht remarks that instead of casting the poet as a fat drunkard in the type of Diktonius (a writer whom Brecht had met in Finland), Lang had chosen a man in the mould of Ganghofer (a third-rate Bavarian popular writer, popularly known as Hofgänger on account of his notorious loyalty to the Emperor), genial and vain and delighted with the phrase 'invisible torch'. So the worker is expressing himself in the cliché images the bourgeoisie had outgrown; and the bourgeoisie accepted them back from him with emotion.

By 20 January Brecht is declaring that the sight of the intellectual deformation makes him physically sick. He has had to telephone the Screen Writers' Guild because Lang and Pressburger do not want to credit him for his work on the screenplay (compare Lang's assertion that this was Wexley's doing, not his and that it was on his advice that Brecht sought the help of the Guild). Wexley himself was now sitting in the conference room of the Screen Writers' Guild, armed with half a hundredweight of manuscripts, and maintaining that he had hardly ever spoken to Brecht.

There is no doubt that the screen credit on this film would have helped Brecht to find work in films at a time when he was desperately hard-up.

Brecht's last reference to the film comes on 24 June 1943. There are always compensations: Lang's film – now called *Hangmen Also Die* – had helped him write three plays: *Die Gesischte der Simone Machard, Die Herzogin von Malfi* and *Schweyk*.

LANG'S COUNTER STATEMENTS
A journalist who had had the opportunity to see Brecht's working diaries before publication, asked Lang for his comments on the foregoing. The gist of his reply was:
(a) To reiterate his emphatic reasons for using American actors for Czech characters and European actors for the Nazi roles, in order to demonstrate more vividly to

American audiences what an occupation was like.

(b) He felt no need to make a screen test with Helene Weigel since he had used her in small parts in films (e.g. *Metropolis*) even before her marriage to Brecht.

(c) Lang speaks of Brecht's plan for the elaboration of the hostage scenes into a 'documentary' film to be used after the war, and says that he approved the idea.

(d) He reiterates that the reason for an estrangement was that he, Lang was obliged to cut the script at short notice, when Pressburger announced that for unforeseen financial reasons the shooting would have to be brought forward by three weeks. It was no longer possible to do the work with Wexley and Brecht as planned within the time available, eight days; and Lang had been obliged to cut the script with difficulty from 280 pages to a manageable 192, with the help of a young writer called Gunsburg. The cuts had involved the hostage scenes, so that the main action could be left intact.

(e) According to Lang there was never any differences of opinion over the content of the film, since he and Brecht had drawn up the main outlines together.

(f) At the time Lang had not foreseen any likelihood of differences between Brecht and Wexley, or that Wexley would claim sole authorship for himself. This was patently absurd because of the typically Brechtian quality of many of the scenes. So it was natural for Lang to defend Brecht's claim before the arbitration court of the Screen Writers' Guild, as did Hanns Eisler who had advised Lang on the resistance scenes, as well as providing the music for the 'Never Surrender' song. Lang in fact yielded his own rights as author of the idea and original story in order to allow the credit to go to Brecht after the irreversible verdict in favour of Wexley.

(g) The reason why the film could not be called *Never Surrender* was that a book of this title had been published during the period of shooting.

20 Ministry of Fear (1943)

The Lang structure has never been so elaborate, particularly in The Ministry of Fear, *the world of which is built up with hardly any help from lighting or decor effects, just like the world of Kafka . . . The spectator identifies completely with the principal character, and undergoes with him all the evil surprises, all the traps that are set.*
Luc Moullet: *Fritz Lang* (1963)

Lang seems rejuvenated. In fact he is merely true to himself: more than twenty years later, The Thousand Eyes of Dr Mabuse *will be in much the same style, the style of* The Spiders . . . *we are full speed ahead for action. This is the cinema conceived from the image, detailed, nervous.*
Francis Courtade: *Fritz Lang* (1963)

This is a film for which Lang says he had not much feeling, though he liked Graham Greene's original novel, and eagerly accepted when his agent called him in New York to tell him of Paramount's offer of the film. Normally Lang himself negotiated with the producers, but in this case his agent drew up the contract, and neglected Lang's habitual clause retaining his right to make such changes in the script as he considered necessary. The producer and writer, Seton I. Miller, a former saxophonist and bandsman, was resistant to the changes proposed by the director.

Despite this, and his lack of enthusiasm for the cast (he had suggested Tonio Selwart, who had been admirable as a Gestapo official in *Hangmen Also Die* for the role of Willy Hilfe), Lang managed to make the film his own, full of menace and mystery. It is, of course, a thriller, a definite part of the *film noir* tradition, full of typical Langian concerns: the ambiguity of guilt, a breaking through a moral trap towards redemption and redefinition of identity, a realistic nightmare where seemingly secure certainties give way suddenly. It is also something more than this: Lang wanted to make another anti-Nazi statement; and his realist fantasy is used to good effect. The film has the ring of truth: even such a character as Dr Forrester, who has published a book on Nazi psychology was in no way fantastic, as later events and the discovery that certain prominent persons had been spies during the war, were to prove.

The film starts on a dark evening in England somewhere about 6 p.m. The film opens with no other sound but the ticking of a clock in the silence. The image fades in: all that is seen in the shadow is the old carved

Ministry of Fear (1943): the waiting

black clock case with a pendulum that seems to swing backwards and forwards too slowly. Then the camera draws back to reveal a room sombre in twilight, and a young man sitting staring silently in a chair, as if waiting.

The door opens and a shaft of light from the brilliantly lit hall outside cuts across the dimness of the room. The person who enters tells the young man that he is now free, and leads him to a gate that is heavily barred. A remark that the young man should keep away from the police now, and his reply that he will lead a quiet life at first suggests that this is a prison; but as he passes along the gloomy walls a large sign tells us that this is LEMBRIDGE ASYLUM. Everything is uncertain: in the dark night we are prepared for the nightmare to begin in an atmosphere made even more tense by our ignorance of what the young man has done. Nor will that particular part of the mystery be cleared up until much later in the film, thus keeping the moral equilibration of events to come always a bit askew.

At the deserted war-time station the young man, Stephen Neale (Ray Milland) is told that the train will be another hour late. Hence he is drawn by the distant sound of fairground music to where a group of charitable middle-class ladies in print dresses and silly hats are struggling to make a success of their 'Mothers of Free Nations' charity bazaar. Neale guesses the weight of a prize cake ('made with real eggs' – a rarity in those days of rationing) and is drawn into the clairvoyante's booth. In the dark tent the clairvoyante, Mrs Bellane, absurd in her turban and jewels, reads his palm with her flashlight. When she tells him that he has made a woman very happy, he sharply draws his hand away and says that they should leave the past to itself. Mrs Bellane explains that it is illegal to talk about the future, but reveals to him one thing: the weight of the cake.

Urged by Mrs Bellane, Neale wins the cake, among the congratulations and laughter of the apparently harmless charitable ladies, though a few of the bystanders seem unaccountably startled. As Neale sets off with his cake for the station, a well-dressed man (Dan Duryea) gets out of a taxi. Suddenly everyone pursues Neale, telling him that it was a mistake: the newcomer, who has just come from the clairvoyante's tent, has guessed the weight of the cake more correctly. Neale however stubbornly insists on his prize.

As Neale waits in his darkened train compartment, a strange, staccato tapping noise is heard in the mist of smoke billowing from the engine. It is revealed to be the stick of a blind man, who enters the compartment. Neale kindly offers him a piece of cake for the journey, but as he is bending over to cut it, the spectator realises with shock that the blind man is *looking* with eager curiosity at the cake. Neale, too, is startled when the man instead of eating his cake crumbles it as if looking for something. The train stops on account of an air raid; the blind man hits Neale over the head with his stick and rushes off into the darkness with the cake. Recovering, Neale starts off in pursuit. In the fog the blind man shoots aimlessly at him, until the sudden explosion of a bomb leaves nothing of the mysterious man but a fragment of his revolver. All this is done with the utmost economy; using his effects of light and fog, Lang only gives us the bare facts we need.

Ministry of Fear: the clairvoyant

On a murky London evening Neale visits the seedy
office of a private detective – one of Lang's comic
characters. Surprised taking a swig from his brandy bottle,
he indignantly reproaches that an appointment is necessary, but anxiously drags Neale back when money is
mentioned. Together the two of them go to the offices of
the 'Mothers of Free Nations', where everything seems
innocent and normal, and they meet two Austrian
refugees, brother and sister, Willy and Carla.

They follow the trail to the address of Mrs Bellane, who
turns out to be a handsome, elegant woman not in the least
resembling the stout and overdressed clairvoyante at
Lembridge Fair. Now Neale is involved in a seance as
effectively orchestrated as a scene from the Mabuse films.
The circle of people around the table is mysteriously
illuminated by a central light as the camera pans from one
to the other. Among them is the elegant Mr Costa – the
man in the taxi at the fair. A whispering sound grows

clearer: the medium's spirit guide speaks to Stephen about poison, and about the clock with its loud ticking. His nerves give way, he pulls his hands from the circle and leaps up just as a shot rings out. Mr Costa lies on the ground. Another of the guests, Dr Forrester, says that no doctor is needed now; only the police; and a hysterical old lady points accusingly at Neale as the killer.

The atmosphere has been built up with masterly use of image, sound, lighting, accumulation of detail – all logical, laconic and nerve-racking.

Aided by the kindly Willy, Neale makes his escape and returns to the office of the detective, Rennit, The door creaks ominously as he enters the dark room. The place has been ransacked, and Rennit is nowhere to be seen. In the street outside a sinister dark figure stands calmly cleaning his nails with a file.

Now on the run, Neale meets the young Austrian refugee, Carla (Marjorie Reynolds) who is to take him to a safe place of concealment. The meeting takes place in an air-raid which Lang documents with care – pyjama-clad people dragging their bedding and needless belongings to the tube station shelters. Here Neale reveals to Carla what preys upon his mind. His incurably ill wife asked him to get her poison to end her sufferings. He bought the poison, and though he would not give it to her, she found the hiding place and took it. For a whole night he held her hand, watching the clock and its slowly swinging pendulum, until her torment ended and a happy smile crossed her face . . .

The mysterious man with the nail file appears, but, seeming not to notice Neale who covers his face with his hat – takes the first morning train. As it passes through the station, its lights flicker over the hunched figures lying on the station.

Hidden by a German bookseller, Neale discovers Forrester's book on Nazi psychology, and realises that this was the man at the seance. The bookseller asks Carla and Neale to deliver a suitcase of books to the same Dr Forrester, emphasising that they should bring back the case ('leather is so rare these days'). Arriving at the address given they discover only a deserted flat occupied, says the porter by a Mr Travers. Mystified, Neale opens the case cautiously; smoke fills the room, and Neale is only just in

243

Ministry of Fear: Travers (Dan Duryea) and Neale (Ray Milland)

time to pull Carla to safety before the bomb inside explodes.

When he comes round he is in bed, watched over by the man with the nail file. He is not, as the spectator fears along with Neale, a Nazi, but a Scotland Yard detective, who accuses Neale of the murder not of Costa, but of Rennit the detective, who has been found with his head smashed. Neale's whole story is met with disbelief until the site of the munitions factory where the 'blind' man died is searched. The fragments of cake scattered around reveal nothing, until two quarrelling birds lead Neale to a wall onto which a piece of cake containing a reel of microfilm has been thrown.

The trail of the vanished Dr Forrester leads them to his tailor, Travers, who turns out to be none other than Mr Costa, still very much alive and brandishing a huge pair of scissors, menacingly. The scene reveals Lang at his most virtuoso. Travers uses his scissors to dial one number after

244

... the discovery of the body

another on the phone, in order to inform an unknown customer that his suit is going to be delivered and that while the shoulders seem to be fitting well they should be carefully checked all the time gesticulating threateningly with the scissors – leading both Neale and the spectator to believe he is about to attack. Then he suddenly dashes away, bolting himself in his private office. When the inspector and Neale break down the glass door, he has killed himself with the scissors. Neale dials the telephone number which Travers had called, and the voice that answers is Carla's. Once again a certainty dissolves, and the spectator, like Neale, begins to suspect Carla.

A delivery man arrives and reveals the address of Travers' customer. Neale rushes there by taxi, observed, as the spectator realises, by Dr Forrester who has been waiting in his car. The door is opened by Carla's brother Willy who, Carla reveals she has just learned, belongs to the Nazi gang and intends to shoot both her and Neale. In the fight that ensues, Neale tries to snatch Willy's revolver, but Carla gets it and threatens her brother. Neale forces Willy to remove his jacket and starts to examine the shoulder padding. Willy snatches it back and dashes off shouting to Carla, 'You won't shoot your own brother!'. Carla shoots through the door, and then opens it to find Willy dead on the ground. This shot was particularly difficult. Lang had to make the hole cut by the bullet visible at exactly the right angle. It took $1\frac{1}{2}$ hours to set up. Then, because of union rules, Lang was not allowed to drill the hole himself, nor let any of the crew do it. The entire door had to be sent to the studio joinery, while the entire cast and crew waited for the hole to be drilled and the door returned to its position.

Neale now finds in the shoulder padding of the dead man's jacket a further piece of microfilm which should correspond to that portion from the cake. Carla and Neale rush for the lift, just as someone else is ascending in it. Footsteps are mounting the stairs also. Desperately the couple, shot from above, escape onto the roof. The police arrive just as Dr Forrester emerges menacingly . . .

The epilogue shows Neale and Carla on their honeymoon, driving through clear sunshine; the darkness and nightmare have been dispelled. And yet, Carla mentions their wedding without wedding cake, and Neale says with a shudder: 'Cake? No, no cake!'

I have described the content of the film at length to show how in a film reckoned as one of Lang's minor works, taken from a Graham Greene novel and scripted by a different author, an adventure story has become a typical Lang film – directly in the line of *Mabuse* and *Spies* with its seamless functioning action, its strict logic, an atmosphere which combines fantasy and documentary realism, its ability to control a multiplicity of incident – in short the work of a perfectionist who makes each film he works on his own.

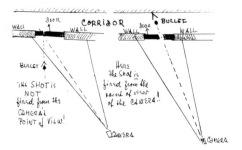

21   The Woman in the Window (1944)

Within the apparent structure of a police film, overlaying an insupportable anxiety, Fritz Lang allows himself an inquisitive walk into the subconscious of a professor who is convinced of the infallibility of his theories. He believes that all the confused images, symbols and mad dreams can be made lucid, thinks he has the key to all our mysteries, and finds himself one day unwittingly trapped by the fascination exerted over him by the portrait of a beautiful woman. This face, which works with the help of phantom images, is the starting point of an infernal adventure, which is lived as intensely as if it had really happened. And this revelation, which was so much criticized at the time the film appeared, makes us understand that the whole thing was only a dream, suddenly elucidates two meanings with equal passion: the knowledge that nothing is protection against the internal demons, and that so-called human wisdom, ripening with age, is only deception, a kind of social convention.
Henry Chapier, *Combat*,
22 April 1972

'When I made *Woman in the Window*,' wrote Lang in his article 'Happily Ever After' (*Penguin Film Review*, No. 5, 1948):

I was chided by critics for ending it as a dream. I was not always objective about my own work, but in this case my choice was conscious. If I had continued the story to its logical conclusion, a man would have been caught and executed for committing a murder because he was one moment off guard. Even were he not convicted of the crime, his life would have been ruined. I rejected this logical ending because it seemed to me a defeatist ending, a tragedy for nothing, brought about by an implacable Fate – a negative ending to a problem which is not universal, a futile dreariness which an audience would reject. *Woman in the Window* enjoyed a considerable success, and while it may be hindsight on my part, I think that with another ending its success would have been less.

This statement characterises the development Lang had undergone in the United States. He is no longer working strictly within the formula of 'man trapped by fate' of his early scripts and German films.

The origin of the script, I. H. Wallis's novel *Once Off Guard* has a tragic ending. Lang's decision to give it a happy ending was not a concession to the box office (both the producer and the writer, Nunnally Johnson, at first opposed the idea), but in accordance with his own feelings. The professor, after all, is not Chris Cross of *Scarlet Street* or the similar figure in the Georg Kaiser play *Von Morgen bis Mitternacht*. Those critics who have insisted that *Scarlet Street* is some sort of remake of *Woman in the Window* with a tragic ending have failed to see the very real differences between the two in terms of character, motivation, and action; perhaps they have simply been deceived by similarities of casting and theme. From the very start *Woman in the Window* was intended as a nightmare, based on the notion of 'assuming that . . .' Why should a good family man have to end his life in suicide because of a wish-dream? He does not even visit a night club, his only excess being an extra drink or two at his club.

At the very beginning, Lang provides the clues to all that will follow (or, in truth, *not* follow). The professor remarks with a smile to his friends, the doctor and the district attorney, in their club that he would not visit a burlesque show, although

If one of the young ladies wishes to come over here and perform I'll be only too happy to watch . . . But if it means leaving this chair . . . (He shakes his head).

So the professor of psychology and expert on criminology will have been shaken out of the smug certainty of his his arm chair. The temptations of the subconscious are chimaeras ironically dreamed up by a man who considers himself an expert on matters of the mind. By the end he will have been shaken out of the snug certainty of his theories, about which we have seen him lecturing to his students at the beginning of the film. And afterwards, back in the lap of his respectable family, he may well occasionally experience a longing for, or a fear of, those dangerous forces within him which were the source of his dream. Thus, while the ending is a happy one in a certain sense, it is ultimately an ambiguous one.

The adventure begins when the professor (Edward G. Robinson, clearly responding to the chance to play an intellectual as a change from gangster roles) pauses to look at a picture of a beautiful woman in the window of an art gallery. The two friends who are accompanying him to the club tease him for his faraway thoughts; she is their 'dream girl' too. In the club the three ageing men discuss the proposition that 'Life ends at forty' – which surely is a bit early. Nonetheless, the professor insists that:

That sort of shenanigan is out for us. To me it is the end of the brightness of life, the end of the spirit of adventure.

The District Attorney answers that there is still the *demon de midi* which can ruin ageing men. Thus, the premises have been stated.

Two drinks more than usual and a few moments spent reading Solomon's 'Song of Songs' – the quintessential love poem – and the professor is asleep. Woken, a bit

. . . the adventure has been described with an assiduous deliberation that gives it an almost dreamlike quality: everything seems real yet surely it cannot be. But the sleeper is not to waken and nightmarish sequels . . . arrive with the same, inexorable, ominously charged momentum. It is only with the entrance of the blackmailer that his momentum begins to slacken; the sense of accumulating fatality is not matched by a gathering intensity of rhythm, the inevitable begins to hover on the edge of the obvious. Yet this was perhaps Lang's intention, for knowing the trap is bound to close, one is still fascinated to learn exactly how and when.
Gavin Lambert, 'Fritz Lang's America', *Sight and Sound*, Autumn 1953

The next significant film I made was again directed by Fritz Lang: Woman in the Window *with Edward G. Robinson. Its success equalled that of* Man Hunt, *and ours seemed a most fortuitous working relationship.*
Joan Bennett; *The Bennett Playbill*, by Lois Kibbee, 1970

Woman in the Window (1944): the meeting

dazed, by the club waiter, the professor stumbles into the dark street. Gazing once more at the portrait, he sees reflected in the glass window – almost like a momentary hallucination – the real-life original, the double, of the face in the picture. They talk; she explains that when she is feeling lonely she goes to the window to watch the reactions of passers-by. In a bar, the woman (Joan Bennett) asks if he would care to see the sketches for the portrait back at her apartment. 'I'm not married. I have no designs on you,' she reassures him. The elegantly dressed and obviously sophisticated woman is no cheap call-girl. In her refined speech and her glittering dress she is difficult to place socially, and Lang thus introduces an unresolved ambiguity.

The professor's demurrance is token ('I don't think I should. I was warned against the siren call of adventure.'). Characteristically, Lang moves the action ahead by ellipsis. A dissolve, and the professor is helping the woman from a taxi and entering her apartment. Another dissolve, and the portfolio of sketches has been moved from the coffee table where the professor studied it; he is about to open a bottle of champagne. The cork breaks and the woman brings a pair of scissors to get it out. The conditions and the tools for the coming action are now established.

For the initial street scene Lang made a note in the script: 'No Rain'. As a new taxi drives up outside the apartment building, rain is pouring down. It is the kind of rain that produces an unnerving insecurity and hints at potential catastrophe. Horror and brutality are about to invade the cool, civilized interior of the luxury apartment. We are also about to learn more about the rather detached woman who lives there among her countless reflections in the many mirrors lining the walls. (Lang's characterisation of the woman is expertly done; later when she phones the professor, for example, there is a mirror placed over her bed, so that décor, as Lang has always insisted, leads the spectator to discoveries about the people who inhabit them.)

The man who gets out of the taxi enters the apartment with his own key. Rushing into the room he slaps the woman and throws himself upon the professor. Nearly strangled, the professor reaches out and grabs at the scissors offered by the woman and blindly plunges them again and again into the back of his assailant.

The man is dead. The professor's first reaction is to phone the police; a homicide in self-defence is, after all, justifiable. His reasons for replacing the phone after the operator's repeated 'Hello' is clear enough without the sequence in the script which Lang quite rightly cut:

Montage of transparent figures, his wife's face looking at him in anguish, begging him: 'you didn't, Richard, you didn't'

followed by superimpositions of the entreating faces of his two children.

The woman is anxious. She begins to reveal more of herself. The man's name was Howard, a rich man she met on a train. While he kept her, she learned little about him; they never went out anywhere together; she only saw him when he turned up as he did that night, unexpectedly. The professor conceives a plan. If he takes the corpse away in his car and dumps it, no one will connect either of them with the killing. At this decision, the line of self-defence is invalidated and the strict logic of fate and its ramifications begins to operate. Yet, the woman is uneasy; she has no reason to trust anyone:

> But if you get out of here like that why should you ever come back?
> . . . I don't think there's a man in the world who wouldn't get out of a mess like this if he could.

Her experience with men has evidently not been uniformly a happy one. Before he leaves to get his car from the garage, she persuades him to leave his waistcoat. While one senses that she would not inform on the professor, her character is still somewhat ambiguous; she removes the professor's initialled pencil from his pocket and hides it, carefully wrapped, in a drawer. She also ignores the professor's advice to throw away the dead man's watch; she places that as well in the drawer. Later, she will attempt to keep back some of the blackmail money for herself. Clearly, she has a somewhat firmer grip on reality than has the theoretician professor. Whatever their differences, however, each has his destiny marked out in common.

Driving along dark, rain-drenched glistening streets, the professor is stopped by a police car: 'Don't you ever turn your lights on at night?' The spectator's nerves are strained along with the professor's, and the tension is kept up by a ritardando characteristic of Lang. Returning to the house, the professor is just about to carry out the body when the tenant from the floor above drives up and catches a glimpse of the woman who has opened the door to see that the coast is clear. Her appearance does not surprise him so much as her sudden retreat, which makes him hesitate on the stairs to look back. Even with such a false track, so beloved of Lang, we are made aware of the possibilities of sudden discovery of the crime.

Nor is Lang shy in heightening his moments of drama: there is a thunder-clap just as the professor leaves the house with his ominous burden wrapped in a dark cover. Two stunning images stand out of the precipitation of incidents. As always with Lang, they are an organic part of the situation. The woman watches the body being placed in the car by the professor who then brings back the cover to her and returns to sit in the driver's seat. At first we see her

Woman in the Window: hiding the corpse

face reflected (once again) in the glass of the front door, then at a reverse angle behind the glass, with raindrops slithering down the pane, and the light from a street lamp weaving glittering reflections. In this liquid, distorted imagery she looks even more beautiful and seductive than in her portrait. This is at once the climax of fascination and an underscoring of the strangely ambiguous atmosphere of dream. Yet, it must be remembered, all of this is created without a single erotic incident between the two.

Having already acted suspiciously when stopped earlier by the police, the professor again reveals his nervousness when the toll-gate collecter misses the hastily thrown dime and the professor is obliged to back-up to fumble for another coin. The danger involved is emphasised by a quick shot of the pale and bloated face of the dead man on the car floor.

Nor does Lang allow either the spectator or the professor a respite from the tension. There are constantly new sources of unease and obstacles: a stop sign which the professor almost misses, and near it a motorcycle policeman flashing his light. Everything glitters and glints in the rain-sodden darkness. The glistening wet foliage of the bushes – concealing the barbed wire which catches some tell-tale threads from the professor's jacket when it cuts his arm – recall the bushes of *The Last Will of Dr Mabuse* in their taking on a life of their own. And, again, we are given two shots of the awful face of the corpse that looks out of sightless eyes.

The evidence piles up. There are the footprints and tyre marks in the wet clay soil. Rashly the professor mentions murder to the distinct attorney when the other man has no more than commented that a financier has disappeared. When the professor is invited along, socially, to watch the police investigation he makes the mistake of moving directly towards the spot where the body was found before he is told where it was. He cannot keep his explanations simple: he claims his arm was cut when he was opening a tin, and then as it becomes inflamed from the sumak poison of the bush, he must talk about a search for a lost golf ball. While he can burn his jacket, he cannot remove the already discovered imprints in the earth. Lang obviously enjoys playing the game of circumstantial evidence. He is also fond of red herrings: a woman arrested in a cheap hotel whom he tried to avoid turns out not to be the professor's 'dream girl' at all; another toll-gate attendant has replaced the one who might have identified him.

If, however, the professor is more or less managing to deal with the police, these are only delaying tactics. The trap springs from an entirely different direction. The dubious bodyguard, ironically hired by the dead man's business partners to protect him against his own hot temper, suddenly appears with a blackmail demand. The demand follows a characteristic moment of relief: the professor is at first terrified when the woman telephones him, but she only wishes to congratulate him on an academic promotion which had been announced in the newspaper. He has time only to put down the receiver, reassured, when the blackmailer (Dan Duryea, an actor Lang liked a good deal and used whenever he could) rings her door-bell. The first demand for 5,000 dollars goes up when the official reward is placed at twice that sum. The blackmailer finds the professor's pencil, although the woman has managed to keep the newspaper article from him by agreeing at once to his demands.

The professor has gotten a prescription from his friend the doctor for a heavy tranquilizer – with the warning that too many will cause a sudden heart attack without leaving a trace. So now the two, once having killed by accident, are ready to murder in earnest. The blackmailer is too clever, however, to drink the drugged glass offered by the woman. His demands grow heavier when he discovers the dead man's watch.

The woman desperately calls the professor, but he has run out of cash and valuables. He hangs up and takes the rest of the tranquilizer himself. Hearing shots, the woman runs into the street. In a disquieting tilt-shot, the hunched-up body of the blackmailer is discovered, outside a basement entrance, with the incriminating watch and 5,000 dollars; when the police had approached he had panicked and shot first. Oddly enough, Police Inspector Jackson, who has observed the professor during the investigations, comments:

'. . . that's very funny, I was beginning to get an entirely different idea about it . . .'

When the woman tries to telephone the good news to the professor there is no answer.

Lang employs virtuoso camerawork for the transition from catharsis to the reality which succeeds the dream. The camera angle carefully calculated, we see the professor in an armchair in his bedroom beside the photographs of his family. The camera pans close to the unconscious man who vaguely reacts to the ringing of the telephone, then draws back. The professor is now asleep in his chair in the club, and the hand touching his shoulder is that of a club servant, waking him: 'It is half past ten, Professor Wanley.'

In a letter, put at my disposal by Pierre Rissient, Nunnally Johnson writes, on 23 January 1969, about how the initially resistant producer-writer came to accept Lang's intentions:

Our association couldn't have been pleasanter. The script was completed when it was offered to him and when we went over it together I can remember only one conflict of opinions. But conflict is not exactly the word. It might better be described as a different opinion about the treatment of the story within the story. I did not want this inner story to be a dream . . . I wanted it to be a story told by someone, though I can't remember how I worked out such a presentation. But Fritz preferred the dream, and it would have been presumptuous of me to disagree with him on such a small point in view of his experience and eminence. He was more likely to be more right than I was.

The picture provided Fritz with one of the most ingenious shots, possibly the most ingenious that I have seen. It is when Edward G. Robinson must be brought out of his dream back into reality. Robinson has taken some kind of poison that is putting him to sleep when the telephone rings. If he can summon the strength to reach out and pick up the 'phone the audience knows the mystery has been solved and that he can in all possibility take some antidote to the poison. This is where the dream must end.

As the 'phone continues to ring and Robinson begins to expire, Fritz moved the camera closer and closer until it was almost a head shot. Robinson is now presumably dead. Then a hand is pressed urgently on his shoulder and he opens his eyes, awakening from his dream. Fritz then pulled the camera back and a steward is reminding him that he wanted to be called at 11 o'clock.

This shot which involved a complete change of wardrobe and set was done without a cut. It was so perfectly done it had to be explained to me. Robinson was wearing a break-away suit of clothes and in the few seconds of the head shot an assistant crept up under the camera and snapped it off, leaving him in the suit he was wearing when he fell asleep, and in the same few seconds the crew had substituted the club set for the room in which he had taken the poison. It was that sort of ingenuity that helped to make Fritz the great director he was.

When he is awakened, the professor rises and goes out. We now see the irascible financier and the cunning blackmailer in their everyday shapes. They had evidently lingered in the professor's subconscious from previous encounters. The 'financier' is the obsequious cloakroom attendant; the 'blackmailer' is the club doorman, his face now, like the other man's, without anything sinister about it. Outside, a streetwalker asks for a light in the traditional first gesture of a solicitation, while just in the background is the mysterious and ambiguous portrait of the 'dream girl' with her smile of a thousand possibilities. He flees, shouting 'No . . . not for a million dollars!' It is the satyr play after the tragedy; it is the release from the nightmare, not an arbitrary or imposed happy ending.

22   Scarlet Street (1945)

Scarlet Street *is Lang's most European American film . . . its surface is very similar to that of* Woman in the Window, *with the same cameraman (Milton Krasner) creating some dark texture impressions of an anonymous, melancholy urban world. A long-held shot introduces* Scarlet Street *itself – nocturnal, rainy, vaguely raffish with a barrel-organ playing while a few couples stroll past.*
Gavin Lambert, 'Fritz Lang's America', *Sight and Sound*, Autumn 1955

I did a couple of films after that, neither of which pleased me very much, and it was then Walter, Fritz and I formed an independent producing company and arranged to distribute through Universal . . . We called the company Diana Productions and our first film as an organisation was Scarlet Street, *with a cast headed by Edward G. Robinson and me. It was another hit and a good omen for the newly formed company.*
Joan Bennett: *The Bennett Playbill*, by Lois Kibbee, 1970

So far as he recalls, Lang held 55 per cent of the stock of Diana productions, while Joan Bennett had ten per cent and Walter Wanger none, being hired as the firm's vice-chairman with a 40,000 dollar fee for every film, since he had arranged Lang's financial backing.

Looking about for a subject for their first production, Lang heard that Paramount had acquired the rights of the Renoir film *La Chienne* (1931) which had been based on the novel by Georges de la Fouchardière. Lubitsch, however, had dropped the idea of a remake because he couldn't find a way of making the subject palatable to American audiences. Lang, on the other hand, saw the possibility of transposing the film to a Greenwich Village setting and still retaining the atmosphere. Dudley Nichols, who knew Renoir's film, liked the idea, and Lang recalls:

The two of us were agreed to make a new film and not just a copy of the Renoir film which we had seen in the Thirties. We wanted to use the idea in a new way with reference to the Greenwich Village atmosphere and the American characters – 'Lazy Legs' (Joan Bennett) and Chris Cross (Edward G. Robinson).

(The name 'Lazy Legs' rather indicates a prostitute who is almost too lazy to follow her trade, while 'Chris Cross' is a man who criss-crosses his way through life.)

Before Nichols started to work on the script, he, Lang, Wanger and Joan Bennett met to find a suitable title; a literal translation of *La Chienne* would clearly not be acceptable. 'We talked and talked and could not find what we wanted until I suddenly had a brainwave and said "Scarlet Street?" and everyone was enthusiastic.' Lang says he did not know exactly what the title meant, but that afterwards he remembered the passage in the Apocalypse of St. John where the whore of Babylon is described as 'the

257

woman arrayed in purple and scarlet' and thinks that perhaps that image might have been in the back of his mind.

In Renoir's film the girl is clearly a *putain* from the lowest ranks. When Michel Simon tries to rescue her and strike her pimp who has thrown her to the sidewalk, she goes for him angrily and screams at him in vulgar French. When she allows him to take her home, there is no doubt what she is: she tells him openly that she lives with her pimp, Dédé. Thus Simon has no illusions; he accepts their fate as something natural.

Joan Bennett's Kitty is a better-class girl, but not because of the Hays Office. Lang intends to make something else from the material, and the romantic illusions of Chris are a necessary part of that plan. The script says that 'she lives with her friend Milly who designs belts for a boutique where Kitty herself worked before she met Johnny'. While Lang has kept references to this in the film, we come into the story after she has become Johnny's adoring slave; he allows her to keep him. The scene in which he beats her up because (Lazy Legs that she is) she has earned only fifteen dollars in an evening is self-explanatory. Still, except with Johnny, she has some pride and ambition. She is more than happy to have Chris believe her story that she is an actress who has been attacked by a purse-snatcher. Later, when she begins to have professional success as a 'painter', she will even be able to parrot back Chris's second-hand opinion about the 'Work of art that grows organically' when she talks to an art critic.

Lang's Chris is very different from Simon in the Renoir film. Simon is half-primitive, yet cunning enough not to be completely defenceless – almost a bourgeois mutation of *Boudu sauvé des eaux*. His Sunday painting is more a hobby than a passion, and unlike the timid and 'considerate' Chris he has a real, sexual affair with the prostitute. At the end, after killing her in a fit of rage, he becomes a tramp, but it is less tragic downfall than release, an anarchist freed at last from all bourgeois restraints. The cynicism of this ending was only possible in the liberal French atmosphere which still preserved a good deal of the scepticism of Anatole France. In the United States of 1945, Lang had to at least make a gesture toward the demonstration that 'crime does not pay'. Nonetheless, Lang

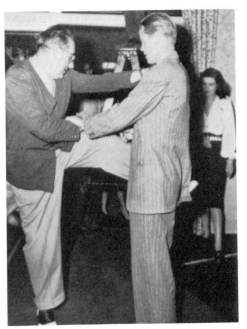

Scarlet Street (1945): Lang with Dan Duryea and Joan Bennett (*right*)

had a somewhat different conception of what that might mean from that of the Hays Office. He declares that Chris suffers neither from the death of Lazy Legs nor from having sent an innocent man to the electric chair. He suffers only from a jealousy which cannot be assuaged even by the death of the two people involved. He still hears their love talk, is tortured by it, and this is what turns him into a bum. Lang further points out that this was the first Hollywood film in which an innocent man is executed, yet no single review commented on the fact; nor, evidently, did the Hays Office object, although that Office had earlier found the intrigue against Czaka in *Hangmen Also Die* 'immoral'. Was this because Chris's downfall seems ambivalent, and because Lang shows it with such intensity and atmospheric anxiety? Did no one object to Johnny's execution because he was so unpleasant? If the film itself is sometimes ambiguous in the Lang fashion, the reactions to the film on the part of critics and censor were ambiguous in quite another way.

Renoir's film is in parts almost vaudeville, drastic naturalism with occasional tragic overtones. Lang's film with its chiaroscuro compositions reveals the deep tragedy of a man hurt by life. Chris has a heart; something unique in the film. He trusts Kitty deeply and forgives her everything. He destroys Kitty, and himself, because she has destroyed his love, his trust, his illusions. It is a long way from Montmartre to Greenwich Village.

The film opens on a rain-sodden night in which the headlights of cars are reflected in puddles, in which the lights from restaurants barely penetrate the dark, in which the pavement seems to slide away under one's feet and temptation (and doom?) is waiting at every street corner. Thin music from a barrel organ is wafted away in the thin breeze. An elegant car containing a beautiful woman draws up outside a restaurant; a discreet chauffeur murmurs something to the head waiter who, in turn, passes the message along to the boss, who then speeds up to conclude the presentations to celebrate the cashier's twenty-five years with the firm. The lady can't be kept waiting.

The office staff, a little tipsy, crowd to the window to wonder at the boss's companion – not, certainly, his wife. The timid, little cashier, slipping away from the party with his friend and fellow-worker confides:

I feel kind of lonely tonight . . . I wonder what it is like . . . to be – well, loved by a girl like that?
. . . No one ever looked at me like that, not even when I was young.

When he was young this gentle, helpless man dreamed of being a painter. Now, after twenty-five monotonous years as a bank cashier (his only reward, tonight's gold watch and a hurried presentation), he is married to a shrew who never misses a chance to compare him unfavourably to his predecessor whose picture (with a genuine life-saver's medal pinned to its chest) glares at him in the sitting room. Chris in a woman's apron, afraid to invite his friend home, washes the dishes and listens to her threats to give his paintings to the junk man because she can't bear the smell of turpentine and oil. Detail is piled upon detail to create a picture of his domestic life in all its stuffiness, all kept by Lang in chiaroscuro. The one bright spot in Chris's life is his painting – done on Sundays locked in the bathroom –

Scarlet Street: Chris (Edward G. Robinson) and wife

paintings which are strangely primitive, without perspective as his whole existence is without perspective.

The encounter with Kitty is the fulfilment of undefinable longings. With her, the Sunday painter who thinks she is an actress, becomes a real painter. The flower she gives him acquires a magic: he paints it, but his wife throws it into the garbage. Yet, even early in their relationship there is a stirring of suspicion. As Chris and Kitty part, he asks her who is the Johnny for whom she asked the barman, but seems satisfied with her explanation that he is the boyfriend of Milly. In fact it is at Johnny's instigation that Kitty begins to soak the apparently rich painter.

Chris becomes entangled in easy stages. First a loan for a few clothes so she can be presentable when she visits 'agents and producers'. Then a bright, modern flat, which Kitty will live in but where Chris can come to paint in peace away from his wife, Adele. To get the necessary

Scarlet Street: discovering the pictures

money, Chris first steals bonds which his wife had
inherited from her first husband. Soon, he is robbing his
employer too. He is so besotted that he is not even angry
when he discovers that Kitty is signing his paintings ('It's
almost like we were married.') and selling them to a
gallery. This leads to a comic passage. Chris's wife sees the
pictures in the window of the art gallery and assumes her
husband had copied the work of this 'Katherine Marsh'.
She dashes home to demand 'How long have you known
Katherine Marsh?' Hard at work cutting meat, Chris not
realising she knows nothing of his relationship with Kitty,
brandishes the knife in Adele's face – obviously remembering all the newspaper stories he has read with relish about
wives being murdered.

For the scene before the gallery, Lang had an ingenious
technical idea. To give the impression of an intense street
life reflected in the window of the gallery, he made a back
projection with moving traffic and passers-by which he

then *reflected* in the window which, being dimly lit from the other side, provided a partial mirror.

Chris finds that he will not have to murder Adele to be rid of her. The supposedly lost husband returns to demand blackmail money to leave Chris in happy possession of Adele. Instead, Chris delightedly tricks him back into the marriage trap. Now free to marry Kitty, he rushes to the apartment with his suitcase.

In the Renoir film, Simon found the girl in bed with her lover. In Lang's film, Chris sees the two through a glass door rushing into each other's arms and kiss, and hears

Oh Johnny! Oh Johnny!

Lazy Legs! (*half in mockery*)

Jeepers I love you Johnny!

The gramophone needle has stuck in a groove of the refrain of Kitty's favourite 'Melancholy Baby': 'I love . . . love . . . love . . . love'.

Johnny hears the front door as Chris runs away. Angry with Kitty's negligence, which may have lost them the source of their income, Johnny stalks out. Having got a bit drunk in a saloon, Chris returns to tell Kitty he is free, that he forgives her and understands that Johnny forced himself on her. She buries her head in her pillow, her shoulders shaking. 'Don't cry, darling. Please don't cry.' At which point she turns on him, laughing:

How can a man be so dumb . . . I've been wanting to laugh in your face ever since I met you. You're old and ugly and I'm sick of you – sick, sick, sick!

He retreats, horrified. The ice-pick Johnny had borrowed from the ice-man downstairs for a champagne celebration of his purchase of a new car falls to the floor. Chris mechanically picks it up to replace it. As Kitty buries her face in the blankets, he hacks like an enraged machine at her body.

The stairwell is lit in a tragic chiaroscuro. Johnny, drunk, drives up in his new car so recklessly that he almost runs down the ice-man:

Just look out, Johnny, you will kill somebody.

Chris comes down the stairs like a sleepwalker. When Johnny's shadow appears on the frosted glass of the front door, silhouetted by the lamp outside, Chris hides at the side of the stairwell. Impatiently, Johnny rattles the bolted door, then smashes the glass to get in. As Johnny runs up the stairs, Chris slips out unnoticed.

The circumstantial evidence against Johnny the pimp piles up: he stole the dead girl's jewelry; just before her death Kitty rang Milly who warned her Johnny was drunk and threatening Kitty with violence; Johnny hardly makes a good impression when he insists that Chris ('He ain't as dumb as he looks.') did the 'Katherine Marsh' paintings while both Adele and Chris claim that Chris was only capable of making bad copies – so bad they had been destroyed.

Nichols' screenplay already provides for the stylisation of the scene of cross-examination:

In this succession of quick wipes we see only the witness chair and part of the judge's bench. But at intervals we hear the audience and the judge's gavel. The prosecutor who asks the questions we do not hear, becomes the CAMERA. We, the audience of the film are the audience of the court-room.

It is interesting to compare this with other Lang court-room scenes, and the solutions he finds elsewhere to the problems of showing multiple interrogations.

The script contained a further scene of hallucination: in the night, as Johnny goes to the electric chair, Chris drives to Sing Sing. He climbs up on an insulation tower from which he can watch how the voltage drops when the switch is pulled. Lang rightly felt that this might have an unintentional comic effect on the audience and eliminated it. The scene must have been shot, however, as there is a surviving still photograph showing Robinson overlooking the death house from the vantage of the pole.

As the film now exists, there is only the sequence of his return journey by train. He is politely addressed by the journalists who recognise him from the trial as 'Mr Cross', though he has already begun to look shabby and unshaven. He hears one of the passengers remark 'Nobody gets away with murder' – there is always the conscience – 'No one escapes punishment'.

Yet, when Chris collapses in the miserable Bowery hotel room, without even a curtain, it is not because of guilty conscience. Lang's suggestive powers transcend the script. A neon sign outside flashes on and off, lighting in

sequence cut from film (*left*); Chris in the dreary hotel room (*right*)

uncannily regular intervals the gloomy room through the curtainless window, torturing his already sore nerves. He finds himself unable to stop involuntarily whistling Kitty's favourite 'Melancholy Baby', and then another sound comes in as if from another dimension: the words he heard the lovers speak:

Oh Johnny, Oh Johnny!

Lazy Legs!

Jeepers I love you, Johnny!

The words are repeated again and again with the flashing light, more terrifying than the footsteps heard in the mind of Joe Wilson in *Fury*. Everything suddenly stops and Chris screams out 'Kitty!'

There is a cut to the door of Chris's room; the grubby porter and another client push open the door from behind which there has just been the noise of a falling chair. Through the open doorway we see the outlines of a hanging man, or rather the dark shapes of his legs in the twilight. The failed suicide is shown as starkly as a newsreel.

The final act, the slow decline of an obsessed man who has lost everything is shown by means of an ellipsis. On a snowy night the police find the tramp asleep on a park bench. One tells the other that the tramp is a bit crazy. He wants to be arrested:

he has the crazy idea he killed a couple of people. Always tryin' to give himself up, wants to be tried and executed. You know these nuts.

As they make him move along, they conclude that probably he just wants a warm place for the night.

Through the wintry night Christmas carols and jingle bells can be heard in the distance. The tramp is shuffling past the art gallery when the door opens and Kitty's alleged self-portrait is carefully carried into a waiting car. The gallery owner discusses it with a fat woman:

Well, there goes her masterpiece. I really hate to part with it . . .

For twenty-five thousand dollars you shouldn't mind, Mr Delarow.

It is almost as if Chris has not heard. He shuffles on towards the Bowery, picks up a cigarette stub, shuffles on again. The original script continued, eerily:

A gust of wind whines in the street, making a swirl of snow around him like ghost figures and we hear Kitty's voice whispering: 'Johnny, I love you Johnny'.

Lang goes even further. As the jingle bell music continues merrily, and as the voices of the lovers again haunt Chris, there is a dissolve. All of the other people on the street have disappeared, and Chris's profound loneliness is made concrete in the image of him slowly, listlessly, shuffling off, becoming smaller and smaller in the distance.

23   Cloak and Dagger (1946)

Peace? There's no peace! It's year one of the Atomic Age and God have mercy on us all! . . . if we think we can wage other wars without destroying ourselves.
Script by Albert Maltz and Ring Lardner, Jr.

Cloak and Dagger is a less romantic title than at first appears; it was the actual name for the intelligence work and wartime secret service activities of the Office of Strategic Services – OSS – in Washington. *Man Hunt, Hangmen Also Die*, and *Ministry of Fear* are all, in addition to their other aspects, anti-Nazi films made during the Second World War. *Cloak and Dagger* was made in 1946, when the Nazi regime had, in principle, been destroyed; it was thus meant as a kind of concluding commentary on the terror of the Reich. There is, however, more to it than simply that: the sentiments from the script quoted above, for example, were central to the film and put into the mouth of the film's hero Alvah Jasper, played with human simplicity by Gary Cooper. This ending, a warning against the new-born terror of the spread of the destructive capabilities of atomic power, was Lang's central purpose in making the film. While it was filmed, it was removed, with the entire last reel of the film, by the production company, and was destroyed before the film's release. No complete copy of the film as intended has survived.

In Lang's previous anti-Nazi films, the enemy are sharply characterised. In *Cloak and Dagger* the Nazis and Fascists are treated more summarily and vaguely. Like the bomb itself they remain a dim, hard to grasp, menace; in the original film and script, the menace is no longer localized, but has spread to international proportions.

The Gestapo kidnap Dr Katerin Loder, a famous Hungarian physicist, who has fled to Switzerland rather than work for the Nazi atomic weapon. Before Jasper can save her, she is shot by a Nazi nurse. Before dying, she is able to reveal that an Italian physicist, Dr Polda, is working for the Nazis. The rather unworldly Jasper, recruited to

OSS to establish contact with Dr Loder, realises he now has a larger task: he must go to Italy to discover why the once liberal Polda is working with the Nazis. Like Jan and Mascha in *Hangmen Also Die*, he is to be transformed into a committed fighter.

Although the script is ascribed to Albert Maltz and Ring Lardner, Jr. (both to become victims of the McCarthy witchhunts in Hollywood), Lang's influence and logic are evident in the mosaic structure. In a Basque restaurant a switchman and his colleague are sending messages to England about loads of pitchblend being shipped from Czechoslovakia to Germany. In the middle of their radioing, the Gestapo surprise and kill them. Meanwhile, in Washington, the interrupted message has been monitored.

Jasper explains to his cloak-and-dagger friend the significance of the shipments of pitchblend and monicite – uranium and thorium: the Nazis, like the Americans, are working on an atomic bomb.

> ... this is the first time I am sorry I am a scientist. Society is not ready for atomic energy. I'm scared stiff.

Whatever his ultimate feelings about the bomb, however, one thing is immediately clear: the Nazis must not develop the bomb.

Disguised as a German scientist, Jasper reaches Polda (after an adventurous landing by submarine in Italy) to find that he is being forced to work with the Nazis. His daughter is in their hands and his house is heavily guarded by Fascists. When Jasper reveals his real identity, the terrified Polda rings for his guards; but reminded by Jasper of his former statements about science and humanity, merely mumbles a request for matches when the Fascist Luigi appears. Luigi will later become suspicious when he finds a box of matches already on Polda's desk.

Here, as well as in other incidents like the 'accidental' encounter in Switzerland of Jasper with an American adventuress who is actually a Nazi agent, the sudden tying together of seemingly trivial or unconnected details in their causal connections is sometimes reminiscent of *The Spy*.

Polda will make his escape with Jasper only if his daughter is first saved, so that Jasper must stay in Italy instead of leaving within twenty-four hours as ordered. He

Cloak and Dagger (1946): the subtle menace of the Nazis

is put under the protection of the lovely resistance fighter Gina, played by Lili Palmer with the actress's usual deliberate coolness which is here not inappropriate to the role. At first, the two are to stay together in the same room until they receive the signal – a newspaper obituary notice for a lieutenant Rinaldi – that Polda's daughter is safe.

Here, Lang's instinct for suspense and his economy of means comes into play. Jasper can't stand the meowing of a hungry cat outside the door. Gina coldly replies that 'When people are hungry, it's natural cats should be too.' When it stops, she remarks 'here even cats learn it's no use to cry'. Yet when the meows begin again, she softens and allows the cat to come inside the room. Thus we are given the situation which has made Gina's assumed hardness necessary and shown that there is another, softer, side to her character. But the cat serves yet another purpose: in the morning the janitor comes looking for his cat and discovers Jasper. While the introduction of Jasper as Gina's new husband works for the moment, Jasper obviously cannot register with the police, and they are forced to flee. They move from one precarious refuge to the next, with Jasper learning more and more about Gina's anxieties and fears brought about by her hard and dangerous life. She begins to relax and to trust Jasper's basic decency and sympathy:

Don't make love to me! Don't be someone I like . . . In my work, I kiss without feeling . . . When you fight scum you become scum.

Nothing is what it appears; danger is everywhere. Two nuns knock at the door of their hiding place collecting money for war orphans. Trusting no one, Gina watches them when they leave and sees them stop at a car parked down the street. They were agents, and Gina urges Jasper that they must again move on. While he is not convinced of the danger, he recognises her terror and tries to calm her by taking her into his arms. She clings to him:

I *want* you to like me – I want you to think I am nineteen, with a white dress, a girl who has never been kissed before.

This, however, is no sentimental boy-meets-girl situation. Lang very carefully directs the scene so that it is perfectly natural, two human beings clinging to one another for support and warmth in a nightmare world which has devalued human emotions and the heart.

Their next refuge is a bombed house. Then Jasper must hide under a bridge. The nightmare is increasing in intensity and the alternatives for survival are diminishing. Finally the obituary notice is in the newspaper, and Jasper and Gina set off to fetch Polda from his appointment with his anti-Fascist dentist. The danger has not passed however. A typical Lang set piece follows. Luigi, suspicious, has followed Polda's car and must be got out of the way.

Gina passes him with swaying hips, apparently not even noticing him, then stops in a doorway to fix her stocking. While Luigi's attention is thus elsewhere, Jasper is able to get near enough to force him at gun-point into the doorway. From outside we can hear street music. Luigi resists, jumps at Jasper and claws at his face. The wild struggle is all the more frightening for taking place in total silence, save for the strains of music from the street. Jasper kills his enemy with a well-aimed karate blow. At that moment a ball rolls down the stairs, step by step, heralding the arrival of someone unseen. Jasper, who has already tried unsuccessfully to hide the body behind some boxes in the hall, only to find that the feet and legs stick out too much, seats Luigi on one of the boxes, and sits behind him, opening up a newspaper in front of the two of them as if they are reading together. The owner of the ball, a small boy, and his mother come down the stairs and out the door.

Gina has meanwhile found Polda. Jasper leaps into the car with them just as Luigi's body, no longer supported, slowly slides down from his box, exciting the curiosity of passers-by. (Lang recalls that Gary Cooper insisted on playing the entire scene himself – including the fight – although he had a sprained hip at the time.)

Jasper, Gina, and Polda reach the lonely farmhouse where the resistance fighters await them, only to find that the girl whom they have 'saved' is not Polda's daughter Maria, but a Nazi agent who has taken her place. She reveals with malicious pleasure that Maria has been dead for six months; it was easy to fake the childish writing of the letters to Polda.

It is a trap. The Germans who have followed her now

attack. The cloak-and-dagger Pinkie who brought Jasper to Italy shows him a secret exit from the house through which he can take Gina and Polda. When Jasper asks why they cannot all escape this way, Pinkie declares 'sometimes a guy carries the ball, sometimes another' in a speech reminiscent of the 'take the torch' speech in *Hangmen Also Die*, and:

> Because the only way you can make it is if we do enough shooting to convince them we're still here.
> My orders were to get you into this country and get you out again.

Dragging the dazed Polda with them, Gina accompanies Jasper to the plane which is waiting to take them to the United States. Gina has already explained she must stay in Italy where she is needed:

> After the war – I'm coming back for you.
> Things change, people too . . .
> (*calling after him:*) Come back for me!

The film as it now exists ends here on this equivocally happy ending. In the original version as filmed, Polda dies in the plane just as he is about to reveal to Jasper the locations of the four main plants where the Nazi atomic bomb is being tested. Unable to finish, he takes a photograph from his pocket just as he dies. It shows him and his daughter in a lake landscape with wooded hill and unusual mountain formation in the background. From this the OSS are able to identify the fourth plant, the only one Polda had not named, as Grünbach in Bavaria.

An operation is mounted. Mysteriously, RAF reconnaissance planes sent in advance encounter no resistance. When Jasper and the task force arrive, they find the secret factory is deserted. Where is the work on the bomb being continued? In Spain? The Argentine.?

It was at this point that Jasper made the speech which was for Lang the *raison d'etre* of the film:

> God have mercy on us if we ever thought we could really keep science a secret – or even wanted to. God have mercy on us if we think we can wage other wars without destroying ourselves . . . And God have mercy on us if we haven't the sense to keep the world in peace.

Emerging from the cave that leads to the underground factory, Jasper takes a deep breath, then sees a paratrooper tossing pebbles and gazing at the sky. The paratrooper remarks:

Cloak and Dagger: Lang with Vladimir Sokoloff (Polda) and Gary Cooper
(Jasper) and (*below*) the set

Nice sky.

Sure is.

Looks like the sky over my part of Ohio. I want to go back there, take off my suit and never climb into it again.

That's a good want. I hope you make it.

Blue sky and birds singing. Guess I'll see my girl soon.

Yeah. Guess I will too.

Does Jasper's sudden smile on this line anticipate a better end; or does this evocation of the normal life actually underscore the fears he had expressed moments earlier; is it, as in *Hangmen Also Die,* NOT THE END?

As usual Lang surrounded himself with experts for the preparation of this film. Two former OSS men gave him advice based on their own cloak-and-dagger experiences during the war – Milton Sperling, the producer, and Mike Burke who had actually had the task of smuggling out of Italy an Italian admiral who had invented an electronic torpedo device which the Allies wanted to prevent the Fascists from having. Jasper's views in his 'God help us' speech were based directly on the anxieties expressed by the famous physicist Oppenheimer, who had anticipated the disastrous consequences of the development of the atom bomb.

Thus, even in its present truncated form, the film represents Lang's consistent careful balance of documentary foundation with necessary adventurous narrative elements.

When I mention psychoanalysis in connection with Fritz Lang, I mean to say that he is better than anyone else in discovering its poetry and dreamlike power. Anyway, the film starts like a dream from which one awakens . . .
What is superb is Lang's personal style, the treatment he gives to this story, the plastic beauty of his structures, his flight into an imaginary world. The reconstruction of rooms which were the theatre of famous murders is the shock sequence of this film. There is a baroque profusion which reminds us of the aesthetics of Josef von Sternberg, but Fritz Lang imbues it with that Germanic coldness of the delirium which has the purity of a diamond . . .
Henri Chapier: *Secret Beyond the Door*, in *Combat*, 20 February 1968

On 1 February 1947, Lang wrote to me on notepaper with the heading of Diana Productions:

I started shooting *Secret Beyond the Door* this week ... I am experimenting with using superimposed sound for the 'thought voices' of the leading characters, and I find the idea intriguing to work out.

Later he explained that his first idea had been to let the thought voice of Celia (Joan Bennett) be spoken by a different actress, but in the end Joan Bennett insisted on doing it herself. Lang was endeavouring with his superimpositions of thought voices to do something which O'Neill's *Strange Interlude* had failed to achieve on stage. The words of the subconscious are not like asides in a play but are somehow placed on a different plane, belong to a different dimension. Because of this, and their intensity, they tightly integrate the whole structure of the action and, importantly, prepare us for the latent Freudian undertones. At the same time, paradoxically, they free the action from its improbabilities, reinforcing Lang's 'fantastic realism'. Emotional reactions are revealed, and what we hear enables us to explore the furthest ramifications of inner thought. Along with this, the camera acquires an astonishing degree of subjectivity: we follow the action through the heroine's own eyes. When at the decisive moment of the reversal of fortunes, at the climax of the drama, her partner's thought voice tells us almost unspeakable things, the atmosphere of dream reaches a density that is still completely natural.

The film starts with a waking-up from a kind of dream pool. The script says:

I have tried to approach the murderer imaginatively to show him as a human being possessed of some demon that

FADE IN – pool, clear sunlit water sending out widening ripples. A

Secret Beyond the Door (1948): shadow play: Joan Bennett as Celia

girl's voice is heard warm and vibrant . . . When a girl dreams of a ship, she will reach a safe harbour, when she dreams of daffodils, she is in great danger. And then: 'This is my wedding-day. When somebody drowns he sees his whole life floating'.

So when Celia enters the church, fragments of her life rush before her imagination; and the thought voice makes these flashbacks seem possible, natural, organic in their connections.

The rich heiress who has turned down many suitors is now suddenly marrying, in the little baroque Mexican church, a stranger of whom she knows nothing except that he is an architect and edits a magazine. They had met at a Mexican fair, where the spoilt Celia gazed spellbound at two gypsies fighting a knife duel over a woman. Her thought voice tells us she was also transfixed by the sense of eyes gazing at her. The stranger speaks to her:

I heard his voice and then I didn't hear any more because the beating of my blood was louder.

has driven him beyond the ordinary borderline of human behaviour . . .
Fritz Lang: *Why I am Interested in Murder* (Newspaper clipping, 1947, quoted in Eibel: *Fritz Lang*)

I remember he wouldn't use doubles for Michael Redgrave and me for a sequence in a burning house. We fled terrified, through scorching flames time and again and it wasn't a fire for toasting marshmallows.
Joan Bennett: *The Bennett Playbill*, by Lois Kibbee, 1970

276

Lang, intent on achieving subtle shades of tonality, shows us the stranger's lips moving, but we do not hear his words, only the thought voice takes us into the unknown and vague, deep waters unbounded by shores seem to carry us along. A wishing well, surrounded by candles, into which people throw coins merges into the stream of awareness. We share with the young woman the tempting, seductively dangerous experience of making decisions against her own will.

'Joan Bennett and Michael Redgrave', continues the 1947 letter, 'are starred, and I think it will be an interesting picture.' Redgrave, with his ambiguous charm and equivocal sexuality, the rather sulky, protruding lower lip, his occasionally almost childlike, hesitant tenderness, is an ideal partner for the austere Joan Bennett, who turns into an adoring sleepwalker; but then regains her old active self, which makes plausible the psychoanalytic cure of the unstable man.

The patio of the Mexican villa recalls the idyll of the Valley Tavern in *You Only Live Once*, though here everything is more sensuous and sultry. Celia intends only a joke when she says 'Mark, darling, you are inhibited. You are touched in the head'. In the next scene she has locked herself in the room, to tease her husband. A close-up shows the handle turn once, then twice. The dark corridor – seen with a subjective camera from Celia's point of view – is empty. When Celia subsequently asks Mark if he came upstairs while she was dressing, he denies it, not looking at her (or at the camera). His glass shatters in his hand ('his kiss was cold'). Still looking away he says he must go at once to Mexico City; a telegram has brought a good offer to buy his magazine.

'And then I was alone.' Lang expresses forcefully the restless walking up and down, the thoughts in the dim, candle-lit room, the tension when Paquita, the servant says, 'There was no telegram. Telegrams do not come to this loneliness.' Celia throws herself on the bed; the music echoes the thought voice: 'Why did he go away? Why did he lie to me?'

At Mark Lamphere's estate, Lavender Falls, his sister Carrie tells Celia he has not yet arrived. Standing by the entrance to the house, she sees a curtain move briefly. Perhaps it is the strange child, David, who Celia learns is Mark's child by a previous marriage. She goes upstairs, past the eerie South Sea and Indian masks on the wall. Everything about the house is sinister. None of Celia's doors has a key, and seeking Carrie to ask her about this, Celia encounters the mysterious Miss Robey in Mark's studio. Miss Robey wears a shade to hide the scar received in rescuing little David from a fire in the summerhouse. This adds to the sinister atmosphere; she is not unlike creatures from the American horror films of Paul Leni.

It seems to be the old Mark who runs to meet her next morning when he arrives at the railway station; yet when he sees the lilac twig she has in her lapel, he freezes and makes an excuse to get away from her.

The house-warming party is suddenly interrupted by a thunderstorm; and Carrie suggests that Mark should entertain the chattering guests by showing his collection of 'felicitous rooms'. Celia's lawyer, Bob, takes the opportunity to reproach Celia for having given Mark power of attorney over her fortune. 'Look, Bob, I know Mark would never do anything unfair.' At the very moment Celia is thus reassuring Bob there is a shrill burst of laughter – typical Langian irony – followed by a remark of a passing society woman:

Mark's a lucky fellow. First wife's money runs out . . . She dies. Second wife with plenty of cash . . .

The 'felicitous rooms', which Mark is showing his guests with sadistic joy, all turn out to have been distinguished by the violent deaths of women: a Huguenot countess stabbed by her husband on Bartholomew's night; an old mother tied to a chair to drown in a flood for the sake of her life insurance; several Hacienda wives strangled with the suave Don Ignazio's flowered scarf: murder à la De Quincey as a fine art! As in the trial scene in *Fury*, Lang shows only a selection of cases. Mark stops before the last door, upon which the hat of a garrulous guest casts an ominous shadow; but this one is locked. 'A man must have at least one secret', he smiles.

Later alone with Celia, he explains that 'felicitous' is only another word for 'appropriate', to indicate the unholy emanations of a room. When Celia charges him with morbidity, he grows cool; and when she asks what is in the seventh room he shows irritation: 'I won't be badgered, Celia. I never lived my own life.' There have always been women – his mother, Carrie, then Eleanor his first wife.

Next day she learns from Carrie and the gardener that Mark's mother loved lilac and had bushes everywhere in the garden. After her death Mark had them all torn out. He had been a sensitive child, almost like David. Once he was beside himself with rage when Carrie locked him in his room for fun. Told by little David, 'He killed my mother', Celia's thought voice demands again and again 'How did Eleanor die?'. A characteristic Lang series of dialogue overlaps takes up the question. 'She was tired of living', declares Carrie. 'Mr Mark is the soul of kindness', says the chambermaid; and the next shot shows Mark, through the window, caring for a run-over dog. The chambermaid adds the sinister information that Mark always gave Eleanor her medicine himself. Celia's thought voice adds, 'He keeps his mind locked like his door'.

Secret Beyond the Door: door no 7

Breaking some wax off a candle, she sneaks into Mark's dressing room to make an impression of the only key in the house. The shorter candle disturbs Mark's pathological sense of symmetry; and Celia has to lie when he asks if she has just been to his room.

Late at night,

The door opens . . . a shaft of light breaks the darkness. Celia comes out, turns down the corridor towards the stairs. At the top of the stairs, she stops, looks down into the blackness and directs the beam of her flashlight into the pitch-black stairwell. Moving shot of the CAMERA PASSES in the dim indirect light . . .

The eerie native masks and grim family portraits recall *The Last Will of Dr Mabuse.* The script continues with an almost Expressionist touch:

. . . in the weird light the furniture of the library looks immense and threatening.

Objects seem to assume a life of their own, and Celia becomes a tiny distant figure. Far-off church chimes are

Secret Beyond the Door: the flight through the fog

heard. Stills show that the library scene was shot in this way, though the copies of the film existing in France pass at once to Celia standing in front of the iron grilled door which sighs as it is opened. In the dark corridor the beam of the flashlight moves along the walls until it stops at the locked door. 'Close-up of No 7, then of the lock.'

When she finds the room behind the curtained doorway, her thought voice at first tells her it is Eleanor's room – poor Mark feels such guilt at not having loved her that he thinks he actually killed her. Only then does she realise: the room is a duplicate of her own and is waiting for her, Celia. Terrified, she flees past Don Ignazio's room and passes with difficulty through the iron door which has shut itself. Then we see a shot of Mark's legs, and Don Ignazio's scarf trailing behind him. As Celia reaches the stairs, Miss Robey's door opens. No longer hostile, Miss Robey gives her a coat and the keys of the car when the terrified girl cries: 'I want to go away.' On the bottom stair, she sees Don Ignazio's scarf.

In the dark garden, tree trunks menace through the haze. Just as she reaches the end, a dark figure appears. There is just a scream, and then a fade-out.

The sequence which follows, with its complexity and abstractions, could only have been brought off by a director of Lang's assurance, the experience of his German days, his grasp of 'fantastic realism' – and above all by a director working for his own production company. It is the following morning. Mark is coolly shaving, and holding Don Ignazio's scarf. Now Mark's thought voice is used for the first time, while his schizophrenia and anxieties are given visual form. Grey-on-grey we see a ghostly court-room, with the distant dark shadow of the judge and the equally faceless silhouettes of the jury.

I tried not to kill her . . .

I love her but I still have to kill her

The superimposed thought voice of Celia comments on and interprets events objectively. Mark's is much more direct and subjective. His assumption of the role of both prosecutor and defence echoes his schizoid state.

The faint music is at once disembodied and insistent, with themes suggestive of grief and torment. The faceless judge gives a hollow knock with his gavel to announce the

Secret Beyond the Door: the dark shadow of justice: Michael Redgrave as Mark

death sentence . . . and the knocking merges into Sarah's knock on the door: Miss Carrie asks if he is coming down to breakfast. There he finds that Celia has not gone away:

I thought you left last night?

I did. I ran into Bob (*the dark figure in the garden*).

Why did you come back?

Because I love you.

Mark dismisses Miss Robey for having tried to come between him and Celia, and the woman supposes that Celia has broken her promise not to reveal to him that the supposed scar behind her veil had been in fact removed by surgery long ago. 'So she told you', is her only, resentful, response.

Later Celia and Mark are left alone in the house, in a thunderstorm and Mark's thought voice declares: 'I can't be alone with her.' He says he must go to New York and insists she move to a hotel so as not to be alone. At the station however – atmospheric with the smoke, lights, and raging storm – Mark suddenly turns back.

At the house the telephone rings. It is Miss Robey, and Celia tells her Mark has gone to New York. Then she goes to Eleanor's room with a large bouquet of lilacs. She leaves the key in the lock and waits. Mark appears, Don Ignazio's scarf in his hand. Celia, to stay alive, must talk to him.

This 'lesson in psychoanalysis' has been criticised; and Lang himself would today agree that the whole story is too simplified, and Mark's cure improbably abrupt. Still the situation had been prepared. When Mark was showing his rooms, a woman psychoanalyst explained the murders and their motivation. Mark immediately afterwards tells Celia, 'Murder comes from a strong emotion, more direct than love'. On the Mexican patio, Celia has told Mark, jokingly, that he is 'inhibited'.

As Henri Chapier has written, Lang's achievement here is not simply to *exteriorise* psychoanalysis but to steep it in a poetic-dreamlike fluidum which gives credibility and logic to events which would otherwise be only melo-drama. We must remember too the period in which the film was made: psychoanalysis was just becoming popular, both on and off the screen, in America. Lang admits to a certain influence by *Rebecca*, and we are also reminded of *Spellbound*. In the atmosphere of subconscious suspension which Lang has created, it becomes believable that Celia prises Mark's long-suppressed secret out of him – the associations of lilac and locked doors – just as he is about to strangle her; that he now realises what is buried deep inside him and drives him to murder the people he most loves; that he is freed of his murderous desires when he saves Celia from the burning house, fired by the incendiary Miss Robey. With the burning of the ominous rooms, his obsessions are laid and he is free.

A degree of improbability is allowed for in the epilogue, when Mark and Celia are again together on the Mexican patio; and Mark very deliberately is made to state that he has still some way to go before he is again completely well. Celia answers: 'We have to go this way together.'

25   The House by the River (1949)

Made after Secret Beyond the Door and following immediately after, The House by the River takes up the same themes in a manner that is perhaps even stricter and more precise. A film of fear in which desire leads to strangulation, a film of the night in which the scream augments in relation to the image, Lang's main erotic obsession is here displayed more clearly than in any other of his films. Secret and House together form a singular enclave in his oeuvre, the perfectly achieved climax of a way of directing partly abandoned in favour of the search for greater nakedness which was not a regression, but an evolution towards a different goal.
Michel Mourlet: 'Billet Londonien' in Cahiers du Cinema, No 102, December 1959

House by the River constitutes, in the oeuvre of Fritz Lang, one of those moments of pause like Moonfleet or Rancho Notorious, in which, with the help of a story based on fear, the author of The Big Heat gives free rein to a

Lang recalls very little about this film, and its subject matter seems unfamiliar to him, though he finds it interesting. It is easy to see the attractions of the story for Lang: the transition from good to evil 'with the speed of thought', as the Devil in Lessing's *Faust* remarks; the 'once off guard' theme, the how and why of a man's becoming guilty, here presented even more mercilessly than in the nightmare of *Woman in the Window*; his favourite idea that in certain situations very little distinguishes a peaceful citizen from a law-breaker; the half-tones, the doom-laden and dream-like atmospheres, hinted in the script and strengthened in the realisation.

The opening of the script already establishes the atmosphere – perhaps too markedly, for Lang generally does not like beginnings which too clearly evoke and anticipate later events:

A row of old and dignified houses of early Victorian architecture is seen from the opposite bank of a river. As CAMERA MOVES IN CLOSER and PANS DOWN the river we are aware of a peculiar lack of activity; no tugs go by, no one is in sight.

CAMERA concentrates on the rushing water of the river; hinting at dark things, passion and death and furtive cruelties, and all that sense of secrecy and crime which clings to the riverside of cities. Somehow there is a feeling of expectancy and disaster – as if horrible things might easily be accomplished beside these dark waters, then hidden and condoned by the river, carried away to oblivion in the sea. CAMERA HOLDS: a few twigs and scum and masses of seaweed float by. Suddenly a sodden, heavy mass of something floats into shot, half submerged in the water. CAMERA FOLLOWS as it hits a brighter patch of water and we see that it is a dead cow. With dingy light-coloured hide and bloated belly, it flows down drowned and forgotten on the water. As it begins to float down out of shot, a woman's VOICE IS HEARD O.S.

House by the River: Stephen tries to strangle his wife

profound romanticism. Yet through this romanticism which gives us wonderful structures and vibrant nature studies, Lang keeps his lucid critical eye . . . In The House by the River *he deals with the notion of guilt, one of his main obsessions . . .* House *differs from* Beyond . . .*, on account of the dream like quality of its atmosphere. Afterwards one wants to go back, as to those dreams whose endings one can foresee, back to that astonishing peace which reigns in the first scenes of the film, on a summer's evening, near the stream. Anxiety grows rather from tenderness than from cruelty.*
Bertrand Tavernier: 'Lettre de Bruxelles', *Cahiers du Cinema*, No. 132, June 1962

Mrs Ambroise's Voice (O.S.): 'I hate this river!'

Louis Hayward plays the novelist, Stephen Byrne, good-looking, but weak and glib in his charm. He is not a very successful writer: the post laid on his desk by the maid Emily includes a rejected manuscript.

Emily asks if she may use the upstairs bathroom, since the plumber has not been to repair her own in the basement, and Mrs Byrne is away with friends in the country. Stephen agrees, and continues to battle with his writing in the garden. A blot falls on the sheet; he crumples it, then makes more blots on a fresh page, folding the sheet to create patterns. From time to time he glances up at the bathroom window with light shining through its curtains. A beetle crawls over the paper, and Byrne carefully replaces it in safety on the grass. This detail is characteristic of Lang (he recalls he had personally to search for a beetle for the scene) in serving at least a dual purpose: to illuminate Stephen Byrne's character at the moment and to provide an ironic comment on his morality: the man who cannot hurt an insect will five minutes later kill a human being.

Stephen has entered the house. We hear the bathroom door open, and see a streak of light fall on the wall opposite. Emily, in her bathrobe descends the stairs – at first the upper part of her remains in the shadows, and starts at the sound of a glass clinking on a tray. 'Oh, Mr Byrne! You've frightened me.' Stephen stops her, playfully taxes her with using his wife's scent, then passionately kisses the astonished girl on the mouth. When he starts to embrace her, she struggles, then begins to scream hysterically.

Afraid that his gossipy neighbour Mrs Ambroise will hear, Stephen presses his hand to her mouth, and as she continues to scream, grasps her neck, and peers anxiously out of the window to see if Mrs Ambroise has heard. When the screaming stops, and he lets go, Emily's body falls limp. The Hays Office modified Stephen's 'Merciful God!' to 'Good Heavens!', as he realises he has killed her.

Stephen's brother John appears, seen through the panels of the front door. When the frightened Stephen does not answer, John comes in the back way. Quite undeceived by Stephen's attempts to lie, John wants to call the police; but

287

House by the River (1949): lowering the sack into the river

for the sake of Stephen's wife, Marjorie, who Stephen claims is expecting a baby, reluctantly agrees to help his brother out of one more scrape.

Stephen's search for a sack in the dark cellar, with a candle throwing grotesque shadows on the wall, gives Lang opportunity for an atmospheric scene. As the two brothers are about to carry their sacked burden to the river, Mrs Ambroise engages Stephen in conversation while John is forced to stand in the shadows with the sack: Is Marjorie home yet? What should she wear for the party to which they are all invited . . .

Finally they are able to take out their little rowing boat in the rain, with clouds hiding the moon. As they are lowering the sack, a fish jumps – its white belly flashes in the moonlight – and startles Stephen, who is almost pulled into the water by the weight. He is startled again when he returns to the eerily silent house: just as he is contemplating his tormented face in the mirror, a naked foot descends the stairs. His first thought is 'Emily!' But it is Marjorie who has come back unexpectedly soon, and wants Emily to help lace up her corset (it is the Victorian age). The flash of the silver hairbrush reminds him of the flashing belly of the fish jumping in the moonlight; and he has to plead a headache to explain his agitation. Nevertheless he goes to the party: while Stephen is unaccountably gay and noisy, John is depressed.

Emily's disappearance remains mysterious: Marjorie is encouraged by Stephen to blame the apparent runaway for the disappearance of her opal earrings; and Stephen does not defend her even though the publicity surrounding her disappearance begins to benefit his career. He does not, as is his habit, read to his wife and John the new novel, *The River*, on which he is assiduously working ('I've had enough of your criticisms!') Stephen flourishes; John becomes increasingly forlorn, and Marjorie complains of her husband:

There is such a peculiar look that comes on his face when he talks about Emily . . . It's almost as if he were actually enjoying it . . . He fancies this whole affair as a great big melodrama – with himself in the leading role.

One day as Stephen is working in the garden he hears Mrs Ambroise's off-screen voice again: 'I hate this river! . . . That horrid thing floated by again!' Realising it is the sack which has surfaced, Stephen takes out the boat. His boathook tears the sack, now back on the river bed; and a woman's long fair hair tumbles out. Stephen confides to his brother what has happened. John has meanwhile realised that his own name is stencilled on the sack, which he had himself lent to Stephen. He has also learned from Marjorie that Stephen's story that she is pregnant, by which he had won John's sympathy and help, is false.

Again Stephen is writing in the garden when a policeman arrives with the empty sack. Stephen admits that he borrowed it from his brother, but says he had been unable to find it; and pretends shock on learning that it had contained the body of Emily Gaunt. At the subseqent inquest, Stephen is suave, undisturbed, self-righteous; while John's former housekeeper tries to incriminate the employer who has dismissed her.

After the inquest (treated, like other Lang court-room

scenes, with concentrated economy) Stephen begins to hint to Marjorie suspicions of John – a cripple who could hope for nothing more than a servant girl. Marjorie is contemptuous of her husband, and goes to John whom she finds on the point of leaving as a result of the persecution he is suffering. She persuades him to remain.

Her fears that John may commit suicide evidently give Stephen an idea. While Marjorie is out of the house, he takes the missing earrings from a secret drawer in his desk. Surreptitiously he moves about the darkened house, hiding in the bathroom when Marjorie returns, until she disappears into her room. We first see the curtain stirring with the draught of the door's movement. We see Stephen's silhouette against the window of John's room, then the brief flash as he drops the earrings into the grandfather clock.

At night, with no sound but a faint, distant foghorn, John is standing by an abandoned pier, staring into the water, when Stephen – sent by Marjorie who is worrying about John – comes up behind him. John reassures him that he would not commit suicide, which would only convince people of his guilt. Stephen confides:

In spite of everything that has happened and everything that's going to happen . . . I want you to know that I've gained something . . .

All his life, he explains, he has been afraid of people and of people's opinion. This has been the trouble with his writing:

But now I'm not afraid any more, and I've written something good, because it's real.

JOHN: It took a murder to do that . . .

STEPHEN: Doesn't this justify the end?

JOHN: You must be very, very, ill, Stephen . . .

STEPHEN: Ill?

JOHN: Yes, sick. Otherwise you wouldn't think as you do . . .

STEPHEN: I can't understand my own brother sharing my wife with me . . .

Whereupon John hits him on the jaw and makes to leave. Stephen grabs an iron chain lying on the pier, moves after the limping John and brings it down on the back of his head. John crumbles, and Stephen rolls him, still apparently alive, off the pier edge. We hear a heavy splash.

Stephen enters Marjorie's room, sees her reading his manuscript now entitled *Death on the River*, and calmly asks how she likes it.

MARJORIE: (almost inaudibly) How can you ask me that?

STEPHEN: (*with a half smile*) Can't you appreciate its quality . . . quite apart from its content?

MARJORIE: (*in the same low voice*) Not when it says that my husband is a murderer . . .

STEPHEN: John must love you very much . . . letting everybody believe he did it. (*smiling*) No, he loved you very much . . . he was old-fashioned . . . he believed in chivalry.

Marjorie makes to rush for the door, but Stephen holds her back:

STEPHEN: Don't you see, Marjorie . . . your reading the script has solved everything . . .
She had used your perfume . . . she looked rather pretty and I wanted to kiss her. I didn't mean to kill her . . . I hardly touched her.
(*His hands go up to Marjorie's neck*)
But I didn't realise that it would be so easy . . .
(*His hands go round her throat*)
. . . so very easy.

Marjorie struggles helplessly. Suddenly there is a sound, of a heavy, limping tread. The back door is open; a gaslight burns in the hallway. The tread becomes clearer:

CAMERA PANS to wet muddy footprints; it is the long shadow of John as he slips up the stairs. CAMERA PANS UP – the staircase is deserted – only the curtains at the top of the stairs flutter in the draught . . .
Marjorie is fighting for her life, Stephen's thoughts are elsewhere, he listens, it appears as if the strangling has become of secondary importance to him. The background is lost in shadows, lit only by the reflection of the one dim gaslight through the open door to the corridor.
Stephen seems to witness an – apparition. John appears dripping wet and matted with blood on one side of his head, he is haggard, muddy to his knees.
Stephen's grip slackens – full of horror he believes to see his brother's ghost. He lets Marjorie drop, dashes into the corridor, runs towards the staircase. The bathroom door opens slowly and the draught blows the long white curtains out. Viewed by the dim single gaslight, it is ghostly and weird.
With an expression of extreme horror he stares in the direction of the bathroom door. The billowing curtains stream out with the draught, Stephen thinks he can see a white body – Emily with floating hair.

House by the River: the re-appearance of John

... the avenging curtains

With this second apparition his brain cracks completely, he rushes towards the staircase, but now the heavy curtains from the balcony are blown out towards him, they appear to entangle him.

In a panic he struggles frantically to disentangle himself, in his effort to free himself Stephen goes backwards over the banister. There is an agonised scream.

John and Marjorie are standing down below. CAMERA PANS AWAY from them – one sees the title page of Stephen's manuscript, *Death on the River*, while the other pages are scattered on the floor.

The late Victorian period, with its heavy draperies, plush sofas, gaslights, antiquated telephones, tight-lacing and the claustrophobic atmosphere in which erring husbands went secretly to prostitutes, is an appropriate setting for an action in which it is the shame and fear of discovery of a minor offence, and the secrecy demanded by petty bourgeois morality, that leads a man to crime. Lang emphasises all the baroque elements of the Victorian age; and the camerawork of his excellent director of

293

photography Cronjäger relishes the shadow and chiaroscuro, the monochrome shades of grey and white, the bright flash of the jumping fish or the glitter of a silver hairbrush. This black and white film seems to anticipate the colour work of *Moonfleet*, a later essay in period recreation.

The melodrama is transformed into a work of art; not only in the formal shape and composition, but in the themes and their treatment. Lang's treatment of guilt, for example, is characteristically ambiguous. The 'once off guard' motif, the drama of a man trapped by circumstance or fate (which is partially character, after all; if the plumber had come in time, would Stephen have still become a murderer?) is given more depth, and acquires more point from being set in this milieu and the most bourgeois of all ages. Lang seems this time less than sympathetic to his 'once off guard' character; Stephen becomes entangled in more and more acts of cowardice as he continues to scheme and turn everything to his own advantage. Yet with Lang there are always imponderables; shortly before his psychopath brother tries to murder him, John suggests mitigating circumstances, when he says: 'You must be very sick'. Are there also such mitigating circumstances for John? To what degree is John also guilty as he aids and abets his murdering brother? Wanting to help one's brother, not wanting to upset his supposedly pregnant sister-in-law, calmly accepting blame which is not his: all these are virtues, doubtless, until they are offered as reasons for dumping a dead girl in the river and saying nothing. If the 'nice' people in the film must accept partial responsibility for the murder in their bourgeois morality, Lang also suggests that their system of justice leaves much to be desired. A girl disappears at the same time as a pair of earrings; it is assumed (with Stephen's help admittedly) that she has stolen them. The most circumstantial evidence makes John guilty of the murder in the eyes of his fellow citizens.

We have, then, returned to the beginning with the river of dark things, furtive cruelties, secrecy and crime running alongside the dignified houses of respectable society. The melodrama has turned into a moral nightmare.

26 American Guerrilla in the Philippines (1950)

The many scenes, actually
photographed in the islands, of
tattered hordes of fleeing
refugees strung across strange
and rugged landscapes, of
marauding Oriental troops, of
bearded, unkempt American
fighters inhabiting alien hovels
in alien land and dauntlessly
improvising devices and
designs as they go – all have a
timely appearance in this film.
The New York Times, 8
November 1950

Background and native
customs caught in
Technicolor give this
attraction an interesting and
different flavour.
Motion Picture Herald, 18
November 1950

When Lang was asked about *American Guerrilla in the Philippines*, he answered: 'It was also offered to me – and even a director has to make a living! Honestly, I needed some money. Directors are often blamed: "Why did you do this? And why did you do that?" But nobody ever says, "Even a director has to eat."' Admittedly the film is not among his best and most personal projects. Yet, given Lang's drive for perfection and his authority over every aspect of his medium, it would seem impossible for him to make a film which was totally without interest or which did not reflect in some way his personal vision.

Che Guevara's diaries reveal how war is more often a matter of daily incidents in the struggle for survival, than confrontation with an enemy; and Stendhal's description of Waterloo in *La Chartreuse de Parme* illustrates how tiny a sector the spectator placed in the centre of a battle can see. Lang's *American Guerrilla in the Philippines*, based on the book by Ira Wolfert with a script by producer Lamar Trotti, is, equally, made up of countless small interwoven episodes.

Lang seems without hesitation to have chosen to shoot on location in Subic Bay, Bataan Peninsula, Barras and Manila; while critics constantly speak of his liking for the studio, it would never have occurred to him to build a studio on a Japanese island, as did Sternberg for *The Saga of Anatahan*. This, with Lang's passion for documentary detail, and the sporadic character of the plot structure, gives the film an admirable directness.

It is interesting to see how typical Lang themes and concerns work outside the studio. The basic situation is like those in *Man Hunt, Hangmen Also Die, Ministry of Fear,* and *Cloak and Dagger.* The hero is suddenly in a situation

295

where the enemy is everywhere. All activity is forced underground; all 'normal' activity becomes impossible. Slowly each character moves from passive action (escape, survival) to the more active and positive movement towards fighting back in the hope of the final restoration of complete freedom of activity in a 'normal' way. While the situation remains the same, the setting tends to alter the coloration of the situation. *Man Hunt*, for example, takes on the quality of a nightmare partially because the city, the fog, and the urban night act as part of an ever-shifting and sinister trap. In the open, island locations, however, the very presence of the sky, the sea, the jungle and the open fields tends to offer more alternatives for escape and survival. While the strangeness of the island for the main characters tends to limit these alternatives, it is still not surprising that their movement towards positive action comes sooner than it does for their urban colleagues.

The film opens with the bombing of a motorboat by Japanese aeroplanes; eight survivors reach the shore. The unpretentious, precise, understated commentary constantly cuts into the action and drives it on:

For sixty-five days we took it – and gave back the best we had . . . And then – we got it!

This was the Philippines in the spring of 1942, and this was the last of Motor Torpedo Squadron X, which broke through the Japanese lines to clear the way for General MacArthur . . .

But now she was done, and we were out of business – here in a strange island, with wounded to be cared for and dead to be laid to rest in lonely graves, eight thousand miles from home . . .

Jim Mitchell (Tom Ewell) one of the survivors tries in vain to start his battered radio. Only when he kicks it does it give out first a blare of dance music, then the news that Bataan has fallen to the Japanese. The survivors decide to split up so as not to be conspicuous, and to make for Del Monte Airfield, from which they can get a priority lift to Australia.

Mitchell goes with Chuck Palmer (Tyrone Power):

There was a lot of walking for us after that – over mountains – through jungles – in equatorial heat and rain – sometimes waist-deep in water . . .

among refugees, threatened by Japanese soldiers.

296

An American Guerrilla in the Philippines (1950) : Chuck Palmer (Tyrone Power)

An American Guerrilla in the Philippines: (Micheline Presle)

For two weeks and ten days we were on the jump until at last we came towards a town.

At the mission school of Tacloban on the island of Leyte, Chuck learns that the Japanese have taken Del Monte Airport. Advised to stay and surrender according to orders, Chuck determines to press on for Australia. He borrows money from the sceptical Colonel whom he also persuades to give a permit for a woman to enter the over-crowded hospital for a cesarean operation.

Despite further dissuasion from Jeanne (Micheline Presle), the cousin of the pregnant woman, Chuck and eight other men provision a small rowing boat. Notwith-standing inexperience and the mutiny of a piglet – part of the provisions – they get under way.

Wrecked in a storm, they swim for hours, but are picked up by a Filipino fishing boat, and nursed back to health by the Filipinos of Leyte. Despite trouble with the traitorous Politico, they make their getaway with the aid of a Filipino, Miguel, when the Japanese arrive. Arriving in Tacloban they again encounter Jeanne, with her husband Martinez who persuades Colonel Grenada to get them a boat if Chuck will first lead his men on a perilous mission to contact the guerrilla leader Colonel Philip.

Hijacking a Japanese motor launch, they cross the Gulf of Leyte and the difficult, insect-infested Djuta mountains to reach Philip. Philip sends Chuck and his men back to Leyte ('We don't want men in Australia, we want them *here*') to take charge of radio operations. When they return, the Free Leyte Provisional Government has been set up:

We were starting from scratch, but the people of Leyte were quick to respond, offering what they had freely ... We printed our own money.

So finally Chuck is following Jeanne's original advice to stay and fight. Her husband Martinez assists with the radio station, and pays with his life when he refuses to betray its whereabouts to the Japanese. Again Lang does not show the torture directly. Martinez is dragged back, off camera. We hear blows; and a Japanese officer tells Jeanne 'This is the way we treat guerrillas', as she turns her head away. The next scene is Martinez's funeral.

Back in the jungle, it is by now Christmas. Jeanne improvises a Christmas tree out of a tropical plant, sings a French carol for Chuck; and they exchange their first kiss. Not unlike Jasper and Gina in *Cloak and Dagger*, their emotion is partially born from the situation of being thrown together into the dangers of war. At this moment Miguel is brought in gravely wounded. Chuck's primitive surgery is unable to save him.

That Christmas somehow, marked the beginning of a change on Leyte. For one thing, our subs were coming in regularly now, bringing with them guns and all manner of supplies. For another, our guerrilla armies were going on the offensive everywhere.

Chuck accomplishes a near suicidal mission to establish a radio observation post behind enemy lines. Later, when the Japanese return to the village, the population barricade themselves in the church, from the windows of which Chuck and a choirboy keep up a valiant defence with one tommy gun and a pistol. The siege is becoming desperate when suddenly there is the noise of aircraft, and the Japanese hastily withdraw. General MacArthur has kept his word: the reason for the siege on the church was a Japanese officer's picking up of a chocolate bar dropped by a frightened Filipino boy. On it was inscribed 'I shall return – MacArthur'. In a final scene we see Chuck and Jeanne driving in a jeep through a jubilant crowd as the American and Filipino flags flutter side by side in the wind.

Ira Wolfert's book was based on the real experiences of an American guerrilla leader in Leyte, David Richardson. Lang turns the loose recital of often apparently unrelated episodes into a *chanson de geste*, reminiscent of Brecht's epic theatre. Like the song in *Rancho Notorious*, the commentary is used to concentrate and comment on the situation, in a tone of cool but sympathetic understatement.

The Lang of *American Guerrilla* is unfamiliar. His passion for precise research and documentation have paid off, despite the speed with which the film was made, in working on location instead of in the studio and in depicting an unfamiliar country and its people. Lang does not, however, aim for a picture-book exoticism: the exotic details emerge organically from the action – for instance the Filipino dance between poles which occurs during a relaxed moment in the film. The Filipino struggle for liberty must have appealed to the director of *Hangmen Also Die*; but the creation of a free country is shown without sentimentality, demonstrated in a thousand small details of guerrilla warfare, or the printing techniques involved in establishing a paper currency.

300

27 Rancho Notorious (1951)

We love Westerns in proportion to whether they offer us just enough surprises to make us experience the pleasure of seeing images we have seen a hundred times before. Fritz Lang respects here the rules of the game which he has insidiously complicated by introducing an unusual reality into the cinematic medium: time . . . by accepting the age of his interpreter he shows the two myths it illustrates: that of the Western and his own. This is why there is an unknown emotion, a sort of derisory and tragic complicity with the film women – who suddenly resemble the women in life and ourselves.
Claude Mauriac: *L'Amour du Cinema*, Albin Michel, Paris 1954

Rancho Notorious is unique among Westerns, going beyond even the school of the 'psychological Western'. The subject matter is clothed in half tones, the course of the action is kept in a minor and at the same time ironic key. It is seen in depth, new aspects are opened up by imponderables; the 'once upon a time' of a melancholy fairy tale is mingled with a crude reality in which values have lost their meaning. Moral certainties and a peaceful life are torn apart at the beginning of the film, an average 'normal' man is corrupted by hate, but nothing is restored to its former state by the end. The dark undertones of *The Return of Frank James* and *Western Union* have here come to the foreground; there will be no possibility of a return to a pastoral existence, no happy ending. Whatever redemption is possible for the characters is here only partial and carries the taste of 'bitter and evil fruit'. At once unsentimental yet full of gentle nostalgic longing for the past, it is the saga of an aging but still very desirable dance hall girl and an old gun hand who is no longer as quick on the draw as he once was. It is still the myth of Marlene, yet with the goddess facing maturity: resignation tempers the triumphant pose of the *femme fatale*. A similar type of woman would have ruined men in earlier Lang films: here she throws herself into the path of the bullet intended for her old lover.

Howard Hughes, who financed the film, changed the admirable title *The Legend of Chuck-a-Luck* (from the name of the vertical roulette wheel of Western bar-rooms) because he believed Europeans would not understand it. The title *Rancho Notorious* means even less to a non-American audience. The film was moreover heavily cut, and the writer Daniel Taradish maintains (cf. Eibel:

Textes, page 68) that the producer boasted of having cut out all the 'ambience'. Fortunately he was unsuccessful: even though he was compelled to use backdrops, painted skies and the Western street of the Republic lot, Lang's experience in working in interiors, together with his excellent production designer, Wiard Ihnen, served him well; and the film is rich in authentic Lang atmospheres. It might even be argued that *Rancho Notorious* would not have worked half so well had it been shot on locations. The world of the film is a closed one, in which moral alternatives are limited, in which literally there is nowhere to go. The painted backdrops, beautiful in themselves, serve to emphasise the moral situation.★

The theme song – 'the old story of hate, murder and revenge' – powerfully reinforces the impact of the film. The 'theme song' used as a continuing and integral commentary was at this time new (Lang invented its use in film a year before *High Noon* was released); and from it *Rancho Notorious* derives the feeling of a ballad, a legend, a saga appropriate to a Western which is a celebration of the pioneer past.

The prologue to the film achieves its impact from its abrupt juxtaposition of moods of tender lyricism and horrifying violence. The little Wyoming town is deserted (everyone has gone to visit the mother of newly born triplets), except for Beth left alone in the general store, and a little boy, Tommy, when Vern rides in to give his fiancée Beth a brooch. After Vern leaves, Kinch and the aged, white-haired Whitey, two outlaws, ride into town. Kinch enters the store, forces Beth to open the safe, and his gaze lingers on the brooch on her seductive shoulder ... Outside little Tommy hears a scream and a shot. Kinch rushes out of the store and the two outlaws ride off. With this violation of the peaceful normality of the town, the values upon which it was founded are also violated. The values are turned into something suspect, as we will see in the town of Gunsight a bit later in the film.

As in *M* we are shown nothing of the rape. When Vern arrives back, Beth is lying dead on the couch, her brooch off, with a piece of her dress, blood staining her shoulder and breast, a limp hand dangling to the floor. The doctor tells him:

★ Further illustration of how such sets can work wonderfully to underscore such moral and ideological concerns can be found in two later Westerns: *The Man Who Shot Liberty Valence* (John Ford, 1961) and *El Dorado* (Howard Hawks, 1967).

Vern, I don't know how to tell you this – She – wasn't spared anything.

While the sheriff leads a posse to the borders of Sioux country, the vengeful Vern rides on alone. He comes upon the dying Whitey, who had wanted to dissociate himself from the rape-murder by taking his cut and riding on alone and was therefore shot in the back by Kinch, and who tells him as he dies that the murderer has gone 'To Chuck-a-Luck':

Now where and what is Chuck-a-Luck?
Nobody knows and the dead won't tell
So on and on relentlessly this man pursues his quest
Through fall – and winter – searching the great Southwest
This thing that drives him like a whip will never let him rest
Night and day, early and late
He looks for a place,
Or a town, or a face
And deep within him grows the beast of HATE
MURDER
And REVENGE . . .

Thus Vern has quickly changed from the innocent lover carrying a brooch to a gun-carrying version of Kriemhild or Joe Wilson; soon he will be so poisoned by his hate that he will be unable to see good anywhere. For him, everyone will be guilty or suspect. During the ballad there is a montage of mute shots of Vern questioning strangers on his way. All shake their heads or shrug. None knows, until, the song ended, he asks in a barber shop and is told by another customer:

I wouldn't talk about Chuck-a-Luck so free if I were you . . . Altar Keane wouldn't like it.

The customer defensively draws his gun – he turns out to be a wanted bandit – and Vern overpowers him to set out on the quest for the mysterious Altar Keane.

Suddenly we see her for the first time, in flashback, as the middle-aged deputy recalls the day in his youth when he was her mount in a ribald steeplechase in which the jockeys were dance-hall girls and the horses their customers. The laugh of the deputy suddenly mingles with the gay hearty laughter of Altar riding the younger deputy. She is blonde, rouged, bejewelled, leggy and handsome. In short, it is Marlene in all her glory, vic-

Rancho Notorious (1951): the ribald steeplechase

Rancho Notorious: Altar (Marlene Dietrich) with Frenchy (Mel Ferrer) and
Vern (Arthur Kennedy) – a publicity photograph

torious as she and her miner 'horse' take all the obstacles
in the chase – a stepladder, a rope held by two men, tables
and chairs. Unscrupulous, she kicks a rival with her long,
beautiful legs, stops another with her arm. The whole
sequence is without dialogue; the shouts and laughs
mingle with the music, for there is no need of dialogue: the
focus of the scene is Marlene, as supremely the apogee of
womanhood as when sitting on the barrel in *The Blue
Angel*. The whole passage glitters, its visual impact as
powerful as a blow. Lang knew exactly how to use the
presence and the myth of Marlene; Vern will now try
everything to find this Altar Keane.

Vern encounters other recollections of Altar. In Dodge
City her former friend Dolly recalls how Altar would
have shut the door on a cattle baron if she had a fancy for a
cowpuncher. In Baldy Gunder's shabby saloon in Tascosa
he learns she was fired after she kicked a man in the jaw for
fondling her knee while she was singing and because 'you

don't smile enough!'. Almost cheated out of her winnings by Baldy on his own fixed roulette wheel. Frenchy Fairmont (Mel Ferrer) – the fastest draw in the West who once rode with General Lee – protected her that night, taking her home without asking himself for 'payment'. Since then, Altar and Frenchy had met again. Baldy takes malicious delight in revealing that Altar's cosy liaison with Frenchy has come to an end, and that the gunman is waiting to be hanged:

Now the trail that goes to Chuck-a-Luck, Chuck-a-Luck
Leads to a jail down Gunsight way.

The theme song and the flashbacks which Lang structures so organically and rhythmically, have thus created a mosaic impression of the myth of the youthful, glamorous Altar Keane, to prepare us for the woman of later years.

As Vern arrives in Gunsight, an election is in progress, with the slogan 'Throw the grafters out of town! Vote Law and Order!' prominently plastered in the centre of the little town. The small town election, however, is an ironic inversion of the values of the earlier small town in Wyoming. Like the citizens in *Fury*, the 'Law and Order' party plans to rid its town of evil (the grafters) by doing evil (lynching the ousted politicians). In seeing moral corruption everywhere, Vern is here, at least, accurate. Vern manages to get himself thrown into jail by shooting up the bar (gone 'dry' for the election period), and is put in Frenchy's cell. Together they break jail, using the horses prepared for their fellow-prisoners, three corrupt local politicians. As Vern has planned, Frenchy takes him to Altar Keane's Chuck-a-luck ranch.

Altar is wearing faded denims and a simple shirt. When Frenchy tells her about the jail-break, and how Vern 'used his head and used his guts', she comments sardonically, 'Uses his eyes, too, doesn't he?'. She allows him to stay at the ranch:

Once you agree to the rules –
We don't have any fighting here
We don't ask any questions.

Vern spends his time learning sharp-shooting from Frenchy, and studying the outlaws who surround Altar.

Rancho Notorious

Ironically, while he shoots at a silver dollar obligingly spun by Kinch, whom he does not suspect, he comes to the conclusion that the lady-killer, Wilson, may have been Beth's murderer.

He is attracted to Altar, and not merely because he hopes to use her to find the murderer. He is attracted both by what he had learned about her (the romantic myth) and by her honesty and more mature beauty. His courting her casts a shadow on his relationship with Frenchy. Talking about his days with General Lee, Frenchy says 'I just don't like to lose anything . . . even a war'. His significant glance indicates he is speaking of Altar. Vern is warned by Frenchy:

'Lately I see you trying everything I do.'
'If I keep on I might be able to outdraw you some day.'
'Don't ever try it.'

The rivalry for Altar is intensified during her birthday

party ('and don't ask me how old I'll be tomorrow . . .
Every year is a threat to a woman.') when she sings a song
with a special significance:

A young man is reckless and ready
A young man is handsome and vain.
He's young and intense, but he hasn't the sense
To come in out of the rain.

Get away – get away
Get away, young man, get away

A young man is full of adventure
And eager to do what he can.
He may be a joy, but don't send a boy
To do the work of a man . . .

Before she sings the third verse, she pulls off her scarf to
throw it to Frenchy, revealing Beth's brooch on her
dress.★

The look-out reports riders approaching the ranch, and
the men all ride out. Vern however returns, and is in time
to save the situation when the marshal's men notice that
horses are missing from the corral. Vern's calloused
cowboy hands convince the marshal that he is not a
gunman. When Frenchy returns and finds Vern and Altar
together, his suspicions are aggravated: now the song
moves from illustration to commentary, and the immediacy with which it grows out of the situation serves to
demonstrate Brecht's 'epic' theory:

Oh, there's trouble in the air at Chuck-a-Luck! Chuck-a-Luck!
And death is waiting at every turn
There's jealousy and fear, and suspicion here
And a woman with love to burn.
And he somehow feels that in this place
He'll meet the killer face to face
Which one . . . which one will die for
HATE
MURDER
And REVENGE?

The resentful Frenchy takes Vern along on a bank
robbery. Kinch, who has now realised who Vern is from
the way he mounts his horse, tries to shoot him during the
raid, and sets off a gun battle from which the robbers
retreat with their lives and their money. Frenchy however
is missing. Vern rides back to the ranch with Altar's share

★ It is interesting to
compare Lang's use of the
motif of the brooch and
revenge with that of John
Ford (*My Darling
Clementine*, 1946) and of
Henry Hathaway (*Nevada
Smith*, 1966).

of the loot. He asks her to put on her dress; and tells her the significance of the brooch. As he flings his share of the loot at her feet, in exchange for the brooch, the last words of the song are heard –

HATE
MURDER
And REVENGE

Vern confronts Kinch with the brooch in the saloon, and tells him he will kill him. Kinch is too cowardly to fight however and Vern hands him over to the sheriff:

I've tracked you for a year and a half . . . All I wanted of life was to kill you . . . But something has happened to me . . . Maybe I'm just not a killer

Frenchy returns to the ranch wounded and exhausted, to find Altar leaving. She explains that she wants to go away and be a dance hall girl again; and denies that she is going with Vern: 'He wouldn't have me'. Meanwhile the outlaws, having freed Kinch on his way to jail, return to settle scores with Altar whom they suspect of betraying them. Vern comes back in time to assist Altar and Frenchy. In the gun battle which ensues, Frenchy kills Kinch before he can shoot Vern. Altar sees the outlaw Wilson draw on Frenchy, and throws herself in front of Frenchy to protect him. Vern shoots Wilson but too late to prevent his bullet hitting Altar. The gun-battle over, Altar is dying.

The two men whom she loved in different ways ride off tired and aimlessly:

Now revenge is a bitter and evil fruit
And death hangs beside it on the bough
These men that lived by the code of hate
Have nothing to live for now . . .
And the legends tell that when Custer fell
They died with him in the fight.

So Frenchy, who once rode with Lee for a lost cause, and Vern who has lost everything that made his life worth living, go off together to the hoplessness of a lost battle.

There is much more to this beautiful film than the familiar Lang themes of violence, revenge, wrong and right, justice, the *femme fatale*, the efficiently functioning outlaw organisation and its guiding boss. The organic

fusion of psychological motivation and adventure spring-
ing from them, produces a sense of harmony and tragedy
which is instinct, never exteriorised.

Fury already revealed a profound and mature understanding of the vanity of violence. Here it is even more
evident, emphasised by the use of the theme song to
summarise and to anticipate events, to supply the film's
structure as a ballad of the old frontier. Its rhythm merges
with the rhythm of the action and the vibrant reactions of
the characters. The new role of the *femme fatale* – saving the
life of her lover, rather than ruining him – suggests that
Lang's pessimism has matured and changed: he understands better the complexity of existence and the
impossibility of reducing it to formulas of implacable fate.

28 Clash By Night (1951)

Lang finds himself forced to comply with the modern New York theatre which indulges in the display of human misery. Yet here, where the New Yorkers blame the misery on some kind of undefined ananke, somehow linked with the social constitution of the United States . . . Lang insists on the concept of responsibility. Destiny again represented by the movement of the waves, is fused with the realistic document.
Luc Moullet: *Fritz Lang*, Editions Seghers, 1963

Clash by Night was based on a Clifford Odets success of the early forties, and both Lang and Jerry Wald, the film's unofficial producer, were very fond of the play. Nevertheless the focus is considerably altered in the screen vision. In the original the action centred on the social background of the thirties, unemployment and the relation of these conditions to the cuckolded husband's final murder of the wife's lover. The film is concerned essentially with the more personal aspects of the plot: the adulterous relationship of a married woman; and its denouement is both more dramatic and less conventional. At the end the woman returns to her husband.

Wald wanted to change the scene of the action from a small mid-American town to a fishing village. To establish that Lang, the European, could grasp such a milieu, the director took his cameraman Nicholas Musaraca to Monterey (which he knew well and which had already been the setting of Steinbeck's *Cannery Row*). Some remnants of the once flourishing sardine fishing industry still survived there. Lang and Musaraca came without actors, and watched the fishing boats return, and the way the catch was thrown from underwater pipes on to a moving conveyor belt and thus straight into the canning factory.

They shot enthusiastically and discovered that in three days they had used some 10,000 feet of film. Anxiously they sent the voluminous material to Wald, and instead of the rebuke they expected they received a congratulatory telegram from the producer. The material they shot provided the introductory sequence of the film. Swarms of seagulls fly in the sun on a clear sky, waves break on the shore, a big fishing boat glides along, the masses of glittering fish are pumped by pipeline into the holding tanks. Inside the cannery women briskly process them into canned food. The atmosphere is so airy and sunny, the impressions all so glittering that it is hard to realise it is not in colour. In some copies of the film in circulation today, this splendid opening is incomplete.

The open-air atmosphere, the density of natural exteriors established here contributes to the film's escape from the theatricality of the stage original; and in this respect too the change of plot in the script by Alfred Hayes (and Lang, naturally) is effective. It is not the imposition of a happy ending by the producer that has resulted in the happy ending, but Lang's desire for verisimilitude, as well as his natural abhorrence of violence. The only result of having the husband kill her lover would be to make the wife hate him. Instead of an unnecessary act of revenge we have only the fierce quarrel in the projection room. Lang would not find it true for the simple and kindly husband, Jerry D'Amato, who knowingly married a woman with a past, to strangle his rival and suffer the punishment for it. It is enough that the friend he worshipped – an equally complicated character who in his own way also loved the woman – steals her from him. There is no reason to blow a simple tragedy up to unnecessary dimensions.

Jerry (Paul Douglas), the owner of a sardine fishing boat, conducts the trade of his Sicilian forbears in a patriarchal way, projecting his personality on a bigger scale in the new country. Mae Doyle (Barbara Stanwyck), always hopeful, always disappointed, perhaps a cut above Jerry socially, and who says that 'home's where you come to when you run out of places' is at first reluctant to accept his proposal ('You don't know anything about me. What kind of animal am I? What kind of jungle am I from?'). Only after a final scene at the dance hall with Earl Pfeiffer, the film projectionist (played with a somewhat mephis-tophelean cast by Robert Ryan) does she accept Jerry's offer. She has meanwhile confided to Earl that the only man who ever gave her what she needed had died –

a man who didn't tear a woman down. He made her feel confident – sure of herself.

She marries Jerry with the best of intentions, perhaps because he might give her something like this. She rightly

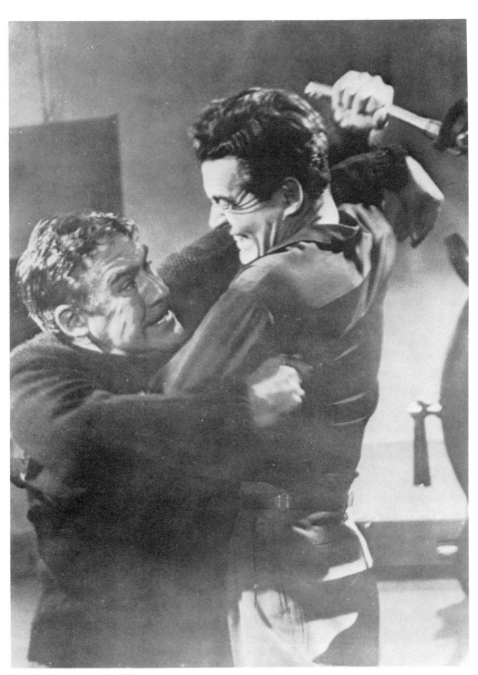

Clash By Night (1951): the fight

senses that Earl is as unstable as herself and so is dangerous for her. Jerry is indeed sad that she behaves harshly to his friend. Accident nevertheless throws them together. Earl having been divorced from his fickle wife collapses dead drunk at Jerry's house, and stays the night. The next morning, after Jerry has gone to work, the inevitable happens despite Mae's resistance. Succumbing to Earl's passion, she determines to leave Jerry, taking their child with her. It is when Earl tries to persuade her to leave the child behind with Jerry that she realises how selfish his passion is:

You'll come home – I'll be tired – the kids'll cry – there'll be dishes in the sink . . .
   And I'll have to be pretty all the time. I want to be loved ugly, tired, dull . . .
EARL Like Jerry loved you? (laughs cynically)
MAE Yes. Like Jerry loved me (slowly).

   Her return to Jerry – who has meanwhile taken the child to the safety of his boat – is treated tactfully and without sentimentality. At first Jerry is unwilling to believe her:

JERRY You never loved me. Bein' safe – bein' taken care of – that's all you wanted. And my fault was savin' you – all right – if that's the way she loves me I'll take it that way.
MAE People change. You find out what's important and what isn't. What you really want.

When Jerry still does not believe her, she calls out:

MAE Am I the only woman in the world who thought she was in love with a man and then found out she wasn't? Maybe certain things are unforgiveable.

Reluctantly Jerry relents.

JERRY You've got to trust somebody. There ain't no other way. Go take your child home.

The script concludes:

Mae turns slowly towards the bunks.

Here Lang has added, significantly:

She turns and smiles at him.

   People who question whether Mae would go back to Jerry when she realises how selfish is Earl's love should recall that twenty years later, another film Bergman's *The Touch* shows an unfaithful wife returning to her husband

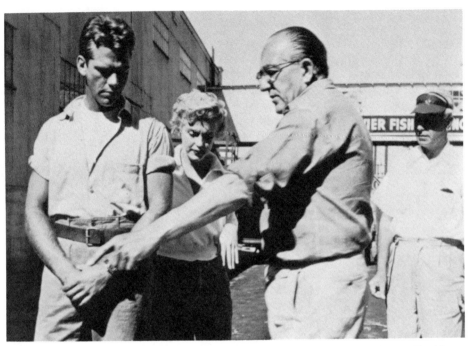

Clash By Night: Lang directing the young Marilyn Monroe

for similar reasons. Neither director can be suspected of choosing this ending simply for box-office considerations. The two directors interpret the situation differently. In both cases the decision is made not from a desire to get back to bourgeois security, but from an understanding that everyone should behave responsibly to others, and that it is not possible simply to run away from moral obligations. Bergman takes an easier way out, in not showing how the adulterous wife returns to her husband: we merely see her back in the home. Lang with his sense of logic and matter of fact shows all the consequences of the action.

The Odets play provides a parallel and counterpoint action in the story of Mae's brother Joe (Keith Andea) and his bride, who was played by the young Marilyn Monroe. Lang recalls that it required a lot of patience to deal with her. Shy and unsure of herself, she would arrive late for work – either out of stagefright or because unconsciously she was nervous of her more experienced colleagues. At the same time she was clearly aware of her sexual appeal. While Paul Douglas clearly resented this comparatively inexperienced starlet being made to act the star, Barbara Stanwyck was exceptionally kind to her, and patient even when Marilyn's fluffs and errors meant frequent retakes.

Lang remembers one particular example: a difficult scene in which Stanwyck had to deliver important dialogue and take washing from a line at the same time. Monroe was particularly bad, so the scene was retaken innumerable times to everyone's frustration except the professional Stanwyck who took it all in sympathetic stride.

Marilyn was ambitious and keen too, and asked Lang if she could have her personal coach Natasha Lytess with her. He agreed as long as Miss Lytess did not coach her at home, but when he realised that she was trying to make suggestions about how Monroe should act in front of the camera, he withdrew his permission. The result of Lang's patience and Stanwyck's unselfish and comradely help was a performance that seemed free and spontaneous and earned Monroe some excellent reviews. In contrast to the near-tragedy of Jerry and Mae, Joe and Peggy provide a tender comedy of the taming of a shrew. The high-minded Joe also adds a complication to the main plot.

Subsidiary characters are real and vivid: Jerry's father, upright and eager to work but wandering the bars with his concertina and getting drunk, since he cannot get a job; Jerry's drunken and cadging uncle, a burden upon Jerry and less harmless than the father with his hostility to the intrusion of Mae and the child, and his attempt to incite Jerry to murder his rival.

An exceptional complexity and variety in the editing corresponds to the psychological subtlety of the film, and the final shooting script reveals vividly the careful logic of Lang's direction and the precision with which every detail is planned and worked out in advance. Lang received proper praise for this even from the usually undiscerning Paul M. Jensen who declares that:

the director gets close to his characters both physically and psychologically . . .

and mentions:

the mobility of his camera as it pans and tracks, unobtrusively pulling

Clash By Night: Lang's drawing

in towards the actors and then backing off again . . .

and notices:

the tendency to cut to different angles at dramatic moments instead of allowing a scene to unfold from a single point of view.★

★The book by Jensen was written under such unusual circumstances, and has in Lang's opinion so distorted his work and personality, that it must be commented on. Apparently Jensen sent Lang a manuscript copy of his university thesis. Lang was immediately more offended by the huge number of errors of simple fact than he was by the accompanying letter demanding that the director correct the thesis, in spite of

The drawing reproduced here, by Lang himself, shows how he worked in one scene, using two back projection screens to the right and to the left of a big rock on the beach. Thus he could make a panning shot without a cut by first showing the young lovers Joe and Peggy playing on the beach, then let them disappear behind the rock and then re-emerge to climb the steps to the restaurant. All this happens under the eyes of Earl who sits on the terrace, following their movements with a cynical expression on his face. He subsequently flirts with Peggy while Joe has gone to get her sweater, but is distracted because Mae is trying to dance with the clumsy Jerry. Such shots, where the geography is dictated by the psychology, reveal the precision and economy of Lang's mind and method.

The symbolic use of the high waves to reflect emotions and underline the passions are unobtrusive, and never merely decorative, but necessary and meaningful in a drama which is orchestrated by images of air and storm. It is no longer the symbolism of an independent, autonomous fate as in the early German films. Tragedy can be averted by an act of free will on the part of the protagonists. Jerry knows what he wants. Mae has learned how empty and meaningless adventures can be. Now the two of them have to put their joint efforts into making a good marriage for the sake of their child. Everyone is responsible for his own destiny. The 'happy' ending summarises the problems of existence, and reflects that maturity and experience which we shall find echoed in Godard's *Le Mépris*.

the author's praising Lang's films. Some time after Lang's refusal to have anything to do with the project, the thesis was published. While most of the factual errors had been corrected, the author had assumed a whole new attitude towards Lang and his films. To this day, Lang who has never minded honest criticism of, even attacks on, his work, refuses to allow anyone to bring the book into his presence.

29 The Blue Gardenia (1953)

I would like to say – not to diminish the film's merit – that in this scenario Lang perhaps saw no more than a pretext, and tried harder to work out the characters than to justify the facts. Yet what richness of observed detail, what a delightful representation of the life of three young American employees . . . What a modern conception of cutting in the flat sequences . . . Fritz Lang fights neo-realism on its own ground . . .
'Maurice Scherer' (Eric Rohmer): *Un realisme méchant* in *Cahiers du Cinema*, June 1954

While Lang was shooting *Clash by Night* Howard Hughes – who still owned RKO and had financed *Rancho Notorious* – told him through his associates that 'the future held great things in store for him'. *Clash By Night* was finished on 3 November 1951. After that months went by, but Lang received no offers from anywhere. Eventually Lang's solicitor heard what the trouble was. Lang had been placed on the Hollywood black-list, not as a communist, but as a *potential* communist.

Even before the end of the war there had been signs that certain Americans would have preferred to fight the Soviet Union on the German side; and after the death of Roosevelt the cold war against the Soviet Union began in the United States. When Joseph McCarthy became senator for Wisconsin in 1948, he quickly recognised the House Committee on Un-American Activities, founded the year before, as a valuable political stepping-stone. Hollywood was his finest showplace. The so-called Black List contained the names of liberals as well as out and out communists, which is why Fritz Lang, Walter Wanger and even Thomas Mann found themselves on it. Lang of course had been a friend of such known left-wingers as Brecht and Toller, had worked with Hanns Eisler, and used the scriptwriters Ring Lardner Jr. and Albert Maltz – both included in the Hollywood Ten – on *Cloak and Dagger*. So he was informed that there was no longer any work for him.

Only after eighteen months of enforced idleness was Lang offered work, by a producer named Adolf Gottlieb. Gottlieb wanted to use the title *The Blue Gardenia* which had been suggested to him by the *nom de guerre* of a prostitute who had recently been brutally murdered,

'Black Dahlia'. The script had no prostitute, but it had a murder; and Gottlieb hoped to cash in on the title as quickly as possible before the sensational murder was forgotten. *The Blue Gardenia* served its purpose of getting Lang back into work. In 1953 Harry Cohn of Columbia gave him a year's contract, and testified before the House on Un-American Activities Committee that Lang had never been a member of the Communist party.

Apart from this Lang has no particular affection for *The Blue Gardenia*. It had to be shot in twenty days which left little time for the preparation and revision of the script, though he was able to modify the dialogue and, in one important particular, the action. Nor did it have the kind of social message which he preferred. For all that the film is remarkably vivid and substantial, with the world of the telephone exchange – a busy harem of girls with their individual preoccupations and troubles, all ready to pounce on the first man that enters – and the world of the tiny apartment in which the three girls live a cheerfully irritable spinster life. The cramped space (in which the opening of the bathroom door leads immediately to bumping somebody's bottom) and subtle angles seem to focus the characters: the worldy-wise Crystal just starting to flirt again with her divorced husband Homer; the childlike Sally, engrossed in the world of paperback thrillers and dating the drugstore librarian; the gentle, romantic Norah.

It is Norah who is caught 'once off guard' and drawn into the whirlpool. Alone in the apartment on her birthday, she sits down to a prettily laid table facing a photograph of her fiancé who is a lieutenant in faraway Korea. As she drinks her champagne, she opens and reads his latest letter. He has suddenly broken the engagement; he has met a nurse and is going to marry her. Norah is distraught and vulnerable when the phone rings. It is the famous fashion designer, Harry Prebble, who has met the girls while sketching in the telephone exchange. While hoping to date the lively (and 'easy') Crystal, when he learns she is dining with her ex-husband, he settles for Norah instead: to him it is all the same.

Lang instantly evokes the sultry and intoxicating ambience and cheap exoticism of the Blue Gardenia restaurant where there is always too much rum in the

The Blue Gardenia (1953): the birthday table scene

Polynesian Pearl Diver cocktails. In a characteristic and ingenious shot, a tilted mirror behind Nat King Cole, who is singing in the background, reflects his piano keyboard and behind the whole restaurant. Prebble persuades the now tipsy Norah to go to his flat on the pretext that he has invited some friends. There – with the concealed lighting casting strange shadows of the tropical plants, and the gramophone playing 'The Blue Gardenia' – he slips her more rum in the coffee she drinks to sober her up. She falls asleep on the couch, and when she awakes to find Prebble making advances to her, she at first thinks in her confusion it is her boy-friend; then starts to struggle. Prebble has pushed her to the fireplace; there is the glint of the fire irons; she awkwardly seizes the poker, which crashes into the mirror.

At this point the script as written looks temptingly effective for any director:

Norah swings the poker downwards to Harry in front of the broken mirror. We SEE the distorted vision of the piece of mirror. The piece of mirror falls and we HEAR Harry's hoarse yell. Flash of Harry with his arm trying to protect his face, he stumbles over a table or low chair and falls to the floor.

Sound of falling poker. On soundtrack, crash of the mirror, the music of the record and Harry's yell melt into the distant ringing sound as though a doorbell is ringing in Norah's mind. The ringing of the door bell repeats and changes into knocking. Norah slowly collapses in a faint on the floor, around her inert body (CAMERA MOVES DOWN with her) trick black waves wash in and out from various angles, sometimes blackening her out, sometimes leaving her face free. When they cover her face all SOUND comes to a *complete silence*. But when they leave her again the SOUND TRACK contains a *medley of distortion, blurred voices, knocking* and the rain outside.

Finally the black waves retreat. Norah looks vacantly up to see: in the remaining piece of glass we see the reflection of two vague and indefinite figures moving . . .

Lang's cinematic instinct told him that to show the audience the clever distortions, the ringing, knocking, entering of another person and so on would have killed every bit of suspense and revealed the solution. He therefore simplifies all this: Norah falls to the floor after the breaking of the mirror. Whirlpools of waves envelop her, and neither Norah nor the spectator know what has happened. Norah wakes up as if from a fever dream, and without looking round runs out into the thunderstorm, leaving her shoes behind.

Next morning she wakes with a leaden head. Her only recollection is a flash of her own distorted face in the mirror, which recalls the evening before. At the telephone exchange the girls who had been sketched by Prebble the day before are interviewed one by one by police investigating his murder. A pair of shattered sunglasses startle her; and in a characteristic ellipsis, the shot leads Lang to Prebble's apartment and the investigation there, treated in cool documentary style: the police, cameramen, a journalist called Casey Mayo, the inspector who is exasperated by the conscientious charlady who has polished away all fingerprints ('that's what I'm paid for'); the discovery of the incriminating size $5\frac{1}{2}$ court shoes and a lace handkerchief.

The spectator shares Norah's fears that she is guilty, and experiences all the shocks of her shattered nerves. Leaving

The Blue Gardenia: the smashing of the mirror

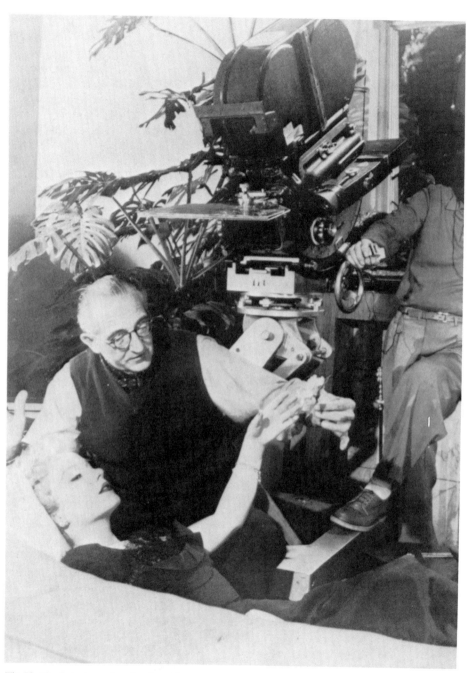

The Blue Gardenia: Lang directing Anne Baxter

the apartment she bumps into a policeman – but he is only looking for the janitor. About to burn what she takes to be the incriminating taffeta dress she had worn that evening (a characteristic Lang touch: it is wrapped in a newspaper with Prebble Murder headlines), she is stopped by another cop – 'Lady, don't you know it's against the law to burn an incinerator at night?'. On the point of telephoning Casey Mayo who has offered his help to the unknown suspect, in his newspaper, she sees the car of a deputy sheriff outside the telephone kiosk, and flees.

Reminiscent of the blind street hawker in *M*, the blind flower woman from the Blue Gardenia tells the police about the taffeta dress: 'Taffeta has a voice of its own. It rustles like no other material'. Yet just when Norah has succeeded in burning her new dress, Inspector Haynes tells Mayo:

The taffeta dress isn't much of a clue, Casey. My wife tells me they're all the rage this year . . . Shoes are different . . .

Casey Mayo, who has pinned his ambitions on to solving this case, decides to base his investigations on the shoes. His open letter to The Girl of the Blue Gardenia is written to keep alive the sensation. In a Lang montage that again recalls *M* we watch all sorts of people read the letter in the newspaper. As Norah reads the letter, we hear Mayo's own voice on the sound track:

I hope you will read this letter . . .
I want to help you . . .
But I do care . . .
You can trust me

Alone in his office, Mayo sits answering endless phone calls from hysterical women (including one who confesses, a humorous touch typical of Lang, to the murder because of a 'big passion', but is dismissed because her feet are equally big, size $8\frac{1}{2}$). Norah, the only one to give the right shoe size, makes an appointment to come to see him. On her arrival Lang uses a characteristic shock lighting effect, when Casey suddenly turns on the bright light in the dark office. Norah unconvincingly relates the incidents that happened 'to a friend'. Mayo drops some ash on her dress so that he can see her handkerchief: it is not a lace one, like the handkerchiefs dropped in Prebble's flat and in the telephone box from which Norah unsuccessfully tried to call Mayo.

Still unaware that Norah is the Blue Gardenia, since his preconception of the mysterious girl is of someone no better than she ought to be, he arranges with her to meet her 'friend' the next afternoon. It is not Mayo, however, who betrays her to the police, but the unpleasant barman, Bill, who overhears the conversation at their rendezvous, when Norah reveals the truth.

Unhappily, Mayo sets off from the airport to his next assignment. Suddenly hearing a record on the coffee-shop juke box, he realises it is the one that was on Prebble's phonograph when the cleaning woman discovered the body, and not 'The Blue Gardenia', which Norah remembered playing as she blacked out. Investigation in record shops to discover where the disc was bought leads to an aging woman, Rose, with whom Prebble had had a brief (and at the time apparently insignificant) telephone conversation early in the film. Just as Haynes is trying to dissuade Mayo from his wild goose chase, Rose is found in the ladies' room with her wrists slashed. (The apparently harmless telephone conversation will find an echo in a similar call in Beyond a Reasonable Doubt.)

Rose's hospital-bed confession is shown as a series of flashbacks, which only now reveal the events hinted in the elaborate sequence prescribed much earlier by the script: she had burst in on Prebble while Norah lay unconscious, and despite his efforts to calm her by putting on her favourite phonograph record, had killed him in the fury of being scorned. The epiloque is light-hearted. When Norah is released from prison she is cool with Mayo, not because she still thinks he betrayed her, but because Crystal has given him her (their) telephone number. Mayo however demonstates his intention of fidelity by handing over his 'little black book' of telephone numbers of call-girls and Crystal-types to the delighted Haynes.

30 The Big Heat (1953)

With The Big Heat . . .
Lang found a subject – a small
town dominated by a racketeer
and a young detective's
determination to break his
tyranny – in which he could
combine American 'realism'
and the more abstract, symbolic
menace of his most
characteristic melodrama . . .

From the opening shot, the
close-up of the revolver . . .
lying on the table, there is a
morose intentness on violence.
The killings and outrages . . .
are not presented with great
physical emphasis or detail –
several of them occur off-screen
– but they determine,
menacingly, the course of the
action.

In its great variety of human
comment, and its more
intimate observation of
character, The Big Heat
marks a development in
Lang's work . . . these are
unusually rounded portraits
presented more acutely and
vividly for themselves than is
usual with Lang . . . The
texture of the film is richer and
more concentrated than in any
of his works since the 30s.
Gavin Lambert: *Fritz*
Lang's America, in Sight and
Sound, *Autumn* 1955

Every film, says Lang, has to have its own rhythm. The rhythm of *The Big Heat* is a relentless action, spurred by hate, murder and revenge (there is a parallel to *Rancho Notorious* in that the detective is more keenly motivated to his investigation following the murder of his wife). Here Lang had an excellent script, by the crime reporter, Sidney Boehm, and one which he could regard as serious in theme: a real accusation against crime and the criminal. The script must also have appealed to him in its treatment of the spread of corruption throughout society on both sides of the law.

A letter to Lang from his producer Robert Arthur, dated 10 April 1953 suggests that the Breen Office may be thanked for the extreme effectiveness of the opening scene: the censors thought it too gruesome to show the suicide directly, so stimulated Lang into a scene of suggestive intensity. We see a close-up of a pistol on a desk. A hand comes into the picture, then an arm. The hand takes up the pistol and the camera moves back to reveal the back of the man's head and the raised weapon. A shot; and the man's head and arms slump to the desk. The camera pans to a bulky envelope addressed to the District Attorney, and beside it a police sergeant's badge.

Wakened by the shot, the wife of the suicide comes downstairs. She shows no emotion, simply opens the letter, glances through the pages and picks up the telephone:

Mr Logana!
I know it's late – wake him up!
Tell him it's Tom Duncan's widow.
Yes, I said, widow.

Woken by his secretary and bodyguard, the millionaire

329

racketeer Logana, thanks Bertha Duncan for the news, and says they should meet. It is clear that she intends to use the letter, which she puts into a safe place, against Logana.

Logana tells his secretary to call up Vincent Stone (Lee Marvin), and we see some of Logana's gang. Vince, gruff, rugged and apparently self-assured, is goaded by his girl friend Debbie (Gloria Grahame) about his subservience to Logana:

I always like to tell Vince you're calling – I always like to watch him jump.

she tells Logana. Later on she tells one of the gangsters:

Ever go to the circus, Larry? You should – and take Vince. The man in the big hat holds up the hoop, cracks the whip! – Come Vince! Up! Over! Come Larry! Up – over!

This not only tells us about the inter-gang relationships, but also reveals a good deal about Debbie: outspoken, clear-sighted, and honest, even about herself. In return Vince charges this frivolous yet worldly-wise mistress:

Six days a week she shops . . .
On the seventh she rests – all tired out!

The clues to future relationships are laid. With characteristic economy, Lang has sketched in present relationships and laid clues for the future.

Police Sergeant Dave Bannion (Glenn Ford) suspects nothing as he interviews Bertha Duncan, who claims that Tom killed himself because he was suffering from an illness. Here Lang adds to the script, in his own large handwriting:

Bertha stands at mirror, fixes her face . . . Knock at door – she assumes tragic pose: 'Please come in'
Dave enters in mirror.

Thus before the interview begins, the audience is prepared: Bertha is going to lie.

Lucy Chapman, a bar hostess, arouses Bannion's suspicions that it is not a case of simple suicide when she tells him about Tom Duncan's excellent health, his house in Lakeside, his impending divorce and affair with herself. When she accuses him of:

covering up for a cop's widow! You don't want to find out anything that'll change her story

The Big Heat *distinguishes itself by the simplicity of its style, in the image of its heroes, by its rejection of artificiality and by the violence of its action.*
Luc Moullet: *Fritz Lang*, Editions Seghers, 1963

he retorts brutally, 'I want facts'. He returns of his own accord to question Bertha further. She acknowledges her husband's infidelity, but rejects all other implications, especially those having to do with the source of the money which paid for the big Lakeside home and the Duncan's luxurious life style.

Returning to his office, he learns that Lucy Chapman has been murdered; while his cautious lieutenant has been given orders that Bannion is to leave Mrs Duncan alone. Logana's payroll is clearly a big one; and when Bannion receives a threatening telephone call he knows who he has to see. He goes to Logana in the luxurious house of which the gangster is so proud:

This is my home.
I don't like dirt tracked to it.

When Bannion talks to him about Lucy Chapman's death, he is turned out of the house, after first knocking down the bodyguard who touches him.

One of the surprises of this film is the warmth of the domestic scenes. Contrasting with the Logana house, Lang shows the home of Bannion and his cheerful wife Katie (later described by Bannion as a 'real Irish blow-top, a sampler, she'd take sips of my drinks – taste my food and take puffs of my cigarette') and their little girl Joyce who insistently demands that Bannion tells her the story of the three kittens.

The poignancy of the end of the sequence is thus under-scored, and we are made to feel something of the same rage and emotional shock as Dave Bannion himself. Katie leaves to fetch the babysitter in the car while Bannion tucks in little Joyce. There is an explosion. Bannion rushes out; the car – blown up by the Logana mob – is already on fire. When Bannion smashes the car window in order to open the buckled door, the lifeless body of Katie falls into his arms. We are now ready to join Bannion in his implacable determination to destroy Logana, his gang, and its corrupt supporters. He knows now that he will have to work outside the corrupt police system, and that if Bertha Duncan is killed, the letter she is using to control Logana will reveal everything:

With you dead the big heat follows!
The big heat for Logana, for Stone – for the rest of the lice.

The Big Heat (1953): the scarred Debbie (Gloria Grahame) with Vince (Lee Marvin)

('The big heat' is a slang term for concentrated police activity against criminals; it is a powerful title which carries the implication of a settling of accounts, from which derives the French *Reglement de Compte*; the German title Heisses Eisen – Hot Iron – means nothing.

Bannion challenges the Chief of Police, Higgins, with being on Logana's payroll, and throws in his police badge – refusing to hand over his pistol, which is his own property. Higgins has remorse enough to put a police guard on the house of his brother-in-law who is keeping the child.

Lang (and Boehm) fill the world of the film with people who make that world come alive. Bannion's trail of the killer of his wife leads him far from the 'respectable' homes of the Duncans and Loganas, to the underworld of 'scared rabbits who never see a thing'. The denizens of the car graveyard are perfect examples of Lang's ability to surprise us with characterisation. The fat, scared owner is indeed a 'rabbit' ('When it comes to my bread and butter I stay careful.'), but the elderly, limping Selma – who might so easily be just a sinister type – turns out to be sympathetic and helpful, courageously so. Such honest characters turn up again and again in the film when we least expect them; the whole world has not been corrupted. Selma sends him to the same bar where he had met Lucy Chapman (ironically called The Retreat). Vincent Stone is playing dice with a girl, and in his pathological rage at losing, he burns her hand with his cigar. Bannion challenges the startled Stone:

Maybe you're the one that worked over Lucy Chapman!
Get out!
Now! While you can still walk!

When Stone leaves, Debbie offers Bannion a drink. In spite of his refusal ('with Vince Stone's money, I'd choke on it!') she follows him out. When they get into his car, they are followed by a Logana man. Debbie is clearly not prepared to reveal anything about the gang. Her only intention is to make Stone angry and jealous; and the weary Bannion tells her:

I'll put you in a cab.

Again Lang shows a lying woman through a mirror: Debbie is primping her pretty face while she denies where she has been to Stone, who is playing cards with Higgins, Larry and another municipal official. She gives herself away, however, when she reveals that she is aware of Bannion's hatred for Stone. Stone twists her arm, and throws an urn of scalding coffee in her face. Higgins is made to take her to a doctor, but Debbie runs away to Bannion, knowing that Lucy Chapman's fate awaits her otherwise.

Now Debbie is prepared to tell all and to give Bannion the lead to a man he has been seeking, Larry Gordon. Larry confirms Bannion's suspicions of Logana and Stone. A little later we learn that he is dead. Next Bannion goes to Bertha, but her warning call to Logana brings two protecting patrolmen sent by Higgins. Bannion is obliged to leave.

He returns to Debbie in the hotel hideaway where he has put her; and Lang provides an unsentimentally touching scene between the disfigured girl and the lonely cop who paternally makes her eat and take her pills. Debbie tells him:

... Guess a scar isn't so bad not if it's only on one side. I can go through life sideways ...

Just sitting here and thinking is pretty rough when you've spent most of your life not thinking.

When she asks him about his wife, and he answers only:

She was twenty-seven years old, light hair – grey eyes ...

Debbie replies that this is a police description. But she understands, she says, that he doesn't want to talk about his wife with someone like her. Bannion answers, for Debbie's honesty and plight have touched him as they have us, 'Not with anyone'.

Bannion confides to Debbie that with Bertha Duncan he has run into a brick wall. She is the only thing that stands in the way of the conviction of the gang, since she holds Duncan's confession, which she is using to blackmail Logana. 'I almost killed her an hour ago', he says. Then Debbie replies, with her usual clarity of vision:

I don't believe you could. If you had, there wouldn't be much difference between you and Vincent Stone.

Bannion's brother-in-law calls him to tell him that

Higgins has removed the police guard from the apartment where Bannion's little daughter Joyce is staying: Higgins intends to leave the way clear for Logana to get at the child to threaten Bannion. Bannion throws a revolver on Debbie's bed for her protection, rushes out, but is overpowered by an unidentified man on the first floor landing in his brother-in-law's house. The spectator believes with Bannion that it is a member of the gang: in fact it is the brother-in-law's wartime buddies whom he has brought in to protect them. Bannion is able to tell little Joyce the story of the three kittens again before going down to the street more calmly, to find that two of his own former colleagues have mounted their own guard of the house; not all human beings are scared rabbits.

Meanwhile Debbie has gone to Bertha's apartment ('We're sisters under the mink, Bertha') and shot her dead. When Vince Stone returns to his apartment, she is already waiting for him, too, and throws boiling coffee in his face, before telling him,

Bertha Duncan's dead!
No more insurance for you and Logana.
The lid is off the garbage can.
And I did it.

Stone whips out his Luger and shoots Debbie, just as Bannion breaks in the door. Shots are fired; but when Stone's gun is empty Bannion disdains to kill him and hands him over to his police friends:

Guess I was a cop too long. I almost said, You're under arrest, to him.

His action here parallels that of Vern when he captures the murderer Kinch in *Rancho Notorious* save that Dave is not so poisoned by hatred. He kneels beside the dying Debbie, and gently tells her about his wife ('I like her – I like her a lot.'), which he has hitherto refused to do.

Sergeant Bannion is back in the Homicide Department. When he is called out on a hit-and-run case, he is just about to drink his coffee. 'Keep it hot, will you, Hugo', he grins.

Sidney Boehm's excellent script is masterly constructed by Lang, and is recounted here in some detail because it is so typical of Lang's method and approach. As we have seen the characters in the film are not merely gangsters and cops, but real people, and this gives the film its remarkable density.

The Big Heat: disdaining to kill

According to Lang, Bannion's story is a personal affair between himself and crime. Bannion becomes the audience, and Lang constantly uses the camera from the viewpoint of the protagonist, until the audience involuntarily follows him and identifies with him. Even more than Joe Wilson in *Fury*, Bannion is Joe Doe. As a loner like Wilson or Vern in *Rancho Notorious*, he takes the law into his own hands and pursues his private revenge. But when the big heat starts, he understands that it is not for him in the final resort to exercise justice, but that he must hand the criminals over to the official organs of justice, which he has been instrumental in awakening. Earlier he has been warned by his colleague Detective Burke:

You've decided people are all scared rabbits and you spit on them, you're on a hate binge.

This is an attitude which Lang examines again and again.

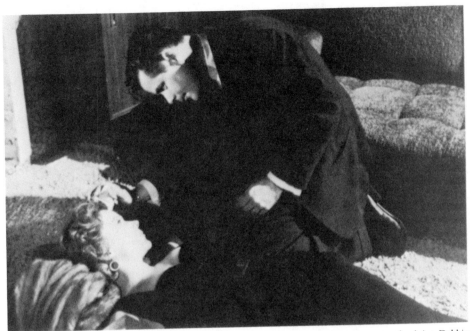

. . . the dying Debbie

He shows the results of violence rather than the violence itself, activating in this way an absolutely legitimate dramatic element. The way leads from *M* to *Fury*, to *Rancho Notorious* and *The Big Heat,* as Lang heroes move towards a maturity and wisdom which no longer contains bitterness or contempt for their fellow men.

Lang and his scenarist Alfred Hayes chose the same quotation from Zola as Renoir had done to preface their film:

There dwells in each of us a beast, caged only by what we have been taught to believe is right or wrong. When we forget these teachings, the beast in us is unleashed in all its fury.

In Zola's naturalistic view all the characters of *La Bête Humaine* act according to natural instincts and a realistic theory of genetics; and Renoir, facing no prior restrictions, was able to follow the novel closely in his film version. Lang – having already remade one Renoir film, *La Chienne*, as *Scarlet Street* – was eager to arrive at a completely personal conception, and accordingly asked the Cinémathèque Française for a copy of Renoir's original film. The creator of *M* would certainly have found an interesting solution of the ambivalences of the story in a mentally sick character, as he had done a few years earlier in *Secret Beyond the Door*, working for his own production company, and was to do later in *While The City Sleeps*, where the murderer is again a psychopath like the hero of *M*. In *While the City Sleeps* however, the psychopath is not the main character, but a minor figure who is run to ground by the hero. In *Human Desire* Lang transfers that tragedy to a different plane. He emphasises the tragic existence of the aging husband, who, as in Zola, sinks deeper and deeper, since every crime brings its own revenge.

Lang and his writer inevitably encountered difficulties in making this subject in Holywood. The Hays Office frowned on sex maniacs or epileptics in main roles. The American hero had to be sympathetic and normal, as a

La Bête Humaine *(Renoir) is made up of long sequences and short scenes while* Human Desire *(Lang) is all in short sequences and long scenes and thus has a completely different rhythm . . .* Human Desire, *coming after* Woman in the Window *and* Scarlet Street *possesses the same qualities which are characteristic of Fritz Lang . . . It is a solid and strong film, a beautiful block whose sharp edges follow the classical rules of cutting, the images are frank, brutal, each of them has its own beauty . . . The confrontation of these two works is extremely rewarding since it reveals how two of the greatest men of the cinema treated the same subject diverging in their conception of content and of form while each of them succeeded in making one of the best films of their careers.* François Truffaut: Desir Humain, *in* Arts, *July 1955*

Whereas Renoir's The Human Beast *is the tragedy of a doomed man caught up in the flow of life, Lang's remake* Human Desire *is the nightmare of an innocent man enmeshed in the tangled strands of fate. What we*

remember in Renoir are the faces of Gabin, Simon and Ledoux. What we remember in Lang are the geometrical patterns of trains, tracks and fateful camera angles. As Renoir is humanism, Lang is determinism. As Renoir is concerned with the plight of his characters, Lang is obsessed with the structure of the trap.
Andrew Sarris: 'Films', *The Village Voice*, 7 December 1967

prerequisite of the American dream. Glenn Ford, following his performance in *The Big Heat* was chosen for the main role, in which Columbia, carefully guarding their star's 'image' insisted he present a completely normal and hard-working person. For the producer Jerry Wald – who detected sexual symbolism in everything, not least in trains entering tunnels – a married woman who is determined on seducing a man was purely and simply the human beast.

Rita Hayworth was originally intended for this role, of the ambivalent Vicky (possibly to reunite the Ford–Hayworth team again). When the location shooting was rescheduled for Canada, however, Hayworth bowed out (legal difficulties and a divorce and child custody proscribed her leaving the States). Gloria Grahame (fresh from her teaming with Ford in *The Big Heat*) took the role and was no doubt a better choice. She conveys all the character's sexual instincts, and exactly fits the script description:

on the surface she seems contained, easygoing and affectionate natured. It is only in the sudden changes of expression in her eyes and in certain unfinished gestures that one can sense the complexity that exists under the surface.

Vicky's husband, Carl Buckley, is dismissed from the railway company because of a quarrel. He persuades his wife to go and plead with the powerful Owens. Suspicious at her long absence, he forces out of her a confession about her former connection with Owens. The jealous husband forces Vicky to write a letter to Owens saying that she will join him in his sleeper to Chicago, since her husband will be away in Edmonton.

As in Zola, the husband murders Owens on the train, in Vicky's presence, and takes his watch and wallet to suggest the murderer was a simple thief. In Zola, however, the incriminating letter from Vicky to Owens remains in the papers of the murdered man, to incriminate the murderer – even though the judge will hush up the matter, so corrupt were the times. In Lang's film the use of the letter is more logical: Carl finds it and keeps it as a permanent hold over Vicky.

As Carl and Vicky are returning to their compartment after the murder, they see the relieved engine driver, Jeff Warren, travelling back as a passenger and waiting for a

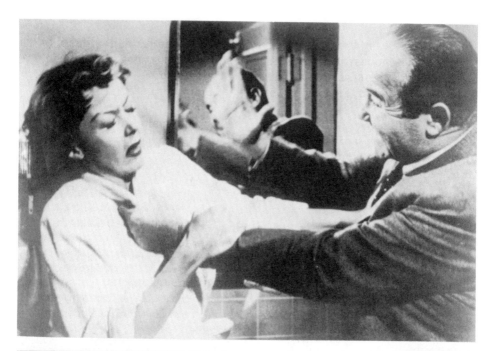

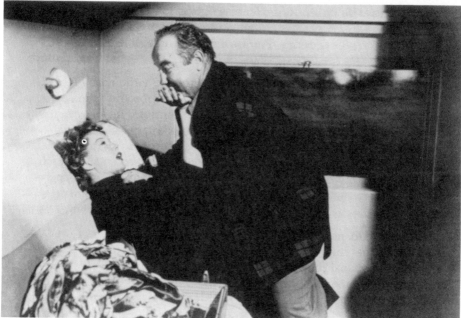

Human Desire (1954): scenes of violence: Broderick Crawford and Gloria Grahame

free compartment. Carl sends Vicky, who is unknown to Jeff, to lure him from the place he is standing in the corridor, so that Carl can safely regain his compartment while the two are having a drink in the dining car. Later, in the court-room where the passengers from the train are assembled for investigation, he catches Vicky's imploring eyes, and denies that he saw anyone coming from the murder compartment; now he is implicated, and has made the first step towards their guilt. All the major characters are now caught in a trap of their own making (fate is character).

The usually jealous Carl deliberately throws Vicky and this new friend together. At first she insists to Jeff that she found Owens dead in the compartment; then, as they become more intimate later she tells the truth about the murder, but claims that she had been seduced by Owens when a sixteen-year-old virgin. Jeff realises how deeply he is involved when Vicki tries to persuade him to kill Carl. He finds the incriminating letter in Carl's pocket when he picks him up, drunk, from the railway tracks. He gives it to Vicki who thus feels herself free of Carl, but is desperate when Jeff tells her their affair is over. In despair at not being able to hold Jeff, Vicky takes a train to leave Carl and when he breaks into her compartment she tells him another version of the Owens seduction:

Owens seduced me – yes, because I wanted him to! I wanted that big house he lived in. I wanted him to get rid of that wife. He knew what I was after. And you know what? I admired him for it.

When she tells him that he will never be sure of her because new men would always desire her, Carl strangles Vicki. Jeff returns to the loyal girl who tried to tell him in the beginning that he should find the right girl.

Lang and Hayes transplanted Zola's story into an American milieu and the present time. Jeff has just come back from the war in Korea; but the lesson of how to kill has not stuck with him enough for Vicki to be able to seduce him into killing Carl. The day of the steam train, moreover, is finished: Jeff drives an electrical-powered diesel engine; and his assistant – father of the girl he will eventually return to – is no longer a stoker.

Lang had difficulty in persuading a railway company to cooperate in the shooting. The Santa Fe Company refused

Human Desire: the lovers

when they learned that the original novel had a murder in a sleeping car; and the company appears to have passed on its warning to all the other American railroad companies. In the end Lang found a small company in Canada – where the weather at the beginning of December was distinctly un-California-like – to agree. Despite the problems Lang gave a characteristic authenticity to his railway milieu – endless travellings along the rails, top shots of the carriages, rolling wheels that translate speed into visual terms. His images are never gratuitous or simply decorative; always they are logical and functional. Touches of detail and mood give the background life an authenticity; the metallic shimmer from the tracks in the darkness of the railway yard lend a distinctive lyricism to the love story of Jeff and Vicki. The purely documentary introduction to the film has almost the same power as the sardine fishing shots in *Clash By Night*.

Lang captures Zola's own feeling of the speed of the

trains as a symbol of unbridled passions. Characteristically Lang again leaves the details of the murder of Owens to the imagination of the spectator: Carl enters the compartment after Owens has let in Vicki; we see only the speeding train, the locked door, and then, after the murder, just a glimpse of part of the body. On the other hand Carl's strangling of Vicki can be shown directly – partly because it is not actually bloody, but also because it is important we are aware that Carl's fate is sealed, that he will meet the consequences of murder, and the murder of Owens, too, will be atoned for.

Renoir followed Zola's ending: the engine-driver and stoker fight in their hatred and are thrown from the train and killed. The driverless train crashes, and all in it perish. Lang's film, subtly understated, abandons this ending for the possibility of a happy one. In Hayes' eighth draft of the script, Jeff sits in his engine as the tracks stretch into the darkness. Lang noted in his characteristic large handwriting: 'Day or night?'. Ultimately he chose broad daylight, as for the beginning of the film: the nightmare has passed with the morning: Jeff smiles at Alec and looks at the tickets for the railwayman's ball which Alec's daughter has given him. The dark, after all, had grown naturally from the subject: the murder, the illicit meetings of the lovers. Thus Lang's delight in chiaroscuro comes into play. The moral twilight calls for atmospheric night. Occasionally even the story of the good girl, Ellen, Alec's daughter, is taken into twilight. Jeff lies on his bed, with streaks of light from the half-closed shutters throwing dark stripes across the room. Ellen comes in to tell him that Mrs Carl Buckley is on the telephone. She goes on to remind him how he had talked to her about the simple life he wanted when he came back from the war – a little fishing; a night at the movies. She tells him he forgot one thing: the right girl to take to the movies. How, he asks, 'do you tell a girl who's right for you from the one who's not'. Thus in this room in which darkness struggles with light, he has doubts for the first time.

Moonfleet (1954)

32   Moonfleet (1954)

The sets are themselves a means of creating the horror which makes them reflect the mental world of the characters . . . Even the most glowing colours of Dorset, the splendid tonalities of the deserted places make one feel uneasy because of their density. The sea, with its waves, presents a concrete image of the inaccessibility of fate. But this frightening universe is not without the natural charm which is revealed in the novel as in all adventure stories. The critical mind takes away the romantic aura from the facts of the past, and reveals their base motivations, identical to those of our own times . . . On the other hand Lang always remains sensitive to the romantic elements which characterise his early films. Like all of Lang's masterworks, Moonfleet owes its success to a very strong expression of the two components of his dialectics . . . The film achieves in this way a great subtlety of tone and rhythm.
Luc Moullet: *Fritz Lang*, Editions Seghers, 1963

It was gratifying to Lang to be approached by MGM to do *Moonfleet*, since the company had not used him since his original contract expired, despite the success of *Fury*. He was presented with a finished script, but was able to follow his usual habit of careful preparation and modification. In the outcome MGM did not retain the montage he had planned; and it is only recently that Lang has come to have a higher opinion of the film.

Moonfleet opens with a highly Langian scene, which was in fact in the original script. Eleven-year-old John Mohune has strayed into the overgrown graveyard of Moonfleet. Overhead the sky is heavy and stormy, painted in deep purples and brilliant yellows, with menacing clouds. The boy is alarmed by a crudely carved wooden angel which looms between the crooked gravestones, looking more like an evil demon, and appearing to grow more and more gigantic. Suddenly a shadow rises out of a grave. The terrified boy, who has just taken off his boot to ease his sore feet, tumbles into a hole and loses consciousness. This sequence, as well as many other aspects of the story, remind one of Dickens' (if not Lean's) *Great Expectations*, in both atmosphere and theme; this resemblance is all the more striking when one recalls the problems of Dickens with the two endings of the novel.

When he wakes, we see from his viewpoint a frog's eye view of a half circle of smugglers, with grimacing faces, who surround him like a pallisade. From now on the action will be seen very much through the eyes of the brave little boy who, innocent and unsuspecting, is drawn into a world of dark intrigues, the murderous desires of the smugglers and the vices of a depraved aristocracy. At the same time it has the tone of a ballad, with the theme of the

Moonfleet (1954): Lang and his cinemascope format

strong, loyal friend to whom the dying mother has
entrusted her child, the romantic fantasies and adventures,
and the melancholy charm of a lost age.

In his treatment of period, the director of *Destiny* and
Liliom is again recognisable. The painted sky produces
effects half surrealist, half baroque, which serve to make
the characters more real to us. Composing in groups and
colour contrasts, Lang admirably copes with the Cinemascope format which was forced on him, and which he
regards as only suited to 'snakes and funerals'. The settings
(particularly the tavern inspired by a Hogarth picture)
built in the studio and on the lot are created dynamically in
the Cinemascope proportions. Lang's careful preplanning
and innate sense of composition are present even in the
antipathetic ratio.

Typically, Lang's success in making the characters real is
due to his refusal to romanticise them simply because they
appear in a romantic context. These figures from a *Liaisons*

Dangereuses world are at the same time realistic, and portrayed in critical, contemporary terms: the rake Jeremy Fox (Stewart Granger), unscrupulous and grown cynical yet still courageous and somehow a gentleman; the corrupted Lord Ashwood (George Sanders), more cynical than Fox and totally villainous; Lady Ashwood (Joan Greenwood) simply greedy for money and pleasure.

When John Mohune meets his prospective but very unwilling guardian, Jeremy, for the first time, he says with innocent trust: 'It's nice to have a friend'. Next morning he thinks he has been kidnapped when he is driven off to a far-off school, and escapes, to burst inopportunely into a dinner party at Jeremy's house. Nevertheless he pleases Jeremy by attacking Lord Ashwood when he supposes he is insulting his new friend Jeremy ('If the boy's heart is set on a career of rascality, there's no man in England can set him a better example').

Left alone the next day, he begins to learn some of the secrets of the past: how the arrogant Mohunes had set the dogs on Jeremy for his interest in John's mother; the legend of the Mohune diamond; the eerie secret of 'Redbeard' Mohune's coffin in the churchyard, which spills out its macabre and intriguing contents. Investigating the tomb of his ancestors, John finds, among the scattered bones, a locket. Hearing footsteps coming near, he hides in a corner; this is the smugglers' hide-out.

From their conversation John learns that Jeremy is the leader of the organisation. Trying to escape from the tomb, John finds that the smugglers have blocked the entrance with a huge rock. His cries for help only bring the smugglers. Aware he has heard their secrets and knows their identities, they plan to drown him in the sea. Realising that John can be trusted to keep the secret, Jeremy rescues him. The incident, however, provokes a showdown between Jeremy and his villainous men; and the Fairbanks-like swashbuckling battle which follows, with everything in the inn being brought in as improvised weapons, is a tribute both to Stewart Granger's aptitude, and, much more, to Lang's virtuosity in *mise en scène*.

Jeremy plans to send John off to the colonies in the charge of Mrs Minton, his mistress; but the jealous Mrs Minton, realising that it is the memory of John's dead mother that stands between her and Jeremy (his affairs with Lady Ashwood and the gypsy girl are of no consequence next to that lost love), denounces him to the military. Jeremy, wounded, nevertheless escapes from the soldiers after a cliff-top fight. John accompanies him, but Jeremy realises that they must separate for the boy's safety.

Meanwhile they succeed in deciphering the message involving verses from the Bible with deliberately wrong reference numbers written on an old parchment concealed in a locket which John retrieved from the coffin of 'Redbeard' Mohune, and recaptured from the smugglers. It reveals that the Mohune diamond was hidden in the well of the fortifications which Redbeard used to command. With the help of the servant girl from an inn and a stolen Colonel's uniform, Jeremy and John find the well-head, and John is lowered down to find the diamond in the locket. Jeremy risks his life to save the boy when the true owner of the uniform suddenly turns up and they are almost captured by the troops in the fortification; a sequence which is at once excitingly swashbuckling and comic.

The boy plans to start a new life in the colonies with Jeremy, thanks to the diamond, but while he is safe and sound asleep in a fishing hut by the sea, Jeremy leaves him, taking the diamond, and leaving behind a note written on the back of his own arrest warrant:

Go back to your mother's house – for her sake. She was wrong to put her trust in

J.F.

Making off with his friends Lord and Lady Ashwood, Jeremy is saved when the carriage is stopped by the soldiers looking for him, thanks to Lady Ashwood who embraces him thus hiding his face. Ashwood explains that it is his daughter and her new husband. The Ashwood coat-of-arms on the coach are enough to cow the military.

The conversation turns to John. ('What did you do with him? Kill him to be rid of him?' 'Yes, you approve?') Suddenly Jeremy demands that the carriage is turned back. When Ashwood and his coachman resist Jeremy knocks out the coachman and shoots Ashwood, but not before he has himself received a mortal wound from Ashwood's sword-stick. Nevertheless he makes it to the hut where John is still asleep. He tears the note he had left, so that only the first sentence remains; and slips the locket with the

Moonfleet: Jeremy (Stewart Granger) and Ashwood (George Sanders)

diamond into the boy's pocket. The boy wakes:

JOHN: Time to go sir?
JEREMY: Our plans are changed.
JOHN: Shall we be able to go home?
JEREMY: Would you like that? (with difficulty)
JOHN: Yes, if you think it's best.
JEREMY: It's best.

He quietly closes the door behind him, and through the window we see him in a boat with a red sail (dragged into the water with what must have been great difficulty). He lies down in the boat, his hand still holding on to the sail. As the boat sails out of shot, the hand drops down.

This was the ending which Lang intended, having shot and omitted a happy ending provided by the script. In this we see John and his little playmate Grace walking with the honest parson. When the parson comments that it is the first time he has seen the great gates of the manor house open, the young owner declares:

They must be open! There's no telling – when he'll come home . . .
PARSON: Jeremy Fox? You're sure that you'll hear from him –
some day?
JOHN: He's my friend.

Lang was initially angry that this ending was added to
the film after the preview against his will. Today, as ever
scrupulously fair, he is prepared to revise his opinion:

I think now that I was completely wrong, because I can see that the
script motivated the return (Jeremy's note; the last dialogue between
Jeremy and John) strongly.

The current ending, as Lang must be aware, is ambiguous
in its 'happiness' anyway. John is happy, but he does not
know what the audience knows; for the spectator the
ending then, is bitter-sweet.

It is the Rake's Progress towards the better; but the
ending is not conventional or cliché; Fox's change of heart
is motivated; the man who was once the lover of John's
mother still retains the remnant of a conscience despite the
years' accumulated cynicism; and it is the boy's trusting
nature that has succeeded in reactivating it. It is achieved
without conformism or sentimentality. As in *Clash By
Night* and *Human Desire* Lang's logic perceives that
resolutions which tend towards a happy ending are the
only possible solutions.

33 While the City Sleeps (1955)

Lang . . . is as sharp as the edge of a razor. His icy detachment is that of the naturalist or the ethnologist. He describes a flock of crows which devour a corpse, and from his description grows a judgment without appeal . . . Lang draws a limited case of social pathology, he constructs, if you will, the 'ideal type' of a current phenomenon of social corruption by money . . . It is a question of analysis which only retains certain essential details and whose object is to destroy the myth of the journalist as a defender of widows and orphans.
Jean Domarchi: 'Lang le Constructeur', *Cahiers du Cinema*, October 1956

It is myopic to see this film – as at least one German critic did – as no more than a 'thriller'. Lang was not concerned with a 'who-dunnit' mystery. As in *M* he reveals the identity of the murderer from the start; even before the credits we see him in action (though true to his usual principle, Lang refrains from showing the murder itself).

The concern of the film is rather the effect of the murder upon the other characters. It exposes the world of American newspapers and the sensational press, the treachery and disloyalty that can divide friendly colleagues caught up in the rat-race for position, the advantages to be won by being the one to discover the murderer. The scheming is developed in a series of chessboard moves; the tension comes not from external incident or conventional mystery suspense, but from the internal motives that drive on the action. This time the question is not 'what makes the murderer tick?': Lang composes his film so that we understand this from the start. Again as in *M* Lang's sympathy or empathy for the murderer's disturbed mentality admits that this murderer, too, cannot help it.

The other people involved could behave in a different way from what they do, yet they are more incurably ill than the murderer, driven on and on against one another by 'the bloody spur of ambition' and senseless competitive rivalries.

A French critic has complained that the murderer is 'misunderstood Freud'; yet Lang's 'lipstick killer', based on real events, is very much more convincingly motivated than, say, Losey's neurotic murderer in his weak remake of *M*. If the character from time to time seems conventional, despite his tics and manias, it must be blamed less on the director than on John Barrymore Jr, an incorrigibly mediocre actor whom Lang found he could teach nothing.

There were certain modifications of Charles Einstein's original book *The Bloody Spur*. Einstein's killer writes on the bathroom walls with his victim's lipstick: 'Help me for God's sake' (which, in turn, was based on a real killer who wrote 'stop me before I kill more'). The Hays Office would no doubt have resented the request to the Lord; and Lang's killer, a student who delivers drugstore parcels in the evening, knows enough about psychoanalysis to write, 'Ask mother'. One of the four journalists in the novel is a notably colourless character, and Lang has reduced them to three ('decent men corrupted by the bloody spur of ambition', says the original paperback blurb).

Lang and his writer Casey Robinson make other changes. Perhaps to avoid similarity with *M*, the murderer's victims no longer include a child; nor is his third assault against an elderly woman who resembles his mother. Recalling the 'Letter to the Blue Gardenia' the crack reporter unscrupulously uses his own fiancée as bait, and through television challenges the murderer, appealing to his vanity and inciting him to give himself up.

This reporter, Mobley (Dana Andrews) is thus made a more substantial character. At first he seems more decent than the others because he declares himself to be without ambition. Eventually however he proves as unscrupulous as his colleague Casey Mayo. Not only is he prepared to risk his own fiancée's life in this way, but he yields quite readily to a nymphomaniac when it proves opportune.

Lang brilliantly evokes the atmosphere of the newsroom where everyone is crowded and a glass wall is the greatest privacy the privileged can claim; the buzz of noise, work and intrigue is worked out with characteristic instinct for rhythm and tension. We are really aware of people and of a great news empire – on the line of Hearst's – at work. In spite of echoes of *M*, this is, after *The Big Heat*, Lang's most American film, with its concern with cynicism and self-assertion, the women who are never unaware of the irony of their easy favours. In an amusing incidental scene (based on a real experience of Lang's) Mildred (Ida Lupino) the gossip columnist sets out to seduce Mobley, with her own lover's connivance. At the bar, she makes coquettish play with a stereoscope which

While the City Sleeps (1955): the lipstick killer

we are led to suppose contains pornographic pictures. When she drops the gadget, we see, with the inquisitive barman, that it is only a picture of herself as a baby lying naked on her tummy. This ironic little scene was almost cut by the producer, who could see neither point nor humour in it, in spite of positive reactions from preview audiences.

Lang's critics have affected to see in the film both misogyny (odd since the male characters are less sympathetic than the female) and an aversion to journalists. But Lang sees only the truth: journalism is a hard profession, and people must be tough to survive in it. Lang is realistic about his heroes. They are no longer like the ideally noble human Freder in *Metropolis*. Lang's heroes are no longer immaculate, but seen in all their weaknesses, great and small.

When the old newspaper tycoon Walter Kyne dies, there is no sentimentality: the long-ready obituary is got out for the next edition, and a new power struggle is on. His heir, the spoilt son Walter Kyne Jr (Vincent Price) finds his only means of domination is to stimulate competition and hatred. Only the picture editor Harry Kritzer (James Craig) thinks that his affair with Kyne's wife Dorothy (Rhonda Fleming) saves him the necessity of effort. Neither Kritzer nor Dorothy are deceived by the nature of their relationship.

'I'll play it my own way as Walter's best friend,' he tells Dorothy.
'With Walter's best wife.'
'I don't want to involve you, darling,' he replies.
'My hero!' is her ironic and rather cynical answer.

The only apparently neutral man is Mobley, and the slick and cynical Mark Loving of Kyne News Service (George Sanders) thinks he can win his support by getting his girl friend Mildred to seduce him. At once pleased by the opportunity and irked by his disregard for their affair, Mildred cheerfully obliges. Of all of them perhaps Jon Griffith (Thomas Mitchell) a hard drinking, hard working Irishman is perhaps the most honest in his motives: he needs the money.

Even Mobley's fiancée, Nancy (Sally Forrest) is neither innocent nor free of the cynicism of the other two women, though in deference to the League of Decency she is at least

While the City Sleeps: the newsroom

less sophisticated than in the original novel, in which she declares 'I like my men experienced'. This very seeming lack of sophistication, however, serves to make her even less sympathetic in the film. She is constantly making sly remarks full of sexual innuendo, and is something of a sexual tease. A certain coquetry finally serves to save her. When the murderer tries to gain entry to her room by pretending to be Mobley, she will not let him in because she is jealous over the affair with Mildred.

The intrigue of the film is frequently better planned than in the book – for instance the incident in which Mrs Kyne, on her way to a date with Harry Kritzer, is almost killed because Nancy has refused to let the murderer into her room, which happens to be in the same house as Kritzer. This replaces the scene in the original where the murderer almost kills the woman who resembles his mother.

The incident of the murderer's flight into an underground tunnel is so typical of Lang, that it is tempting to think that Einstein, writing *The Bloody Spur* in 1953, might have been inspired by *Man Hunt*, released twelve years before. 'Manners bolts into the blackness', says the script; '. . . the light hits a distant figure – Manners.' We hear 'the roar and clattering of the oncoming train . . . (which) blocks from cameraview' the two men wrestling with each other. Then, 'the lights of the southbound train are flickering over them'. Finally, 'the sound of the north-bound train is heard, it comes closer and closer'. We see the headlights; Mobley is 'propelled across the express tracks'. Manners, having broken free, runs up the spiral stairs to the emergency exit, into the hands of the police.

Lang orchestrates light and sound easily, heightening the tension to breathtaking intensity; yet where the action itself contains suspense enough, and is driven on by the dialogue, he makes little use of idiosyncratic virtuosity. Only the pre-credit sequence, of the first murder, and the scene in which the murderer listens to Mobley's television speech are shot in Lang's typical chiaroscuro. Lang is seeking a real environment instead of revealing 'mysterious' atmosphere. The French word *ambiance* – untranslatable though it is, with its implication of a social component – best expresses his intentions, in showing how the violence of other people is triggered off by one man's violent actions. The starting point could well be something else besides a murder story. Rather than showing him as misogynist or hater of pressmen, *While the City Sleeps* shows more forcefully than any other of Lang's films the loneliness of an individual.

While the City Sleeps: Mobley (Dana Andrews) in the underground

34 Beyond a Reasonable Doubt (1956)

Beyond a Reasonable Doubt presents an ever more difficult dramatic problem than *Liliom* – in which the hero dies halfway through the film. Here a hero who throughout the film has seemed altogether sympathetic and against whom we have seen false evidence deliberately fabricated, is at the last moment revealed as the murderer. Lang's last film in the United States, it is very characteristic, even though it was somewhat cut by the producers. It has often been taken as a tract against capital punishment, but Lang was seeking in it something more universal. In the summer of 1969 he explained his intentions to me. At the time he had read a lot of scripts during the period he was editing *While the City Sleeps*. Gradually it dawned on him why they all seemed so devoid of interest:

'Social' themes, such as the exposure of corruption and similar subjects seemed passés to me.

How many more films on that subject?

People enjoyed these films, having become indifferent to VIOLENCE (not by watching films or by daily life around them!) – a 'social' film serves no other purpose but that of killing time. It was an unconscious escape from monotonous daily routine of work and life into the unreality of daydreaming.

More and more over the past few years I pondered the question: *what* or *who* is the cause or the reason of people's increasing alienation?

Is it the double standards of our society – of the establishment – which accepts for instance that a man may do certain things for which a woman would be condemned?

These double standards which campaign against the immorality of street prostitution by laws and prison sentences allow the better-paid call girls to follow their trade, and even formally tax them on their 'wages of sin'.

Laws against homosexuality, against abortion – discussions on the 'morals' of judges or politicians . . . and so on, ad infinitum!

Lang, as is well known, always searches for the truth beyond appearances, and here he searches for it beyond improbabilities. It is perhaps a vain task to contrast this last film of Lang's with some of his earlier ones like Fury *or* You Only Live Once . . . *Here innocence with the appearance of culpability, there culpability with all the appearance of innocence . . . Beyond appearances what is culpability or innocence? Is one in reality ever innocent or guilty?*
Jacques Rivette: 'La Main *(Beyond a Resonable Doubt)*', *Cahiers du Cinema*, November 1957

It is the personal selfishness of the contented 'respectable citizen', his lack of concern for the suffering of others, the lack of understanding, the cold indifference *unless one is involved oneself.*

It is not merely the arrogant self-righteousness of bourgeois 'morality' and its prejudices, it is the intolerance of the mistakes or offences committed by other people, the unwillingness to understand the worries, feelings and sufferings of their fellow human beings!

AS LONG AS IT ISN'T A QUESTION OF ONE'S OWN SKIN

Lang cites instances of epileptics or accidents on the New York sidewalks when passers-by walk on rather than get involved, or the case in which a woman was assaulted and killed in the street while people looked on without troubling to telephone the police: 'They might have had to be witnesses in court – what a waste of time'. He continued:

In fact people do not want to know who or how they really are, and they are certainly not interested in knowing their fellow human beings.

The basis of their actions is the deeply rooted personal dishonesty of which the younger generation quite rightly accuses the older generation.

As Brecht said: 'Man is not good. Man is evil'.

I was pondering all this in Autumn 1955 when I was offered *Beyond a Reasonable Doubt*; and when I asked myself whether the public would accept the fact of the sympathetic 'hero' of the film, Dana Andrews, turning out to be an unsympathetic murderer at the last moment, I began to wonder who – was the worse human being – the murderer or the unscrupulous blackmailer who is after his money with egotistical singlemindedness and without a moment's thought for the possibility that she is ruining his whole career and his future life?

This is no excuse; yet it may be an explanation. Or is it the woman with whom the murderer is in love? Does she really love him? Did she ever love him? To leave a man who has committed a murder is perhaps understandable, but to betray him, to hand him over so that he ends up in the electric chair is a completely different matter. Which of the two is the worse character? Or which out of all three of them?

Or out of all four, if we include the journalist who is in love with Susan, since he removes a rival for her affections simply by telephoning the warden? Who then is the worse human being? The man who is driven by his nature to murder, the blackmailer who is only interested in money and is indifferent to the ruin she may effect to his life; or the two philistines who do not even make the effort to understand what might have driven the man to the murder; first, *because one does not do things like that*; and secondly because by handing over to the executioner 'as he deserves', they smooth the way to their own respectable marriage bed.

WHICH IS THE MOST DESPICABLE CHARACTER OUT OF THE FOUR?

This was the problem which Lang set himself to investigate, and he now asks himself whether he wholly or partially succeeded, when the audience condemns the murderer who agrees to play the role of a fictitious murderer in order to help the newspaper tycoon Austin Spencer in his campaign against the death penalty, and incidentally to rid himself of the blackmailer without risk, since he knows that when he is put on trial he will be acquitted, and thereafter safe from further trial for the offence. Partly Lang's interest was the same as in *While the City Sleeps* – the comparable guilt of the murderer and of those who are prepared to profit financially or professionally from the hunt after the murderer.

The approach indicates less misanthropy in Lang than a sympathy with the sufferings of unstable personalities that goes back to *M*. Nor is his decision to open the film with an execution in the electric chair a mark of sadism:

I was very keen on this first scene, because I wanted to impress Dana Andrews (and of course the audience, too) with the heartlessness and illogicality of a process which forces other people – by switching on the fatal electric current – to commit the very same action as the person who is condemned to death – that is, *to kill a human being*.

When Lang explained this to the producer, he remarked, 'Fine, Fritz; make it very realistic'. Lang asked if there might not be trouble with the front office and distributors, and was assured, 'Don't worry, that's my business'. During the shooting of the sequence, one of the usual innumerable studio spies informed the front office, and the producer was summoned. When he returned to the stage where Lang was shooting the scene of the convicted man waiting in the death cell, adjacent to the execution room, the producer was enraged: 'Why did you shoot the electric chair scene so explicitly. You're not at UFA now. Here in America we don't like these sadistic scenes'.

Lang did not reply: it was not the first promise the producer had broken. When the shooting was finished the producer exercised all his charm in order to ensure Lang would excise all the so-called cruel scenes. Lang, however, left the cutting in the charge of his reliable cutter and friend

Gene Fowler, Jr. who would save what he could. 'But Fritz, we are friends', wailed the producer; 'You can't do that to me; you can't leave me now!'

The camera pans along the cells of the Condemned Row, affording glimpses of the inmates. Two condemned men in separate cells play chess on a board placed outside, beside the bars of their two cells (this was based on an incident Lang had seen in a real prison during his research). This small touch – authentic or 'cruel' according to the point of view of the spectator – is much more effective than the original script which refers to a prisoner bent over his bunk in silent prayer, another in an adjoining cell pacing helplessly up and down, a third in the farthest cell crouched like a wild animal.

For *Beyond a Reasonable Doubt* there exists an early version of the script, which reveals the extent to which Lang worked over his scenarios before starting to shoot. Apropos of a scene in which Stephen Garrett (Dana Andrews) listens to a conversation between Austin Spencer, his prospective father-in-law and the pig-headed District Attorney, Thompson, he notes that Stephen should not listen in such an indifferent way:

I don't think that Dana Andrews can sit through the whole scene without taking sides, or say something important; not just a weak line 'What's wrong with that?'

Moreover he wants the scene between the two rivals to be less amicable; one must feel that Austin is a genuine opponent of capital punishment and the District Attorney supports it:

There should be some fireworks, accusations by Beall* who's *emotionally* involved! It's an old feud! . . . Garrett as a writer must have some opinions about the whole question. He is too *indifferent* . . . a writer always wants to meet interesting characters . . .

Lang also demands:

more about Beall's point of view! The audience must be intrigued by what Beall is standing for

Lang in other words wants to give this scene better motivation from the start – an indication of his constant insistence on the deeper psychological implications of every scene, of his objective approach to the characterisation of people and events. Lang himself dictated the

* The name of the Austin Spencer character in the early versions of the script.

Beyond a Reasonable Doubt (1956): establishing an alibi

entire immensely important introductory sequence in which Stephen is taken along by his prospective father-in-law to watch the execution. The writer Douglas Morrow had simply a scene in which the jury condemns a man on circumstantial evidence. (This scene was actually filmed for use in countries like England where the censor would have banned the showing of an execution.) Lang has Spencer say:

He's trying to reach the governor's chair over the bodies of executed men. I'm fighting against capital punishment. That's why I wanted you to see that execution this morning . . .

Apart from Eddie in *You Only Live Once*, none of Lang's heroes is very young. Garrett is in his middle or late thirties, ruggedly handsome, casually but conservatively dressed. His fiancée Susan is conventional, ambitious, with expensive tastes. Not very sexual, she does not allow pre-marital intimacy, which is not accepted in her circles.

Between the two of them there is always a certain distance, a noticeable restraint. Susan, too, is apparently the more active partner in the engagement. From the start Lang and the scenarist make clear her character: such a girl will not stick to her fiancé, but will betray him without qualms rather than risk a scandal.

The very cool engagement scene is interrupted by a telephone call. It is left unexplained, but makes Stephen nervous (we know later it is from the blackmailing Patty Emma). With his hobby horse of capital punishment, even Spencer is surprised at the newly engaged man's eagerness to talk about the subject. Garrett readily agrees to Spencer's proposition that he shall allow himself to be framed for an as yet unsolved murder of a dancer in a cheap amusement club (while Garrett postpones the marriage date for unknown reasons), in order to demonstrate the dangers of circumstantial evidence and of capital punishment.

Lang goes on methodically to show the fabrication of the evidence against Garrett, and at the same time the progress of the police investigation as they question associates of the murdered girl. Characteristically, Lang makes each authentic in accent, posture, type. One, still innocent, lived with the murdered girl, and is contrasted sharply with a flamboyant type with dyed blonde hair. This second girl, brassy and confident, has nothing good to say about Patty Gay: 'she was a real creep'. Only the third girl, a bit more intelligent, has a description of the murderer: 'He had a grey tweed coat and a brown hat on . . . and he was smoking a pipe.' On the basis of such vague evidence, Spencer has little difficulty in manufacturing a suspect. Arrested and convicted Garrett waits in prison for the photographs which Spencer had made of each item of fabricated evidence. Then comes a ritardando so typical of Lang. As Spencer drives out of his garage to take the photos to court, a lorry hits it. Spencer is killed and the films entirely destroyed.

The proof of Garrett's innocence thus gone, Susan dutifully sets out to fight for her fiancé, aided by a journalist who is in love with her. Their enquiries reveal the surprising news that the murdered girl, Patty Gray was really called Emma Bloker.

Just when everything seems hopeless, Austin Spencer's

Beyond a Reasonable Doubt: the car crash

partner returns from a European trip, and an envelope is
found in which Spencer had made a written record of the
whole plot, for use in the event of some such accident as has
occurred. At this last moment of reprieve, however,
Garrett, worn out by worry, is caught off guard. He tells
Susan:

He should have found out who *really* killed Emma instead of putting
me through all this . . .

Susan is startled to learn that he knows the murdered girl's
real name; and recognises that he is the killer. He confesses:
he had been made to marry Emma when he was only a boy
(she had cynically pretended to be pregnant), had lost sight
of her, but had recently been blackmailed by her after the
success of his writing and the announcement of his
engagement.

Garrett attempts to regain Susan's shaken loyalty to
him:

Beyond a Reasonable Doubt: Susan (Joan Fontaine) with the journalist

'And you proved your love by fighting for me.' 'I thought you were innocent.' 'You'd have fought for me anyway . . . if you had known why I did it.'

She breaks away from his embrace and seeks advice from the journalist:

If . . . I were accused of a crime . . . and if you thought I might be guilty . . . would you still help me?

His answer does not please her:

How could I love you and not do anything I could?

But when she explains the situation, his nobility suddenly dissolves. He sees a way to have Susan: it is her duty to inform the authorities, for if Garrett were acquitted he could never again be convicted. She is still undecided; she picks up the phone, puts it back. Lang introduces a touch of irony: Garrett tells a reporter who asks if he will resume his writing:

I guess so. That's the way I make my living . . .

On the word 'living' the telephone call of Susan's journalist friend reaches the Governor who is just about to sign Garrett's pardon. The Governor puts down his pen:

Warden . . . have Mr Garrett taken back to his cell. There will be no pardon.

Why is this hero so unsympathetic while the hero who kills or wants to kill for the sake of ambition in Sternberg's and George Stevens' adaptations of Dreiser's *An American Tragedy* does not strike the spectator as at all unsympathetic? Perhaps it is because Garrett calculates the whole affair so coolly; or because the audience has become so certain about his innocence. Perhaps he should have told Susan more about his reasons and about the way he suffered to keep her and our sympathies. Perhaps we are not sufficiently taken into his confidence about the suffering which brought him to his action.

Lang says he was interested not in the characters but in the subject. He was again fascinated by questions of guilt and innocence, by the vague ambiguities and ambivalences of the subject. Throughout his films he again and again asks the same question: What is guilt, and what is innocence?

The ending was perhaps inevitable. The conclusion of *While the City Sleeps* had still the possibility of not being tragic; *Woman in the Window* was only a nightmare from which the hero could wake; the equivocal ending of *Scarlet Street* permitted the real murderer – the dupe – to throw all the blame on the pimp, the worse human being. In *Beyond a Reasonable Doubt* the conformist Susan and her journalist will live on happy ever after. The father who crusaded against capital punishment will be forgotten. For Lang is in accord with Brecht: man is not good at all.

35 Working Methods and Style: The American Period, 1934–1956

Other Countries – Other Methods

Lubitsch came to Hollywood in 1923, at the height of twenties' optimism and movie prosperity. Despite initial troubles with Mary Pickford and occasional hostility, in the aftermath of the War, this adroit and highly commercial director triumphantly made his way. Murnau, too, lured to Hollywood late in the twenties, was given comparative freedom on his first film *Sunrise*, though later commercial compromises and pressures were to prove too much for him and he was to give up the struggle against money interests to escape to the South Seas.

1929 was the year of the stock market crash. The carefree twenties with their prosperity were succeeded by a period of social crisis and mental anguish, the turmoil of the troubled thirties.

Fritz Lang arrived in Hollywood from a Germany which was ostensibly stabilised, which was eager to forget the anguish of the early twenties, and which looked forward (despite the rising numbers of unemployed) to Hitler's promised economic miracle; a Germany equally willing to overlook certain rather sinister 'problems' in the hope of material improvements. He found an industry technologically far in advance of the German studios, but in which the director's position was very different: here he was not a twentieth century prince, but just another employee of the big film companies, no longer commanding unlimited money and manpower.

In Germany Lang had been used to writing his own films, in collaboration with Thea von Harbou. In Hollywood a script was often the confection of a whole

367

number of writers, working simultaneously or in succession. Lang had been used to cutting his own films; in Hollywood the rushes were entrusted to an editor. He had been accustomed to shoot on at the end of the day, to go on making retakes until he was content. In Hollywood he found regular working hours and strict control of breaks for the crews. Yet, even in the departmented studios, Lang was often, rather surprisingly, able to manage a good deal of control over his scripts, editing, sets, and other aspects of the films he made. He also attempted as much as possible to follow his practice in Germany of maintaining something of a repertory company of technicians and actors. Although stars were often forced on him, it is enlightening to examine the credits in his filmography; one finds again and again the same names among both the technical and casting credits.

Lang shared the unhappy experiences of other European film people at MGM. At first the company found him no work; they thought his shyness 'Germanic'; and when his first film was a surprise success, they were rather more uncomfortable than pleased. Lang found himself struggling all the time. He discovered Zanuck, a writer himself, possessed understanding of art, though easily influenced by sycophants. Other, lesser producers often believed Lang too idiosyncratic or too perfectionist; hence his constant moves from one studio to another, apart from three successive films for Twentieth Century-Fox.

He found himself dragged into the muddy waters of the witchhunts and blacklists. To avoid unemployment he was forced to take whatever work he could get. Even working for his own company did not make things easy. When finally, after major films like *The Big Heat* and *While the City Sleeps,* he at last turned his back on Hollywood in order to realise an old cherished dream in a new Germany, a remake of *The Indian Tomb,* he faced disappointment. Lang's outlook on life has been called pessimistic; perhaps a more fitting word would be 'disillusioned'.

Yet the United States have given Lang a lot; and he returned much to the country of his choice. It is not without reason that he is known as 'a director's director'. The director of *M* never deviated from the path along which his character and his talent led him.

Subject Matter

Lang wrote to me, in relation to *The Spy*:

There are two kinds of detective novels or better, to use the English expression, 'Whodunnits'. There is the type *I never liked* in which the reader is made to solve riddles and where in the end after long and boring chapters the action is finally explained and the identity of the culprit revealed.

Or the second kind: *showing both sides*, that of the criminal as well as that of the people who oppose him. I always found it much more interesting to show, *as in a game of chess, the moves of both partners,* how in an interlocking logic one move *necessitates* the next while occasionally one side seems to prefer the short cut of violence. Whether this – in its original sense – *mental* struggle between the two minds has to be developed in psychological terms seems to me more than doubtful . . .

* François Truffaut, although speaking specifically about one film, sees quite clearly Lang's constant method and theme:

One sees that this film is at once both subversive and daring, constructed as it is on the principle that 'respectable' people can be morally repugnant. In fact, it is the duty of the artist to show us beauty where we had thought only ugliness existed. Fritz Lang, throughout *You Only Live Once*, underscores the contrast between the servility of people within 'society' and the nobility of the 'anti-social' couple.
'Fritz Lang en Amerique', *Les Films de Ma Vie* Flammarion, Paris 1975

** Alternatively he could refuse: after *Fury* he turned down a script about a Jewish school teacher who was lynched after being accused of raping a pupil. He did not want to be typed as a director specialising in lynching films.

Though these statements are directly applicable to *The Spy* and the *Mabuse* films, in the States Lang also retained this principle of showing both sides.

Lang is often described as ambiguous; and he points out that he is by birth a Sagittarian, a discordant nature. Already in *M* he raises his favourite problem of guilt. It is explored more deeply in his American films: in *Fury* the innocent victim of a lynching almost becomes guilty in the end. Films like *Secret Beyond the Door, Beyond a Reasonable Doubt, While the City Sleeps* are further variations of the question.*

The subjects of Lang's films are very varied – often he accepted subjects that were offered him** (though always there had to be something in the story to appeal to him, to offer 'possibilities'). Yet there are always inner connections: whether in the preliminary preparation or the studio work, they were turned into Lang subjects.

One means by which this was achieved was his characteristic stress on detail. The accumulation of detail, the power of the camera to isolate it at once gives him his spontaneity and his realism: 'detail produces authenticity' said Stendhal. In his American films detail is no longer symbol as in his German period. In *Fury* symbols may still be important (the gossiping women paralleled with the images of ducks; the number '22' which pursues Spencer Tracy in the dark street) and even in *You Only Live Once* there is the frog image; yet their significance is deeper.

Lang once wrote to the present writer that his first three American films formed a trilogy, but that the later ones, *Woman in the Window, Scarlet Street, The Big Heat* and *While the City Sleeps* were directly connected with this trilogy. These films of social problems are all the inevitable followers of earlier work like *M*.

The Finished Script and other matters

The Bogdanovich interview occasionally gives the impression that Lang at times had to take over 'finished' scripts in America. People who know and have worked with Lang insist that there was never a case when he did not meticulously work over a script, even when he had to shoot quickly. Even in his so-called 'final' scripts, there are always dialogue changes to make characters more consistent, and reorganisation of whole passages of action for the sake of logic. He writes in a letter:

What is a finished manuscript? It is not, as might be assumed, a manuscript ready for shooting. It is a manuscript of a story which is far from being a manuscript ready for shooting.

Never in my life have I been given a manuscript I could have filmed straightaway. This applies to *House by the River* as much as to *Moonfleet*.

It is a long way from a 'finished' manuscript to a final screenplay and almost always did I have to work hard – sometimes not so hard – to turn it into a final screenplay.

In a later letter Lang adds that the fine writer Dudley Nichols who wrote *Man Hunt* and *Scarlet Street* always said 'A script is only the blueprint for a future film'. Many years before, too, an article signed by Lang, 'Wir über uns selbst', in *Film-Künstler* (1928) speaks of Thea von Harbou as:

an invaluable collaborator who out of a profound understanding of my intentions creates the manuscripts which are the basis of my work.

Lang has often described how he worked with a scriptwriter. If he liked a story offered him he would ask to meet the scriptwriter at an early stage. He reckoned himself a pretty good script doctor. He is rarely credited by name for the script: it was more important to him to arrive at the best scenario ready for shooting and which would enable him to maintain, as required, the studio shooting schedule.

Each script, of course, was a different case. On *Fury* he is credited; and passages like the pursuing '22' are unmistakeably his. Sometimes – as on *Hangmen also Die* – the original idea was his own. For *While the City Sleeps* he took a screenplay in which he saw possibilities, though he felt certain passages lacked the necessary logic. He introduced the author to *M* and showed him a newspaper clipping about a real-life sex murderer who had left a message on a mirror: 'Please catch me before I kill more'.

Lang saw the relationship with the scriptwriter as essentially a *collaboration*. When it worked well, Lang might conceive one scene, the writer another. Moreover he encouraged the writers to include suggestions for camera angles and positions if they wished. 'I could always change it if I wanted to.'

Camera Angles

I always proceeded as follows: on one or two evenings before I went into the studio to shoot the sequence in question, in the mornings I sat at home at my desk, after having seen the rushes, going over the floor plan of the scenes to be filmed in the morning and decided every single camera angle.*

I chose not only the angles, but also the kind of lens – whether 28, 30 or 40 – that was to be used.

This method of not working out the angles in the studio just before shooting had two big advantages:

1) When we had rehearsed the sequence and the actors knew it inside out, we could shoot the sequence out of the chronological order which the audience sees later on. Then everything that had to be filmed in *one* direction was shot first and then the shots in the *opposite direction*. This meant that the lighting had to be *changed only once* and saved us a lot of time.

2) When I sat every evening say about *two hours* only working out the various angles I had to shoot the next day I saved those two hours in the studio. For a film with 40 days of shooting I thus saved 80 hours of shooting time spent in preparing angles. With an 8-hour working day I thus saved 10 days of studio work (80 divided by 8) and the result was naturally a considerable reduction in the cost of a film.

Everything in other words is planned and fixed before work in the studio begins. There are no longer experiments and improvisations as in the early German period when everything had still to be invented. Only rarely would a camera angle be changed in the studio, if Lang suddenly perceived something that made for a better

* Lang was a sufficiently well-trained architect to be able to make up the floor plans for himself from the set drawings, if he did not have the designers' own floor plans; and he was enough of a painter to be able in turn to visualise the composition from the plans.

371

Lang at the camera

atmosphere or was more suitable to the lighting.

The Rational Camera

Lang constantly emphasises that every movement of the camera has to have a reason. He told Bogdanovich that he tried to get his cameramen to use the camera where possible to make the audience see the action as if from the viewpoint of the protagonist. In this way the spectator can identify directly, think with him and – we should also say, in terms of Lang's philosophy, suffer with him.

Despite the subtlety of lighting, the mastery of atmosphere learned in Germany, Lang dislikes virtuoso camera work (hence, for example, his rejection of the zoom lens as 'not natural'). Striving for authenticity, for 'spontaneity' and documentary verisimilitude, he demanded from his cameramen the 'newsreel' method already often mentioned.

Every tilt shot has its reason. In *The Blue Gardenia*, for instance, the use of the crab dolly subtly emphasises the cramped space of the girls' bedroom. His most extensive use of a variety of camera angles is in the psychologically complex *Clash by Night*. Lang does not permit himself to be seduced into camera tricks by the script. Fascinating as they are on paper, Lang rejects the elaborate scenes prescribed by the script of *The Blue Gardenia* (p. 370).

Josef von Sternberg was accustomed to claim that he had operated the camera on all his films, and that the cameramen credited were merely assistants. Lang, in contrast, constantly stresses in his letters the excellence of his cameramen. Only once, when I praised the angles and camerawork of *Secret Beyond the Door* during Joan Bennett's nocturnal wanderings through rooms and corridors did he reveal how much preparatory work he had himself put into achieving these effects.

Working With Actors

There are, said Lang in a letter, apropos his silent films, 'actors and actors. Some are serious about their work, others are overconscientious, others have no idea what it's all about and others again are only interested in silly jokes!'.

Generally the most intelligent and the most modest actors understood Lang's intentions, his perfectionism, the fact that he demanded as much from himself as he did from

Lang editing *Hangmen Also Die*

them. Edward G. Robinson has praised Lang's understanding of dramatic action, his rare energy and enthusiasm. He admits it was not always easy to work with him and his high demands, precision over detail, contempt for the mediocre, occasional tyranny to those who did not measure up to his level. Shortly before his death, the actor told David Overbey in an interview that Lang was to him one of the great ones, a true innovator. If he was hard to work with, it was because he was so different from what actors had been accustomed to in the United States. Yet for his great skill he was highly respected, so that actors and technicians alike were prepared to accept his domineering methods. He was part of everything, not only the director of actors. He would even sweep the floor of the set (*Scarlet Street*) if he was dissatisfied with the way it was done. 'He could be extra precise, meticulous with externals, dominating, autocratic for the sake of the work we were doing. He knew what he was about.'

Dan Duryea gives a similar impression (cf. Eibel, p. 121). It could be a difficult test for an actor, yet it opened up a bigger dimension. He worked with an actor, he acknowledges, but he also worked for the actor.

Other actors have recorded less complimentary views. Marlene Dietrich, who may have been influenced in her comments by the souring of a personal relationship with Lang, says (cf. Eibel, p. 121) that she did not like working with him because everything was already fixed and constructed in his mind before the actor came along, and would make no concessions. Even though he was rarely as excellent as in the two films he made with Lang, Henry Fonda (cf. *Cinema 66*) seemed not to comprehend the working methods of Lang, whom he found incomprehensibly unyielding. More recently (*Sight and Sound*, Spring 1973) he has said that working with Lang was a 'bad experience compared to the way in which John Ford allowed the actor his head. He was not prepared like Boyer to be told when to open or shut his eyes, as in *Liliom*; 'but I must admit it is effective on the screen'.

Fonda also mentions endless retakes of the scene in *You Only Live Once* showing the dirty plates of the newlyweds' meal:

He would dolly back and shoot, then he would stop and take the spoon from my dessert, move the ice cream a little bit and dirty the dish etc. etc. He would do it fifty-five times . . .

Amusingly, Lang in writing about another film confirms this in his article 'The Frog and I':

I was once criticised for spending an hour in arranging a pile of dirty plates and left-overs in an apartment sink, yet one brief look which the camera took at that sink explained to the audience much more about the woman who owned that apartment than lines of dialogue.

(As he has said elsewhere: 'Out of detail is created atmosphere'.) Despite his reservations Fonda admits, 'He is a great director'.

In a letter to David Overbey, Joan Bennett, who has elsewhere stated that she was never better than when working with Lang, goes into detail about Lang's relationship with actors:

An ordinary day with Fritz Lang as director was ordinary in just one respect: it was invariably handled as he alone could. For me, this was extraordinary. He was thoroughly meticulous, with a complete grasp of where he was going, exactly what he wanted and precisely how he wanted his actors to perform. My confidence in him was absolute and unquestioning. There were no demonstrations, discussions or analyses of character. Fritz told his cast what he wanted – and that was it. He was fanatical about realism. Just as he demanded that Michael Redgrave and I do the actual shot of running through the burning house in Secret, the one fearful moment I had in Scarlet Street was the stabbing scene. I would have welcomed a double except for Fritz's insistence on the real thing and my confidence in him and his integrity. Fritz was a demanding director, but working with him was well worth the experience. As you well know, his camera techniques were distinctive, original and revolutionary in the motion picture industry. He had one – I suppose you might call it a trick – that he seemed to use with me alone. He habitually stood behind the camera during shooting and would motion to me with his hands for small movements which would improve camera angles. He's the only director I ever worked for who did this, and while it seemed to be a source of annoyance to others I've worked with, I accepted it Trilby-like because of the consummate confidence in his ability.

Rhonda Fleming (cf. Eibel, p.122) perhaps sums up most succinctly:

He was strict, occasionally almost severe – he is never gentle in his attempts at getting results yet with him work gets done and it gets done well.

A Perfectionist

When Lang was shooting American Guerrilla in the Philippines a Naval Commander said to him, ambiguously:

'They say you are a . . . perfectionist!' Eibel quotes a number of his associates who all confirm the stories of long preparation, meticulous work on the script, pre-planning of camera work, discussions with designers, architects and cameramen; above all his immense knowledge of technical means and possibilities, his indefatigable energy and stamina. Even when it led to conflicts, his best associates respected the need to be as he was.

Joseph Ruttenberg, cameraman of *Fury* praises the help to the operator of Lang's precise and subtle knowledge of the camera and his preparatory work: improvisation would take up too much time in the studio. Arthur Miller, cameraman of *Man Hunt* also talks about Lang's technical knowledge and says that every scene he shot was given the profile which alone gave it strong dramatic emphasis. Nicholas Musuraca, camerman of *Clash by Night* and *The Blue Gardenia* praises Lang's enormous professional ability, and Ernest Laszlo, the cameraman of *While The City Sleeps*, also praises his professionalism, and ability to know and get what he wants.

Most significant are the statements of Gene Fowler Jr. He had been warned that Lang had the reputation for 'devouring cutters alive'. Rather, he demanded:

of everybody who worked with him a willingness to contribute to his search for perfection – and in most American studios the word perfection is looked at askance.

Fowler says that Lang taught him three things: that he had still a lot to learn himself; that it was easy to work with Lang once one admitted this; and finally how many things could be expressed in film if it were cut correctly. He mentions Lang's interest in realism, his care for detail, his expertise concerning the lens to be used for every shot, the way his sets are always adapted to the size of the lens (a particularly interesting comment: with Lang the angle and the respective lens size are always dependent on the composition); his unrivalled knowledge of the crane and its uses in specific situations. Fowler speaks as a cutter, who has particular opportunity to appreciate the procedures which precede the editing.

Atmosphere and Style: Shooting on location
Lang relates in a letter how the magic forest of Siegfried was built:

I remember how Thea von Harbou and myself tried, at first near Dresden, then in the Harz mountains, to find a forest that seemed to fit the intended stylisation of the *Nibelungen*. We could not find a 'heroic' forest. Somehow I was thinking of Boecklin's *Schweigen im Walde*, and after discussions with my working crew Vollbrecht, Hunte and Kettelhut, we decided to build the forest. And all the other external shots were built, apart from the sand dunes down which the Huns rush on horseback. (Somewhere around Berlin there was a suitable sand dune in those days, though it was eventually swallowed up by building sites.) I also shot the Tower of Babel scenes for *Metropolis* there.

As far as I can remember I never filmed on location in Germany except in the grounds of Woltersdorf.

(Woltersdorf was used in *The Spiders* and perhaps *Harakiri*.) On another occasion Lang told me that if he had known the great American Redwoods he would probably have used them for Siegfried's forest. Yet ultimately he preferred building his sets in the studio or the studio grounds, because it gave him greater control of atmosphere and mood by means of lighting.

In the United States Lang mostly stuck to this practice – usually out of necessity. The prison in *Fury* was built against the studio walls; and Lang explains in a letter that the highway and the forest scenery were built:

perspectively by the very gifted art director Alexander Taluhoff i.e. they were designed from the point of view of the camera. And this was done in a way that they could be livened up by cars and people, yet from a certain point onwards – looked at from the camera as focal point – the life-size street was built in a constantly diminishing scale, i.e. finishing off perspectively.

The same procedure was used for the exterior shots of *You Only Live Once* which was filmed in and around the studios. Because of the perspective building, there was always a point beyond which actors could not move into the set without appearing in altered scale. Lang confirms also that:

For *Man Hunt* the port and all the other exterior shots (the forest in the dried-out river bed in front of the cave into which Thorndyke has escaped) were shot on the Fox Studio grounds.

The architect here was Wiard Ihnen, who also created the backdrops and painted skies for *Rancho Notorious* which unlike Lang's earlier two Westerns, was not shot in natural exteriors. For *Moonfleet*, too, only the scenes by the sea and on the shore were shot outside the studio, on location south of Marineland.

378

Lang selecting models for *You Only Live Once*

French critics often talk of a 'vase clos' in reference to Lang's German films; and Gavin Lambert sees in the American films Lang's love for abstraction and construction. I would feel tempted to replace the word 'abstract' by 'absolute': Lang's films have the perfection of an 'absolute composition' in the architectural and logical sense.

Surprisingly few critics have mentioned Lang's genuine exterior shots however. Gavin Lambert says that the landscapes of *The Return of Frank James* are soft and luminous, with a rich idyllic glow; and praises the rarely equalled subtle shading of *Western Union*; yet he believes that Lang, the painter, was mostly interested in the exploratory use of Technicolor. Even Lang's least perceptive critic, Jensen, notes that 'the proximity to such raw natural forces – the pounding waves, moulds the characters and their reactions', that the intervention of nature is necessary, and that the fine documentary introduction of the sardine

379

fishery in *Clash by Night* was more than simply a virtuoso exercise.

Yet in general Lang's critics are still captivated by his earlier formula of 'Man trapped by Fate' (although even in the earlier films 'Fate' is based on character), seeing the heavy nocturnal chiaroscuro of the streets of *Woman in the Window*, *Scarlet Street* and even *Fury*; and the night-time assignations of *Human Desire*. Yet his remarks in the article 'Happily Ever After' (*Penguin Film Review*, no 5) reveal that he is not only interested in tragedy, the nocturnal menace, the *huis clos* atmospheres created in the studios. Tragedy has become for him the Greek idea, of 'character is the daimon of man', rather than the earlier 'Man trapped by fate'.

In one of his most recent letters he cites a quotation he had found in Democrates:

Everywhere man blames nature and fate, Yet his fate is mostly but the echo of his character and passions, his mistakes and weaknesses.

Outlook: Germany or America?
It is an academic question – and as trivial as the favourite German dispute between the relative greatness of Goethe or Schiller – whether Lang's German films or his American period are to be valued more highly. Gavin Lambert regards the peak as being the German films, with the American period – apart from *Fury* and *You Only Live Once* – as a decline. American reviewers (who rarely know the German films adequately) tend to consider his American works as an evolution in his *oeuvre*.

The discussion leaves out essential elements of the matter: the American films were made in a different time and a different environment. There is doubtless, a profound difference in perspective, but there is also a firm continuity of vision. Lang, of course, matured as a natural process of aging common to all men, and the change in environment of course played a part in this maturation. The first films, then, are not exactly the same as the later films, but the same man made them all; both periods are always related in essentials (*Big Heat*, for example, can be taken to correspond to *M* in many ways).

French critics always pride themselves upon their eccentricity: for them the apogee of his career is the second German period, and particularly the Indian diptych.

Meditating

APPENDIX

In a copy of the screenplay of *Rancho Notorious* may be discovered a short note to Daniel Taradash, the writer, which illustrates much about Lang's working method. Generally his comments are brief and written in his large, energetic writing. In this longer note, he is notably tactful, beginning (using his own modification of Taradash's nickname, 'Dash' or 'Dachs' as Lang called him):

'Ach, Herr Dachs,* I think it is pure insolence to criticise the script.'

For all that, his criticisms are to the point:

1) My main impression is that from the birthday party onwards the story leads away from its proper subject because the scenes are too long and elaborate and divert from the story.

The shooting practice. We know from earlier scenes that Vern cannot shoot. The scene with Vern and Frenchy should end on p. 72 with Frenchy's words to Altar: 'That's right. I will be', and merge into the silver dollar scene on page 74, where Vern is the good shot.

* The note is in German; 'Dachs' is the word for 'badger', the animal.

2) Vern should never suspect Frenchy, because we know Frenchy as a gentleman-outlaw and consider him incapable of a brutal murder of a woman (p. 70). The tension between Frenchy and Vern should only arise out of Frenchy's jealousy because of Altar (page 75).

3) I think Vern is quite logical in his search for the murderer. He knows that three men* were in on the act. He knows from Tommy that the wounded man has long, blond hair. He should look for the friendly pairs among the outlaws. Kinch and Geary are often seen together. The Wilson brothers too are together. He doesn't even notice that Kinch is suspicious of him, though Kinch attacks him (p. 74). Even during the bank raid he is not aware of Kinch's shooting him.

4) The preparations for the bank raid (at the ranch) and the raid itself are very long.

5) Further to point 2: Vern says to Frenchy in jail that he is from Wyoming and asks him if he has ever been there. Frenchy says, no. Even if Vern thinks that Frenchy is lying, his acts of friendship must convince him that Frenchy is not the murderer.

* At first there were to have been three men; but in later versions of the script there were only two, one of whom rapes and murders Vern's fiancée.

Part III: The Second German Period: 1959–1960

The circle is closed.

Fritz Lang in conversation with the author

36 Der Tiger von Eschnapur; Das Indische Grabmal (1959–60)

On a visit to India Lang had made some notes and done some research for a film about the Taj Mahal, a monument to eternal love. The plan came to nothing and he returned to the United States. The subjects he was offered did not interest him, and a film on the tapping of private telephones by the FBI and local police stations – a fascinating foreshadowing of Watergate – ran into surprising (or not surprising) difficulties.

In 1958 he eagerly accepted an offer from Arthur Brauner in Germany to film *The Tiger of Eschnapur* and its sequel *The Indian Tomb*, with the promise of a completely free hand. Perhaps it still rankled that thirty-seven years before this subject, written by Lang and von Harbou, had been taken over by Joe May on the pretext that Lang was too young to direct this subject.* This fulfilment of so old an ambition had an almost mystical significance. He felt the circle had closed.

He was attracted by the adventure, the romanticism, the exoticism, above all by the *recherche du temps perdu* of Indian legend. He recognised too that he had to make a big popular success, by creating fairytale splendour for a Germany that was still not rich. In this he succeeded: the films were an instant popular success, though the reviews were negative. German critics at that time certainly seemed to have a barely conscious resentment of the emigrés of the thirties, like Lang and Dietrich. More recently, there is evidence of a new understanding of Lang, but in 1958 he was wryly amused to find 'Yankee Go Home' chalked on walls both of the studio and locations.

The quotation at the head of this chapter is perhaps a partial explanation of the strongly contrasted enthusiasm for the films in France, where there is a delight in elements

The great director Fritz Lang made these films ten years ago in Germany. They were then considered disturbing, even ridiculous. Later on one realised that Godard likes them. . . . Looking at them studiously as if they were difficult avantgardist works, leads to the discovery of something over and above their ideological content and the non-existent psychology of an exotic and romantic story: the classical lucidity of construction, the stylisation of figures and situations, the meaningful glances, the continuity of space, the nostalgia, a kind of paralysis, an almost uncanny abstraction. H.F. *Süddeutsche Zeitung*, 13 November, 1968

* It is one of the ironies of film history that, just as the May film had been edited into one incomplete feature in 1922 when it was released outside of Germany, the Lang films were released in America and England in a mutilated single feature version called *Journey to the Lost City* (USA) or *Tiger of Bengal* (UK). See filmography.

384

Der Tiger von Eschnapur (1958): Debra Paget in the dance sequence

essentially related to the noble classicism of Corneille, or the rationalist lucidity of Descartes. The work has a crystal-clear composition which is not the creation of an old man, but the crowning of maturity. When I complained to Chabrol about the vagueness of the praise showered on the film by the French critics, he pointed out the mastery with which Lang presented the young architect's search for the dancer from chamber to chamber, with gathering intensity and the balancing of colours and structures. It is the formal perfection, the masterly use of decor and spatial structuring, on which the extreme admiration of the Indian films is based.

Occasionally the stylisation and deliberate abstraction recall the *Nibelungen*. Here too situations and sequences are often set pieces of courtly splendour; sometimes the subject demands a static treatment. At the same time there is rich visual variety, as for instance in the subtle variations introduced into the two separate temple dance scenes performed by Debra Paget – the first in the temple grotto, and the second in which she is threatened, and apparently even hypnotised by a snake. Again Lang's *mise en scène* achieves mastery in the sequence to which Chabrol made reference – the young architect's search through state-rooms, terraces and halls for the dancer Seetha. The camera is very mobile, and we follow him almost breathlessly through heavy gates which mysteriously close one after the other behind him. Again Lang produces a symphony of colours, a feeling for space and dimension, a fusion of spatial units. Again the sequence is paralleled in the second part, where the dancer walks similarly from room to room with Chandra's hostile brother, in order to reach the dungeon where her beloved lies. There is yet a different aspect of the situation when the architect's sister is also seeking Seetha, to help her in her quest for her brother.

Individual images are memorable for their formal perfection: the palace surrounded by water and seen against a vast expanse of sky; a hall with avenues of stone elephants jutting like a pier into the water; the panorama of an Indian town overlooking a bay; water, stone, reflections, opalescent shimmer. Reflections in the water are shattered by a pebble or a jumping fish; the sandstorm; the mesmeric rhythm of galloping horses (which Lang had already used in his Westerns); vultures in a burning sky; the fugitive's desperate gesture of shooting at the merciless disc of the sun which appears in his sand-blinded eyes as yellow and brown haloes; inevitably the grottoes, heavy with mystery, with their strangely mingled colours; the silent army of lepers which noiselessly menace from their depths; the deep circular shaft in which the chained architect is imprisoned.

The silent moments in this film have a resonance that produces new spatial dimensions. The phosphorescent colours melt together in the temple grotto, as the misty haze and billowing smoke rise slowly up to veil the gigantic limbs of the goddess, then clearing to reveal them again so that she seems to come alive. Although the spatial and atmospheric effects are so strongly characteristic of Lang, they were produced in spite of a rather intractable camera. One regrets that the director was not able to use the cameraman of his choice, Fritz Arno Wagner, who had so memorably shot *Destiny*, *The Spy*, *M* and *The Last Will of*

Der Tiger von Eschnapur: the grotto passage

Dr Mabuse. Instead he was given Richard Angst, celebrated for his memorable scenic photography for the 'mountain' films of Arnold Fanck and Leni Riefenstahl. Disappointed in not being allowed to work with Lang, Wagner accepted a job on an indifferent film that was being shot in Geiselgasteig near Munich, and fell to his death in the course of shooting.

In this admirable spectacle, Lang remained true to his principles of what should constitute an adventure film: sustained suspense, without psychological treatment of character, or analysis of emotional reactions. He endeavoured to modernise the subject, working over it with a German writer (Werner Jörg Lüddecke), and entirely reforming the original Lang–Harbou scenario. Now the ending has Chandra discovering in the face of his defeated enemy that hatred and revenge are hollow. While the architect departs in a caravan, with Seetha, his sister and his brother-in-law, we see the once-powerful maharaja

The Hindu Tomb: the strangling: Lang demonstrates (*above*)

transformed into the humble servant of a Buddhist priest.

Lang had to deal with a not very understanding producer, Arthur Brauner, whose own film *Morituri te salutant* – based on his experiences in a concentration camp, and of which only the intentions were good – had failed commercially. His eye was therefore obsessively on the box office. Nonetheless, while Lang took great joy in delivering exciting adventures which would be popular, he never failed to make such adventures an organic part of the story as seen from his own personal viewpoint. The astonishing use of the rope trick in the film is an example. Exciting in itself, it leads logically to the basket trick. A court magician shoves sharp knives into a basket containing a servant woman. After the trick – at first seemingly a success – blood begins to ooze from the basket. While the scene is exciting and popularly exotic, it also allows Lang to make a serious point about both the character of the maharaja (who is punishing Seetha's faithful servant) and the age of absolutism.

37 Die Tausend Augen des Dr Mabuse (The Thousand Eyes of Dr Mabuse, 1960)

After the popular success of the Indian films Arthur Brauner proposed a remake of the Nibelungen, an idea which Lang, now back in the States, rejected as absurd.* Already, just after the war he had refused Eric Pommer's proposal of a remake of *Destiny*: he did not like to repeat himself. When Brauner came back with a suggestion for a remake of *The Last Will of Dr Mabuse*, Lang agreed instead to film a new variation on the Mabuse theme, almost thirty years after *The Last Will*. He was attracted by the idea of using a realistic modern style, new technological notions, and an idea he had picked up from documents about a hotel microphone system the Nazis had planned to use after the war to spy on foreign diplomats.

As a thriller Lang's last film is masterly: elated by his love of whirlwind adventure, Lang produced a film which stands up well against the work of his preceding American period. Yet it is more than a thriller: Lang was concerned with sounding a warning on dependence upon technology, the benefits of science that can turn into a menace in an age when one maniac might press a button and set off a nuclear holocaust.

Lively, spontaneous, thrilling, the film has nowhere the appearance of an old man's work. Lang himself feared that the opening was too long-winded; but his fears seem groundless: the present-day spectator, to whom Mabuse is quite unknown, requires certain background information.

Echoing the famous scene of the murder of Dr Kramm in *The Last Will*, a man sits in his car as another car glides up beside him. In the back seat is No. 12 (Howard Vernon), the executor of the new gang, his fingers tapping nervously on a violin-shaped box. There is a cutaway to the police station where the inspector sceptically listens to a

He makes films with ideas rather than films of ideas. As he remarked recently 'I live through my eyes', and in the end it is his power to embody his ideas visually which accounts for the lasting effects of his films. The main conflict in them is not primarily on the intellectual level, between good and bad, order and disorder, but on the intuitive between darkness and light. Light is never in Lang used merely decoratively, atmospherically, but always psychologically to convey emotional states.
John Russell Taylor: 'The Nine Lives of Dr Mabuse, *Sight ind Sound* Winter 1961–2

* He did not see how the problem of proper dialogue for the characters could be solved. Were they to *speak* the same dialogue that appeared in the silent titles, he thought they would sound ridiculous.

Die Tausend Augen des Dr Mabuse (1960): the blind clairvoyant

From its audience, The Thousand Eyes asks both greater innocence and infinitely greater sophistication than most of us bring to the movies nowadays.
Roger Greenspun: 'Film Favourites: The Thousand Eyes of Dr Mabuse,' Film Comment, March–April, 1973

telephone call in which the clairvoyant Cornelius predicts a car murder. On the word 'murder' there is a quick cut back to the cars, and the executioner who pulls an unusual rifle from his case and aims. When the traffic lights turn to green, all the cars move on – except one. The main difference between this scene and the murder of Dr Kramm is that in *The Last Will* the noise of the shot was smothered by the concert of motor horns playfully tooted by the impatient drivers; we only find out later why Lang did not use this detail again.

In *The Last Will* we were already aware of who Dr Kramm was and exactly what was happening. In *The Thousand Eyes*, however, Lang maintains suspense by keeping us ignorant at several points. Thus we learn after the murder who the victim was, but not yet why he was killed. A tearful woman announcer appears on television to announce that the popular reporter Peter Barter, who had promised a sensational scoop, died of a heart attack

391

Dr Mabuse: the executioner (Howard Vernon)

while driving his car. A quick cut takes us back to the murder car where the chauffeur expresses curiosity about what 'the doctor' looks like. The executor tells him that similar curiosity was the reason why an American was found with his throat cut. Soon the police and Interpol discover that Barter was shot with a weapon that fires a steel needle without sound, an American Army secret weapon which was stolen by a soldier who was later found with his throat cut. Thus we begin to get at least the outlines of a conspiracy as details begin to dovetail together. A search of Barter's apartment reveals that every scrap of tape or paper that might give a clue has been removed. All that remains is a photograph of a girl friend.

The film is constantly kept on the move by Lang's characteristic overlapping, ellipsis, rapid cutting. If someone mentions a person, an object or an event, the next shot will show us something about this person, object or event. A question is taken up and unexpectedly answered

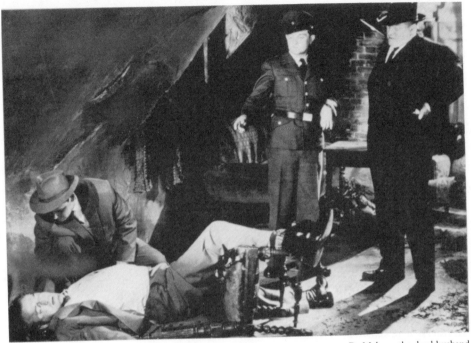

Dr Mabuse: the dead husband

in the succeeding shot. The device produces a breathtaking pace and immediacy, which never sacrifices precision or clarity.

Now the name of Mabuse begins to be mentioned. The technique of the car murder reminds someone of the mastermind of crime who died before the Hitler regime. We see his overgrown grave; then in quick cuts, a room with the police file 'Dr Mabuse'; but then immediately afterward are taken into the gangster headquarters where a man – of whom we only see a close-up of a clubfooted leg – is giving orders to the gang, using the name of Dr Mabuse.

In a monitor van two gangsters are told to watch the American millionaire Henry B. Travers (Peter van Eyck). Henry Travers is seen carrying on discussions about taking over the Arar Atomic Works, in his hotel – the Luxor. At police headquarters there is talk of the mysterious crimes and accidents that have all centred on the Luxor Hotel.

Then immediately we see the facade of the hotel with its clearly lettered sign. The camera pans back: a young girl is on a ledge, threatening to jump, watched by a thrilled crowd. She ignores the hotel manager and detective who are trying to help, but from an adjacent window Travers manages to grab her hand and pull her to safety. This dramatic 'accidental' meeting recalls the scene in *Spies* where Sonja bursts into the hero's hotel room, having apparently just shot a man.

After this the story becomes an intricate mosaic of interlocking incidents. Soon after 'saving' Marion (Dawn Adams), Travers meets Cornelius ('Lupo Prezzo'*) a blind clairvoyant who 'foresees' an automobile accident and a problem with a business transaction in Travers' future. Soon both come true: an 'accident' with Travers' car and a truck; and explosion at the Arar Atomic Works which Travers was negotiating for. Intrigued by Cornelius, Travers accepts an invitation to a seance, which is also attended by the odd Mistelzweig (Werner Peters), and by the inspector with his 'wife' who turns out to be Barter's friend. During the seance, accompanied effectively by a thunderstorm, Cornelius changes places with the inspector, warning him of danger. A shot comes through the window and hits the chair where the inspector was sitting. Cornelius insists it was meant for himself.

Travers is shown, by a greedy hotel detective, an empty suite where it is possible to watch what is happening in the next room through a two-way mirror. By this time Travers and Marion have begun to fall in love. She receives a message from Professor Jordan (Wolfgang Preiss*) that the husband she hates and fears is on his way to find her. She flees from Travers' suite. Travers watches the meeting of the two; her clubfooted husband threatens her, and he is about to cut her face, Travers crashes through the mirror which he has been watching, grabs the husband's revolver and shoots him.

Jordan arrives with mysterious rapidity; he will take the body away with the help of the hotel detective, and they will claim that the husband died of a heart attack. Marion is free to marry Travers. Mistelzweig, however, suspects Marion. Cornelius' dog was friendly with Marion, but refused his own overtures of friendship.

Mistelzweig, still in the guise of an insurance agent,

* The same actor played Cornelius and Jordan; Wolfgang Preiss used the Italian translation of his own name for his second role. The make-up is so good that even Roger Greenspun in his otherwise perceptive article did not notice the single actor in both roles. Although Lang rarely played the 'whodunnit' game, in this case he simply did not want the opening credits of the film to give the plot away.

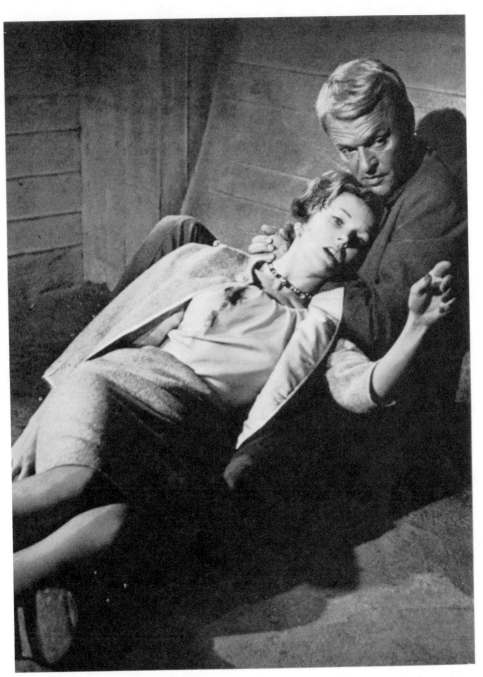

Dr Mabuse: the wounded Marion with Travers

tricks Cornelius into revealing that he can actually see. Meanwhile, in the ambulance carrying away the 'dead' husband, the clubfoot begins to move under the sheet. The spectator suddenly realises the whole scene had been staged. Yet the executor raises his gun; Marion must remain free.

The lovers are about to go away together. Yet Travers still has doubts. Marion finally breaks down and confesses: she had been forced to take part in the plot. Mabuse wants her to marry Travers; then back in the States, he would be killed and Mabuse would hold all the power of his economic empire. But now they must flee the hotel where every room has eyes and ears, where in every ornament there is hidden a television camera.

They get into the lift. In the lobby Mistelzweig notices that the lift continues to descend past the ground floor. The lift door opens on a lower level and the two lovers are trapped in the giant spy center with television screens for monitoring everything that happens in the hotel. In the centre is Professor Jordan, who explains that the entire system was built by the Nazis, but that it is now his realm as the rightful heir of Dr Mabuse.★★ Locking them in the hidden dungeon with a revolver to kill themselves before they die of hunger, Jordan takes off his disguise. Walking calmly through the lobby unnoticed, he is betrayed by the joyful recognition of his own (Cornelius') dog. He escapes with his faithful executor. There is a wild chase, and their car suddenly goes out of control and breaks through the railings to drop into the swirling water of the river below.

The television centre has been discovered and the lovers are released. In the hospital where the wounded Marion is being treated, Travers takes her hand; the scene is purposely silent.

★★ For publicity reasons Brauner wanted to make Mabuse's spiritual heir his real son. 'Son of Mabuse' seemed, rightly, ridiculous to Lang and he refused. Brauner later made the claim in the original programme anyway.

38   Lang's Statements About Himself: *Le Mépris*

There are innumerable published 'interviews' with Lang; but as has been pointed out these have to be approached with caution – particularly those from the earlier periods. Lang is conscious how often his remarks have been misunderstood and misinterpreted. Even alleged tape-recorded interviews are not always above suspicion: for instance the interview which *Cahiers du Cinema* published with the claim that it was taped by Gretchen Berg (*Cahiers* Nos 169 and 179, August 1965 and June 1966) turned out to be a skilful confection of statements from Lang's article 'Happily Ever After' and other interviews, articles and remarks made by Lang to Gretchen Berg and her father Hermann G. Weinberg in informal meetings.

The best clues to Lang's complex personality are his own articles – though he has always insisted a film director should express himself through his films and not through writing or talking. Of the articles, 'Happily Ever After', which has already been quoted earlier, is the longest and most revealing. Of the audience Lang says:

I respect the audience, which I believe to be moving towards better standards and higher truths on the screen as well as in life.

Nobody except the producer believes in the gullibility of a public prepared to accept anything:

I am always suspicious of assumptions which discredit the audience, because they are used for lazy, unintelligent or inept productions.

The article explains Lang's appeal to contemporary young people, who still find him entirely modern:

I believe in artistic rebellion. I think new approaches, new forms are needed to reflect the changed world we are in . . .

. . . But I don't think the only alternative to sugar is poison (and this explains also why he is against unnecessary violence).

For Lang, 'the film creators are responsible to our own time'. Contrary to the view of many critics – including Lambert, Bogdanovich and Moullet – who stress Lang's pessimism, in this article he takes a stand against negativism and despair:

Open City and Hangmen Also Die show man . . . in his own sense of dignity. Both of them . . . proclaim the solution through man's courage and sacrifice for those who live after him. This is not man as the victim of fate or man dying for nothing.

Later, in Mépris, he expresses a similar view: 'Death is no solution'. Such a statement reveals the American films in a new light, showing his own transformation, the philosophy of a man who insists, in the same article, 'The highest responsibility of the film creator is to reflect his time'.

The 1946 article 'The Frog and I', which relates the frog incident from the shooting of You Only Live Once (1936) contains two significant statements on style:

. . . a director must pay attention to detail because out of detail is created atmosphere and atmosphere sets the mood and tempo which condition the whole action of the film.

Spontaneity is what every director tries to achieve, perhaps it is because I learned film making in a country where detail was always thought important . . . that I say spontaneity comes from minute attention to detail and constant practice. That careless jerk of the thumb that halts the passing motorist, that flick of the wrist that empties the glass and sends the barman back for another . . . these are the fruits of long endeavour. And in film making, too, spontaneity like atmosphere can only be created by piling detail on detail.★

Some of Lang's views on censorship appeared in an article in the Los Angeles Daily News of 15 August, 1946, headed 'Director presents his case against censorship of films'. The statement was stimulated by the cutting by the Oregon censors of the scene in Woman in the Window in which Joan Bennett tries to poison the blackmailer Dan Duryea, on the grounds that there had been a recent real-life murder by poison. Lang quotes Voltaire's 'I disapprove of what you say, but I will defend to the death your right to say it'. His arguments are characteristic: aside from the fact that censorship, in denying freedom of speech, is

★ The importance of detail and décor to character in film is emphasised as well by Lang in his essay 'Ameublement et Caractère', written in 1968 for the book by Barsacq. (See Bibliography).

Fritz Lang (1967) (photo by Axel Madsen)

clearly unconstitutional, does it solve any problem? (cf: 'Death is no solution').

Censorship is an attempt to gloss over the sources of social ills, which, if they could be wiped out, would make censorship unnecessary. Failing to eradicate the real roots of crime – poverty, disease, unequal opportunity, inadequate education (including sex education) – we attempt with censorship to ignore and deny results of this failure.

Truth is always constructive; and where the young are concerned, 'should youth actually be kept from facing life?'

I am not opposed to censorship because I wish to make sensational or sordid pictures. I hate bad taste and dirty jokes. But if stronger language or more outspoken description appear necessary to me in order to give a true characterisation of a particular man or woman, I want to be in a position to use what is necessary, irrespective of rules designed to appease political censors.

Lang expresses similar views in the longish article 'The Freedom of the Screen'. He quotes a phrase from a novel by Michael Blankfort: 'Reform is always the dream of the young and the nightmare of the old'.

The way of real security and progress lies neither in the blind acceptance or rejection of new ideas; they should be scrutinised, tested and, if found of value, adopted. The censors would deny us the very rights to examine what is new.

To limit or prevent the spread of ideas or suggestions which might evoke a dangerous or unhealthy response among the immature, illiterate or irresponsible or pretend they do not exist and to deny them an honest treatment on the screen is to treat people like children and prevent them from reaching maturity.

As to education in sex:

the danger, as always, does not lie in telling the truth, but in telling half-truths.

Film must draw strength from life, for only by modelling themselves on the ever-shifting patterns and conflict of society can they continue to interest, to stimulate, and by dramatizing society's problems, indicate the solutions.

In an article in the *Los Angeles Herald Express* of 12 August, 1947 Lang published an article which appeared under the heading: 'Director Tells of Blood Letting and Violence – Vicarious guilt complex amuses and tortures "M" Man' (Lang was not responsible for the title). He develops the views on censoring expressed earlier, and writes about the fascination of murder, already discussed on page 113.

Why has the crime of murder such a patent clutch on the imagination of all humans? Why does a juicy murder shave even war events off the front page? And why is Shakespeare who wrote hardly a play without a murder in it the greatest dramatist.

(The article was written at the same time that *Secret Beyond the Door* was made 'to show how a compulsion to murder can be averted'.)

Lang also discusses the cinema in more general terms:

Drama begins with emotion, strong emotion and with conflicts of desire and temperament. Given a group of human beings, hemmed in by circumstances, driven by urges conscious or unconscious, their actions must march to a climax and from that climax to a resolution.

In Shakespeare's plays death always speaks the last line. In his own films, writes Lang, he always:

tried to approach the murderer imaginatively, to show him as a human being possessed of some demon that has driven him beyond the ordinary borderline of human behaviour, and not the least part of whose tragedy is that by murder he never solves his conflicts.

When a disappointed lover shoots his mistress – what does he gain? He has removed the last chance of possessing her body. And when he shoots his rival, he only earns the girl's unending hate.

For such reasons Lang found a new solution to tragedy in *Clash By Night*; and in *Scarlet Street* so effectively exposed the punishment of the murderer that neither the Hays Office nor any other censorship body could find fault.

Another Lang Article, 'A Person from Porlock' is a wryly ironic treatment of interventions and objections he suffered during the shooting of his films; while in his 'Preface to Famous Films' Lang paraphrases Lincoln: 'The cinema is the art of the people, by the people, for the people'. The cinema after all had started in the nickelodeons, and was a collective art. It represented a new language. Inevitably it had its clichés, but so far people had barely touched the surface of the medium's expressive potential.

Finally, Lang has discovered among his papers some previously unpublished notes concerning, he writes, 'the mental processes during the making of a film':

One has an idea . . .

a notion of something . . .

an inspiration . . .

One of these inspirations (or notions or ideas) is somehow dream-like, situated between reality and unreality and it is a very long process of developing and revealing the visionary idea which we have seen with our inner eye and to ultimately put it into 'life-giving' words.

Yet words have become impoverished in our time . . . they are like worn-out coins, it would probably have been impossible to describe a *visionary beauty* like Botticelli's Venus in her shell, *before* it was created on the canvas.

If I am honest I have to confess that I never quite succeeded in turning the wealth of visions I intended to film into actual films.

In Paris I was once asked in an interview where a creative idea (what is called a directorial touch in English) comes from . . . and suddenly I had the idea that I did not really know myself and I said: 'I do things intuitively without much thinking, because they seem right at the moment', and added, 'Maybe a film maker should be psychoanalysed when he has just finished a film, if he wants to find out, why he had one *particular* idea and not another, and used it.

Perhaps I should describe in more detail how my films originate and how I make them.

Almost as if I were sleepwalking.

This is the only expression I can find for this process, because I have had no models, no masters whose style I tried to imitate.

Yet from the first moment of my cinematic career I consider filming *the* art of our time and it is therefore only logical that the cinema should be an expression of its time, in other words, 'reflect its time'.

When, in 1922, I made my first Mabuse film I called it *Dr Mabuse – the Gambler*, a picture of our time . . . and I believe that *all my films* are somehow a picture of their time'.

Lang and 'Le Mépris'

How does the self-portrait presented by these views accord with the image of Lang – a sort of 'archive picture' – in Jean-Luc Godard's *Le Mépris*? When he set out to film Moravia's book, Godard confided to Mary Meerson of the Cinémathèque Française, that his dearest wish was to get Lang to act the role of the film director. Lang was at first hesitant because the film director was a fascist; and only agreed because Godard assured him the part would be tailored to suit him, and because ever since Truffaut's *Les Quatre Cents Coups* Lang had been keenly interested in the *nouvelle vague*, and had closely followed Godard's career.

Because Godard is accustomed to work without a script and because of Lang's ease in the role, I at first assumed that Lang's statements in the film were his own, improvised by himself. Later Lang assured me that the quotations from Dante, Corneille, Brecht, and even Hölderlin, however appropriate they seem to him, were part of a real script (not merely an outline) which Godard sent to Lang when he arrived in Italy.

It is fascinating to observe this confrontation of two directors of diametrically opposed approaches. Lang says that he never thought of himself as a director in this film, merely as an actor. He seems in the film, more of an observer; indeed his function is similar to a Greek chorus. He rarely added anything to the text even when Godard asked him to. One of his contributions was the sentence 'Death is no solution' which is a remark he makes to Michel Piccoli, who does most of the talking, as they walk together in a wood, and which becomes a summing-up of the Bardot character's fatal car accident. The final sentence, also, 'One has to finish what one has started' is, of course, also Lang's.

Nevertheless the Hölderlin quotation which Godard puts into Lang's mouth when the director is attacked by the unpleasant producer (unpleasantly played by Jack Palance) who says, 'When I hear the word culture I reach for my cheque book' is totally appropriate:

Fearless remains the man whenever he can. Alone with God, his simple mind protects him. He needs no arms and no cunning. As long as God's help is near . . .

Such behaviour by a producer cannot have been an unfamiliar experience for Lang; and his imperturbability seems as natural here as when Godard has him quote Brecht's lines (with reference to the scenarist who has compromised himself to please the producer) to the effect that every morning he goes to market and hopefully joins the queue of people waiting to sell their lies.

The few shots – gigantic marble heads or a statue – of the Ulysses film the director is supposed to be shooting do not look at all like Lang; they might come rather from a Cocteau film. (Godard was prevented by lack of money and bad weather from showing more of the film.)

More important for us is his television interview with Godard, after the filming of *Le Mépris* and his subsequent remarks to me, which make it clear that he considers the essential difference between himself and the Godard of that period to be that Godard improvises while he meticulously prepares everything in advance. He was astonished that Godard does not show the car accident as action – as he himself had done, for instance in *Beyond a Reasonable Doubt* – but only as *result,* that is, he simply shows the dead bodies in the car, revealed in flashes cut into the reading of Bardot's farewell letter. This single point vividly illustrates the difference between the two creators.

Lang, a *grand seigneur,* wise as one of the seven Greek sages, modestly followed Godard's 'Intentions'. As a final gesture of his career he was content to play the role of an imperturbable observer of life.

This led to the television interview between Lang and Godard, with no third person to intermediate or meddle: an interview between a dinosaur and a baby, between an Indian chief retiring to meditate and the younger son who will take over the warpath.

Both admitted romantics, despite their passionate quest for truth, they met in their love of the cinema. Both regard

403

themselves as workmen who know their trade. Both fight against censorship, and admit that they cannot say why they make films, only that they have to. Godard remarks on Lang's astonishing youthfulness, and Lang replies that what matters is youth and its progress. Lang declares again that a film has to have a theme, that it must offer food for thought and discussion. To which Godard, in near Maoist terms already, adds – for action and intervention.

In the final resort, it is necessary to finish what one has started.

Bibliography

BELLOUR, RAYMOND: 'Sur Fritz Lang', *Critique*, 226 (March 1966).

BERG, GRETCHEN: 'La Nuit Viennoise', *Cahiers du Cinéma*, 160 (August 1965), 179 (June 1966).

BOGDANOVICH, PETER: *Fritz Lang in America*, Studio Vista (London, 1967).

BUÑUEL, LUIS: 'Textes (*Metropolis*)', *Cahiers du Cinéma*, 223 (August/September 1971).

COURTADE, FRANCIS: *Fritz Lang*, Eric Losfeld/Terrain Vague (Paris, 1963).

EIBEL, ALFRED and MICHEL MOURLET: *Fritz Lang: Choix de Textes*, Présence du Cinéma (Paris, 1964).

EISNER, LOTTE H. : 'Notes sur le Style de Fritz Lang', *La Revue du Cinéma*, 2nd series, 5 (February 1947).
'The German Films of Fritz Lang', *The Penguin Film Review*, 6 (April 1948).
'Le Style de *M le Maudit*', *L'Avant Scène*, 39 (July 15–August 16, 1964).

FERGUSON, OTIS: 'Fritz Lang and Company' (23 June 1941).
'Behind the Camera: Lang' (30 June 1941).
'Fritz Lang, Continued' (7 July 1941), reprinted in *The Film Criticism of Otis Ferguson*, Temple University Press (Philadelphia, 1971).

FRANJU, GEORGES: 'Le Style de Fritz Lang', *Cinematographe*, 2 (March 1937).

GANDERT, GERO: 'Ein Interview', *Kinemathek*, 3, Ausgewählte Filmtexte, Marion von Schröder Verlag (Hamburg, 1963).

GUILLEMINAULT, GILBERT, and PHILLIPE BERNERT: *Les Princes des Années Folles*, Plon (Paris, 1970).

HYMSON, JOSEPH: 'Fritz Lang's *M*', *UCLA Daily Bruin* (7 November, 1969).

JENSEN, PAUL M. : *The Cinema of Fritz Lang*, Zwemmer (London, 1969).

KRACAUER, SIEGFRIED: *From Caligari to Hitler: A Psychological History of the German Film*, Princeton University Press (Princeton, 1947).

LAMBERT, GAVIN: 'Fritz Lang's America', *Sight and Sound* (Summer, 1955; Autumn, 1955).

LANG, FRITZ: 'Happily Ever After', *Penguin Film Review*, 5 (January 1948).
'Ameublement et Caractere', in Léon Barsacq, *Le Décor de Film*, Seghers (Paris, 1970).

MAMBER, STEPHEN: 'The American Films of Fritz Lang', *UCLA Daily Bruin* (15 October, 1969).

MINISTRO, MAURIZIO DEL: 'Introduzione a Lang Expressionista', *Letteratura*, no. 85–87, Gennaio–Giugno/De Luce (Rome, 1967).

MOULLET, LUC: *Fritz Lang*, Seghers (Paris, 1963).

OVERBEY, DAVID L. : 'Fritz Lang's *Death of a Career Girl*', *Sight and Sound* (Autumn, 1975).

PHILLIPS, GENE D. : 'Fritz Lang Remembers', *Focus on Film*, no. 20 (Spring 1975).

RHODE, ERIC : *Tower of Babel*, Weidenfeld and Nicolson (London, 1966).

RIVETTE, JACQUES, and JEAN DOMARCHI : 'Entrevue avec Fritz Lang', *Cahiers du Cinéma*, no. 99.

SCHRÖDER, PETER : 'Ornament und Ideologie: Zu Einer Fritz Lang Retrospektive in Bad Ems', *Film*, no. 8 (June/July 1964).

SCHÜTTE, WOLFRAM : 'Kolportage, Stilisierung, Realismus, Anmerkungen zum Werk von Fritz Lang', *Film Studio*, no. 44 (September 1964).

TAYLOR, JOHN RUSSELL : 'The Nine Lives of Dr Mabuse', *Sight and Sound* (Winter 1961/62).

TRUFFAUT, FRANÇOIS : 'Fritz Lang en Amerique', in *Les Films de Ma Vie* Flammarion (Paris, 1975).

VERBAND DER DEUTSCHEN FILMKLUBS : *Retrospektive Fritz Lang: Dokumentation* (Bad Ems, 1964).

WEINBERG, HERMAN G. : *An Index to the Creative Work of Fritz Lang*, Index Series No. 5, Special Supplement to *Sight and Sound* (February, 1946).

ilmography

he following filmography was based on a number of published (see bibliography) and unpublished sources. 'he most important of the latter was, of course, Lang himself and his personally corrected and updated copy f the Weinberg 'Creative Index'.

In the early period (1916 to 1917 or 18), Lang wrote a number of scenarios ('. . . in those days I wrote a script a four or five days—don't forget no dialogue and shorter films . . .') some of which were doubtless lost and ave since been forgotten even by Lang himself. According to Erich Pommer, the first script Lang ever rote was *Peitsche* (1916), but no one now knows if it was ever made into a film nor what it was about.

ie Hochzeit im Exzentrick Klub Wedding in the Eccentric Club)
17
irector: Joe May. *Writer*: Fritz Lang. hotographer: Carl Hoffmann.

oe Debbs (Series)
ecla-Bioscop, 1917
irector: Joe May. *Writer*: Fritz Lang. 'ast: Max Lande, Harry Liedtke.

ilde Warren und der Tod (Hilde Varren and Death)
ecla-Bioscop, 1917
irector: Joe May. *Writer*: Fritz Lang. 'ast: Mia May (Hilde Warren), Fritz ang (Death, an old priest, a young essenger, and a fourth role Lang no nger can recall).

alb-Blut (Half-Caste)
ecla-Bioscop, 1919
irector/Writer: Fritz Lang. *Photographer*: :arl Hoffmann.
'ast: Ressel Orla, Carl de Vogt, Gilda anger, Carl-Gerrard Schröder, Paul lorgan.
remiere: Early April 1919. Marmorhaus, erlin

est in Florence (Plague in lorence)
ecla-Bioscop, 1919
irector: Otto Rippert. *Writer*: Fritz ang. *Photographer*: Willy Hameister. *Art* irectors: Franz Jaffé (exteriors and lorentine constructions), Hermann Varm (interiors), Walter Reimann, Valter Röhrig (murals and backgrounds). *Music*: Bruno Gellert.
'ast: Otto Mannstaedt (Cesare), Anders Vikman (Lorenzo, his son), Karl Bernhard (his confidant), Franz Knaak Cardinal), Erner Hübsch (Monk), heodor Becker (Franziskus), Marga Zierska (Julia), August Prasch-Grevenberg (Servant), Hans Walter Friend to Julia), Julietta Brandt (The 'est).
he script for this film, as for *Totentanz* nd *Die Frau mit den Orchideen*, were vidently written before the making of falb-Blut but were themselves filmed fterwards. Released October 23, 1919.

Totentanz (Dance of Death)
Helios Film, 1919
Director: Otto Rippert. *Writer*: Fritz Lang. *Photographer*: Willy Hameister. *Art Director*: Hermann Warm.
Cast: Sascha Gura, Werner Krauss, Joseph Röhmer.

Die Frau mit den Orchideen (The Woman with the Orchid)
Decla-Bioscop, 1919
Director: Otto Rippert. *Writer*: Fritz Lang. *Photographer*: Carl Hoffmann.
Cast: Werner Krauss, Carl de Vogt, Gilda Langer.

Der Herr der Liebe (The Master of Love)
Decla-Bioscop/Helios Film, 1919
Director: Fritz Lang. *Writer*: Oscar Koffler. *Photographer*: Emil Schünemann.
Cast: Carl de Vogt (Disescu), Gilda Langer (Yvette), Erika Unruh, Fritz Lang. Released: Mid-September, 1919. Richard Oswald Lichtspiele, Berlin.

Die Spinnen (The Spiders). *Part One*: Der Goldene See (The Golden Lake)
Decla-Bioscop, 1919
Director/Writer: Fritz Lang. *Photographer*: Emil Schünemann. *Art Directors*: Otto Hunte, Carl Ludwig Kirmse, Hermann Warm, Heinrich Umlauff.
Cast: Carl de Vogt (Kai Hoog), Ressel Orla (Lio Sha), Lil Dagover (Priestess of the Sun King), Paul Morgan (Expert), Georg John (Dr. Telphas), Bruno Lettinger (Terry Landon), Edgar Pauly (Four-finger John), Paul Biensfeldt. Original length: 1900 metres. Released: 3.10.1919, Richard Oswald Lichtspiele, Berlin. Lang later made a novel from the material of *Der Goldene See* which was first serialized in the Berlin *Film-Kurier* and then published in book form.

Hara-kiri
Decla-Bioscop, 1919
Director: Fritz Lang. *Writer*: Max Jungk (from the play, *Madam Butterfly*, by John Luther Long and David Belasco). *Photographer*: Max Fassbaender. *Art Director*: Heinrich Umlauff (with the assistance of the I.F.G. Umlauff Museum of Hamburg).

Cast: Paul Biensfeldt (Daimyo Tokuyawa), Lil Dagover (O-Take-San), Georg John (Buddhist Monk), Meinhard Maur (Prince Matahari), Rudolph Lettinger (Karan), Erner Hübsch (Kin-Be-Araki), Kaete Jüster (Hanake), Nils Prien (Olaf J. Anderson), Herta Heden (Eva), Loni Nest.
Original length: 2525 metres. Released: Late December, Marmorhaus, Berlin. 1919. After *Hara-Kiri*, Hermann Warm, Walter Reimann and Walter Roehrig submitted a story to Lang and Erich Pommer: *Das Cabinet des Dr Caligari*. The popularity of the first part of *Die Spinnen* was so great, however, that Pommer decided Lang had to begin the second part at once. Lang's idea that the expressionistic story be framed by a normal prologue and epilogue was retained by the writers of the script (Karl Mayer and Hans Janowitz), and *Caligari* was then directed by Robert Wiene and released by Decla in February 1920.

Die Spinnen. *Part Two*: Das Brillanten Schiff (The Diamond Ship)
Decla-Bioscop, 1919
Director/Writer: Fritz Lang. *Photographer*: Karl Freund. *Art Directors*: Otto Hunte, Karl Ludwig Kirmse, Hermann Warm, Heinrich Unlauff.
Cast: Carl de Vogt, Ressel Orla, Lil Dagover, Paul Morgan, Friedrich Kuehne, Georg John, Meinhardt Maur, Gilda Langer, Paul Biensfeldt.
Shooting: October/November 1919.
Original length: 2219 metres. Released 1920. Early February 1920. Theater am Moritzblatz, Berlin. This section of *Die Spinnen* was originally called *Das Sklaven Schiff* (The Slave Ship) in Lang's original four-part cycle; Parts Three (*Das Geheimnis der Sphinx*—The Secret of the Sphinx) and Four (*Um Asiens Kaiserkrone*—For Asia's Imperial Crown) were written by Lang but never filmed.

Das Wandernde Bild (The Wandering Image)
Joe May Company, 1919
Director: Fritz Lang. *Writers*: Fritz Lang, Thea von Harbou.
Cast: Mia May, Hans Marr.
Shooting: July 1919. Released 1920.

Working title: *Madonna im Schnee (Madonna of the Snow)*. 25.12.1920, Tauentzienpalast, Berlin.
1920. Lang wrote a four-part serial *Der Silberkoenig* (The Silver King) for the Joe May Company. Some of the material was subsequently filmed by Lothar Mendes.

Vier um die Frau (Four Around a Woman)

Decla-Bioscop, 1920
Director: Fritz Lang. *Writers:* Fritz Lang, Thea von Harbou,
Cast: Carola Tölle (Madame Yquem), Ludwig Hartau (Mr. Yquem), Anton Edthofer (The Swindler), Rudolph Klein-Rogge.
Working title: *Kaempfende Herzen (Fighting Hearts)*. Released: Early February. Marmorhaus, Berlin.

Der Müde Tod (The Weary Death)

American/British title: **Destiny.**
French title: **Les Trois Lumières**
Decla-Bioscop, 1921
Director: Fritz Lang. *Writers:* Fritz Lang, Thea von Harbou. *Photographers:* Erich Nietzschmann, Fritz Arno Wagner, Hermann Saalfrank. *Lighting:* Robert Hegerwald. *Art Directors:* Hermann Warm, Robert Herlth, Walter Röhrig.
Cast: Bernhard Goetzke (Death), Lil Dagover (Young Woman), Walter Janssen (Young Man), Rudolph Klein-Rogge (Girolamo), Georg John (Magician), Eduard von Winterstein (Calife), Max Adalbert, Paul Biensfeldt, Karl Huszar, Hermann Vallentin, Erika Unruh, Wilhelm Diegelmann, Lothar Müthel, Hermann Picha, Hans Sternberg.
Shooting: 9 weeks. Original length: 2306 metres. Released: October 1921. The film was given a very brief American release in July 1923 as *Between Two Worlds* by Artclass. Released: 7.10.1921. Mozartsaal and U.T. Kurfürste Kürfurstendamm, Berlin.

Das Indische Grabmal (Part I: Die Sendung des Yoghi; Part II: Das Indische Grabmal) (The Hindu Tomb)

Joe May Company, 1921
Director: Joe May. *Writers:* Fritz Lang, Thea von Harbou. *Art Director:* Martin Jacoby-Boy.
Cast: Mia May, Conrad Veidt, Lya de Putti, Olaf Fonss, Erna Morena, Berhard Goetzke.
Lang and von Harbou had written this screenplay in 1920 with the idea that Lang would direct the film. At the last moment, May decided to direct it himself. While in Germany the two parts were shown on consecutive evenings, for foreign distribution it was edited into a single eight-reel feature and called *Mysteries of India* (later changed to *Above All Law*). The scenario was filmed a

second time under Hitler's government as *The Indian Tomb* (1938) by Richard Eichberg. Lang finally directed the material himself in 1958/9 (see below).

Dr. Mabuse, der Spieler (Dr. Mabuse, the Gambler) (Part one: *Dr. Mabuse, der Spieler—Ein Bild der Zeit—Dr. Mabuse, the Gambler—A Picture of the Time;* Part Two: *Inferno—Menschen der Zeit—Inferno—Men of the Time)*

Ullstein-Uco Film-Decla-Bioscop-Ufa.
Director: Fritz Lang. *Writers:* Fritz Lang, Thea von Harbou, from a novel by Norbert Jacques. *Photographer:* Carl Hoffmann. *Art Directors:* Otto Hunte, Stahl-Urach.
Cast: Rudolph Klein-Rogge (Mabuse), Alfred Abel (Count Told), Aud Egede Nissen (Cara Carozza), Gertrude Welcker (Countess Told), Bernhard Goetzke (Von Wenck), Forster Larrinaga (Spörri), Paul Richter (Edgar Hull), Hans Adalbert von Schlettow (Chauffeur), Georg John (Pesch), Grete Berger (Fine), Julius Falkenstein (Karsten), Lydia Potechina (Russian Woman), Anita Berber (Dancer), Paul Biensfeldt (Man with Gun), Karl Platen (Told's Servant), Karl Huszar (Hawasch), Edgar Pauly (Fat Man), Julius Hermann (Schramm), Lil Dagover, Adele Sandroch, Max Adalbert, Hans J. Junkermann, Auguste Prasch-Grevenberg, Julie Brandt, Gustave Botz, Leonhard Haskel, Erner Hübsch, Gottfried Huppertz, Alfred Klein, Erich Pabst, Hans Sternberg, Olf Storm, Erich Welter, Heinrich Gotho, Willy Schmidt-Gentner.
Shooting: (*Mabuse*) 8 weeks, (*Inferno*) 9 weeks. Original length: (*Mabuse*) 95 minutes, (*Inferno*) 100 minutes. Released (with tinted night sequences and shown on consecutive evenings): April 1922. (*Mabuse*) 27.4.1922, Ufa Palast am Zoo, Berlin, (*Inferno*) 26.5.1922, Ufa Palast am Zoo, Berlin.

Die Nibelungen (Part One: *Siegfrieds Tod (Death of Siegfried)*; Part Two: **Kriemhilds Rache—Kriemhild's Revenge)**

Decla-Bioscop-Ufa, 1923–24
Director: Fritz Lang. *Writers:* Fritz Lang and Thea von Harbou, based on *Die Nibelungen* and Norse Sagas.
Photographers: Carl Hoffmann, Günther Rittau, and Walter Ruttmann (for the animated 'Dream of the Falcon' sequence). *Art Directors:* Otto Hunte, Erich Kettelhut, Carl Vollbrecht.
Costumes: Paul Gerd Guderian, Anne Willkomm. *Armour and weapons of the Huns:* Heinrich Umlauff. *Make-up:* Otto Genath. *Music:* Gottfried Huppertz.
Cast: Paul Richter (Siegfried), Margarete

Schön (Kriemhild), Rudolph Klein-Rogge (Etzel, King of the Huns), Georg August Koch (Hildebrand), Theodor Loos (Gunther), Bernhard Goetzke (Volker von Alzey), Hans Adalbert von Schlettow (Hagen Tronje), Georg John (Mime Alberich, I; Blaodel, II), Gertrude Arnold (Queen Ute), Hanna Ralph (Brunhild), Rudolph Rittner (Rüdiger), Fritz Albert (Dietrich), Hans Carl Müller (Gerenot), Edwin Biswanger (Giselher), Hardy von Francois (Dankwart), Frieda Richard (Lecturer), Georg Jurowski (Priest), Iris Roberts (Page), Grete Berger (Hun), Fritz Alberti, Rose Lichtenstein.
Shooting: (I) 15 weeks; (II) 16 weeks. Original length: (I) 3216 metres; (II) 3576 metres. Released (with subtitle *Ein Deutsches Heldenlied* and shown on consecutive evenings): January, 1924. During the production, Decla-Bioscop merged with Ufa. In 1925, Ufa released outside of Germany a shortened version (9000 foot) of *Siegfried* with music from Wagner's *Der Ring des Nibelungen* arranged by Hugo Reisenfeld, and in 1928 a shortened version (9000 foot) of *Kriemhilds Rache* followed. In 1933, Ufa released an even shorter version (2258 metres) of *Siegfried* with sound effects and the Wagner music. Needless to say, these short versions, particularly with Wagner music which Lang dislikes, were not authorized by the director.
(*Siegfried*) 14.2.1924, Ufa Palast am Zoo, Berlin, (*Kriemhild's Rache*) 26.4.1924, Ufa Palast am Zoo, Berlin.

Metropolis

Ufa, 1926
Director: Fritz Lang. *Writers:* Fritz Lang, Thea von Harbou. *Photographers:* Karl Freund, Günther Rittau. *Special effects photographer:* Eugene Schüfftan. *Art Directors:* Otto Hunte, Erich Kettelhut, Carl Vollbrecht. *Sculptures:* Walter Schultze-Middendorff. *Music:* Gottfried Huppertz.
Cast: Brigitte Helm (Maria), Alfred Abel (John Frederson), Gustave Fröhlich (Freder Frederson), Rudolph Klein-Rogg (Rothwang), Heinrich Georg (Foreman) Fritz Rasp (Grot), Theodor Loos, Erwin Biswanger, Olaf Storm, Hans Leo Reich, Heinrich Gotho, Margarete Lanner, Max Dietze, Georg John, Walter Kuhle, Arthur Reinhard, Erwin Vater, Grete Berger, Oily Böheim, Ellen Frey, Lisa Gray, Rose Lichtenstein, Helène Weigel, Beatrice Garga, Anny Hintze, Helen von Münchhoten, Hilda Woitscheff, Fritz Alberti, 750 secondary actors and over 30,000 extras.
Shooting: 310 days, 60 nights—1925–26.
10.1.1927, Ufa Palast am Zoo, Berlin.
The novel *Metropolis* by Thea von Harbou would seem to have been written (as it was published) after the film, rather than the film having been 'based on a

ovel by von Harbou'. When originally
nown, *Metropolis* ran for two hours (4189
netres). After its initial release (January
927), the film was considerably cut
0,400 feet), both abroad and in
Germany; no complete copy is now
nown to exist.

pione (The Spy)
ritz Lang-Film-G.M.B.H. (released by
Jfa), 1927-28
Director/Producer: Fritz Lang. *Writers:*
ritz Lang, Thea von Harbou.
Photographer: Fritz Arno Wagner. *Art
Directors:* Otto Hunte, Carl Vollbrecht.
Music: Werner R. Heymann.
Cast: Rudolph Klein-Rogge (Haighi),
Gerda Maurus (Sonja), Willy Fritsch
Detective), Lupu Pick (Masimoto), Fritz
Rasp (Ivan Stepanov), Lien Deyers
Kitty), Craighall Sherry (Burton Jason),
Julius Falkenstein (Hotel Manager), Georg
ohn (Train Conductor), Paul Rehkopf
Strolch), Paul Hörbiger (Valet), Louis
Ralph (Hans Morriera), Hermann
allentin, Grete Berger, Hertha von
Walther.
hooting: 15 weeks at Neubabelsberg
tudios, Berlin. Original length: 4364
netres. 22.3.1928, Ufa Palast am Zoo,
Berlin.

rau im Mond (Woman in the
Moon)
ritz-Lang-Film-G.M.B.H. (released by
Jfa), 1928
Director/Producer: Fritz Lang. *Writers:*
ritz Lang, Thea von Harbou.
Photographers: Curt Courant, Oskar
ischinger, Otto Kanturek. *Special effects:*
Constantin Tschetwerikoff. *Art Directors:*
Otto Hunte, Emil Hasler, Carl
ollbrecht. *Backdrop photographs:* Horst
on Harbou. *Music:* Willy Schimdt-
Gentner. *Technical Advisors:* Hermann
Oberth, Willy Ley.
Cast: Gerda Maurus (Frieda Venten),
Willy Fritsch (Professor Helius), Fritz
Rasp (Walt Turner), Gustav von
Wangenheim (Hans Windegger), Klaus
Pohl (Professor Georg Manfeldt), Gustl
tark-Gstettenbaur (Gustav), Margarete
Kupfer (Madame Hippolt), Tilla Durieux,
Hermann Vallentin, Max Zilzer,
Mahmud Terja Bey, Borwin Walth
Financiers), Max Maximilian (Grotjan),
Alexa von Porembsky (Flower Vendor),
Gerhard Dammann (Foreman), Heinrich
Gotho, Karl Platen, Alfred Loretto, Edgar
Pauly, and Josephine the Mouse.
hooting: 13 weeks. Original length:
4356 metres. 15.10.1929, Ufa Palast am
Zoo, Berlin. *Frau im Mond* has also been
nown in the United States and England
under the titles *By Rocket to the Moon* and
The Girl in the Moon.

M
Nero Film A.G.-Ver. Star Film-

G.M.B.H., 1931
Director: Fritz Lang. *Producer:* Seymour
Nebenzal. *Writers:* Fritz Lang, Thea von
Harbou. *Photographers:* Fritz Arno
Wagner, Gustav Rathje. *Camera Operator:*
Karl Vash. *Art Directors:* Carl Vollbrecht,
Emil Hasler. *Backdrop Photographs:* Horst
von Harbou. *Music:* excerpts from *Peer
Gynt* by Edvard Grieg ('murderer's
theme' whistled by Fritz Lang). *Sound:*
Adolf Jansen. *Sound Editor:* Paul
Falkenberg.
Cast: Peter Lorre (Franz Becker), Otto
Wernicke (Karl Lohmann), Gustav
Gründgens (Schraenker), Theo Lingen
(Baurenfaenger), Theodor Loos
(Commissioner Groeber), Georg John
(Peddler), Ellen Widmann (Madame
Becker), Inge Landgut (Elsie), Ernst
Stahl-Nachbaur (Police Chief), Paul
Kemp (Pickpocket), Franz Stein
(Minister), Rudolf Blümner (Attorney),
Karl Platen (Watchman), Gerhard Bienert
(Police Secretary), Rosa Veletti (Servant),
Hertha von Walther (Prostitute), Fritz
Odemar (The Cheater), Fritz Gnass (A
Burglar), Heinrich Gretler, Lotte
Löbinger, Isenta, Leonard Steckel,
Karchow, Edgar Pauly, Kepich Günther
Neumann, Krehan, Almas, Kurth,
Balthaus, Leeser, Behal, Rosa
Lichtenstein, Carell, Lohde, Döblin,
Loretto, Maja Norden, Josef Damen,
Wulf, Bruno Ziener, Walth, Wanka,
Wannemann, Otto Waldis, Eckhof,
Mascheck, Else Ehser, Matthis, Elzer,
Mederow, Trutz, Stroux, Swinborne,
Faber, Margarete Melzer, Ilse
Fürstenberg, Trude Moos, Gelingk,
Hadrian M. Netto, Goldstein, Nied, Anna
Goltz, Klaus Pohl, Heinrich Gotho,
Polland, Hadank, Rebane, Hartberg,
Rehkopf, Hempel, Reihsig, Höcker,
Rhaden, Hoermann, Ritter, Sablotski,
Sascha, Agnes Schultz-Lichterfeld.
Shooting: 6 weeks. 11.5.1931, Ufa Palast
am Zoo, Berlin. Upon its original release
(May 11, 1931) *M* ran for two hours.
Since then the film has often been
shortened; it is now most commonly
shown in a version of 89 minutes,
although rare, complete prints do exist.
A 1933 dubbed version was released in the
United States with only Lorre speaking
his own lines. In 1951, Superior Pictures-
Columbia released a version of *M*
produced by Seymour Nebenzal, directed
by Joseph Losey, with a screenplay by
Norman Reilly Raine, Leo Katcher and
Waldo Salt. Although obviously based on
the original screenplay and film, neither
Lang nor von Harbou are credited, which
given the dubious quality of the film may
be just as well.

Das Testament von Dr.
Mabuse/La Testament du Dr.
Mabuse (The Last Will of Dr.
Mabuse)

Nero Film-Constantin-Deutsche
Universal, 1932-33
Director/Producer: Frita Lang. *Writers:*
Fritz Lang, Thea von Harbou, based on
characters from a novel by Norbert
Jacques. *Photographers:* Fritz Arno
Wagner, Karl Vash. *Art Directors:* Carl
Vollbrecht, Emil Hasler. *Music:* Dr. Hans
Erdmann.
Cast: Rudolph Klein-Rogge (Mabuse),
Oskar Beregi (Dr. Baum), Karl Meixner
(Landlord), Theodor Loos (Dr. Kramm),
Otto Wernicke (Karl Lohmann), Klaus
Pohl (Müller), Wera Liessem (Lilli),
Gustav Diessl (Kent), Camilla Spira
(Juwelen-Anna), Rudolph Schündler
(Hardy), Theo Lingen (Hardy's friend),
Paul Oskar Höcker (Bredow), Paul
Henckels (Lithographer), Georg John
(Servant), Ludwig Stössel, Hadrian M.
Netto, Paul Bernd, Henry Pless,
A. E. Licho, Gerhard Bienert, Josef
Damen, Karl Platen, Paul Rehkopf, Franz
Stein, Eduard Wesener, Bruno Ziener,
Heinrich Gotho, Michael von Newlinski,
Anna Goltz, Heinrich Gretler.
A French version was shot simultaneously
with the same technical crew. The
scenario was adapted into French by
A. René-Sti.
Cast: Rudolph Klein-Rogge, Oskar
Beregi, Karl Meixner, Jim Gérald
(Lohmann), Thomy Bourdelle, Maurice
Maillot, Monique Rolland, René Ferté,
Daniel Mendaille, Raymond Cordy,
Ginette Gaubert, Sylvie de Pédrillo,
Merminod, Georges Tourreil, George
Paulais, Jacques Ehrem, Lily Rezillot.
Shooting: 10 weeks. Forbidden in
Germany, censorship card dated
29.3.1933. When the Nazis banned the
film, unassembled footage of the French
version was smuggled out of Germany
and edited in France by Lothar Wolff into
a less complete version than Lang's own
German version. It was the French
version which was released in the United
States in 1943 for which Lang wrote a
special foreword.

Liliom
S.A.F-Fox Europa, 1933
Director: Fritz Lang. *Producer:* Erich
Pommer. *Writers:* Fritz Lang, Robert
Liebmann, Bernard Zimmer, based on the
play by Ferenc Molnar. *Photographers:*
Rudolph Maté, Louis Née. *Art Directors:*
Paul Colin, René Renoux. *Music:* Jean
Lenoir, Franz Waxman. *Assistant Director:*
Jacques P. Feydeau.
Cast: Charles Boyer (Liliom), Madeleine
Ozeray (Julie), Florelle (Madame
Muskat), Robert Arnoux (Strong Arm),
Roland Toutain (Sailor), Alexandre
Rignault (Hollinger), Henri Richaud
(Commisionary), Richard Darencet
(Purgatory Police), Antonin Artaud
(Knife Grinder), Raoul Marco
(Detective), Alcover (Alfred), Leon Arnel

(Clerk), René Stern (Cashier), Maximilienne, Mimmi Funés, Viviane Romance, Mila Parély, Rosa Valetti, Lily Latté.
Shooting: 57 days, starting December 1933 at St. Maurice Studios, Paris.
Original length: 2 hours. Released: May 15 1934, Paris.

Fury
Metro-Goldwyn-Mayer, 1936
Director: Fritz Lang. Producer: Joseph L. Mankiewicz. Writers: Fritz Lang and Bartlett Cormack, based on the story 'Mob Rule' by Norman Krasna.
Photographer: Joseph Ruttenberg. Art Director: Cedric Gibbons (assisted by William A. Horning, Edwin B. Willis). Costumes: Dolly Tree. Music: Franz Waxman. Editor: Frank Sullivan. Assistant Director: Horace Hough.
Cast: Spencer Tracy (Joe Wheeler), Sylvia Sidney (Katherine Grant), Walter Abel (District Attorney), Bruce Cabot (Kirby Dawson), Edward Ellis (Sheriff), Walter Brennan (Bugs Mayers), Frank Albertson (Charlie), George Walcott (Tom), Arthur Stone (Durkin), Morgan Wallace (Fred Garrett), George Chandler (Milton Jackson), Roger Grey (Stranger), Edwin Maxwell (Vickery), Howard Hickman (Governor), Jonathan Hale (Defense Attorney), Leila Bennett (Edna Hooper), Esther Dale (Mrs. Whipple), Helene Flint (Franchette), Frank Sully (Dynamiter).
Original length: 94 minutes. Released June 5, 1936.

You Only Live Once
Wanger-United Artists, 1937
Director: Fritz Lang. Producer: Walter Wanger. Writers: Gene Towne, Graham Baker, based on a story by Towne.
Photographer: Leon Shamroy. Art Director: Alexander Toluboff. Music: Alfred Newman. Song 'A Thousand Dreams of You' by Louis Alter, Paul Francis Webster. Editor: Daniel Mandell. Assistant Director: Robert Lee.
Cast: Sylvia Sidney (Joan Graham), Henry Fonda (Eddie Taylor), Barton MacLane (Stephen Whitney), Jean Dixon (Bonnie Graham), William Gargan (Father Dolan), Warren Hymer (Mugsy), Charles 'Chick' Sale (Ethan), Margaret Hamilton (Hester), Guinn Williams (Rogers), Jerome Cowan (Dr. Hill), John Wray (Warden), Jonathan Hale (District Attorney), Ward Bond (Guard), Wade Boteler (Policeman), Henry Taylor (Kozderonas), Jean Stoddard (Stenographer), Ben Hall (Messenger), Walter De Palma.
Shooting: 46 days. Original length: 86 minutes. Released January 29.

You and Me
Paramount, 1938
Director: Fritz Lang. Writer: Virginia Van

Upp, based on a story by Norman Krasna. Photographer: Charles Lang, Jr. Art Directors: Hans Dreier, Ernest Fegté. Set Decorator: A. E. Freudeman. Music: Kurt Weill, Boris Morros. Songs: 'The Right Guy For Me' by Weill, Sam Coslow: 'You and Me' by Ralph Freed, Frederick Hollander. Musical Advisor: Phil Boutelie. Editor: Paul Weatherwax.
Cast: Sylvia Sidney (Helen Roberts), George Raft (Joe Dennis), Barton MacLane (Mickey), Roscoe Karns (Cuffy), Harry Carey (Mr. Morris), Warren Hymer (Gimpy), George E. Stone (Patsy), Guinn Williams (Cab Driver), Vera Gordon (Mrs. Levine), Carol Paige (Torch Singer), Bernadene Hayes (Nellie), Egon Breecher (Mr. Levine), Joyce Compton (Blonde), Cecil Cunningham (Mrs. Morris), Willard Robertson (Dayton), Roger Grey (Attendant), Adrian Morris (Knucks), Joe Gray, Jack Pennick, Kit Guard, Fern Emmet, Max Barwyn, James McNamara, Paul Newlan, Harlan Briggs, Blanca Vischer, Hetra Lynd, Jimmie Dundee, Teryy Raye, Sheila Darcy, Margaret Randall, Jack Mulhall, Sam Ash, Ruth Rogers, Julia Faye, Arthur Hoyt.
Shooting: 45 days. Original length: 90 minutes. Released June 3.

The Return of Frank James
Twentieth-Century-Fox, 1940
Director: Fritz Lang. Producer: Darryl F. Zanuck. Associate Producer: Kenneth Macgowan. Writer: Sam Hellman. Photographers (Technicolour): George Barnes, William V. Skall. Art Directors: Richard Day, Wiard B. Ihnen. Set Decorator: Thomas Little. Costumes: Travis Banton. Music: David Buttolph. Editor: Walter Thompson.
Cast: Henry Fonda (Frank James), Gene Tierney (Eleanor), Jackie Cooper (Clem), Henry Hull (Major Rufus Todd), J. Edward Bromberg (George Rynyan), Donald Meek (McCoy), Eddie Collins (Station Agent), John Carradine (Bob Ford), George Barbier (Judge), Ernest Whitman (Pinky), Charles Tannen (Charlie Ford), Lloyd Corrigan (Randolph Stone), Russell Hicks (Agent), Victor Kilian (Preacher), Edward McWade (Colonel Jackson), George Chandler (Roy), Irving Bacon (Bystander), Frank Shannon (Sheriff), Barbara Papper (Nellie Blane), Louis Mason (Mose), William Pawley, Frank Sully, Davidson Clark.
Shooting: 46 days. Original length: 92 minutes. Released: August 16.

Western Union
Twentieth-Century-Fox, 1941
Director: Fritz Lang. Associate Producer: Harry Joe Brown. Writer: Robert Carson, based on a novel by Zane Grey.

Photographers (Technicolour): Edward Cronjager, Allen M. Davey. Art Director: Richard Day, Wiard B. Ihnen. Set Decorator: Thomas Little. Costumes: Travis Banton. Music: David Buttolph. Editor: Robert Bischoff.
Cast: Robert Young (Richard Blake), Randolph Scott (Vance Shaw), Dean Jagger (Edward Creighton), Virginia Gilmore (Sue Creighton), John Carradine (Don Murdoch), Slim Summerville (Herman), Chill Wills (Homer), Barton McLane (Jack Slade), Russell Hicks (Governor), Victor Kiligan (Charlie), Minor Watson (Pat Grogan), George Chandler (Herb), Chief Big Tree (Chief Spotted Horse), Chief Thundercloud (Indian Leader), Dick Rich (Porky), Harry Strong (Henchman), Charles Middleton (Stagecoach Rider), Addison Richards (Captain Harlow), J. Edward Bromberg, Irving Bacon.
Shooting: 56 days. Original length: 93 minutes. Released: February 21.

Man Hunt
Twentieth Century-Fox, 1941
Director: Fritz Lang. Associate Producer: Kenneth Macgowan. Writer: Dudley Nichols, based on the novel Rogue Male by Geoffrey Household. Photographer: Arthur Miller. Art Directors: Richard Day, Wiard B. Ihnen. Set Decorator: Thomas Little. Costumes: Travis Banton. Music: Alfred Newman. Editor: Allen McNeil.
Cast: Walter Pidgeon (Captain Thorndike), Joan Bennett (Jenny), George Sanders (Quive-Smith), John Carradine (Mr. Jones), Roddy McDowall (Vaner), Ludwig Stössel (Doctor), Heather Thatcher (Lady Risborough), Frederick Walcock (Lord Risborough), Roger Imhof (Captain Jensen), Egon Brecher (Whiskers), Lester Matthews (Major), Holmes Herbert (Farnsworthy), Eily Malyon (Postmistress), Arno Frey (Police Lieutenant), Fredrik Vogedink (Ambassador), Lucien Prival (Man with Umbrella), Herbert Evans (Reeves), Keith Hitchcock (Bobby).
Original length: 105 minutes (longest existing version 102 minutes). Released: June 20.

Confirm or Deny
Twentieth-Century-Fox, 1941
Director: Archie Mayo (and uncredited Fritz Lang). Producer: Len Hammond. Writer: Joe Swering, based on a story by Samuel Fuller, Henry Wales. Photographer: Leon Shamroy.
Cast: Don Ameche, Joan Bennett, Roddy McDowall, John Loder.
Mayo took over when Lang suffered a not unfortunate illness (he never liked the film and was merely fulfilling his contract). Lang: 'I directed practically nothing.' Length: 73 minutes. Released: December 12.

Moontide

Twentieth Century-Fox, 1942
Director: Archie Mayo (and uncredited
Fritz Lang). *Producer:* Mark Hellinger.
Writer: John O'Hara, based on the novel
by Willard Robertson. *Photographer:*
Charles Clarke.
Cast: Jean Gabin, Ida Lupino, Claude
Rains, Jerome Cowan, Thomas Mitchell.
Mayo replaced Lang after only four days
shooting. Length: 94 minutes. Released:
May 29.

Hangmen Also Die

Arnold Productions–United Artists, 1943
Director: Fritz Lang. *Executive Producer:*
Arnold Pressburger. *Associate Producer:* T.
W. Baumfield. *Writers:* Fritz Lang,
Bertolt Brecht, John Wexley, based on a
story by Lang and Brecht. *Photographer:*
James Wong Howe. *Art Director:* William
Darling. *Costumes:* Julie Heron. *Music:*
Hanns Eisler. *Song:* 'No Surrender' by
Eisler, Sam Coslow. *Editor:* Gene Fowler,
Jr. *Production Manager:* Carl Harriman.
Assistant Directors: Archie Mayo, Fred
Pressburger.
Cast: Brian Donlevy (Franz Svoboda),
Walter Brennan (Professor Novotny),
Anna Lee (Mascha Novotny), Gene
Lockhart (Emil Czaka), Dennis O'Keefe
(Jan Horek), Alexander Granach (Alois
Gruber), Margaret Wycherly (Ludmilla
Novotny), Nana Bryant (Mrs. Novotny),
Billy Roy (Boda Novotny), Hans von
Twardowski (Richard Heydrich), Tonio
Stawart (Gestapo Chief), Jonathan Hale
(Debège), Lionel Stander (Cabby), Byron
Foulger (Bartos), Virginia Farmer
(Landlady), Louis Donath (Shumer),
Sarah Padden (Miss Dvorak), Edmund
MacDonald (Dr. Pilar), George Irving
(Nezval), James Bush (Worker), Arno
Frey (Itnut), Lester Sharpe (Rudy),
Arthur Loft (General Bertruba), William
Farnum (Viktorin), Reinhold Schüenzel
(Inspector Ritter), Philip Merivale.
Shooting: 52 days. Original length: 140
minutes. Released: March 26.

Ministry of Fear

Paramount, 1944
Director: Fritz Lang. *Producer/Writer:*
Seton I. Miller, based on the novel by
Graham Greene. *Photographer:* Henry
Sharp. *Art Directors:* Hans T. Dreier, Hal
Pereira. *Set Decorator:* Bert Granger.
Music: Victor Young. *Editor:* Archie
Marshek. *Assistant Director:* George
Templeton.
Cast: Ray Milland (Stephen Neale),
Marjorie Reynolds (Carla Hilfe), Carl
Esmond (Willi Hilfe), Dan Duryea
(Costa/Travers), Hilliary Brooke (Mrs.
Bellane), Percy Waram (Inspector
Prentice), Erskine Sanford (Mr. Rennit),
Thomas Louden (Mr. Newland), Alan
Napier (Dr. Forrester), Helene Grant
(Mrs. Merrick), Aminta Dyne (False Mrs.

Bellaire), Rita Johnson ('Real' Mrs.
Bellaire), Mary Field (Miss Penteel),
Byron Foulger (Newby), Lester
Matthews (Dr. Morton), Eustace Wyatt
(Blind Man).
Shooting: 7 weeks. Original length: 84
minutes. Produced before, but released
(16 October) after *The Woman in the
Window* (11 October).

The Woman in the Window

Christie Corporation-International
Pictures (released by R.K.O.), 1944
Director: Fritz Lang. *Producer/Writer:*
Nunnally Johnson, based on the novel
Once Off Guard by J. H. Wallis.
Photographer: Milton Krasner. *Special
Effects:* Vernon Walker. *Art Director:*
Duncan Cramer. *Set Decorator:* Julia
Heron. *Costumes:* Muriel King. *Music:*
Arthur Lang. *Editor:* Marjorie Johnson.
Assistant Director: Richard Harlan.
Cast: Edward G. Robinson (Richard
Wanley), Joan Bennett (Alice), Raymond
Massey (District Attorney), Dan Duryea
(Blackmailer), Edmond Breon (Dr.
Barkstone), Thomas E. Jackson (Inspector
Jackson), Arthur Loft (Mazard), Dorothy
Peterson (Mrs. Wanley), Frank Dawson,
Carol Cameron, Bobby Blake.
Original length: 99 minutes. Released:
October 11.

Scarlet Street

Diana Productions (released by
Universal), 1945
Director/Producer: Fritz Lang. *Executive
Producer:* Walter Wanger. *Writer:* Dudley
Nichols, based on the novel and play *La
Chienne* by Georges de la Fouchardière
(with Mouézy-Eon). *Photographer:* Milton
Krasner. *Special Photographic Effects:* John
P. Fulton. *Art Director:* Alexander
Golitzen. *Set Decorators:*
Russell A. Gausman, Carl Lawrence.
Costumes: Travis Benton. *Paintings:* John
Decker. *Music:* Hans J. Salter. *Editor:*
Arthur Hilton. *Assistant Director:* Melville
Shyer.
Cast: Edward G. Robinson (Chris Cross),
Joan Bennett (Kitty Marsh), Dan Duryea
(Johnny), Margaret Lindsay (Millie),
Rosalind Ivan (Adele), Samuel S. Hinds
(Charlie Pringle), Jess Barker (Janeway),
Arthur Loft (Dellarowe), Vladimir
Sokoloff (Pop Legon), Charles Kemper
(Adele's First Husband), Russell Hicks
(Hogarth), Anita Bolster (Mrs. Michaels),
Cyrus W. Kendell (Nick), Fred Essler
(Marchetti), Edgar Dearing, Tom Dillon
(Policemen), Chuck Hamilton
(Chauffeur), Guss Glassmire, Howard
Mitchell, Ralph Littlefield, Sherry Hall,
Jack Statham, Rodney Bell, Byron
Foulger, Will Wright.
Shooting: 56 days. Original length: 102
minutes. Released: December 28.

Cloak and Dagger

United States Pictures, Inc. (released by
Warner Bros.), 1946
Director: Fritz Lang. *Producer:* Milton
Sperling. *Writers:* Albert Maltz, Ring
Lardner, Jr., based on a story by Boris
Ingster, John Larkin, suggested by a book
by Corey Ford, Alastair MacBain.
Photographer: Sol Polita. *Art Director:*
Max Parker. *Set Decorator:* Walter
Hilford. *Special Effects:* Harry Barndollar,
Edwin DuPar. *Music:* Max Steiner.
Editor: Christian Nyby. *Assistant Director:*
Russ Saunders. *Technical Advisor:* Michael
Burke.
Cast: Gary Cooper (Alvah Jasper), Lilli
Palmer (Gina), Robert Alda (Pinky),
Vladimir Sokoloff (Dr. Polda), J. Edward
Bromberg (Trenk), Marjorie Hoshelle
(Ann Dawson), Ludwig Stössel (German),
Helene Thimig (Katherine Loder), Dan
Seymour (Marsoli), Marc Lawrence
(Luigi), James Flavin (Walsh), Pat
O'Moore (Englishman), Charles Marsh
(Enrich), Rosalind Lyons, Connie
Gilchrist.
Original *release* length: 106 minutes.
Released: September 28.

Secret Beyond the Door

Diana Productions (released by Universal-
International), 1948
Director/Producer: Fritz Lang. *Executive
Producer:* Walter Wanger. *Writer:* Silvia
Richards, based on the story 'Museum
Piece No. 13' by Rufus King.
Photographer: Stanley Cortez. *Production
Designer:* Max Parker. *Set Decorators:*
Russell A. Gausman, John Austin. *Music:*
Miklos Rosza. *Editor:* Arthur Hilton.
Assistant Director: William Holland.
Cast: Joan Bennett (Celia Lamphere),
Michael Redgrave (Mark Lamphere),
Anne Revere (Caroline Lamphere),
Barbara O'Neil (Miss Robey), Natalie
Schaefer (Edith Potter), Paul Cavanagh
(Rick Barrett), Anabel Shaw (Society
Guest), Rosa Rey (Paquita), James Seay
(Bob Dwight), Mark Dennis (David),
Donna Di Mario (Gypsy), David Cota,
Celia Moore.
Shooting: 61 days. Original length: 98¼
minutes. Released: February.

House by the River

Fidelity Pictures (released by Republic),
1949
Director: Fritz Lang. *Producer:* Howard
Welsch. *Associate Producer:* Robert Peters.
Writer: Mel Dinelli, based on a novel by
A. P. Herbert. *Photographer:* Edward
Cronjager. *Art Director:* Bert Leven. *Set
Decorators:* Charles Thompson, John
McCarthy, Jr. *Special Effects:* Howard and
Theodore Lydecker. *Costumes:* Adele
Palmer. *Music:* George Antheil. *Editor:*
Arthur D. Hilton. *Production Manager:*
Joseph Dillpe. *Assistant Director:* John
Grubbs.

Cast: Louis Hayward (Stephen Byrne), Lee Bowman (John Byrne), Jane Wyatt (Marjorie Byrne), Dorothy Patrick (Emily Gaunt), Ann Shoemaker (Mrs. Ambrose), Jody Gilbert (Flora Bantam), Peter Brocco (Attorney General), Howaland Chamberlain (District Attorney), Margaret Seddon (Mrs. Whittaker), Sarah Padden (Mrs. Beach), Kathleen Freeman (Effie Ferguson), Will Wright (Inspector Parten), Leslie Kimmell (Mr. Gaunt), Effie Laird (Mrs. Gaunt). Shooting: 32 days. Original length: 88 minutes. Released: March 25, 1950.

An American Guerrilla in the Philippines

Twentieth Century-Fox, 1950
Director: Fritz Lang. Producer/Writer: Lamar Trotti, based on the novel of the same title by Ira Wolfert. Photographer (Technicolour): Harry Jackson. Special Photographic Effects: Fred Sersen. Art Directors: Lyle Wheeler, J. Russell Spencer. Set Decorators: Thomas Little, Stuart Reiss. Costumes: Travilla. Music: Cyril Mockridge. Editor: Robert Simpson. Production Manager: F. E. Johnson. Second-Unit Director: Robert D. Webb. Assistant Director: Horace Hough.
Cast: Tyrone Power (Chuck Palmer), Micheline Presle (Jeanne Martinez), Jack Elam (Spenser), Bob Patten (Lovejoy), Tom Ewell (Jim Mitchell), Tommy Cook (Miguel), Robert Barrat (General MacArthur), Juan Torena (Juan Martinez), Carleton Young (Colonel Phillips), Chris de Vega, Miguel Azures, Eddie Infante, Erlinda Cortez, Rosa del Rosario, Haty Ruby.
The entire film, including interiors, was shot in the Philippines in 48 days. Original length: 105 minutes. Released: December.

Rancho Notorious

Fidelity Pictures (released by RKO Radio), 1951
Director: Fritz Lang. Producer: Howard Welsch. Writer: Daniel Taradash, based on the story 'Gunsight Whitman' by Silvia Richards. Photographer (Technicolour): Hal Mohr. Art Director: Robert Priestly. Music: Emil Newman. Songs: 'The Legend of Chuck-A-Luck' (sung by William Lee), 'Gypsy Davey', 'Get Away, Young Man' (sung by Marlene Dietrich) by Ken Darby. Editor: Otto Ludwig. Assistant Director: Emmert Emerson.
Cast: Marlene Dietrich (Altar Keane), Arthur Kennedy (Vern Haskell), Mel Ferrer (Frenchy Fairmont), Gloria Henry (Beth Forbes), William Frawley (Baldy Gunder), Lisa Ferraday (Maxine), John Raven (Chuck-A-Luck Dealer), Jack Elam (Geary), Dan Seymour (Commanche Paul), George Reeves

(Wilson), Rodric Redwing (Rio), Frank Ferguson (Preacher), Charles Gonzales (Hevia), Francis MacDonald (Harbin), Jose Dominguez (Gonzales), John Kellog (Salesman), Stan Jolley (Warren), John Doucette (Whitney), Stuart Randall (Starr), Frank Graham (Ace Maquire), Fuzzy Knight (Barber), Roger Anderson (Red), Felipe Turich (Sanchez), Lloyd Gough (Kinch), Russell Johnson (Dealer). Original length: 86 minutes. Released: March 1952.

Clash By Night

Wald-Krasna Productions-RKO Radio Pictures, 1951
Director: Fritz Lang. Executive Producer: Jerry Wald. Producer: Harriet Parsons. Writer: Alfred Hayes, based on the play of the same title by Clifford Odets. Photographer: Nicholas Musuraca. Special Photographic Effects: Harold Wellman. Art Directors: Albert S. D'Agostino, Carroll Clark. Set Decorators: Darrell Silvera, Jack Mills. Music: Roy Webb. Song: 'I Hear a Rhapsody' by Dick Gasparre, Jack Baker, George Fragos (sung by Tony Martin). Editor: George J. Amy.
Cast: Barbara Stanwyck (Mae Doyle), Paul Douglas (Jerry d'Amato), Robert Ryan (Earl Pfeiffer), Marilyn Monroe (Peggy), J. Carroll Naish (Uncle Vince), Keith Andes (Joe Doyle), Milvio Minciotti (Papa d'Amato).
Shooting: 32 days, including locations at Monterey, California. Length: 105 minutes. Released: June 1952.

The Blue Gardenia

Blue Gardinia Productions-Gloria Films (released by Warner Bros.), 1952
Director: Fritz Lang. Producer: Alex Gottlieb. Writer: Charles Hoffmann, based on a story by Vera Caspary. Photographer: Daniel Hall. Music: Raoul Kraushaar. Song: 'Blue Gardenia' by Bob Russell, Lester Lee, arranged by Nelson Riddle (sung by Nat 'King' Cole). Editor: Edward Mann. Special Effects: Willis Cook. Script Supervisor: Don McDougal.
Cast: Anne Baxter (Norah Larkin), Richard Conte (Casey Mayo), Ann Southern (Chrustal Carpenter), Raymond Burr (Harry Prebble), Jeff Donnell (Sally Ellis), Richard Erdman (Al), George Reeves (Officer Haynes), Ruth Storey (Rose), Ray Walker (Homer), Celia Lovsky (Blind Woman), Frank Ferguson (Drunk), Alex Gottlieb, Nat 'King' Cole (Himself).
Shooting: 21 days (December 1952). Original length: 90 minutes. Released: March 28, 1953.

The Big Heat

Columbia, 1953
Director: Fritz Lang. Producer: Robert Arthur. Writer: Sidney Boehm, based on the novel of the same title by

William P. McGiven. Photographer: Charles Lang, Jr. Art Director: Robert Peterson. Set Decorator: William Kiernan. Music: Amfitheatrof. Editor: Charles Nelson. Assistant Director: Milton Feldman.
Cast: Glenn Ford (Dave Bannion), Gloria Grahame (Debby Marsh), Jocelyn Brando (Katie Bannion), Alexander Scourby (Mike Lagana), Lee Marvin (Vince Stone), Jeanette Nolan (Bertha Duncan), Peter Whitney (Tierney), Willia Bouche (Lt. Wilkes), Robert Burton (Gus Burke), Adam Williams (Larry Gordon), Howard Wendell (Commissioner Higgens), Cris Alcaide (George Rose), Michael Grange (Hugo), Dorothy Green (Lucy Chapman), Carolyn Jones (Doris), Ric Roman (Baldy), Dan Semour (Atkins), Edith Evanson (Selma Parker), Linda Bennett, Kathryn Eames, Rex Reason. Shooting: 29 days. Original length: 90 minutes. Released: October.

Human Desire

Columbia, 1954
Director: Fritz Lang. Producer: Lewis J. Rachmil (Jerry Wald). Writer: Alfred Hayes, based on La Bête Humaine by Emil Zola. Photographer: Burnett Cuffey. Art Director: Robert Peterson. Set Decorator: William Kiernan. Music: Daniele Amfitheatrof. Editor: Aaron Ste Assistant Director: Milton Feldman.
Cast: Glenn Ford (Jeff Warren), Gloria Grahame (Vicky Buckley), Broderick Crawford (Carl Buckley), Edgar Buchanan (Alec Simmons), Kathleen Ca (Ellen Simmons), Peggy Maley (Jean), Diane DeLaire (Vera Simmons), Grando Rhodes (John Owens), Dan Seymour (Bartender), John Pickard (Matt Henley), Paul Brinegar (Brakeman), Dan Riss (Prosecutor), Victor Hugo Greene (Davidson), John Zaremba (Russell), Ca Lee (John Thurston), Olan Soule (Lewis) Shooting: 35 days. Original length: 90 minutes. Released: September.

Moonfleet

Metro-Goldwyn-Mayer, 1954
Director: Fritz Lang. Producer: John Houseman. Associate Producer: Jud Kinberg. Writers: Jan Lustig, Margaret Fitts, based on the novel of the same title by John Meade Falkner). Photographer: (Eastman Colour and CinemaScope) Robert Planck. Art Directors: Cedric Gibbons, Hans Peters. Set Decorators: Edwin B. Willis, Richard Pefferle. Costumes: Walter Plunkett. Music: Mikl Rozsa. Flamenco Music: Vincente Gomez Editor: Albert Akst. Assistant Director: Si Sidman.
Cast: Stewart Granger (Jeremy Fox), George Sanders (Lord Ashwood), Joan Greenwood (Lady Ashwood), Viveca Lindfors (Mrs. Minton), Jon Whiteley (John Mohune), Liliane Montevecchi

Dancer), Sean McClory (Elzevir Block), Melville Cooper (Felix Ratsey), Alan Napier (Parson Glennie), John Hoyt (Magistrate Maskew), Donna Corcoran (Grace), Jack Elam (Damen), Dan Seymour (Hull), Ian Wolfe (Tewkesbury), Lester Matthews (Major Kennishaw), Skelton Knaggs (Jacob), Richard Hale (Starkhill), John Alderson (Greening), Ashley Cowan (Tomson), Frank Ferguson (Coachman), Booth Colman (Captain Stanhope), Peggy Maley (Tenant).

Shooting: 45 days (September–October 1954)—locations at Oceanside, California. Original length: 87 minutes. Released: June, 1955.

While The City Sleeps

Thor Productions-RKO Teleradio Pictures (released by RKO Radio), 1955
Director: Fritz Lang. *Producer:* Bert E. Friedlob. *Writer:* Casey Robinson, based on the novel *The Bloody Spur* by Charles Einstein. *Photographer (SuperScope):* Ernest Laszlo. *Art Director:* Carroll Clark. *Set Decorator:* Jack Mills. *Costumes:* Norma. *Music:* Herschel Burke Gilbert. *Editor:* Gene Fowler, Jr. *Sound Editor:* Verna Fields. *Assistant Director:* Ronnie Rondell.
Cast: Dana Andrews (Edward Mobley), Rhonda Fleming (Dorothy Kyne), Sally Forest (Nancy Liggett), Thomas Mitchell (Griffith), Vincent Price (Walter Kyne, Jr.), Howard Duff (Lt. Kaufman), Ida Lupino (Mildred), George Sanders (Mark Loving), James Craig (Harry Kritzer), John Barrymore, Jr. (Robert Manners), Vladimir Sokoloff (George Palsky), Robert Warwick (Amos Kyne), Ralph Peters (Meade), Larry Blake (Police Sergeant), Edward Hinton (O'Leary), Mae Marsh (Mrs. Manners), Sandy White (Judith Fenton), Celia Lovsky (Miss Dodd), Pit Herbert (Bartender), Andrew Lupino.
Shooting: 5 weeks (July–August 1955). Length: 100 minutes. Released: May 1956.

Beyond A Reasonable Doubt

RKO Teleradio Pictures (released by RKO Radio), 1956
Director: Fritz Lang. *Producer:* Bert E. Friedlob. *Writer:* Douglas Morrow. *Photographer (RKO-Scope):* William Snyder. *Art Director:* Carroll Clark. *Set Decorator:* Darrell Silvera. *Music:* Herschel Burke Gilbert. *Song:* 'Beyond a Reasonable Doubt' (sung by The Hi-Los) by Gilbert, Alfred Perry. *Editor:* Gene Fowler, Jr. *Assistant Director:* Maxwell Henry.
Cast: Dana Andrews (Tom Garret), Joan Fontaine (Susan Spencer), Sidney Blackmer (Austin Spencer), Philip Bourneuf (Thompson), Barbara Nichols (Sally), Shepperd Strudwick (Wilson), Arthur Franz (Hale), Robin Raymond (Terry), Edward Binns (Lt. Kennedy), William Leicester (Charlie Miller), Dan Seymour (Greco), Rusty Lane (Judge), Joyce Taylor (Joan), Carleton Young (Kirk), Trudy Wroe (Hat Check Girl), Joe Kirk (Clerk), Charles Evans (Governor), Wendell Niles (Announcer).
Shooting: March 26–April 31, 1956. Length· 80 minutes. Released: September 5, 1956.

Der Tiger von Eschnapur (The Tiger of Bengal)/Das Indische Grabmal (The Hindu Tomb)

A West German–French–Italian Co-production: CCC-Films Artur Brauner-Gloria Film-Regina Films-Critérion Films-Rizzoli Films-Impéria Films Distribution, 1958
Director: Fritz Lang. *Executive Producer:* Artur Brauner. *Producers:* Louise de Masure, Eberhard Meischner. *Writers:* Fritz Lang, Werner Jörg Lüddecke, based on a novel by Thea von Harbou and a scenario by Fritz Lang and Thea von Harbou. *Photographer (colour and ColorScope):* Richard Angst. *Art Directors:* Helmut Nentwig, Willy Schatz. *Costumes:* Claudia Herberg, Günther Brosda. *Music:* Michel Michelet (*Tiger*), Gerhard Becker (*Grabmal*). *Choreographers:* Robby Gay, Billy Daniel. *Editor:* Walter Wischniewsky.
Cast: Debra Paget (Seeta), Paul Hubschmid (Harold Berger—Henri Mercier in French version), Walter Reyer (Chandra), Claus Holm (Dr. Walter Rhode), Sabine Bethmann (Irene Rhode), Valery Inkijinoff (Yama), René Deltgen (Prince Ramigani), Jochen Brockmann (Padhu), Jochen Blume (Asagana), Luciana Paoluzzi (Bahrani—*Tiger* only), Guido Celano (General Dagh—*Grabmal* only), Angela Portulari (Peasant—*Grabmal* only), Richard Lauffen (Bhowana), Helmut Hildebrand (Servant), Panos Papadopoulos (Messenger), Victor Francen.
Tiger (97 minutes) and *Grabmal* (101 minutes) were released in the original German and French versions as a double bill, in July–August of 1959. American International released, in October 1960, a badly dubbed version of the two films edited into one feature of 95 minutes titled *Journey to the Lost City* (US) or *Tiger of Bengal* (UK). Paul Hubschmid

was billed as Paul Christian in the English language version. Shooting: 89 days (27 of which were on location in India). 5.3.1959, Universum, Stuttgart.

Die Tausend Augen des Dr. Mabuse (The 1,000 Eyes of Dr. Mabuse)

A West-German–French–Italian Co-production: CCC Filmkunst-Critérion Films-Cei-Incom-Omnia Distribution, 1960
Director/Producer: Fritz Lang. *Executive Producer:* Artur Brauner. *Writers:* Fritz Lang, Heinz Oskar Wuttig, based on an idea of Jan Fethke and the character created by Norbert Jacques. *Photographer:* Karl Loeb. *Art Directors:* Erich Kettelhut, Johannes Ott. *Costumes:* Ina Stein. *Music:* Bert Grund. *Editors:* Walter and Waltraute Wischniewsky.
Cast: Dawn Addams (Marion Menil), Peter Van Eyck (Henry B. Travers), Wolfgang Preiss (Jordan), Lupo Prezzo (Cornelius), Gert Fröbe (Commissioner Kraus), Werner Peters (Hieronymus P. Mistelzweig), Andrea Cecchi (Berg), Reinhard Kolldehoff (Clubfoot), Christiane Maybach (Blonde), Howard Vernon (No. 12), Nico Pepe (Hotel Manager), David Cameron (Parker), Jean-Jacques Delbo (Deiner), Werner Buttler (No. 11), Linda Sini (Corinna), Rolf Moebius (Police Officer), Bruno W. Pantel (Reporter), Marie-Luise Nagel.
Shooting: 42 days. Length: 103 minutes. Released: May 14, 1960, Gloria-Palast, Stuttgart.

Le Mépris (Contempt)

Films Concordia-Compagnia Cinematografica Champion-Marceau-Cocinor Distributors, 1963
Director/Writer: Jean-Luc Godard, based on the novel *Il Disprezzo (A Ghost at Noon)* by Alberto Moravia. *Executive Producer:* Joseph E. Levine. *Producers:* Georges de Beauregard, Carlo Ponti. *Photographer (colour and Franscope):* Raoul Coutard. *Music:* Georges Delerue. *Editors:* Agnès Guillemot, Lila Lakshmanan.
Cast: Brigitte Bardot (Camille Javal), Jack Palance (Jeremy Prokosch), Michel Piccoli (Paul Javal), Fritz Lang (Fritz Lang), Giorgia Moll (Francesca Vanini), Jean-Luc Godard (Lang's Assistant Director), Linda Veras (Siren).
The Embassy Pictures' American version (subtitled), released in 1964, is three minutes longer than the French version (100 minutes). Paris premiere: December 27. Shooting: April–June in Rome and Capri.

Appendix to Filmography: The Unrealised Projects

In the filmographies, books, and articles devoted to Lang and his work, a good many unfilmed projects are attributed to the director. Most of them are apocryphal, dreamed up by press agents, hopeful producers, and even critics. Lang insists he has never heard of the majority of them. Nonetheless, there are a small number of such projects, authenticated by Lang himself, which he had had the intention of making as films, and which had reached various stages of completion before being abandoned for equally various reasons.

DIE LEGENDE VOM LETZTEN WIENER FIAKER (The Legend of the Last Viennese Fiacre). In 1933, after *Das Testament des Dr Mabuse,* during the dark time of Hitler's rise to power, Lang wrote (without the aid of Thea von Harbou) the outline for a scenario full of humour and gaiety, reminiscent of his Viennese origins and prefiguring to a degree the fairy tale, picture book heaven of *Liliom.*

Lang's story has all the drollery of Raimund, the once famous and popular comedy writer of early 19th century Vienna.

The 'Fiaker' (he shares the appellation with his coach) is a proud proprietor-driver. With haughty graciousness, he gives his lowly 'Waterer' (the man who looks after the horses and gives them water) a lottery ticket which he had been forced to buy, but which he believes is beneath his dignity to keep. Contrary to all expectations, the 'Waterer' wins a huge sum, which he immediately invests in a factory which manufactures the new automobiles which the 'Fiaker' strongly detests. With his new found wealth, the social barriers between the 'Waterer' and the 'Fiaker' dissolve, and the 'Waterer's' son is able to marry his beloved, the 'Fiaker's' daughter.

Only one consolation rests for the 'Fiaker' who is so proud of his horses: those 'damned poor, horseless cars' are not allowed to drive on the principal allée of the Prater. Yet, while the two new fathers-in-law are drinking a toast with new wine ('Heurigen') to the young couple, an 'extra' headline in a newspaper announces that Emperor Franz Josef has given a special dispensation: the automobiles are now allowed on the allée. The news shatters all the 'Fiaker's' illusions; he suffers a stroke.

At the Heavenly Gates, Saint Peter receives the dead 'Fiaker', but when the coachman wants to drive in with his horses and coach, Saint Peter furiously bangs the gates shut, and rushes off to arrange a special concert for Saint Cecile. Although all of the great composers have been invited, Saint Peter can't find them in their bungalows when the concert is about to begin. He finally discovers them all sitting on comfortable clouds, listening in bliss to the 'Fiaker' singing his Viennese lieder. Saint Cecile is waiting; there is only one thing to do: report the entire matter to the Lord.

Our Lord arrives at the gates and speaks to the coachman. As the 'Fiaker' refuses to budge without his horses, the Lord appoints him His special coachman, gets into the fiacre, and proudly the 'Fiaker' drives into Heaven. As the wheels turn, a new constellation is born: The Big Wagon. The story is worth repeating in some detail if only to remind those critics who tend to forget Lang's Viennese background that he is not the total pessimist they sometimes describe him as being.

HELL AFLOAT. In 1934, Lang wrote, with Oliver H. P. Garrett, a story based on the *S.S. Morro Castle* fire in which over a hundred people died. David O. Selznick rejected the story for M.G.M.

THE MAN BEHIND YOU. In 1935, Lang wrote this modern Jekyll and Hyde story concerning a doctor who identifies more and more with the evil nature of man. It is a pity that the director was unable to make the film; it seems a natural subject for the director of *M*.

MEN WITHOUT A COUNTRY. After *You and Me*, in 1939 Lang planned this film for Paramount in collaboration with Jonathan Latimer. It was to have been a story dealing with a secret weapon which destroys eyesight.

WINCHESTER 73. In 1948, Lang worked with Silvia Richards (who had done the script for *Secret Beyond the Door*) on a script of Stuart N. Lake's novel. The film was planned for Lang's own company, Diana Productions, for release by Universal. The film directed by Anthony Mann in 1950 has no relationship to the Lang project. There was never more than the first page of the outline at any rate.

DARK SPRING. In about 1954, Lang planned to shoot a script by Michael Latté, and only gave up his plans to film it when the problem of casting the child's role became insurmountable. The story concerns a girl of eleven or twelve who is to inherit an enormous fortune from her dead father when she comes of age. Her mother marries again. Her second husband is a seemingly successful lawyer, who is being forced to pay a huge sum to a group of gangsters he once cheated. The lawyer attempts to kill the girl three times in order to gain control of the inheritance. Only a friend of the girl, a boy of fifteen, understands what is actually happening. The mother believes her husband when he tells her that Bettina, the girl, is paranoid and is only imagining things. Before he can carry out his fourth attempt at murder, the lawyer is himself killed by a gangster. One is inclined to wonder if it were only casting problems which decided Lang against making the film. While at first glance the subject seems appropriate to Lang, on closer examination certain elements become apparent which might well have made Lang more uncomfortable as the project progressed. Cold-blooded murder for profit has never been central to his work. In *M* and *Secret Beyond the Door*, for example, Lang deals with psychopaths who cannot help themselves; the victim in *Beyond a Reasonable Doubt* is not an innocent girl, but a hardened blackmailer.

TAJ MAHAL. In 1956, the Indian government invited Lang to India to make a film. The project was about the 17th century maharajah who built the Taj Mahal in memory of his love. Lang dropped the project when it became clear that the Indian ideal of beauty was completely different from that in Europe, so that casting became a great problem. This stay of several weeks, however, was of great help later for his German films set in India.

UNTER AUSSCHUSS DER ÖFFENTLICHKEIT (Behind Closed Doors). Although this title appears regularly in filmographies and he has been treated in detail by Alfred Eibel (see bibliography), Lang insists it is a pure invention on the part of Arthur Brauner (Lang's producer on the last three German films) as a publicity stunt for Peter van Eyck in 1960. It was never a Lang project, and the film which was produced in 1961 with the same title has, of course, no connection with Lang.

KALI YUNG and MOON OF DASSEMRA. In about 1960, Lang was offered the chance to make two further films set in India. The projects were finally dropped, however, when the Italian producer insisted on certain script alterations, in spite of his contract with Lang giving the director full artistic control. The *Kali Yung* film would have concerned the greatest criminal conspiracy in Indian history, the Brotherhood of Thugs. More than ten million innocent travellers were strangled with the 'rumal', a kerchief curiously knotted at the corners, presumably in honour of the bloody goddess Kali, in order to rob them of their valuables. The fact that even Mahradschahs and other high level personalities belonged to the secret organisation made it even more difficult for the British authorities to exterminate the evil cult.

Set in 1875, the film centres about a young doctor who runs a cholera clinic. When his Sikhs disappear while bringing him supplies, he requests the resident, a sick old man who wants to avoid trouble, to investigate, the request is refused. The matter is further complicated when the doctor discovers that the girl he had loved in England was already then the resident's wife. A Thug murder is committed and the doctor falls under suspicion. In order to clear himself, he and an Indian companion undertake their own investigation (a dancing girl leads them to the Thugs) and become involved in various adventures. His love and understanding of India prevail, the Thugs are exterminated, and his name is cleared.

...UND MORGEN : MORD! (...and Tomorrow : Murder!). Planned in 1962 (written in Beverley Hills in 1961 and in Munich in 1962), the story deals with a seemingly respectable bourgeois, a severe defender of moral traditions, president of many social associations who in his youth had suffered various repressions which caused him to commit obsessive, sexual crimes. When he is discovered, he commits suicide. Only the police commissioner, with some few others, know the reality behind the lauditory obituary of the dead man.

DEATH OF A CAREER GIRL. In 1964, Lang was president of the Jury at the Cannes Film Festival; Jeanne Moreau was a member of the Jury and suggested that they make a film together. With the actress in mind, Lang wrote a detailed outline of a script. A mature and still beautiful woman, the head of an international economic network contemplates committing suicide because her life and ambitions seem to her to be empty. Her whole life is then seen in flashbacks. Beginning as a young girl working with the French resistance during the Nazi 'occupation', and, like Gina in *Cloak and Dagger*, by 'touching scum becomes scum' in having affairs with Nazi officers. Poor and ambitious she uses men unscrupulously to further her career. As the only man who loves her and treats her with respect sadly explains to her, in the struggle upwards she has lost her soul. At the end of the film, she decides against suicide; as one of the living dead she opens yet another business conference with cold triumph. The agents of Lang and Moreau were unable to settle the conditions of production to their mutual satisfaction and the project was cancelled.*

After this, Lang seriously considered making one last film in spite of his failing eyesight. Claude Chabrol, long an admirer of Lang's work, brought him together in Paris with his own producer, André Génoves, who offered him both complete artistic liberty and an adequate budget. Lang planned a story about contemporary youth, their conflicts and desires, their striving to free themselves from the traditions of the establishment, and their use of drugs. He described to me one beautiful sequence: coloured balls leap from a roof terrace and glide easily down stairs and through the air. A young girl intensely involved in a LSD dream glides down with them. Lang finally decided that his failing sight would not allow him to make the film.

* For an accurate and more complete discussion of DEATH OF A CAREER GIRL, consult the article on the project by David L. Overbey (see bibliography).